Place and Experien

The first edition of *Place and Experience* established Jeff Malpas as one of the leading philosophers and thinkers of place and space and provided a creative and refreshing alternative to prevailing post-structuralist and postmodern theories of place. It is a foundational and ground-breaking book in its attempt to lay out a sustained and rigorous account of place and its significance.

The main argument of *Place and Experience* has three strands: first, that human being is inextricably bound to place; second, that place encompasses subjectivity and objectivity, being reducible to neither but foundational to both; and third, that place, which is distinct from, but also related to space and time, is methodologically and ontologically fundamental. The development of this argument involves considerations concerning the nature of place and its relation to space and time; the character of that mode of philosophical investigation that is oriented to place and that is referred to as 'philosophical topography'; the nature of subjectivity and objectivity as interrelated concepts that also connect with intersubjectivity; and the way place is tied to memory, identity, and the self. Malpas draws on a rich array of writers and philosophers, including Wordsworth, Kant, Proust, Heidegger, and Donald Davidson.

This second edition is revised throughout, including a new chapter on place and technological modernity, especially the seeming loss of place in the contemporary world, and a new Foreword by Edward Casey. It also includes a new set of additional features, such as chapter summaries, illustrations, annotated further reading, and a glossary, which make this second edition more useful to teachers and students alike.

Jeff Malpas is Distinguished Professor at the University of Tasmania, Australia. He is the author or editor of twenty-five books and has published over 150 scholarly articles on topics in philosophy, art, architecture, and geography.

Praise for this book:

'The new edition of this pioneering book remains at the forefront of philosophical engagements with place and space. Profound and challenging, as well as engagingly written, it moves seamlessly across registers – from Proust and Wordsworth to taxi driver knowledge, from Heidegger to analytic philosophy. This is a fundamental work for philosophers, geographers and all those concerned with the question of human experience.'

Stuart Elden, *University of Warwick, UK and Monash University, Australia*

'This expanded and revised edition of *Place and Experience* signifies the enduring importance of Malpas' path-breaking contributions to place and space studies. Eminently readable, full of compelling and illustrative examples, and authoritatively argued, the book masterfully articulates the deep integration of place to human experience.'

Janet Donohoe, *University of West Georgia, USA*

'This important and now classic book is a crucial contribution to our understanding of the deep connections between place and all things human. Transcending disciplinary boundaries, *Place and Experience* offers valuable lessons for architects, urban and environmental designers, and all those willing to challenge the seeming inevitability of homogeneous space and placelessness brought about by our technological civilization.'

Alberto Pérez-Gómez, *McGill University, Canada*

'Ever since Plato, an abiding methodological conceit of philosophy has been to separate conceptual questions from empirical conceptions. Jeff Malpas challenges this conceit. In drawing on literature, anthropology, psychology, and the history of science, as well as philosophy, he opens up new paths and possibilities for thinking seriously about embodied human being in the world and its prospects in difficult times.'

Richard Eldridge, *Swarthmore College, USA*

'This is a book filled with provocative ideas about agency, locality, self, spatiality, past and person. It also established Jeff Malpas as a pre-eminent philosopher of place. If you want to understand the complex unity of place, there is no better book with which to begin.'

Edward Relph, *University of Toronto, Canada*

'Jeff Malpas' beautiful work about place has fed the architecture of my own creative work for many years now. This splendid new edition of his classic text spans from the past of our memories to the future we already live in – thanks to globalization and that thing we call "connectedness" – urging us to more properly locate our thoughts, our actions and our experiences so that we might locate, more entirely, ourselves. A nourishing, inspiring and important book.'

Ashley Hay, *author of* A Hundred Small Lessons

Place and Experience

A Philosophical Topography

Second edition

Jeff Malpas

Routledge
Taylor & Francis Group
LONDON AND NEW YORK

Second edition published 2018
by Routledge
2 Park Square, Milton Park, Abingdon, Oxon OX14 4RN

and by Routledge
711 Third Avenue, New York, NY 10017

Routledge is an imprint of the Taylor & Francis Group, an informa business

First edition published by Cambridge University Press 1999

British Library Cataloguing-in-Publication Data
A catalogue record for this book is available from the British Library

Library of Congress Cataloging-in-Publication Data
Names: Malpas, Jeff, author.
Title: Place and experience : a philosophical topography / Jeff Malpas.
Description: Second edition. | New York : Routledge, 2018. | Includes bibliographical references and index.
Identifiers: LCCN 2017043211| ISBN 9781138291416 (hardback : alk. paper) | ISBN 9781138291430 (pbk. : alk. paper) | ISBN 9781315265445 (ebook)
Subjects: LCSH: Place (Philosophy)
Classification: LCC B105.P53 M35 2018 | DDC 128/.4–dc23
LC record available at https://lccn.loc.gov/2017043211

ISBN: 978-1-138-29141-6 (hbk)
ISBN: 978-1-138-29143-0 (pbk)
ISBN: 978-1-315-26544-5 (ebk)

Typeset in Garamond and Gillsans
by Swales & Willis Ltd, Exeter, Devon, UK

Where does spirit live? Inside or outside
Things remembered, made things, things unmade?
. . .
How habitable is perfect form?
And how inhabited the windy light?

Seamus Heaney, 'Settings', xxii

Contents

Foreword

Edward S. Casey

Jeff Malpas's classic study of place, *Place and Experience: A Philosophical Topography*, first appeared in 1999, the last year of the twentieth century. It capped several decades of work on the importance of place in human experience, and it opened up an efflorescence of further research on the topic – to the point that 'spatial studies' is now an integral part of research and teaching in the humanities and social sciences. For it has become abundantly clear that spatiality (very much including placiality) is indispensable to a full understanding of human experience. The previous priority of time and history, so characteristic in the period extending from Kant through Bergson, has given way to the recognition of the priority of place and space in many fields, ranging from history to sociology, and from psychology to philosophy. In philosophy, Deleuze famously proclaimed in the late 1960s that 'Le Dehors' is the direction that the most productive philosophical work should take. At almost exactly the same moment, Heidegger declared that *Ort* and *Ortlichkeit* – place and placefulness – were what concerned him the most in the third and final phase of his philosophical development. Derrida's *Grammatology*, appearing at the same time, argued for the primacy of written traces over the spoken word – thus for the formative power of spatially determined marks. A little later, Deleuze himself, joining forces with Guattari, explored such spatially distributed models as the rhizome and nomadic movement in terms of a 'smooth space' that is composed of heterogeneous spatialities. Meanwhile, Yi-Fu Tuan, Edward Relph, and others extended spatial studies to geography, Henri Lefebvre reconceived urban studies from a placial perspective, and David Seamon and Robert Mugerauer looked into the architectural dimensions of place considered as the basis for human dwelling.

A complex and rich history of reflection on the centrality of place in human experience was thereby generated, extending over many fields of research and areas of discussion. My own early work was part of this groundswell: *Getting Back into Place* appeared in 1993 and *The Fate of Place* in 1997. It was in 1999 that *Place and Experience* was published. In this masterful book, Malpas drew upon the full scale of contemporary philosophical research, with extensive reference to relevant analytical as well as phenomenological traditions. His approach was as much conceptual as experiential, and one because of the other. The result was a fresh understanding of place as not only pivotal in ongoing experience but as constitutive of the very *idea* of experience itself. For the very first time in the extensive literature on place, a closely argued case was made for place as a necessary structure of human experience – in short, as an *a priori* condition of *all* of this experience, not just of parts or aspects of it. Malpas demonstrates that place is 'the frame within which experience . . . is to be understood'.[1] It is 'integral to the very structure and possibility of experience'.[2]

This strong claim for the priority of place constituted a breakthrough not just in placial/spatial studies in many areas but in philosophy itself. *Place and Experience* is a contribution that is not just important and original but, in its full scope, a text that is indispensable to the understanding of human experience. Lucidly written, this book quickly established itself as authoritative and definitive in the ever-burgeoning field of spatial analysis. The publication of this new edition both acknowledges this fact and makes this remarkable text available to new generations of researchers everywhere.

Its appearance could not be more timely in an era of globalization when, as Marshall McLuhan foresaw, place figures ever more importantly as the effective antipode to, and counterbalance of, transnational corporations and international communications networks. For place is, and will always be, where people live and move and have their being. It is the primary field of lived experience – there where human beings undertake and undergo all that comes their way and all that issues forth from the nexus of past and present experience. As Malpas puts it, 'it is, indeed, only in and through place that the world presents itself – *it is in place, and our own being-in-place, that the world begins*'.[3] By 'world', Malpas means not only one's personal world but whole worlds of history, culture, environment, and nature: all the worlds that matter in human experience (and, for that matter, animal experience).

Of particular relevance to the current moment is Malpas's emphasis on subjectivity and place. Instead of abandoning the human subject in a limbo of cyberspace, he finds myriad ways in which to show that to be a human subject at all – to think, feel, and experience – is to be emplaced. His deep premise is that place is 'that within and with respect to which subjectivity is itself established. Place is not founded *on* subjectivity but is that *on which* the notion of subjectivity is founded.'[4] And it is *grounded* there as well, not in any metaphysical fashion, but in the very concrete ways that call for careful descriptive mapping of the sort at which Malpas is so very adept.[5] He takes Proust as a primal guide: 'Proust's achievement is to display the disclosure of the multiplicity and unity of experience, and therefore of the world, as something that occurs through the spatio-temporal unfolding of place.'[6]

Proust is especially instructive insofar as his celebrated stress on time is shown by Malpas to be tied ultimately to the priority of place. For Proust, temporality and spatiality alike are 'inter-related aspects of the single dimensionality that is integral to activity and fundamental to the idea of place'.[7] What is often construed as Proust's *tour de force* of showing the primacy of temporality in human experience is turned on its head on Malpas's ingenious and persuasive reading. He does not argue that temporality is reducible to placiality (in my own preferred term) but that it is paired with a generic spatiality – in a doublet of lived time with lived space – and that both are enmeshed in a prior matrix whose most fitting name is 'place'.

A corollary of this view is that space – often assumed to be the more encompassing and prior term, as with Newton's idea of Absolute Space or indeed, with any idea of an encompassing cosmic space – is itself dependent on place. If it is true that place itself implies certain spatial modalities (such as measurability), it is more importantly the case that space entails placial locatedness: 'we are forced to look to a way of thinking about spatiality that sees it as embedded within the larger structure, not of a single space, but of a unitary and encompassing place'.[8] From this latter statement we can see clearly that Malpas refuses to reduce place to what Whitehead would call 'simple location', that is, place as a pinpointed locus. Place for Malpas is an immensely and intensely embracing term. For it 'provides the framework within which the complex interconnection of notions of *both* subjective and objective spatiality can be understood'.[9] The framing effected by place – how it functions as a structure – is given an ingenious twist by Malpas when he adds that 'a particular place can appear within the very bounds that it also opens up'.[10] More generally, a given place folds inward toward what is displayed in that place, just as it also folds outward to draw other places into its ambience.[11]

A crucial component of the embrace of place is found in human *agency*. Malpas's conception of the human subject is of an active being that undertakes many modes of praxis. Such praxis is embedded in a spatio-temporal nexus. This nexus is in turn a matter of *embodied* modes of action ('the capacity for action is tied to the capacities of the body, so the particular capacities for action of any particular creature are evident in the particular differentiation of that creature's body'[12]); but more important it is the 'worldly location' in which embodied agency occurs. Such a location is what anchors human actions effected by the kinds of embodied movement described by Merleau-Ponty in his *Phenomenology of Perception*. Place and embodiment are both essential to the possibility of agency. Agency is indispensable to human subjectivity, and so its locatedness via bodily movement becomes essential to this subjectivity. In short, the human subject as an agent does not precede spatiality or temporality but, deploying both, operates within the milieu of places that provide the scene of action. In this deployment, human activity is not only located in places but dynamically reveals aspects of placement that would not come forward without such activity.[13] The set of places thereby disclosed is the experiential equivalent of Heidegger's notion of the Open, that is to say, a clearing in which diverse actions become possible.[14] In part, this is a matter of what we could call 'unity from below';[15] but more completely it is a matter of what J.J. Gibson calls a 'layout of places'. It is in and from this unity and this layout that subjectivity emerges. As Malpas puts it in a characteristically economic but forceful formulation: it is 'in the dense structure of place that subjectivity is embedded'.[16]

It is notable that Malpas is not so much interested in 'place *as* experienced' as in 'place as a structure *within which* experience (as well as action, thought, and judgment) is possible'.[17] This structure is not a formal *a priori* of experience but rather what we could call a *material condition* of that experience in its many forms. As such, it is requisite for that experience: 'such placedness is a necessary condition of our very capacity to experience'.[18]

This basic view carries concrete consequences. Commenting on efforts to argue that place is inherently political – a strong temptation on the part of a number of writers – Malpas remarks that place is not itself political but is rather 'the very frame within which the political itself must be located'.[19] This is a telling statement. It establishes that place is no mere social construct. Nor is it the kind of thing that can be described as such – in a single definitive account, as is possible in the case of a particular human face or a nearby tree. Description of discrete things is classically phenomenological, for it seeks to delineate the discrete characteristics of a given something: a determinate object or event. Malpas's thrust is different; it consists in capturing *the scenography of placement itself*. His concern is not only with place per se – the *what* of place – but also with *how* place situates what comes to be in its midst. This becomes evident in this key passage: 'So, to be a creature that is capable of worldly experience and of thought is not merely to be a creature located in a physically extended space. It is to be a creature that finds itself always situated within a complex but unitary place – a place that encompasses the creature itself, other creatures, and a multiplicity of objects and environmental features.'[20]

Here Malpas spells out the primary features of what I called just above 'the embrace of place'. Place is embracing as 'complex but unitary' and as something that 'encompasses' human beings and other creatures, many objects, and multiple environmental features. In other words, place is neither abstract (as it would be if it were a formal *dimension* of things, as is the case with Newtonian space or clock time), nor is it merely particular (just another piece of the furniture of experience).[21] It is a third thing – something closer to a situational medium, a region within which things and events happen and come to be located. Thus conceived, it is close to what D.W. Winnicott describes as 'transitional space' – a continually accessible threshold for experiences of many kinds – indeed, of *all* kinds if Malpas's model is as broadly applicable as he intends. Otherwise stated, not only is no given experience unemplaced but no *kind* of experience lacks placement in the generous sense spelled out by Malpas.

If this is so, then the main title of the book before is to be construed as deliberately pleonastic: *Place and Experience.* For places are places *for* experiences of every actual or imaginable sort. Conversely, experiences are nothing if not emplaced: without a place in which to be present and to be situated, an experience would evaporate into thin air – thus would not be the experience of an experiencer, a sensing or thinking or feeling subject, and thus no experience at all. With the phrase 'place and experience', we are not talking of a tautology here but of a profound identity or, better, of what Plato called an 'indefinite dyad', in which each term is essential to the other even if the terms of the relationship may not be objectively discernible.

The subtitle of this book is *A Philosophical Topography.* This is no mere gesture or idle metaphor. As Malpas spells out early on, 'topography' is to be construed as a very particular activity that requires the topographer (the surveyor, the cartographer) to be, or at least to imagine herself being, *on the ground*: right there at the surface of the topographic features themselves. True topography is a matter of mapping out a region from within the specificities of the region itself. It is 'precisely through the surveyor's active involvement with the landscape that an accurate mapping is made'.[22] This leads to an extraordinary claim that is at once basic to the ever-expanding field of spatial and placial studies and unique in its apposite formulation:

> The complexity of place is mirrored in the complex process of triangulation and traverse by which the topographical surveyor builds up a map of the region being surveyed. No single sighting is sufficient to gain a view of the entire region, multiple sightings are required . . . The delineation of place can only be undertaken by a process that encompasses a variety of sightings from a number of conceptual 'landmarks' and that also undertakes a wide-ranging, criss-crossing set of journeys over the landscape at issue. It is only through such journeying, sighting, and re-sighting that place can be understood.[23]

This lively description is precisely tailored to Malpas's own conception of place as more like a landscape, a region, a scene than a determinate locus, a simple location.[24] Place is to be compared to Jaspers's idea of the Encompassing (*das Umgreifende*) as that in which many things are to be found but which is not itself found in anything else. Or we might call it a 'plateau' in the spirit of *A Thousand Plateaus*, except that it is a plateau-under-plateaus, comparable to what Deleuze and Guattari call a 'plane of consistency' or a 'plane of immanence'. For in place things and events *con-sist* – sit together – and it is there that they find immanent grounding: a place to be (what they are) and to become (other than what they were), both at once: in the terms of another indefinite dyad.

Place and Experience gives us nothing less than *a philosophical topography of place* – and to be more specific, of *placement*: of the many ways that thoughts and things, events and subjects, become placed. It offers an altogether astute philosophical guide to multiple modes of situatedness in the immanence of place. Or rather *places*; for a major part of Malpas's message is that we always find ourselves in more than one place, whether we consider our experiences in succession or in terms of a given experience:

> Our identities are thus bound up with particular places, or localities, through the very structuring of subjectivity and mental life within the overarching structure of place. Particular places enter into our self-conception and self-identity because it is only in, and through, our grasp of the places in which we are situated that we can encounter objects, other persons, or, indeed, ourselves.[25]

Notice that the primary emphasis here is on 'particular places, or localities' and 'the places in which we are situated'. These make up the reality of place as experienced.

They are what we encounter and undergo in contrast with 'the overarching structure of place' – which latter is the material condition of such things as embodiment and experience itself. And it is the material condition of our own subjectivity: 'it is only within the overarching structure of place as such that subjectivity is possible'.[26] The 'as such' – a phrase singled out by Derrida as designating efforts to find such things as identity or essence[27] – here stands over against the concretions of particular places: places in the plural, places all over the place.

Jeff Malpas's *Place and Experience* takes us to two critical epicentres of human experience: to placial plurality and to place itself – or more exactly, to place as the abiding condition of the plurality itself. In such plurality and such place, we encounter a last indefinite dyad, one that prefigures and configures all that we experience.

This book, here presented in a handsome second edition, represents an indispensable journey into 'the wonder and the fragility of place',[28] rendering its encompassing topography in exquisite descriptive detail. For all this and more, new and returning readers alike will find themselves enlivened by the reappearance of this uniquely instructive text.

Notes

1 Jeff Malpas, *Place and Experience: A Philosophical Topography*, rev. ed. (London: Routledge, 2018), intro., 13. All citations refer to this new, revised, and expanded edition. See also Chapter 1, 45, n47: 'the task undertaken here has a certain "transcendental" character – it is a matter of undertaking an analysis of the structure in which the very possibility of subjectivity and of objectivity, of experience

and self, are grounded'. At Chapter 8, 45, we read that the intimate knowledge of place is 'that in which one's very life is grounded'.

2 Ibid., Chapter 1, 31 (italics in the original).

3 Ibid, Introduction, 12 (italics in the original).

4 Ibid., Chapter 1, 34 (italics in the original).

5 Malpas himself employs the language of 'ground' in several ways, as in a characteristic phrase such as this: 'the fundamental grounding of subjectivity and of mental life in place' (ibid., Chapter 8, 184).

6 Ibid., Chapter 7, 166. Chapter 7, 'The unity and complexity of place', is largely devoted to an analysis of *Remembrance of Things Past*. Later, in the next chapter, Malpas draws upon Sally Morgan's *My Place*, an autobiographical account of living in Western Australia that draws deeply upon the landscapes of that region.

7 Ibid., Chapter 7, 170.

8 Ibid., Chapter 1, 41. Regarding the reverse claim, see p. 40: 'the concept of place cannot be divorced from space, just as space cannot be divorced from time (and so place encompasses time no less than space)'.

9 Ibid., Chapter 2, 74 (italics in the original).

10 Ibid., Chapter 7, 175.

11 On the double folding effected by place, see ibid., Chapter 7, 174–175.

12 Ibid., Chapter 5, 138.

13 'the grasp of space – and so of place – is tied to activity. In this respect, any concrete sense of place is most closely tied to concrete capacities to act and to be acted upon' (ibid., Chapter 7, 173).

14 'Fundamental to the idea of place is the idea of an open and yet bounded realm within which the things of the world can appear and events can "take place"' (ibid., Chapter 1, 33). See also ibid., Chapter 1, 25 and Chapter 7, 172–174. Part of the openness is that a given place allows for *other places* to appear in or through it: see Chapter 7, 175.

15 'Only within place is the unity necessary for subjectivity established' (ibid., Chapter 7, 176). I add the phrase 'from below' (*von unten*: a favourite phrase of Jaspers) to indicate the fact that place *supports* whatever is displayed at its surface.

16 Ibid., Chapter 8, 179.

17 Ibid., Chapter 2, 75 (italics in the original). For other references to place as a 'structure', see ibid., 140, 161, and 188–189.

18 Ibid., Chapter 8, 194.

19 Ibid., Conclusion, 215.

20 Ibid., Chapter 7, 161.

21 When Malpas speaks of 'the unitary dimensionality of place' (p. 185), he is not referring to anything like a formally determined, geometric *dimension* inherent in place. This is confirmed by his statement that 'the identity of any particular place is determined, not in terms of any simple set of *clearly defined parameters*, but by means of a complex of factors deriving from the elements encompassed by that place itself' (ibid., 188, my italics).

22 Ibid., Chapter 1, 38.

23 Ibid., Chapter 1, 40.

24 See the statement that 'self-identity is not thereby tied to any simple location within some purely static space' (ibid., Chapter 8, 181).

25 Ibid., Chapter 8, 180.

26 Ibid.

27 For a discussion of the 'as such', see Jacques Derrida, *Rogues: Two Essays on Reason*, trans. Pascale-Anne Brault and Michael Naas (Palo Alto, CA: Stanford University Press, 2005).

28 *Place and Experience*, Chapter 8, 195.

Acknowledgements

As with the first edition of this book, there are many people to whom I am indebted for assistance in bringing the current edition to publication. Most immediately, I have to thank Randall Lindstrom, my research assistant, who not only made it possible for the new edition to be completed in good time, but whose care in working though the original text has made this a much better book than it was or would have been without him. I am also very grateful to Tony Bruce at Routledge for being so supportive of my proposal for a new and enlarged edition, and for his suggestions as to how that could best be realized. I would like to reiterate my gratitude to all those who were so important in the formation of the thinking that went into this book in its first incarnation: Julian Young, Sue Ashford, Dougal Blyth, Peta Bowden, Andrew Brennan, Marcia Cavell, Felicity Haynes, Onora O'Neill, Charles Spinosa, Reinhard Steiner, Dermot Moran, and Andrew Light, as well as the late Donald Davidson and the late Hubert Dreyfus. I would like to acknowledge again the role of the Australian Research Council, who provided support for this book in 1996–97 and again, in part, in 2017, and the continuing support of the Alexander von Humboldt Foundation over many years. The first edition of this book arose out of a period of thinking and writing while living in Perth, Western Australia; this new edition has been completed in Tasmania where I have lived for almost two decades. The new edition undoubtedly reflects the experience and thinking of that Tasmanian location, and is certainly indebted to my Tasmanian colleagues, students, and friends, as well as those beyond this island, with whom I have engaged since I first came here in early 1999. That group of people includes, especially, Andrew Benjamin, Ingo Farin, Pete Hay, and also, if at more of a distance, Mark Burry, Edward Casey (especially for agreeing to write such a gracious Foreword), Elias Constanopoulos, Steve Crowell, Witi Ihimaera, Bruce Janz, Vasilis Ganiatsis, Juhani Pallasmaa Alberto Pérez-Gómez, Laurence Hemming, David Seamon, and, last but by no means least, Kenneth White.

Introduction

The influence of place

> Is it some influence, as a vapour which exhales from the ground, or something in the gales which blow there, or in all things there brought agreeably to my spirit. . .?
>
> (Henry David Thoreau, *Journal*, 21 July 1851[1])

We are all familiar with the effect of human thought and activity on the landscapes in which human beings dwell. Human beings change the land around them in a way and on a scale matched, for the most part, by no other animal. The land around us is indeed a reflection, not only of our practical and technological capacities, but also of our culture and society – of our very needs, our hopes, our preoccupations and dreams. This fact is itself worthy of greater notice and attention than perhaps it is sometimes given (it is indeed a theme to which I shall return). Yet the human relation to the land, and to the environing world in general, is clearly not a relation characterized by an influence running in just one direction. There are obvious ways, of course, in which the environment determines our activities and our thoughts – we build here rather than there because of the greater suitability of the site; the presence of a river forces us to construct a bridge to carry the road across; we plant apples rather than mangoes because the climate is too cold – but there are other much less straightforward and perhaps more pervasive ways in which our relation to landscape and environment is indeed one of our own *affectivity* as much as of our ability to *effect*.

The relation of person to place is a recurrent theme in Wordsworth's poetry. Following immediately after 'Poems on the Naming of Places', at the end of the second volume of the 1800 edition of the *Lyrical Ballads*,[2] Wordsworth's 'Michael' is explicitly tied to an identifiable place, Greenhead Gill or Ghyll, in Grasmere, Cumbria (see Figure 1) – in what used to be known as Westmoreland. Place is invoked at the very start of the poem with the first lines effectively leading the reader into the landscape to which the poem belongs, and so also into the story of the place and of the shepherd, Michael, after whom the poem is titled:

> If from the public way you turn your steps
> Up the tumultuous brook of Greenhead Gill
> . . . one object which you might pass by,
> Might see and notice not. Beside the brook
> Appears a struggling heap of unhewn stones!
> And to that simple object appertains
> A story. . .[3]

Michael dwelt, we are told, 'upon the Forest-side in Grasmere Vale',[4] and that 'straggling heap of unhewn stones' appears as his unintended memorial. Of Michael's relation to the countryside in which he dwells, Wordsworth writes:

> . . .grossly that man errs, who should suppose
> That the green Valleys, and the Streams and Rocks,
> Were things indifferent to the Shepherd's thoughts.[5]

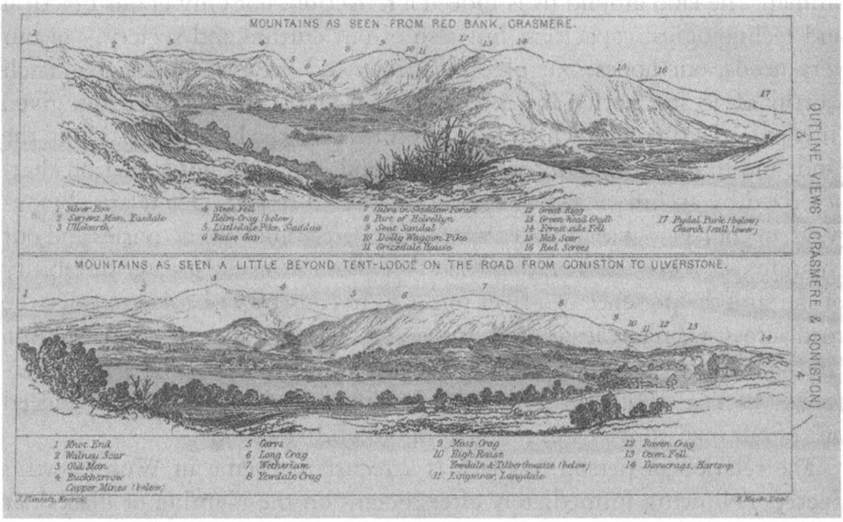

Figure 1 Print, lithograph, 'Outline Views, Grasmere and Coniston – Mountains as seen from Redbank, Grasmere, and Mountains as seen a little beyond Tent Lodge on the Road from Coniston to Ulverstone', by J. Flintoft, Keswick, Cumberland, engraved by R. Mason, Edinburgh, Lothian, about 1900, found at 'Greenhead Gill', in *Old Cumbria Gazeteer*, accessed 28 August 2017, www.geog.port.ac.uk/webmap/thelakes/html/lgaz/lgazfram.htm. Greenhead Gill, marked here as no. 13 in the upper view, is the place named as the location for Wordsworth's 'Michael'.

The point here is not to direct attention to the shepherd's own influence on the landscape around him (though a part of the story focuses around the building of a sheepfold by Michael and his son), but rather to the effect of those surroundings on Michael himself. Wordsworth's concern is to make plain, as Seamus Heaney puts it, the way in which 'the Westmoreland mountains were . . . much more than a picturesque backdrop for his shepherd's existence, how they were rather companionable and influential in the strict sense of the word "influential" – things flowed in from them to Michael's psychic life. This District was not inanimate stone but active nature, humanized and humanizing.'[6] Not only is Michael's own identity bound up with the hills and valleys around him, and which themselves take on an almost personal character, but Heaney seems to suggest that it is the shepherd's very humanity that is bound in this way – nature is both 'humanized and humanizing'. As Wordsworth writes of Michael and his relation to the countryside in which he lived: 'these fields, these hills. . . were his living Being, even more Than his own Blood. . .'[7]

The idea that human identity is somehow tied to location is not, of course, peculiar to Wordsworth, nor even to romantic nature poetry. It is an idea that has both a long ancestry over the centuries and a wide currency across cultures. Indigenous Australians had – and many still have – a conception of human life, and indeed, of all life, as inextricably bound up with the land (something graphically expressed in the image of ancient handprints on rock – see Figure 2). In his historical investigation of the Indigenous shaping of the Australian landscape, Bill Gammage writes of the centrality and intimacy of Indigenous peoples' relation to place or 'country': '[they] felt intensely for their country. It was alive. It could talk, listen, suffer, be refreshed, rejoice. They were on it and others were not because they knew it and it knew them. There their spirit stayed, there they expected to die. No other country could ever be that. Country was heart, mind, and soul. Country was not property. If anything, it owned.'[8] Tony Swain explains how the closeness of the relation between self and country is reflected in Indigenous beliefs concerning conception: 'The mother does not contribute to the ontological substance of the child, but rather "carries" a life whose essence belongs, and belongs alone, to a site. The child's core identity is determined by his or her place of derivation. The details vary; the location might be directly linked with feeling the child enter the womb or, alternatively, dreams or foodstuffs may provide clues as to the site from which the spirit derived. . . Life is annexation of place.'[9] A child's identity is thus derived, on this account, from a particular place and thereby also from a particular spiritual and totemic ancestry. So important is this tie of person to place that for Australian Indigenous peoples the land around them is everywhere filled with marks of individual and ancestral origins, and is dense with story and myth.[10] In traditional

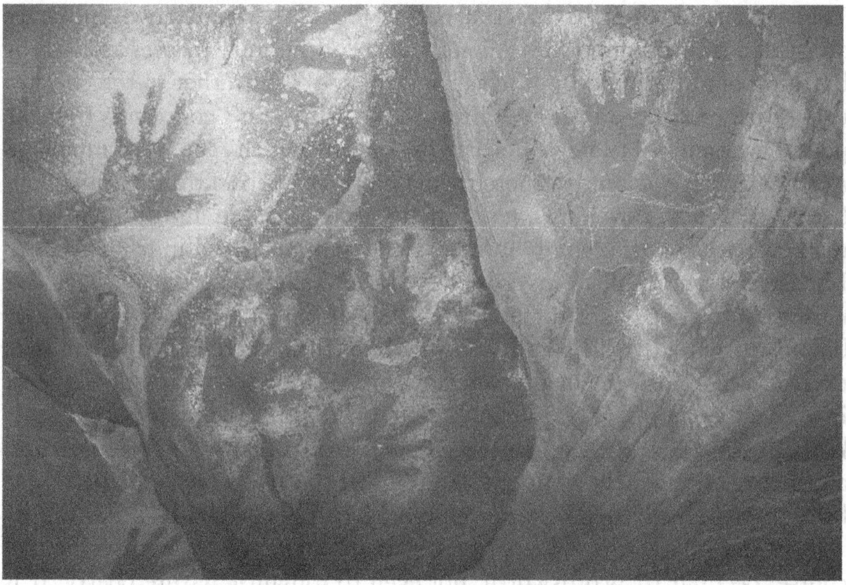

Figure 2 Hand stencils, northern Australia, image courtesy Paul S.C. Taçon.

terms, then, for a person of Australian Indigenous heritage to be removed from that country to which he or she belongs is for them to be deprived of their very substance, and in past times such removal – particularly when it involved imprisonment – frequently led to sickness and death.[11]

While such indigenous views of the relation between persons and place may seem rather extreme or even peculiar to non-indigenous eyes – though perhaps less so in places like Australia where there has been, in spite of entrenched racism and narrowness of vision, a gradually broadening appreciation and understanding of the importance of place and 'country' in Indigenous culture – such views have clear correlates around the globe. Across the Tasman, in New Zealand, Māori beliefs also emphasize connection to place and to the land as constitutive of identity – perhaps most clearly expressed in the idea of *Turangawaewae*, meaning 'a place to stand' and referring to that place in which one is grounded through ties to genealogy and tradition. In *The Coming of the Maori*, Te Rangi Hiroa writes eloquently of the Māori connection to the land:

> In the course of time, the principal tribes with their subtribes came to occupy definite areas with fixed boundaries. The love of their own territory developed to an absorbing degree, for tribal history was written over its hills and vales, its rivers, streams, and lakes, and upon its cliffs and shores. The earth and caves held the bones of their illustrious dead, and dirges and laments teemed

> with references to the love lavished upon the natural features of their home lands. The prestige of the tribe was associated with their *marae* sites and terraced hill forts, and their religious concepts were bound to their *tuahu* shrines. Captives in distant lands have begged for a pebble, a bunch of leaves, or a handful of earth from the home land that they might weep over a symbol of home. It is the everlasting hills of one's own deserted territory that welcome the wanderer home and it is the ceaseless crooning of the waves against a lone shore that perpetuates the sound of voices that are still.[12]

Even if expressed in very different ways in different cultures and traditions, the basic notion of a tie between place and human identity is thus both widespread and explicit in indigenous cultures from Australia to the Americas.

The idea that there is a close tie between place and human being is not, however, peculiar to indigenous cultures alone. It is an important and recurrent theme in Western European thinking, especially Western European art and literature, and more explicitly so over the last two to three hundred years. There is no dearth of examples here, but one especially significant literary instantiation of this preoccupation with place and locality is Marcel Proust's seven-volume *In Search of Lost Time*.[13] One should not allow oneself to be deceived by the apparent focus on time or on the past that is suggested by the title of the work (especially by its original English translation as *In Search of Lost Time*[14]). Proust's work is as much about place and space as it is about anything temporal (a point to which I shall return), and Proust treats the relation between persons and their locations in a manner that is particularly striking. In Proust's work, persons and places intermingle with one another in such a way that places take on the individuality of persons, while persons are themselves individuated and characterized by their relation to place;[15] persons come to be seen, to use a phrase from Lawrence Durrell, almost 'as functions of a landscape'[16] – in some cases, even of a particular room or setting. In fact, the narrator of Proust's novel, Marcel, grasps his own life, and the time in which it is lived, only through his recovery of the places in relation to which that life has been constituted. *Remembrance of Things Past* is thus an invocation and exploration of a multitude of places and, through those places, of the persons who appear with them. As Georges Poulet writes, 'Infallibly, then, with Proust, in reality as in dream, persons and places are united [*lieux et personnes s'unissent*]. The Proustian imagination would not know how to conceive beings otherwise than in placing them against a local background that plays for them the part of foil and mirror.'[17]

The idea that the self is to be discovered through an investigation of the places it inhabits is the central idea in Gaston Bachelard's *The Poetics of Space*.[18] Both the love of place – 'topophilia' – and the investigation of places – 'topoanalysis' – are presented by Bachelard as essential notions in any combined phenomenological-psychoanalytic study of memory, self, and mind.[19] In Bachelard, the life of the mind is given form in the places and spaces in which human beings dwell, and those places are taken themselves to shape and influence human memories, feelings, and thoughts. In this way, the spaces of inner and outer – of mind and world – are transformed one into the other as inner space is externalized and outer space brought within. In this respect Merleau-Ponty seems to express an idea found in Bachelard, as well as in his own work, when he writes that 'the world is wholly inside and I am wholly outside myself',[20] and at the same time suggests a breakdown in the very dichotomy that is invoked. The stuff of our 'inner' lives is thus to be found in the 'outer' places in which we dwell, while those same places 'without' are incorporated 'within' us. Proust's *In Search of Lost Time* can be seen as a special exercise in the exploration of such places, and thus as an exercise in something like the topoanalysis described by Bachelard – although it is an analysis of place that looks, not only to the intimacy of the enclosed spaces of cupboard, room, and home, but also to the larger space of the garden, the village, the city, the plain, the sea, and the sky. And like Bachelard, Proust presents such topoanalysis as an exploration of our own selves as well as an exploration of love through an exploration of place – in Proust we find topophilia writ large.

Proust is perhaps unusual in his almost explicit thematizing of the relation between persons and places, but the same basic idea of human life as essentially a life of location, of self-identity as a matter of identity found in place, and of places themselves as somehow suffused with the 'human', is common to the work of poets and novelists from all parts of the globe and in relation to all manner of landscapes and localities: from William Faulkner[21] to Mo Yan,[22] from Friedrich Hölderlin[23] to Adrienne Rich.[24] Wordsworth regarded poetry itself as having its origins in memorial inscription – in epitaphs and in the naming of places[25] – and the novel seems to have its beginnings in a fascination with the exploration of places and to be, in some respects, an outgrowth of the travelogue.[26] Indeed, in Herman Melville, whose own works can often be seen as instances of the literary preoccupation with place and locale, we find the claim that 'nearly all literature, in one sense, is made up of guide-books'.[27] As Proust's great work, no less than Wordsworth's 'Michael', is an examination of the human through 'humanized and humanizing' place, so too in Melville and V.S. Naipal,[28] in Seamus Heaney,[29] and Louise Glück,[30] the exploration of character and event, of life and love, of culture and of idea is one and the same with the exploration, and often the rediscovery, of landscape, countryside, and place.

It might be thought that the idea of human life and identity as established in some special relation to landscape and place is really just a sort of literary conceit – part of the creative and imaginative technique of the novelist or poet rather than having anything to do with the character of human being as such. Similarly, more generalized conceptions of human identity as tied to human locality, whether amongst Indigenous peoples or others, might be thought to provide evidence of no more than a certain commonplace feature of human psychology – a tendency that is perhaps grounded in biology or evolutionary history, but which may be a purely contingent feature of human character varying as culture and society vary. For my own part, I find such views of the contingency of the connection to place highly implausible – and this is not just because of some personal experience of my own regarding the felt power of the human attachment to place nor of the emotional impact that a particular landscape or locality may bring with it. The idea that human identity is somehow tied to place in a quite fundamental way is given support, both direct and indirect, by a great many purely philosophical considerations as well as by recent work in other more empirical disciplines. Some of these considerations will form the basis for the discussion in the chapters to come, but it is important for now to see the way in which such considerations provide, at the very least, a *prima facie* case for taking the sorts of ideas found, perhaps in somewhat embellished form, in writers such as Proust and Wordsworth, in Indigenous traditions and culture, and elsewhere, very seriously indeed.

Gaston Bachelard, to whom I referred above, is one important philosopher who has treated extensively the role of place (as well of an associated mode of space) in the understanding of human life and mind, but he is certainly not alone in his concern with the significance of such concepts. Within the phenomenological and hermeneutic traditions, the idea of the inseparability of persons from the places they inhabit is an especially important theme in the work of Martin Heidegger. Although Heidegger's *Being and Time* provides a somewhat problematic analysis of the role of spatiality, and so also of place,[31] in the structure of human existence (or properly of *Dasein*[32]), still Heidegger's fundamental conception of human existence as 'being-in-the-world' implies the impossibility of properly understanding human being in a way that would treat it as only contingently related to its surroundings and to the concrete structures of activity in which it is engaged. Heidegger's thinking in the period after *Being and Time* provides an even stronger emphasis on concepts of place and locality – so much so that Heidegger presents the idea of place or site (Heidegger most often uses the terms *Ort* or *Ortschaft* in the German, and sometimes the Greek *topos*) as the central concept in his later thinking.[33] Merleau-Ponty's analyses of embodiment and spatiality in *The Phenomenology of Perception*, while in some respects more inclined towards traditional phenomenology than Heidegger's work, and so more Husserlian (and perhaps even, in a certain sense, more Cartesian) in spirit, nevertheless provides another important instance in which the central role of place, especially as this arises through embodiment, is given philosophical grounding. For Merleau-Ponty human thought and experience is essentially grounded in the corporeal and the concrete and is therefore also intimately connected with the environing world in its particularity and immediacy.[34]

In Heidegger and Merleau-Ponty, it is not merely human identity that is tied to place, but the very possibility of being the sort of creature that can engage *with* a world (and, more particularly, with the objects and events within it), that can think *about* that world, and that can find itself *in* the world. The idea of a close connection between human 'being-in-the-world' and spatiality, locality, and embodiment that can be discerned (though in different ways and with differing emphases) in the work of Heidegger and Merleau-Ponty reappears in the work of many more recent thinkers working in a number of different fields. Sometimes that influence is to be seen in the explicit thematization of notions of place and notions associated with place. This is especially so in relation to the Heideggerian influence on architectural theory, in the work of writers such as Karsten Harries[35] and Christian Norberg-Schulz,[36] and also on geographical thinking, particularly within the framework of so-called 'humanistic geography'[37] and environmentalism.[38] Even aside from the influence of Heidegger and Merleau-Ponty, ideas of place and locality have become almost commonplace in much contemporary work in social sciences and the humanities – including work in areas such as theology.[39] Nor do Heidegger and Merleau-Ponty possess a monopoly on the deployment of place as the focus for philosophical inquiry. Edward Casey, in his book *The Fate of Place*, recounts the story of both the relative decline in the attention given to place over much of the history of philosophy (although Casey's work also chronicles just how important place has often been), along with its re-emergence as a significant notion, not only in Bachelard, Heidegger, and Merleau-Ponty, but also in the work of Derrida, Deleuze and Guattari, and Irigaray.[40]

The concepts of place and space are sometimes taken up as 'strategic' concepts – as tools that have a particular 'political' purpose behind them – rather than as concepts to be investigated in their own right. This seems to be true, for instance, of some of the uses to which Deleuze and Guattari have put their idea of 'nomadism' as developed in *A Thousand Plateaus*.[41] Yet even such strategic uses of place and space provoke the question why those notions in particular should have quite the strategic effectiveness that they seem to possess. It may be that a concept or term is strategically important simply because of its relation to some other term or concept – deconstructive strategies, in particular, look to terms that stand in a relation of binary opposition to one another (as male to female or mind to body) and in which one of the terms is given a privileged role while the other is, in some way, 'repressed'. But at least in the case of concepts of space and place, it seems that the strategic importance of those concepts derives, not merely from their role in any set of binary oppositions or their relation to other sets of concepts, but in large part from their indispensability and ubiquity in human thought, experience, and agency.

This is not just to say, for instance, that we usually experience ourselves, and other things, in relation to place, but that the very structure of the mind is intrinsically tied to ideas and images of place and space. In *Being and Time*, where there is no clear distinction of place from space, Heidegger attempted to explain this as an instance of the inevitable tendency for *Dasein* towards 'fallen-ness' – the tendency always to understand in a way that is forgetful and concealing of the properly temporal character of its being.[42] Only as Heidegger becomes clearer about the nature of place as distinct from any 'Cartesian' notion of spatiality does he comes also to recognize that this dependence of being on place is not merely an artefact of our modes of linguistic articulation or of some ontological forgetfulness, but does indeed relate to the fundamental intimacy of being with place. Within more recent English-speaking philosophy, Mark Johnson has investigated the prevalence of modes of thinking that are reliant on notions of place as well as space as part of a more general thesis concerning the way in which the body, and the structures associated with it, is actually determinative of patterns of thinking and understanding. Thus, he writes that 'as animals we have bodies connected to the natural world, such that our consciousness and rationality are tied to our bodily orientations and interactions in and with our environment. Our embodiment is essential to who we are, and to what meaning is, and to our ability to draw rational inferences and be creative.'[43]

The view that persons must be understood in relation to their worldly surroundings is not restricted, however, to the work of German and French theorists alone. Johnson provides an example of a philosopher working within English-speaking philosophy who finds an important relation of dependence to obtain, if not quite between place and person, then certainly between mind, body, and environmental locality – and in this his approach also reflects a widespread approach within much contemporary cognitive science.[44] Externalist theories of mental content of the sort found in the work of many American and British philosophers – in the work, for instance, of Tyler Burge[45] – also suggest a conception of the person as inseparable from the person's environment. These theories (which can be seen as often having their origins in the later work of Ludwig Wittgenstein) take beliefs, desires, and other attitudes as determined, in large part, by the physical and social surroundings in which the individual person is located.

In the work of Donald Davidson, in particular, externalism of this sort takes on a particularly strong form. Unlike Burge, Davidson is less concerned with the social determination of meaning so much as with the way in which mental life can only be understood in its relation to an external world.[46]

Indeed, one might say that for Davidson, in the absence of such a world there can be no mental life – the mind is itself constituted primarily through its interaction and involvement with the objects and events that surround it. Davidson's externalist approach leads him to reject those standard philosophical dichotomies that, in various ways, set up a contrast between the private world of the mind with the public world of external objectivity – there is no such contrast in Davidson's work.[47] The rejection of that contrast enables Davidson, in a manner reminiscent of both Heidegger and Wittgenstein, to deny that any sense can be attached to the sceptic's claim that perhaps we are mostly wrong in our beliefs about the world, that perhaps there is no 'external world' to which we have access. For Davidson, such a claim can make no sense, since having 'access' to such a world is indeed the primary condition for our own mental life – for our beliefs to fail to be mostly true would be for us to fail even to have beliefs, let alone desires, emotions, or anything more. The very idea that there is some problem of 'access' to a world 'external' to us is itself part of what gives rise to the mistaken problematic on the basis of which scepticism can arise.[48] We must understand ourselves as already 'in' the world if we are to be capable of understanding at all.[49]

As Marcia Cavell writes, providing a neat summary of many of these Davidsonian ideas: 'Without our abilities to move around objects and to see, both of us, the same physical object from different perspectives, to move our tongues and mouths and to make sounds, to remember the past in such simple acts as my recognizing this as the same object we saw a moment ago, to enter into countless forms of communal life, there could be no beginning for those acts of communication that we have said are basic both to interpretation and to thought.'[50] In her own discussion, Cavell also draws on Freudian object-relations theory according to which individual psychological development is always predicated upon the development of relations with others. Cavell thereby suggests another way in which the capacity for mental life might be connected with a localized, 'worldly' existence, since without a grasp of the places and spaces in which others can be encountered it is arguable whether there can be any relation to others at all – and if no relation to others, then no relation to self either.[51]

Another important source in English-speaking philosophy for ideas linking mind and self to the environing world is to be found in a line of thinking that derives largely from Kant. In a range of both pre-critical and critical works, Kant demonstrates a concern to understand human subjectivity as inextricably bound to the world of 'external' objects, and to see philosophical investigation as itself taking the form of an almost geographical or topographical inquiry.[52] This Kantian line of thought is developed further, in work that has its contemporary sources in the work of Peter Strawson and Gareth Evans in particular,[53] through a focus on the way forms of spatial representation are related to concepts of self and to the capacity for mental life in general. Thus, among other writers in this vein, John Campbell argues for a view of the self that ties self-understanding to a grasp of spatial and causal structures,[54] and Quassim Cassam, drawing explicitly on Strawsonian ideas, argues for the view that a grasp of oneself as a thinking creature is also a matter of grasping oneself as an embodied, spatially located creature.[55] Other writers, sometimes reacting against aspects of Strawson's reading, and often influenced by phenomenological approaches, have argued even more directly for a Kantian emphasis on embodiment and situatedness.[56] Kant's own use of geographical and spatial ideas and images reinforce the idea that the Kantian philosophy is indeed topographical or topological in character.[57]

The notion that there is an intimate connection between person and place, and so also between self and environing world, is thus neither a peculiar idiosyncrasy to be found in works of literature nor some sort of 'leftover' from a pre-modern age – and nor does it seem likely to be a merely contingent feature of human psychology. There is good reason to suppose that the human relationship to place is a fundamental structure in what makes possible the sort of life that is characteristically human, while also being determining – even if in a way that requires clarification – of human identity. In that case, it is not surprising that place, and associated notions of spatiality and embodiment, should have come to such prominence in so many different disciplines and in the work of so many different writers and researchers. The ubiquity of place, and the diversity of contexts in which it appears, is thus some testament to the significance of the notion, but just as the concept of place seems to appear in so many different places, so it seems that the concept is also dispersed and fragmented. How do we match up – do we even try to match – the concept of place as it occurs in the poetry of Wordsworth or Heaney (or of James K. Baxter[58] – perhaps the greatest New Zealand poet – or Adrienne Rich, to cite just two further examples) with the idea of place as it might occur in Heidegger or Bachelard? Moreover, how might we connect the emphasis on the self and the mind as always embedded in and dependent on a particular environment as the idea may seem to be suggested in Davidson, for instance, or in Evans, with the emphasis on locality and involvement in Merleau-Ponty or Heidegger or, indeed, in Proust or James Joyce?[59]

One may recoil at the apparent oddity of these juxtapositions – an oddity perhaps all the more strongly felt within the context of contemporary English-speaking philosophy. Yet if we are to take writers like Wordsworth and Heaney seriously in their assertions of the place-bound character of human life and thought, and if are even to begin to admit some recognition, in our own experience, of the presence of something of the Indigenous feeling for the intimacy of the connection to land and locality, then we cannot avoid trying to understand that which might provide the ground for such notions. We cannot avoid trying to think the diversity of issues that surround the idea of place, and our belonging to it, in some sort of unitary fashion. It is just such a project of trying to understand place that is the project, perhaps the overly ambitious project, that I intend to pursue in the following pages. Although I will draw on a variety of sources – some of which are touched on above – my aim will not simply be to present the idea of place as it might appear in different and juxtaposed ways in literature, psychology, geography, philosophy, and so forth. Instead, I will aim to set out a way of thinking about place that, while mindful of the complexity and ambiguity of the concept, explicates its relation to other concepts, including those of space, time, and self, and that also provides some elucidation and explanation of what might be called 'Proust's Principle' (it could equally be Wordsworth's) of the place-bound identity of persons – that the identity of persons is inextricably bound to place, and not merely to place in some general, abstract sense (which would be meaningless), but also, as a consequence, to those *particular* places, multiple and complex though they may be, in and through which a person's life is lived.[60] Moreover, it is not just persons who are tied to place; a central theme in the conceptual explorations undertaken in the following pages is that the very possibility of the appearance of things – of objects, of others, and of self – is possible only within the all-embracing compass of place. It is, indeed, only in and through place that the world presents itself – *it is in place, and in relation to our own being-in-place, that the world begins.*

The way in which human identity might be tied to place is thus indicative of the fundamental character of our engagement with the world – of all our encounters with persons and things – as always 'taking place' in place. The inquiry undertaken here is thus concerned, not merely with the nature of human self-conception and self-identity, but with a certain sort of fundamental 'ontological' inquiry into place as that in which, to use the Heideggerian phrase, human 'being-in-the-world' is grounded (since the inquiry is indeed 'ontological' in this sense, so I do not here attempt any real investigation of the politics or ethics of place that is common to much of the literature[61]). In this respect, of course, the project undertaken here is a thoroughly philosophical one, and one that draws heavily on arguments and concepts derived from the work of philosophers such as Kant, Strawson, Davidson, and Heidegger. Yet although the project is philosophical in its orientation it is no less a project that aims to have relevance to work outside of philosophy and to speak to non-philosophers as well as those within the discipline. For this reason, the book draws upon and combines a variety of sources from both inside and outside philosophy and from a range of philosophical 'traditions'.

The most detailed philosophical work, at least so far as argument and analysis is concerned, takes place in Chapters 3 to 6. It is the material in these chapters that is most important to substantiating the book's basic claims, since these chapters set out an account of certain fundamental concepts of spatiality and agency, subjectivity and objectivity, on the basis of which the significance of place – its significance in relation, for instance, to those questions of human identity that were raised at the outset – can be approached (though the reader should be warned that this discussion, especially in Chapter 5, is also the most philosophically difficult part of the book – readers may find the chapter summaries at the end of the book useful in helping to navigate through these chapters in particular). The adoption of an explicitly philosophical approach, and the orientation of the work towards understanding place and locality in relation to person, self and experience, means that to a large extent the book is as much a foray into the philosophy of mind or 'philosophical anthropology' as of any newly conceived 'philosophy of place'. Indeed, supposing that the fundamental thesis of the book is correct, and there is no possibility of understanding human existence – and especially human thought and experience – other than through an understanding of place (and with it, space as well as time, since neither is properly separable from place, and so has no role independently of place), it follows that the inquiry into the mind or the self will be identical with the inquiry into place. If I can, in this context, be permitted to make use of the term 'experience' in a quite general and non-technical – in other words, *non-empiricist* – fashion to refer to human existence as it comprises capacities to think, to feel, to grasp, to act, and so on (and this is indeed the sense in which I intend the term throughout my inquiry), then this book may be seen to have a double focus: first, on the possibility of 'experience' in the broad sense indicated, and so on place as the frame within which experience (along with conceptions of self-identity) is to be understood; second, on the concept of place and the elaboration of that concept through an understanding of its role in relation to such 'experience'.

Naturally, all of this assumes rather than demonstrates the possibility of providing an integrated account of the philosophical significance of place. That demonstration cannot, however, be given independently of the investigation that is undertaken in the book as a whole and that is set out in the pages that follow. Only through an exploration of the notion of place will the significance of place itself come to light. Yet even to begin such an exploration requires a place from which to set out and some idea of the territory to be covered. This is especially significant given the dispersed treatment of place across so many disciplines and genres and also, as will evident below, because of the relative lack of attention that has been accorded to place, as Edward Casey makes clear, within much of the history of philosophy.[62]

The task of clarifying the terms, concepts, and approaches that are relevant to the discussion is a crucial task (although it is also particularly difficult) for a work such as this. Although this task is, of course, one that inevitably extends to the book as a whole, it is most explicitly and directly addressed in Chapter 1. There I attempt some exploration of the concepts of place and space as they have arisen within the Western philosophical tradition in particular, as a preliminary to the more detailed discussions that follow. Space is an important starting point, not only because place and space are *related* (as are time and place also), but also because place and space are so often *conflated*. Chapter 2 continues this exploration of concepts by looking more closely at the notion of space and, in particular, the distinction between subjective and objective conceptions of space. The analysis of these notions provides the basis for further clarification of the concept of place, while also orienting the inquiry towards an analysis of the idea of subjectivity – along with associated ideas concerning content and agency – that underlies the concept of 'subjective space' and which is the main focus for Chapters 3 and 4. Chapter 5 draws together some of the various threads that have been spun through the preceding three chapters to examine the way in which concepts of agency (already introduced in the previous chapter), spatiality, and objectivity are interconnected.[63] Chapter 6 develops the argument concerning the idea of objectivity further and in particular connection with the notion of inter-subjectivity. Here not only is the relation between objectivity and inter-subjectivity explored, but so too is the connection between those different senses of subjectivity that involve self and other. The crucial role of spatiality in relation to the possibility of social life and of language and conceptuality is also a focus for discussion in this chapter. It is the complex unity of place itself that is the more explicit focus of Chapter 7, although here the topic is taken up, less through abstract analysis, as through literary and poetic example – in particular, the example to be found in the work of Marcel Proust. Chapter 7 recapitulates and connects many of the themes of the preceding discussion in the course of an elaboration of the ways in which space and time combine within the single structure that is place (and in speaking of place as a 'structure', what is intended is to draw attention to the character of place as involving complex interplay of elements, rather than being a single undifferentiated substrate). Chapter 8 returns explicitly to the issue with which I began the discussion here – the question of the relation between place and human identity – attempting to clarify in just what sense persons and places might indeed be tied together and what this might mean for our sense of ourselves. That this issue is taken up once again, in any detailed way, only in the penultimate chapter is indicative of the way in which the treatment of this issue is necessarily dependent on the analysis of the more general 'structure of place' that goes before. Chapter 9, which is not only the final full chapter (it is followed by a brief conclusion), but also represents the largest single addition to the book from its original publication almost twenty years ago, draws out some of the further consequences of the idea of place, and of the connection of place to the human, with particular focus on the character of place in the seemingly displaced world of contemporary modernity. The conclusion of the book briefly addresses the question of the significance of the concept of place, not only for the understanding of experience and subjectivity, but for our conception of philosophy and of the project of understanding. To assist readers in navigating what is at times, a dense and complex set of arguments, each chapter includes, at the very start (as does this introduction), a brief synopsis of the ideas and arguments in the chapter and, at the end, a list of works cited that extend or expand on aspects of the discussion – sometimes offering alternative directions and sometimes providing additional material relevant to the points discussed. Works cited in one chapter will often be relevant to discussions in subsequent chapters.

The question of the relation between place and philosophy with which the book concludes is an important, if not always explicit, issue throughout the volume as a whole. In a sentence that precedes the passage I quoted above, Marcia Cavell writes that 'Philosophy begins in the only place it can, *here*, in the midst of things. . .'[64] This is something to which I shall return. For the moment, however, it is worth reflecting on the way in which the nature and possibility of philosophy (and so of thinking in general) is indeed at issue in the inquiry into the nature and significance of place. Certainly, if philosophy is understood, as a long tradition stretching back at least to Socrates would have it, as essentially concerned with a form of self-examination and self-knowledge, and if human existence is seen as necessarily tied to the nature of place, then the inquiry into place must surely be at the very heart of the philosophical enterprise. Perhaps this is also why the inquiry into place can seem so peculiar and so difficult. Yet it is not merely that this book presents a view of place as posing a special challenge for philosophy. More than just a focus for investigation, place brings with it a specific methodology, embedded in its structure, on the basis of which the inquiry that is undertaken here proceeds. Place is understood as an open region within which a variety of elements are brought to light through their mutual inter-relation and juxtaposition within that region, and the underlying 'method' of the book reflects this very idea. It is a method that is essentially 'topographical':[65] just as a place, or more specifically a stretch of country, is mapped out through the inter-relation of the features within it, so too, I argue, are the objects of philosophical inquiry properly understood only through the inter-relation and inter-connection of distinct, irreducible, but inter-related components.

Notes

1 Henry David Thoreau, *The Writings of Henry D. Thoreau: Journal, Vol. 3: 1848–1851*, ed. Robert Sattelmeyer, Mark R. Patterson, and William Rossi (Princeton, NJ: Princeton University Press, 1990), 318.

2 'Michael' continues the preoccupation with place exemplified by the toponymic poems ('Poems on the naming of places') that immediately precede it. And although 'Michael' is not about the naming of a place, it nevertheless expresses a set of ideas that underpin the significance of such naming.

3 William Wordsworth, 'Michael: A Pastoral Poem', in *Lyrical Ballads*, vol. 2 (London: Longman and Rees, 1800), 199.

4 Ibid., 201.

5 Ibid., 203.

6 Seamus Heaney, 'The Sense of Place', in *Preoccupations: Selected Prose 1968–1978* (London: Faber & Faber, 1984), 145. Heaney's own poetry has also, of course, been strongly characterized by a 'sense of place' – a sense both topographic and historical in its sensitivities and almost 'archaeological' in its preoccupation with history as something buried in the very soil at our feet. On the sense of place in Heaney's poetry, see, for instance, some of the essays in Harold Bloom, ed., *Seamus Heaney* (New Haven, CT: Chelsea House, 1986); as well as Heaney's own discussions of these matters in *Preoccupations* and, of course, the treatment of such matters in his own poems, especially in volumes such as *Seeing Things*. On Wordsworth's 'poetry of place', see especially Jonathan Bate, *Romantic Ecology: Wordsworth and the Environmental Tradition* (London: Routledge, 1991); also: Geoffrey Hartman, 'Wordsworth, Inscriptions and Romantic Nature Poetry' and 'Romantic Poetry and the Genius Loci', in *Beyond Formalism: Literary Essays 1958–1970* (New Haven, CT: Yale University Press, 1970); and John Kerrigan, 'Wordsworth and the Sonnet: Building, Dwelling, Thinking', *Essays in Criticism* 35 (1985): 45–75.

7 Wordsworth, 'Michael: A Pastoral Poem', *Lyrical Ballads*, Vol. II, 203.

8 Bill Gammage, *The Biggest Estate on Earth: How Aborigines Made Australia* (Sydney: Allen and Unwin, 2011), 142. See also Fred R. Myers, *Pintupi Country, Pintupi Self* (Canberra: Australian Institute of Aboriginal Studies, 1986), esp. 51: 'For the Pintupi [the indigenous people of the Western Desert region of Australia] individuals come from the country, and this relationship provides a primary basis for owning a sacred site and for living in the area.' It is significant that loss of connection with the land is one of the significant after-effects of the forced separation of Aboriginal and Torres Strait Islander children from their families (an institutionalized practice throughout Australia from the colonial period right up until the 1970s) that was noted in the report of the national inquiry into the 'stolen generation'. As one submission put it, 'Separation has broken or disrupted not only the links that Aboriginals have with other Aboriginals, but importantly, the spiritual connection we should have had with our country, our land. It is vital to our healing process that these bonds be re-established or re-affirmed' (National Inquiry into the Separation of Aboriginal and Torres Strait Islander Children from their Families [Australia], *Bringing Them Home: Report of the National Inquiry into the Separation of Aboriginal and Torres Strait Islander Children from their Families* [Sydney: Human Rights and Equal Opportunity Commission, 1997]).

9 Tony Swain, *A Place for Strangers: Towards a History of Australian Aboriginal Being* (Cambridge: Cambridge University Press, 1993), 39. Swain notes that in some areas the emphasis on place-identity has been overlain by a turn to a patrilineal principle, but this, he argues, is largely a result of contact with other cultures (ibid., 39–43). It should also be noted that the Indigenous view of conception, in terms of the influence of place, need not imply an ignorance on the part of Australian Indigenous peoples of the role of sexual intercourse in reproduction (although it has often been taken as such), but can be seen rather an assertion of the even more fundamental role to be accorded to the influence of place. On Indigenous views concerning place and conception, focused specifically on the Aranda people of Central Australia, see especially T.G.H. Stehlow, *Aranda Traditions* (Melbourne: Melbourne University Press, 1947), 86–96.

10 See also Deborah Bird Rose, *Dingo Makes Us Human: Life and Land in an Australian Aboriginal Culture* (Cambridge: Cambridge University Press, 1992).

11 As occurred in nineteenth-century Tasmania, where displacement of Aboriginal peoples, as well as the depredations of conflict and disease, was an important factor in the destruction of tribal peoples and forms of life, with Aboriginal lines of descent continuing on primarily among the Bass Strait islanders. See Patsy Cameron, *Grease and Ochre: The Blending of Two Cultures at the Colonial Sea Frontier* (Hobart: Fullers, 2011).

12 Te Rangi Hiroa (Sir Peter Buck), *The Coming of the Maori* (Wellington: Maori Purposes Fund Board, 1949), 381. See also H.-K. Yoon, *Maori Mind, Maori Land, Essays on the Cultural Geography of the Maori People from an Outsider's Perspective* (Bern: Peter Lang, 1986). In 'Taranaki Waiata Tangi and Feelings for Place' (PhD thesis, Lincoln University, 2001), Ailsa Lorraine Smith provides a useful survey of issues and literature relating to Māori ideas of connection to place and land (see esp. chap. 3). The connection with the land, and the invocation of place or locale, is an important element in much Māori writing in English over the last fifty years or so – see, for instance, the work of Witi Ihimaera in novels such as *Tangi* (Auckland: Heinemann, 1973).

13 Marcel Proust, *In Search of Lost Time*, trans. C.K. Scott Moncrieff and Terence Kilmartin, rev. D.J. Enright (New York: Modern Library, 1992). All quotations in the text are from this edition. See also the newer translation (in which different translators undertook different volumes), *In Search of Lost Time*, trans. Lydia Davis, Mark Treharne, James Grieve, John Sturrock, Carol Clark, Peter Collier, and Ian Patterson (London: Allen Lane, 2002), of which the first volume, Lydia Davis's translation of *Swann's Way*, is often thought to be the best and an improvement, at least to modern readers, over the Moncrieff translation. For the original French, see *A la recherche du temps perdu* (1913; Paris: Gallimard, 1954).

14 *Remembrance of Things Past*, trans. C.K. Scott Moncrieff and Frederick Blossom (New York: Random House, 1932–1934). The first volume, *Swann's Way*, appeared with the British publisher Chatto and Windus in 1920. The title is taken from a line of Shakespeare's Sonnet 30: 'When to the sessions of sweet silent thought/ I summon up remembrance of things past...' Proust was horrified when made aware of Moncrieff's translation of the title, by the writer Sydney Schiff, in 1922 – Proust died later that same year – though he was unaware of its Shakespearean provenance. Nevertheless, Moncrieff's rendering of Proust's masterwork is widely regarded as itself a masterpiece, and Proust himself was, in other respects, highly appreciative of Moncrieff's work. See William C. Carter, *Marcel Proust: A Life* (New Haven, CT: Yale University Press, 2000), 794–795.

15 See Georges Poulet, *Proustian Space*, trans. Elliott Coleman (Baltimore, MD: Johns Hopkins University Press, 1977), 19–33; or the original French edition, *L'espace proustien* (Paris: Gallimard, 1963).

16 See 'Landscape and Character', in *Spirit of Place: Mediterranean Writings* (London: Faber and Faber, 1969), 156.

17 Poulet, *Proustian Space*, 27; or *L'éspace proustien*, 42.

18 Gaston Bachelard, *The Poetics of Space*, trans. Maria Jolas (Boston, MA: Beacon Press, 1969).

19 Ibid., 8. Elsewhere, Bachelard quotes from the work of Noël Arnaud: 'Je suis l'espace où je suis' [I am the space where I am] (ibid., 137).

20 Maurice Merleau-Ponty, *The Phenomenology of Perception*, trans. Colin Smith (London: Routledge & Kegan Paul, 1962), 407.

21 See the discussion of Faulkner's 'regionalism' in Michael Millgate, ed., *Faulkner's Place* (Athens, GA: University of Georgia Press, 2009).

22 See *Red Sorghum: A Novel of China*, trans. H. Goldblatt (New York: Penguin, 1994).

23 See Stuart Elden's discussion of the influence of Hölderlin on Heidegger's thinking of place in Elden, 'Heidegger's Hölderlin and the Importance of Place', *Journal of the British Society for Phenomenology* 30 (1999): 258–274.

24 See, among other works, Adrienne Rich, *Your Native Land, Your Life* (New York: W.W. Norton, 1986).

25 See Hartman, 'Wordsworth, Inscriptions and Romantic Nature Poetry.' A great many, perhaps the vast majority, of Wordsworth's own poems can be viewed as instances of just such 'memorialization'.

26 See, for instance, Percy Adams, *Travel Literature and the Evolution of the Novel* (Lexington, KY: University of Kentucky Press, 1983).

27 Herman Melville, *Redburn: His First Voyage* (New York: Doubleday, 1957), 151. The comment appears in a chapter in which the narrator discovers the unreliability of an old, but cherished, guide to

Liverpool. 'Guide-books', he tells us, 'are the least reliable books in all literature; and nearly all literature, in one sense, is made up of guide-books.' See Robert E.Abrams's discussion of Melville's 'Home Cosmography' in *Landscape and Ideology in American Renaissance Literature: Topographies of Skepticism* (Cambridge: Cambridge University Press, 2004), 56–74.

28 See, for instance, Naipal, *Miguel Street* (London: Penguin, 1971); among many other works on place in Naipal's writing, see Rob Nixon, *London Calling: V.S. Naipaul, Postcolonial Mandarin* (New York: Oxford University Press, 1992).

29 From Heaney's own poetry (as opposed to his writing about place in the work of others), see, for instance, some of the poems from *Death of a Naturalist* (London: Faber & Faber, 1966), and *Door into the Dark* (London: Faber & Faber, 1969); see also John Francis Healy, 'From Mossbawn to Staten Island: A Sense of Place in Seamus Heaney's Poetry' (Dissertation, University of Kansas, 1997).

30 See especially *Meadowlands* (New York: The Ecco Press, 1996); see also C.O. Pache's discussion in '"That's What I'll Remember": Louise Glück's Odyssey from Nostos to Nostalgia', *Classical and Modern Literature* 28 (2008): 1–14.

31 See esp. my *Heidegger's Topology: Being, Place, World* (Cambridge, MA: MIT Press, 2006); but also *Heidegger and the Thinking of Place* (Cambridge, MA: MIT Press, 2012).

32 *Dasein* – literally 'there-being', but in ordinary German meaning just 'existence' – is used by Heidegger as the term to designate the mode of being proper to human being.

33 In the Le Thor seminar, held in 1969, Heidegger characterizes the final stage of his thinking as preoccupied with '"the question concerning the place or location of Being" [*Ortschaft des Seins*], from which the name "topology of being" [*Topologie des Seins*] arose...Three terms which succeed one another and at the same time indicate three steps along the way of thinking: MEANING – TRUTH – PLACE (τόπος).' See Martin Heidegger, 'Seminar in Le Thor 1969', in *Four Seminars*, trans. Andrew Mitchell and François Raffoul (Bloomington, IN: Indiana University Press, 2004), 41. See also my *Heidegger's Topology*, 27–37; and my discussion in '"In the Brightness of Place": From History to Topology of Being', in *Heidegger Jahrbuch*, (forthcoming 2018).

34 Phenomenology has been especially important in taking up the question of place. This is partly because of the way the topic appears in the work of Heidegger and Merleau-Ponty (and some would say in Husserl too, at least implicitly), as well as the way it has been taken up as a central concept by more recent phenomenologists such as Edward Casey (see *Getting Back into Place* [Bloomington, IN: Indiana University Press, 1994]) and Edward Relph (see *Place and Placelessness* [London: Pion, 1977]). In fact, the topic seems unavoidable given the phenomenological concern with phenomena, and so with appearing – which always brings place with it (the idea of the horizon that is so central to phenomenological inquiry is itself a topological notion). For an introduction to the range of contemporary phenomenological approaches to place, see Janet Donohoe, ed., *Place and Phenomenology* (London: Rowman and Littlefield International, 2017).

35 See especially Karsten Harries, *The Ethical Function of Architecture* (Cambridge, MA: MIT Press, 1997).

36 See, for instance, Christian Norberg-Schulz, *The Concept of Dwelling* (New York: Rizzoli, 1985); and Peter Zumthor, *Thinking Architecture* (Boston, MA and Basel: Birkhäuser, 1999). A more general phenomenological influence is also evident, sometimes with Heideggerian inflections, in the work of Alberto Pérez-Gómez and Juhani Pallasmaa – see, for example, their contributions in Jeff Malpas, ed., *The Intelligence of Place: Topographies and Poetics* (London: Bloomsbury, 2015).

37 See especially the work of Anne Buttimer and David Seamon, as exemplified, for instance, in Buttimer and Seamon, eds., *The Human Experience of Space and Place* (London: Croom Helm, 1980). Heideggerian influences aside, there is, of course, a long tradition in geographical writing that emphasizes the effect of physical environment on human life, particularly as it affects large-scale social and historical developments. Perhaps the two key figures in this regard are Friedrich Ratzel, in his *Anthropogeographie* (Stuttgart: J. Engelhorns Nachf., 1921–22); and Paul Vidal de la Blanche, in his *Principles of Human Geography*, trans. M.T. Bingham (New York: Henry Holt, 1926). The 'regional' approach of Vidal de la Blanche has been especially influential on twentieth-century French thought, and not only within geography. See Vincent Berdoulay's brief account of the Vidalian legacy in 'Place, Meaning and Discourse in French Language Geography', in *The Power of Place*, ed. John A. Agnew and James S. Duncan (Boston, MA: Unwin Hyman, 1989), 125–128. See also Jean-Yves Guiomar, 'Vidal de la Blanche's Geography of France', in *Realms of Memory*, vol. 2, ed.

Pierre Nora, trans. Arthur Goldhammer (New York: Columbia University Press, 1997), 187–210. Vidal de la Blanche is known for his emphasis on the region as the primary unit of geographical analysis, and his influence is especially evident in the work of Lucien Febvre – see his *A Geographical Introduction to History*, produced in collaboration with Lionel Bataillon, trans. E.G. Mountford and J.H. Paxton (London: Kegan Paul, Trench, Trubner & Co., 1925) – who was himself a founding figure in the *Annales* school of historical inquiry. John Agnew argues that the current emphasis given to spatial and topographic notions, in geography and social science, is much less derived from the work of such as Vidal de la Blanche and more a product of a general turn towards spatialized conceptions of social organization and political power – see John A. Agnew, 'The Devaluation of Place in Social Science', in Agnew and Duncan, *The Power of Place*, 1–28. While Agnew's claim is partly correct (although it may be argued that it leaves out, for instance, the extent to which a figure such as Henri Lefebvre, whose work is often cited in relation to the so-called 'spatial turn', is himself heavily influenced by Vidal de la Blanche), this claim applies more properly to English-language thinking than it does to the French or European. For an overview of geographical thought since 1945, see R.J. Johnson, *Geography and Geographers*, 4th ed. (New York: Edward Arnold, 1991); and David N. Livingstone, *The Geographical Tradition: Episodes in the History of a Contested Enterprise* (Cambridge, MA: Blackwell, 1992). For an excellent general survey of ideas concerning the relation between culture and environment, from ancient times up until the eighteenth century, see Clarence J. Glacken, *Traces on the Rhodian Shore* (Berkeley, CA: University of California Press, 1967). There has often been a tendency to take the emphasis on the environmental or geographic determination of the human to be associated with approaches that are also committed to ideas of race and racial superiority or inferiority. Certainly, a figure such as Ellsworth Huntington, in his *The Character of Races: As Influenced by Physical Environment, Natural Selection and Historical Development* (New York: Charles Scribner's Sons, 1925), provides an excellent example of such an association. It is notable, however, that Ratzel was an active critic of racialist thinking, and although there are thinkers for whom the geographical and biological are indeed connected, there is also a certain tension between the two – see my discussion in *Heidegger and the Thinking of Place*, 137–158.

38 See David Seamon and Robert Mugerauer, eds., Dwelling, *Place and Environment* (New York: Columbia University Press, 1989), for a cross-section of the various ways in which Heidegger's influence has been felt in both geographical and environmentalist circles.

39 See, for instance, Geoffrey R. Lilburne, *A Sense of Place: A Christian Theology of the Land* (Nashville, TN: Abingdon Press, 1989); Mark R. Wynn, *Faith and Place: An Essay in Embodied Religious Epistemology* (Oxford: Oxford University Press, 2009); and Philip Sheldrake, *Spaces for the Sacred: Place, Memory, and Identity* (Baltimore, MD: Johns Hopkins University Press, 2001).

40 Edward S. Casey, *The Fate of Place* (Berkeley, CA: University of California Press, 1996), 197–330.

41 Gilles Deleuze and Felix Guattari, *A Thousand Plateaus: Capitalism and Schizophrenia*, trans. Brian Massumi (Minneapolis, MN: University of Minnesota Press, 1987). Such strategic uses of spatial and topographic notions typically draw on metaphorical more than literal uses of the terms at issue. As a result, their analytical usefulness in illuminating what is at issue in the notions of place and space as such is often obscured. The concept of the nomadic is developed in a very different way, and a way that I would argue is much closer to some aspects of the account of place developed in the work of Kenneth White – see, for instance, *The Nomad Mind*, trans. Sam La Védrine (Liverpool: Liverpool University Press, forthcoming 2018).

42 See Heidegger, *Being and Time*, trans. John Macquarrie and Edward Robinson (New York: Harper & Row, 1962), §70 H369.

43 Mark Johnson, *The Body in the Mind* (Chicago, IL: University of Chicago Press, 1987), xxxviii.

44 Johnson's work with George Lakoff, most notably in *Metaphors We Live By* (Chicago, IL: University of Chicago Press, 1980), is often cited, along with works such as Francisco J. Varela, Evan T. Thompson, and Eleanor Rosch, *The Embodied Mind: Cognitive Science and Human Experience* (Cambridge, MA: MIT Press, 1991), as having had a foundational influence on the development of approaches (usually grouped under the headings of situated, embodied, or extended cognition) that take cognition to be significantly dependent on events and processes in the body (beyond the brain) as well as in the environment of the agent. See also Andy Clark, *Supersizing the Mind: Embodiment, Action, and Cognitive Extension* (Oxford: Oxford University Press, 2008). Although there is a significant

convergence between the approach developed here and that of embodied and situated cognition, it is also the case that my own approach insists on a distinction between place and being-placed (or placedness) that is not so evident in the cognitive scientific literature. Put simply, place comes prior to any being-placed, even though being-placed already implicates place. This may also be seen to mark a point of difference between the way I would characterize my position, and the way Casey does so in his Foreword. My interest here is in both place and 'placement', and I would argue that the latter is impossible to elucidate without the former. On this general issue, see my 'Place and Placedness', in *Situatedness and Place: Multidisciplinary Perspectives on the Spatio-temporal Contingency of Human Life*, ed. Thomas Hünefeldt and Annika Schlitte (Dordrecht: Springer, forthcoming, 2018).

45 See, for instance, Tyler Burge, 'Cartesian Error and the Objectivity of Perception', in *Subject, Thought and Context*, ed. Philip Pettit and John McDowell (Oxford: Clarendon Press, 1986), 117–136; and 'Individualism and Self-Knowledge', *Journal of Philosophy* 85 (1988): 649–663. Burge's earlier papers, such as 'Individualism and the Mental', in *Midwest Studies in Philosophy*, vol. 4, ed. P.A. French, T.E. Uehling Jr., and H.K. Wettstein (Minneapolis, MN: University of Minnesota Press, 1979), 73–121, placed more emphasis on the way mental content is determined by the social, rather than physical, setting. See also Hilary Putnam, 'The Meaning of "Meaning"', in *Mind, Language and Reality: Philosophical Papers*, vol. 2 (Cambridge: Cambridge University Press, 1975), 215–271.

46 Davidson discusses the contrast between his version of externalism and that of Burge in 'Epistemology Externalized', in *Subjective, Intersubjective, Objective* (Oxford: Clarendon Press, 2001), 193–205.

47 See, for instance, 'The Myth of the Subjective', in *Subjective, Intersubjective, Objective*, 39–52.

48 For various presentations of Davidson's arguments on this point, see Davidson, 'Thought and Talk', in *Inquiries into Truth and Interpretation* (Oxford: Clarendon Press, 1984), 168–170; 'The Method of Truth in Metaphysics', in *Inquiries into Truth and Interpretation*, 199–214; 'A Coherence Theory of Truth and Knowledge', in *Subjective, Intersubjective, Objective*, 137–153; 'Empirical Content', in *Subjective, Intersubjective, Objective*, 159–176; and 'Epistemology Externalized', in *Subjective, Intersubjective, Objective*, 193–205.

49 See my 'Self-knowledge and Scepticism', *Erkenntnis* 40 (1994): 165–184.

50 Marcia Cavell, *The Psychoanalytic Mind* (Cambridge, MA: Harvard University Press, 1993), 39.

51 This is an issue I consider in 'Space and Sociality', *International Journal of Philosophical Studies* 5 (1996): 53–79, and parts of that article form the basis for the discussions in Chapters 2 to 6. The issue of inter-subjectivity that is alluded to here is specifically taken up in Chapter 6.

52 See Jeff Malpas, with Günter Zöller, 'Reading Kant Geographically: From Critical Philosophy to Empirical Geography', in *Contemporary Kantian Metaphysics: New Essays on Space and Time*, ed. Roxana Baiasu, Graham Bird, and A.W. Moore (London: Palgrave Macmillan, 2011), 146–166; and also Jeff Malpas, with Karsten Thiel, 'Kant's Geography of Reason', in *Kant's Geography*, ed. Stuart Elden and Eduardo Mendieta (New York: SUNY Press, 2011), 195–214.

53 See particularly P.F. Strawson, *Individuals* (London: Macmillan, 1959); and Evans's own commentary on chapter two of that work, 'Thing Without the Mind', in *Collected Papers* (Oxford: Clarendon Press, 1985), 249–291.

54 See John Campbell, *Past, Space, and Self* (Cambridge, MA: MIT Press, 1994).

55 Quassim Cassam, *Self and World* (Oxford: Clarendon Press, 1997).

56 See, for instance, Hoke Robinson, 'Kant on Embodiment', in *Minds, Ideas and Objects*, ed. Phillip D. Cummins and Guenter Zoeller, North American Kant Society Studies in Philosophy 2 (Atascadero, CA: Ridgeview Publishing, 1992), 329–340; Sarah Furness, 'A Reasonable Geography: An Argument for Embodiment' (PhD Dissertation, University of Essex, 1986); and Angelica Nuzzo, *Ideal Embodiment: Kant's Theory of Sensibility* (Bloomington, IN: Indiana University Press, 2008). The role of embodiment in Kant is also explored in my 'Constituting the Mind: Kant, Davidson and the Unity of Consciousness', *International Journal of Philosophical Studies* 6 (1998): 1–30, in which appear, though in slightly different form, several of the themes taken up in the present volume.

57 See Malpas, with Zöller, 'Reading Kant Geographically: From Critical Philosophy to Empirical Geography', and Malpas, with Thiel, 'Kant's Geography of Reason'.

58 See, for instance, James K. Baxter, *In Fires of No Return* (London: Oxford University Press, 1958). Baxter's poetry reveals a deep sense of place and of the land – many of his poems are tied to

specific places, and, like Wordsworth, his poems often have the almost explicit character of epitaph or memorial. Indeed, as Baxter's vision is often quite dark, so he views the relation to the land as encompassing both tragedy and joy:

> For us the land is matrix and destroyer
> Resentful, darkly known
> By sunset omens, low words heard in branches
> (from 'Poem in the Matukituki Valley',
> in *Fires of No Return*, 22).

59 Joyce's own concern with locality and place is evident in *Ulysses* – both in the idea of the novel as a journey that somehow mirrors that of the original Greek hero, and in its preoccupation with the city of Dublin. On this, see Michael Seidel, *Epic Geography: James Joyce's Ulysses* (Princeton, NJ: Princeton University Press, 1976).

60 In some responses to the first edition of *Place and Experience*, a rather peculiar argument is advanced against Proust's Principle, to the effect that there is a difference between the claims, first, that human identity is constituted by place, and, second, that one's particular self-identity is constituted by particular places – see, for example, N.N. Trakakis, 'Deus Loci: The Place of God and the God of Place in Philosophy and Theology', *Sophia* 52 (2013), 325n30. Oddly, although the first claim is affirmed, Proust's Principle is said to consist in the second of these claims, and to be false (indeed, the claim is that it is self-evidently so). It seems a fairly obvious point, however, that what holds in the general case must also, by that very fact, hold in the particular – so, for instance, the general relation between mortality and the human, if its holds at all, must also hold in the case of any particular human, for instance, in the case of Socrates. Consequently, if it is true in the general case that human identity is constituted by place, then this must also be true in the particular – and so one's particular identity will be constituted by particular places. Perhaps what is intended here, though poorly expressed, is not the denial that the general claim implies the particular, but instead the assertion of a distinction between two general claims: one that place constitutes identity and the other that only certain special places constitute identity. The argument would then be that 'Proust's Principle' consists in the latter claim. Applied to Proust's own work, this would presumably be taken to mean that, of all the places in Marcel's life, only some places, such as, perhaps, Combray are constitutive of Marcel's identity. Certainly, in Proust's work, Combray names a central place in the life of Marcel. Yet not only is this, to some extent, a contingent fact of Marcel's biography (one could imagine a life that is much more geographically dispersed, yet no less determined by place – merely determined differently), but there is also an essential indeterminacy concerning the 'one place' that Combray names. Combray encompasses other places (Swann's Way, the Guermantes way, Aunt Leonie's house, the church of Combray) as well as being itself encompassed by and related to other places, and this is in the nature of place (something developed further in Chapter 7). The complexity and plurality that belongs even to one place (noting, again, the indeterminacy that belongs to this notion of the 'one') is a complexity and plurality that also belongs to identity. The claim that only certain places constitute identity lacks any clear or precise formulation quite apart from any question as to its potential truth or falsity (though the strong tendency is to say simply that it is false). Yet the claim does not, in any case, express what is at the heart of Proust's Principle, and neither is it a claim to be found anywhere in either the current or earlier edition of this book. Indeed, the lack of such a claim in my work more broadly is, in part, what leads Julian Young to argue, almost perversely, that I do not give a central role to place at all (see Young, 'Heidegger's Heimat', *International Journal of Philosophical Studies* 19 [2011], 285–293; and my discussion in *Heidegger and the Thinking of Place* [Cambridge, MA: MIT Press, 2012]), 43–70. Proust's Principle asserts the interdependence of persons and places – an interdependence that will play out in as many different ways as there are places and persons.

61 Although there are ethical and political implications that follow from the nature of the account offered here, and that I have touched upon elsewhere, for instance in 'Is There an Ethics of Place?', *Localities* 2 (2012): 7–32; and 'Thinking Topographically: Place, Space, and Geography', *Il Cannocchiale* 62 (2017): 125–154. The topic is also one that will be more directly addressed in a volume currently in preparation (intended as a companion to *Place and Experience*), tentatively titled 'Ethics and Place', to be published by Routledge in 2019.

62 See Casey, *The Fate of Place*, in which Casey recounts the persistent forgetting of place within much of Western thought.

63 To some extent the arguments developed in Chapters 2 to 5 parallel ideas also to be found, though in different form, in Quassim Cassam's *Self and World* concerning the essential role played by notions of objectivity, unity, and identity in the possibility of self-consciousness. In the discussion here, the focus on objectivity is central to Chapter 5, while the structure of subjectivity and its characteristic unity and identity is dealt with in Chapters 2, 3, and 4.

64 Cavell, *The Psychoanalytic Mind*, 41.

65 Or perhaps 'topological'. Although 'topography' and 'topology' are sometimes used contrastively in some contemporary geographical writing (see, for example, Lauren Martin and Anna J. Secor, 'Towards a Post-Mathematical Topology', *Progress in Human Geography* 38 [2014]: 420–438), as I use the terms in a philosophical context, they have more or less the same meaning – both referring to the writing or thinking of place. As already noted earlier (see this chapter, n23), 'topology' is the term used by Heidegger in discussion of his own work as a 'topology of being'.

Further reading

Agnew, John A., and James S. Duncan, eds. *The Power of Place.* Boston, MA: Unwin Hyman, 1989.

Bachelard, Gaston. *The Poetics of Space.* Translated by Maria Jolas. Boston, MA: Beacon Press, 1969.

Basso, Keith. *Wisdom Sits in Places: Landscape and Language Among the Western Apache.* Albuquerque, NM: University of New Mexico Press, 1996.

Buttimer, Anne, and David Seamon, eds. *The Human Experience of Space and Place.* London: Croom Helm, 1980.

Casey, Edward S. *Getting Back into Place.* Bloomington, IN: Indiana University Press, 1994.

Clark, Andy. *Supersizing the Mind: Embodiment, Action, and Cognitive Extension.* Oxford: Oxford University Press, 2008.

Donohoe, Janet, ed. *Place and Phenomenology.* London: Rowman and Littlefield International, 2017.

Gammage, Bill. *The Biggest Estate on Earth. How Aborigines Made Australia.* Sydney: Allen and Unwin, 2011.

Malpas, Jeff. *Heidegger's Topology: Being, Place, World.* Cambridge, MA: MIT Press, 2006.

Seamon, David, and Robert Mugerauer, eds. *Dwelling, Place and Environment.* New York: Columbia University Press, 1989.

White, Kenneth. *The Nomad Mind.* Translated by Sam La Védrine. Liverpool: Liverpool University Press, forthcoming 2018.

1 The obscurity of place

> If two different authors use the words 'red,' 'hard,' or 'disappointed,' no one doubts that they mean approximately the same thing. . . But in the case of words such as 'place' or 'space,' whose relationship with psychological experience is less direct, there exists a far-reaching uncertainty of interpretation.
>
> (Albert Einstein, Foreword to *Concepts of Space*[1])

It is something of a truism to say that what is closest and most familiar to us is often most easily overlooked and forgotten. To some extent, this is true of the concept of place. We tend to take the notion for granted, yet, at the same time, we are constantly engaged with place. Frequently, that engagement comes to the fore: most obviously when we are displaced or disoriented and in the experience of nostalgia or loss, but also in contemplation, when we attend to our own being-somewhere, or when we attend to that somewhere and are overtaken by a 'sense' of the place, by our own experience of it, by its very presence. Still, in spite of a familiarity with the notion, there are relatively few treatments of place that take it up as philosophically significant in its own right, and this is indicative, not merely of a certain marginalization or forgetting of place within philosophy, but also of the very obscurity of the notion itself.

Certainly, many discussions of place in the existing literature would seem to indicate that the notion is not at all clearly defined. Concepts of place are often not distinguished from notions of simple physical location, and discussions that seem implicitly to call upon notions of place often refer explicitly only to a narrower concept of space. Some writers emphasize a need to distinguish place from space, as when Elizabeth Grosz talks of certain consequences that follow 'unless space (as territory which is mappable, explorable) gives way to place (occupation, dwelling, being lived in)',[2] or when Edward Casey narrates the obscuring of place by space within the history of philosophy.[3] Still, even after the attention that place has received in recent years, it is uncommon to find writers offering any detailed analysis of the concept of place, of the relations between place and concepts of space, or, indeed, of the relations among various spatial concepts themselves.[4]

Even many who are taken as paradigmatical thinkers 'of place' typically assume an understanding of place rather than offer any real elucidation of what it might be. In this respect, Doreen Massey's complaints about the lack of clarity that often attaches to uses of space and of spatial images, and ideas in general, applies as much to the deployment of 'place'. She writes:

> Many authors rely heavily on the terms 'space'/'spatial', and each assumes that their meaning is clear and uncontested. Yet in fact the meaning which different authors assume (and therefore – in the case of metaphorical usage – the import of the metaphor) varies greatly. Buried in these unacknowledged disagreements is a debate which never surfaces; and it never surfaces because everyone assumes we already know what these terms mean.[5]

That the meaning of the terms space and spatial may be contested is an important suggestion to keep in mind. Certainly, in respect of 'place', the term may well be thought so common, and so much a part of our everyday discourse, that its transfer to more theoretical contexts is likely to present an immediate problem.[6] Moreover, it is not just our everyday familiarity with the concept that can give rise to difficulties, but also the complexity and breadth of meaning that seems to attach to the term itself.

Is Bachelard's *Poetics of Space*, for example, really about space – or place? It surely cannot be about the same space of which Newton or Einstein speak – or can it? Michel Foucault claims that 'the present epoch will perhaps be above all the epoch of space', but he explicates this remark in a way that seems to combine a number of different notions: 'We are in the epoch of simultaneity: we are in the epoch of juxtaposition, the epoch of the near and far, of the side-by-side, of the dispersed. We are at a moment, I believe, when our experience of the world is less that of a long life developing through time than that of a network that connects points and that intersects with its own skein.'[7] Here we have references both to the concept of space as a system of locations ('a network that connects points') and to spatial notions that involve concepts of locality and position ('the near and far. . . the side-by-side'), which might suggest connections with broader notions of place.

Part of the complication in dealing with both of these texts is the fact that they appear here in translation, but the French presents a particular point of difficulty. The term translated as 'space' is *éspace*. Yet although the French term is indeed etymologically linked to the English (as the very form of the words suggests), *éspace* carries connotations of place that are not so obvious in the English 'space', at the same time as the French lacks any other term that matches, in its breadth of meaning, the English 'place'.[8] In French, then, there is no simple separation of terms that can be used to mark the distinction of space from place – and this becomes a significant issue given the influence of French thought, and translated French texts, in the English discussion of space and place (it also creates a problem when English discussions are read back into the French). The problems of translation do not mean, however, that the issue of place is absent from French thought (as the work of both Bachelard and Foucault, to say nothing of Proust, Vidal de la Blanche, and many others demonstrates), but rather that the manner of its articulation is different from the manner of its articulation in English.

Discussions of place become more complicated as one looks across different languages, but even if one looks to English alone, perhaps especially if one looks to English, 'place' appears as a complex term – a complexity that belies the simplicity that might seem to follow from the common and seemingly familiar nature of the word. 'Place' carries a variety of senses and stands in close relation to other terms that cover a very broad range of concepts. The *Oxford English Dictionary* says of the noun 'place' that 'the senses are. . . very numerous and difficult to arrange',[9] and its entry extends over some five pages. But in broad terms, one can find five main senses: (i) a definite but open space, particularly a bounded, open space within a city or town; (ii) a more generalized sense of space, extension, dimensionality or 'room' (often, though not always, set in contrast to time); (iii) location or position within some order (whether spatial or another kind of ordering, hierarchical or not); (iv) a particular locale or environment that has a character of its own; and (v) an abode or that within which something exists or dwells.[10]

Clearly, this summary, while it captures most, does not capture all of the shades of meaning that 'place' can carry. Equally clear is the fact that these five broad senses of 'place' are by no means completely independent but overlap and interconnect in various ways. Yet, while some of the notions associated with 'place' are indeed closely connected, others stand in sharp contrast. There is, in particular, a quite definite opposition between the idea of place as merely a *location* – a point that may be specified using, for instance, a grid reference on a map – and the idea of place as a particular *locale* or that 'within which' someone or something resides. One cannot, after all, reside within a grid reference. Place, understood in terms of locale or abode, requires a certain openness, a certain dimensionality, a certain 'room'. Indeed, from the brief summary above, one of the points to be noted is that the concept of place cannot be severed from notions of spatiality and extension – notions themselves at work in the ideas of openness, dimensionality, and room. From an etymological perspective, 'place' (along with related terms in other European languages such as the German *Platz*, Italian *piazza*, and the French *place*) derives from the classical Latin *platea*, meaning a 'broad way' or 'open space', and from the Greek *plateia*, also meaning 'broad way'.[11] A central feature of the idea of place (even if not in all senses of the term) would seem to be that of a certain bounded space or dimension – or perhaps better, a bounded openness or opening. Yet, while the concept of place brings with it notions of openness and spatiality, it is not exhausted by such notions. A place in which one can reside is indeed a place that provides a space for such residing – it 'gives space' to the possibility of residence – and yet a place in which one can reside must be more than just a 'space' alone.

What then is to be said about 'space'? If the English 'place' is an awkward term to clarify, 'space' might be thought to be rather more straightforward (Massey's concerns notwithstanding). Indeed, there is a much narrower range of meanings associated with the term 'space' than with 'place'. 'Space' is often taken to designate only the realm of atemporal physical extension – the realm within which we make sense of the notions of volume, size and shape, of length, breadth, and height, of distance and position, as those notions apply to physical objects. In a broader sense – and perhaps a more basic sense, in as much as it appears to underlie and unify a variety of different uses of the term – 'space' can be taken to mean simply 'room' or extension, whether physical or non-physical (as it is used a number of times in the discussion above). 'Space' thus seems to be tied, first and foremost, to a quite general notion of dimensionality, and so has a range of quite common uses, not restricted to purely *physical* extension or location (as a glance at any good-sized dictionary will indicate), in accord with this. The origin of the English 'space' (and the French *éspace*), can be traced back to the Latin *spatium*, which was sometimes used to translate the Greek terms *stadion*[12] – a standard of length[13] – and conceptually, though not etymologically, it also connects with *distema*, which is most literally 'distance', but also 'magnitude' or 'interval'. Since 'space' can be taken to mean interval or dimension, the term can be used to refer to temporal duration as well as atemporal physical extension. One can thus talk of a 'space' of time, or a 'space' in one's schedule, to mean an interval of time. In German, the word for time is simply combined with that for space – *Zeit* with *Raum* – to arrive at a single term for such a stretch or span of time, a 'time-space', *Zeitraum*.[14]

Although the English terms 'place' and 'space' are etymologically connected to the Greek, discussions of place and space in Greek sources employ entirely different terms that, a little like French, do not clearly separate place from space. The most directly relevant terms are *topos* and *chora*. Contemporary discussions of place and related concepts, including space, sometimes draw quite heavily upon these Greek terms and the ideas associated with them. Recent and contemporary discussions within feminism and deconstruction, for instance, have focused on *chora* – discussions that advance quite particular readings of the ways, not only in which *chora* is deployed within Greek philosophy, specifically in Plato's *Timaeus*, but also in which notions of place and location have been deployed within Western thought and culture.[15] Still, it is important to take heed of the differences between these Greek terms and the English 'place' and 'space'. As they appear in the work of Plato and Aristotle, for instance, both *topos* and *chora* carry important connotations of dimensionality or extendedness (though they cannot be reduced to such notions), while, at the same time, neither *topos* nor *chora* is used other than in relation to particular things. 'All suppose that things that exist are somewhere',[16] Aristotle tells us, and he goes on to characterize *topos* as 'the innermost motionless boundary of what contains'.[17] Consequently, a *topos* is always the *topos* of some body (there must be both a body that is surrounded and a body that surrounds), and similarly, for Plato the *chora*, that which provides 'a home for all created things',[18] is always understood in relation to the particulars that appear or are received within it. These terms are often variously translated into English from the Greek – as both 'space' and 'place',[19] although there is also reason to suppose that both terms are perhaps better understood in terms of place rather than space alone.[20] Certainly, however, recourse to the Greek provides no simple or straightforward way of elucidating the relation of place to space. In addition, there is no good reason, in terms of the relation between these two Greek terms or their appearances in English (*topos* appears in a range of terms from 'topology' to 'topic' and *chora* in 'choreography' as well as 'chorus'), to give precedence to one over the other except inasmuch as *topos* is perhaps more commonly and directly associated, in English, with notions of place. This latter point is evident in my own talk of 'topography' (or sometimes 'topology') to refer to the inquiry that takes place as its central theme.[21]

It is important to achieve some clarification of the various concepts at issue here, but equally, any such clarification must respect the necessary interconnection of those concepts. The vocabulary of place and space, alone, is indicative of the way these are part of a network in which each term is inextricably embedded. Thus, although there is a strong temptation – particularly if one's focus is on the concept of place as *locale* rather than mere *location* – to look to develop a set of clearly differentiated concepts, and, in particular, to look to develop a notion of place that is clearly separated from any narrow concept of space associated with the notion merely of physical extension (something that often motivates authors to look to employ the Greek terms rather than the English), this temptation is one that ought to be resisted. As noted above, place is inextricably bound up with notions of both dimensionality or extension and of locale or environing situation. An exploration of the concept of place, and its elaboration as a philosophically significant concept, must therefore do justice to, and take cognizance of, the complexities of the notion and its necessary implication of concepts of both dimensionality and locale. Consequently, as will be evident in the chapters that follow, the investigation of place cannot be pursued other than in conjunction with an investigation of space. Moreover, as already indicated, time must also be addressed in this same investigation, and just as one cannot assume that place is the same as space nor as simply opposed to it, neither can place be taken as either the same as time or as simply opposed to time (the latter often following from the tendency to treat place as identical with space).

The connection of place with space, while central to any understanding of place, nevertheless presents a problem for the attempt to arrive at such an understanding. The philosophical history of the concept of space in Western thought is a history in which space has been increasingly understood in the narrower terms that tie it to physical extension. This is reflected in the way in which the Greek notions of *topos* and *chora* have gradually been eclipsed in the history of philosophy, so far as thinking of space and place is concerned, by the concept of *kenon* or void. It is this latter notion, the history of which can be traced from its Greek origins,[22] through Medieval and Renaissance thinking,[23] and into the seventeenth and eighteenth centuries, that plays the more significant role in the development of modern concepts of space. The concept of void brings with it the idea of a homogenous and undifferentiated realm of pure extension – the idea of a pure realm of 'containment' of the sort that is arrived at, for instance, when one abstracts the thing from its enclosing surroundings so that what is left is nothing but an empty and open 'space'[24] – precisely the idea that lies at the heart of thinking about space in the work of Descartes and Newton. Thus, we arrive at an understanding of space as a single, homogenous, and isotropic 'container' in which all things are located and, even though modern cosmological physics no longer understands space in the terms developed in Cartesian and Newtonian thinking,[25] the idea of spatiality as primarily a matter of physical extendedness remains.

Parallel with the development of this more refined, and even technical, notion of space is a tendency, in much of philosophical thinking, to make space an increasingly important focus of attention. As Max Jammer notes, 'Space is the subject, especially in modern philosophy, of an extensive metaphysical and epistemological literature. From Descartes to Alexander and Whitehead, almost every philosopher has made his theory of space one of the cornerstones of his system.'[26] In contrast, the concept of place, as distinct from space (even if not independent of it), has a much more ambiguous position in the history of philosophy – particularly in post-Cartesian thought.[27] Indeed, Edward Casey claims that:

> In the past three centuries in the West – the period of modernity – place has come to be not only neglected but actively suppressed. Owing to the triumph of the natural and social sciences in this same period, any serious talk of place has been regarded as regressive or trivial. A discourse has emerged

> whose exclusive foci are Time and Space. When the two were combined by twentieth century physicists into the amalgam 'space-time,' the overlooking of a place was only continued by other means. For an entire epoch, place has been regarded as an impoverished second cousin of Time and Space, those two colossal cosmic partners that tower over modernity.[28]

Just as space has come to be associated with a narrow concept of physical extension, so too has place come to be viewed as a matter of simple location within a larger spatial structure. But place is not separable from the notion of spatiality. Consequently, within a framework in which space is not only given a privileged role, but is also understood within the narrower frame of physical extension, there will also be a tendency towards a similarly narrow and 'spatialized' understanding of place.

This narrowing in the understanding of both space *and* place is evident in Descartes. In the *Principles of Philosophy*, in which there seems to be a degree of differentiation between place and space – or at least between what Descartes terms *loci* and *spatii* – these notions are presented as closely related, but both are essentially properties of bodies. 'The terms "place" [*loci*] and "space" [*spatii*],' writes Descartes, 'do not signify anything different from the body which is said to be in a place; they merely refer to its size, shape and position relative to other bodies. . . The difference between the terms "place" and "space" is that the former designates more explicitly the position, as opposed to the size or shape, while it is the size or shape that we are concentrating on when we talk of space.'[29] Although concerned to distinguish his position from that of Descartes and others, Newton views place as closely tied to space – so closely tied, in fact, that, for Newton, place appears as derivative of space. 'Place is,' writes Newton, 'a part of space which a body takes up. I say a part of space; not the situation, nor the external surface of a body.'[30] Moreover, while seldom explicitly taken up in such a context (though there are some exceptions), the same understanding of place, as a matter of spatial position or location evidenced in Newton, is also a feature of contemporary philosophical discussion. Thus, Richard Swinburne writes that 'A place in the literal sense is wherever a material object is or, it is logically possible, could be. . . a place is identified by describing its spatial relations to material objects forming a frame of reference.'[31] By his account, it would seem that space is the more general and more basic concept.[32] Place is to be understood simply in terms of a particular region of physical space or a location within it, designating a region or location that, in its more precise usage, can be specified within a relativized spatial framework by means of a set of spatial coordinates.

This concept of place, evident throughout so much of the history of philosophy, clearly stands in stark contrast to that implicit in Heaney's talk of the 'humanized and humanizing' place in Wordsworth's poetry (which can also be seen to contrast with certain pre-modern views of place[33]). But it is not just that the narrow understanding of place – as either a matter of spatial location or of subjective affectivity – seems too impoverished to do justice to the sense of place evident in Wordsworth, or in such as Heidegger or Merleau-Ponty. The very understanding of spatiality as paradigmatically a concept of physical theory, and so as primarily tied to physical extension, represents a fundamental obstacle to any attempt to arrive at a view of place as a philosophically significant concept. Place and space are closely related notions (a place must 'give' space and have a certain 'openness' or dimensionality). Consequently, if place is to be explicated in a way that does not simply reduce it to some notion of position or location within physical space, or treat it as secondary to space, then the analysis of place must encompass a broader analysis of space that does not restrict space merely to notions of physical extension and position. Arriving at an adequate account of place, then, requires a rethinking of space – as it also requires, though for different reasons, a rethinking of time, although the widespread tendency to identify place with space means that it is the rethinking of space that has a degree of priority here.

Even in those cases where place is treated as something more than simple spatial location, this is typically arrived at, not through any reconsideration of spatiality, but through the treatment of place as an essentially subjective or psychological phenomenon. While he does not talk of place as such, Max Jammer nevertheless treats the 'primitive' concept of space in just this manner. 'To the primitive mind,' writes Jammer, '"space" was merely an accidental set of concrete orientations, a more or less ordered multitude of local directions, each associated with certain emotional reminiscences. This primitive "space," as experienced and unconsciously formed by the individual, may have been coordinated with a "space" common to the group, the family or the tribe.'[34] It seems that the 'primitive' concept of space is thus a matter of the human appropriation of or orientation to the world, and just such a view is commonly found in discussions of place – all the more so in discussions outside of physical theory.

In the work of many writers who aim to rehabilitate place as a central theoretical concept, place is distinguished from mere location though an understanding of place that takes it to be constituted by the *human response* to physical surroundings or locations. Such writers thus tend towards an account of place in psychological terms that is not far removed from Jammer's account of the 'primitive' concept of space.[35] The difficulty of this approach, however, is that it provides no real explication of the concept of place as such, since it merely conjoins the idea of a part of objective physical space with the notion of some subjective emotional or affective quality, or set of qualities, and so treats place as derivative of these. Moreover, the connection between any particular space and certain emotional or affective responses to that space could turn out to be completely contingent. There is no reason to suppose that it is the experience of specifically *topographic* (or even merely spatial) qualities that are actually at issue in any such emotional or affective engagement.[36] The association of some set of felt qualities with a particular space may be no more than a product of the triggering of particular responses – perhaps in a completely accidental fashion – by some set of physical, and therefore spatially located, stimuli. Consequently, it is not place as such that is important here, but just the idea of a certain physical responsiveness – a responsiveness that need not be grounded in any concept of place as such.

Of course, since human responses to the environment are many and varied, and since the environment has a role to play in almost all of experience, so it is perhaps not surprising that accounts of place in the literature are similarly dispersed. The proliferation of such accounts leads J. Nicholas Entrikin to refer to the 'sometimes competing, and occasionally confusing, claims that have been made and continue to be made about the study of place and region', and he adds that 'one of the reasons for this confusion may be that it is beyond our intellectual reach to attain a theoretical understanding of place and region that covers the range of phenomena to which these concepts refer'.[37] The dispersed character of place, with so many accounts across so many disciplines and writers, provides both an impetus to attempt the development of a more integrated approach to place and, as Entrikin's warning makes clear, an obvious problem for any such attempt. But it should also be clear that if place is to be taken up as a concept in its own right, rather than as a convenient catch-all for what otherwise appears to be a loosely connected set of ideas and problems, then the development of a more integrated account is essential. Indeed, only within the framework of such an account is it possible to give any content to the idea that the set of problems and ideas found in discussions of place are significantly related.

The appearance of place as a central, if problematic, concept is clearest in discussions that touch on aspects of human existence and experience – in contrast, physical theory alone seems to have no need for a concept of place beyond the notion of simple location (perhaps one reason for being suspicious of any purely physicalist approach to human existence and experience). Such emphasis on place as experiential, or as tied to the human response to environment, actually curtails the possibility of giving an adequate account of place as such, but is nevertheless instructive. The crucial point about the connection between place and experience is not, however, that place is properly something only encountered 'in' experience, but rather that place *is integral to the very structure and possibility of experience*. Such a way of thinking about place appears in the work of Martin Heidegger, although, as Edward Casey suggests,[38] in a somewhat 'indirect' fashion.

In *Being and Time*, Heidegger treats human beings, or more properly *Dasein* (used by Heidegger to refer to the mode of being that is proper to human being), as essentially characterized in terms of their 'being-in' the world. This leads Heidegger to distinguish the sense of 'being-in' that is proper to human being from the 'being-in' that is associated with the sense of physical containment that is part of the modern conception of space identified by Einstein and Jammer, and which Heidegger characterizes as 'Cartesian'.[39] Failure to make such a distinction would, it seems, commit Heidegger to understanding the relation between the world and *Dasein* as essentially no different from the relation between, for instance, a box and, say, the apples 'physically contained' within it. It would also seem to entail a view of *Dasein* as existing in a way essentially no different from the way in which the box, the apples, or any other physical objects exist.[40] Such a view Heidegger rejects as inadequate to any proper understanding of *Dasein* – inadequate because it makes problematic the very possibility of a relation between *Dasein* and the world, or the things within that world, and that is clearly evident, according to Heidegger, in the rise of relativistic and sceptical modes of thought.

In this respect, the 'objectivism' that Heidegger associates with the Cartesian view of spatiality is seen as necessarily tied to 'subjectivism',[41] and this would seem to mirror the connection, already noted, between the view of space as primarily a feature of the physical universe, and the view of place, or 'meaningful space', as a human and, in this respect, subjective construct. In distinguishing the spatiality of *Dasein* from the spatiality of objects, Heidegger asserts the impossibility of any purely 'objective' treatment of *Dasein*, one that would treat *Dasein* as no more than an object among other objects, while also rejecting any 'subjectivist' understanding of *Dasein* in its relation to the world. Indeed, since *Dasein* is properly understood as already inclusive of the world, one can see how Heidegger could comment, in his later writing, that '*Dasein* names that which should first be experienced, and then properly thought of, as Place [*Ort*].'[42]

Heidegger provides an important example of a way of thinking that gives to place a central role in the understanding of human being and, so, of human thought and experience. Indeed, something like the Heideggerian thinking of *Dasein as* place is what motivates my inquiry here.[43] However, one need not, as I indicated in the introduction, look only to Heidegger to find examples of such a way of thinking. Externalist theories of mental content, for instance, provide one obvious way in which environment and location can be understood to be directly implicated in the determination of the contents of the mind, and I will draw on such ideas in later chapters. For the moment, however, I simply want to establish the idea of place in such a way that it can begin to be seen, not merely in some narrow sense of spatio-temporal location, nor as some sort of subjective construct, but rather as that wherein the sort of being that is characteristically human has its ground. So far as the idea of experience is concerned, the key point is that understanding the structure and possibility of experience (in the quite general and non-empiricist sense already indicated) is inseparable from an understanding and appreciation of the concept of place. Of course, the exact nature of the concept of place that is at stake here remains to be clarified.

Providing such clarification will be the main task of succeeding chapters, although the direction in which such clarification will proceed should already be evident from the discussion above.

Fundamental to the idea of place is the idea of an open and yet bounded realm within which the things of the world can appear and events can 'take place'. Such a notion of place is broader than the idea of a narrowly defined point or location. Yet even when we think of a place in terms of just such a defined point or location, what is nevertheless also implied is some idea of the place as possessed of enough breadth and space to allow room for oneself within it – room enough to allow an engagement with the world. We can, of course, engage with and grasp places themselves (even from within the very place so engaged with and grasped) as having a character and identity of their own – a character and identity that might be said to derive from the fact that location and orientation in a place brings with it a certain ordering of that very place. This is so, not only in virtue of the way things come to appear within such a place, but also the way in which any such place is always, itself, positioned in relation to other places, thereby providing the possibility of engagement with those places. Places are internally differentiated and interconnected in terms of the elements that appear within them, while they also interconnect with other places. Places are juxtaposed and intersect with one another, even as places also contain places. Thus, one can move inwards to find other places nested within a place, as well as move outwards to find a more encompassing locale. Some of these features of place will become quite important to the ensuing discussion (the 'nesting' of places, for instance, is a significant point of connection between place and memory.)

Just as Heidegger argues that the idea of the 'being-in' of *Dasein* cannot be reduced to the physical containment of *Dasein* 'within' space, so the idea of place cannot be reduced to mere location within physical space, nor can place be viewed simply in relation to a system of interchangeable locations associated with objects. This is not to sever place entirely from physical space. In some sense, place must 'supervene' upon physical space, and upon the physical world in general, such that the structure of a particular place will reflect, in part, the structure of the physical region in relation to which that place emerges. The relation between place and physical space will, however, be no less complicated, and no more amenable to a reductive analysis, than is the relation between the realms of physical theory and everyday talk about our world.[44] Moreover, if place is not to be viewed as a purely 'objective' concept – a concept to be explicated by reference to objects existing in a physical space – neither is it a purely 'subjective' notion. Place, treated as a largely subjective concept, is, as noted earlier, common to many discussions – both those that seek to rehabilitate the concept and those that, even if only implicitly, dismiss it. Yet, although it is certainly not the case that place is constituted independently of subjectivity – or independently of the physical world – neither is it straightforwardly dependent on the existence of an independent subject or subjects. Place is, instead, that within and with respect to which subjectivity is itself established. Place is not founded *on* subjectivity but is that *on which* the notion of subjectivity is founded. Thus, one does not first have a subject that apprehends certain features of the world in terms of the idea of place; rather, the structure of subjectivity is given in and through the structure of place. The argument for this is yet to be provided – the development of that argument is, in many respects, the task of the book as a whole – but the point is such an important and basic one that it deserves to be kept in view almost from the beginning. The connection of subjectivity with place indicates the need to view subjectivity as tied to agency and embodied spatiality, and therefore as constituted in relation to a structure that extends beyond the subject to encompass a world of objects, events, and persons. This structure is determinative, in various ways, of the nature of the subject. It is only within such a place that subjectivity – or, more generally, the structure in which subject and object both appear – is possible. There is, indeed, no possibility of 'appearance' within the space of pure extension, but only within the differentiated and unitary structure of place.

This latter point applies no less to concepts of the social, or the intersubjective, than to the notions of subjectivity or objectivity – place is the frame within which all three must be located. There is, of course, a common tendency to talk of place – and of space and time – as 'social constructs' (a tendency that derives from the more general use of the idea of 'social construction' within social and cultural theory).[45] Although the language of social construction is often itself unclear, and so one can debate whether it really is place as such, or space and time, that are actually at issue (is it just the ideas of these that are socially constructed?), but any such language is particularly inappropriate in the present context. The idea of place encompasses both the idea of the social activities and institutions that are expressed in and through the structure of a particular place (which can be seen as partially determinative of that place) and the idea of the physical objects and events in the world (along with associated causal processes) that constrain, and are sometimes constrained by, those social activities and institutions. There is no doubt that the ordering of a particular place – and the specific way in which a society orders space and time – is not independent of social ordering (inasmuch as it encompasses the social, place is partially elaborated by means of the social, just as place is also elaborated in relation to orderings deriving from individual subjects and underlying physical structures). However, this does not legitimate the claim that place, space, or time are *merely* social constructions. Indeed, the social does not exist prior to place, nor is it given expression except in and through place – in and through spatialized, temporalized ordering – and so the social cannot be that out of which, or solely by means of which, place is 'constructed'.[46] It is within the structure of place that the very possibility of the social arises.

In grasping the structure of place at issue here what is grasped is an open and interconnected region within which other persons, things, spaces, and abstract locations, and even one's self can appear, be recognized, identified, and interacted with.[47] But in 'grasping' such a region, it is not a matter of the subject grasping something of which the acting, experiencing creature is independent. A region or place does not simply stand ready for the gaze of some observing subject. Instead, it encompasses the experiencing creature itself, and so the structure of subjectivity is given in and through the structure of place. Something similar might be said of the idea of objectivity, at least in the sense that objectivity is understood, not merely as consisting in the existence of some physical entity or system, but as precisely *that which can be present to a subject*.[48] In this respect, the idea of the object is something established only within a place, and thereby in relation to a subject – although, in saying this, it must be remembered that *both* subject and object are thereby 'placed' within the same structure, rather than one or the other being the underlying ground for that structure. Of course, the existence of some particular place – of some set of objects or of some subject – will be *causally* dependent on a set of physical processes and structures, but this does not mean that place can be simply reduced to such processes or structures. The language of place, of self and other, of subject and object, describes the world in a way that is tied to the possibility of agency and attitude, not in terms of physical process alone. Indeed, while the existence of a place may be causally dependent on certain physical processes, the capacity to describe, experience, and understand those processes is, in turn, possible only within the framework of place.

One might, nevertheless, claim that the account of space and place given within physical theory is more 'objective' and, in this respect, preferable, in that it treats space and place as existing independently of any subject, whereas, on other accounts, including that already presaged here, in the absence of subjects, there can be neither place nor, in a certain sense, space. Such a use of the term 'objective' already accords a certain priority to physical accounts, but whether this is indeed the primary or most important use of 'objective' is, at the very least, contestable.[49] There is, moreover, a significant difference between an account such as that offered here, which insists on an interdependence between subjectivity and place, and accounts that treat place as simply a product of the subjective apprehension of location (and, accordingly, as a feature of the psychological life of subjects). The relation between place and the existence of the subject, in my account, is analogous to that between truth and the existence of speakers. One can say that only if there are speakers can there be such a thing as truth, yet this does not suggest that truth is somehow a 'subjective' notion, nor does this demand that we seek a more 'objective' analysis that would do away with such dependence. The dependence of truth on speakers is simply a consequence of the way in which the possibility of truth depends on the existence of language, and, since language and speaking arise together, so there is language only where there are speakers.

These considerations notwithstanding, one might accept the notion that experience and thought are to be understood as dependent upon the sort of complex structure that is here at issue in the idea of place, yet query the appropriateness of such talk of 'place' (or any related terms) as nothing more than metaphorical, and, therefore, as a stylistic affectation that obscures rather than illuminates. Of course, whether metaphor is to be treated as a mere 'affectation', rather than contributing additional content of its own, is a moot point. There is, moreover, a common tendency to assume a rather clearer distinction between metaphorical and 'literal' uses of language than is actually warranted, especially, as noted earlier, where spatial and topographical terms are concerned. Yet this aside, to assume that space and place are used literally *only* when employed in relation to the 'objective' language of physics is, once again, already to assume the priority of certain quite particular ways of understanding these terms (including, as I noted above, the notion of objectivity). Not only is such priority questionable, but it can also serve to obscure the conceptual complexity of the terms themselves. The claim that 'place', as it is used here, can remain only a metaphor is simply a reassertion of a particular and fairly narrow view of the nature of place – a reassertion that seems to ill-accord with the complex character of the concept.[50] It is also a claim that remains ambiguous and uncertain so long as the concept of metaphor that it deploys is not itself subject to further inquiry.

The insistence on separating metaphorical from literal usage, and giving priority to the literal over the metaphoric, is often indicative of a style of philosophical approach that looks to reduce complex structures to concatenations of simple components understood in separation from one another rather than in relation to the larger structures of which they are part. On such an approach, one is right to be suspicious of possible metaphorical usages, since such usages may conceal complex structures better analysed in terms of their simpler and more basic components. Here, however, the basic issue is not metaphor, but rather the assumption of a reductive-analytic approach. Such an approach is one that already tends to be antithetical to the very idea of place, since the latter notion is one that tends towards the holistic rather than the reductive, towards interconnection rather than separation. One of the characteristic features of a place is that the elements within it are evident only within the structure of the place, even as that structure is itself dependent upon the interconnectedness of the elements within it – just as it is also dependent on its interconnection with other places. Consequently, the idea of place is the idea of a structure that must resist any analysis that reduces it to a set of autonomous components. One might add that the anti-reductionism that follows from the character of place indicates the problematic nature of any reductive approach to understanding, since understanding is always placed, always proceeds from place, is always constrained by place – a point that lies, even if sometimes left merely implicit, at the heart of hermeneutic thinking.[51]

In the introduction, I referred to Marcia Cavell's insistence that the only place in which philosophy can begin is '*here*, in the midst of things'.[52] As place itself provides the starting point for the present inquiry, the approach adopted is one that looks neither to a place where the subject is abstracted from the world, nor where the world is abstracted from the subject, but rather to the place in which *we*, the inquirers, already find ourselves. This place is one in which both subject and object, both self and world, are presented together. Moreover, this place of departure remains determinative of the entire inquiry, since the investigation aims not to move us away from this place – as is so often the case in philosophical inquiry – but rather to explore it and delineate its structure. Not only does the idea of place provide an important focus for the inquiry into experience, but also a model for the approach that will be adopted and for the structure of the account that will emerge.

Just as the various elements within a place, taken together, give that place its character and identity, and just as each of those elements is dependent for its own identity on the structure of the place as such, so the structural elements, on which the possibility of experience rests, cannot be given any account independent of the overall structure of which they are a part. The way of approaching the question of the structure and possibility of experience is thus one that cannot seek to reduce the structure to a single underlying element or principle. Instead, the structure as a whole must be exhibited as constituted through the interplay of a number of elements. The structure at issue here is exemplified – in an especially appropriate form, given the focus on place – through the relation of topographical features in a landscape, or as delineated in a topographical survey map. Indeed, the practice of topographical surveying provides a neat analogy and model for the inquiry at issue.

Topographical surveying is, according to one British Government textbook on the subject, 'the science, artfully executed, of measuring the physical features of the earth and the art, scientifically controlled, of delineating them'.[53] While the advent of aerial surveying and, more recently, satellite mapping techniques have wrought great changes in the actual practice of surveying – not only over the last one hundred years, but even the last forty – the basic principles for the surveyor on the ground have remained much the same. In the centuries prior to the twentieth, surveyors relied principally on basic sighting and measuring devices, on good eyes and steady hands, and a strong pair of legs. For the surveyor faced with a hitherto unmapped region, and lacking any technical device more advanced than quadrant or theodolite (for sightings and measurement of angles) and odometer or chain (for measurement of distance), the task is to map out that region from within the region itself (see Figure 3). Only by measurement of distance and angle, by repeated triangulation and traverse, can a picture of the topography of the region be built up (the basic method is illustrated in Figure 9 in Chapter 6). For such a surveyor, there is nowhere outside of the region itself from which an accurate topographical rendering can be obtained. It is thus precisely through the surveyor's active involvement with the landscape that an accurate mapping is made. A purely topographical understanding of a landscape does not, furthermore, look to some deeper topography underlying that made evident through our active engagement within it. There is no such 'deeper' topography to be found. The lie of the land is given – almost literally – *on* its surface, rather than being hidden *beneath* it.

Figure 3 Anonymous, portrait of the surveyor Andries van der Wal, with two assistants, circa 1670, oil on wood, Rijksmuseum, Amsterdam. The surveyor is shown using a simple sighting instrument, while in the background, an assistant calculates the angle and height of a tower using a quadrant.

If we take this topographical picture seriously as a guide to our analysis here,[54] then we will similarly come to understand the various elements at issue, not in terms of an underlying structure to which they can be reduced, but rather in terms of their own inter-relation. What the practice of topographical surveying makes evident are certain features of place that has go well beyond the practice of surveying and its own assumptions and aims, at the same time as it also demonstrates something quite general about the way the way the nature of place shapes the nature of any investigation into place.[55] When it comes to the structure by which thought, experience, and knowledge are possible, one of the main consequences to be drawn from the necessity of a 'topographic' mode of analysis is, once again, that the concepts at issue must be understood through their interconnection rather than their reduction, through their complex interdependence rather than their simplification. In this respect, Wittgenstein's comments, in his lectures on the philosophy of mathematics, have a special resonance with the project pursued here: 'I am trying to conduct you on tours in a certain country. I will try to show that the philosophical difficulties. . . arise because we find ourselves in a strange town and do not know our way about. So we must learn the topography by going from one place in the town to another, and from there to another, and so on. And one must do this so often that one knows one's way, either immediately or pretty soon after looking around a bit, wherever one may be set down.'[56] The conception of philosophy suggested here, and given more explicit formulation in my own use of the idea of topography, is something to which I shall briefly return in the concluding section of this book.

The complexity of place is mirrored in the complex process of triangulation and traverse by which the topographical surveyor builds up a map of the region being surveyed. No single sighting is sufficient to gain a view of the entire region, multiple sightings are required, and every sighting overlaps, to some extent, with some other sighting. Thus, the process of topographical surveying is one in which the complex structure of the region is arrived at through crossing and re-crossing the surface of the land and through sighting and re-sighting from one landmark to another. In that process, it may seem as if the region itself is lost sight of – as if it is forgotten in the emphasis on particular views and measurements. In fact, it is only at the end of the process that the view of the region as a whole can emerge in the form of the survey map. Both the complexity of process and the apparent disappearance of region have their analogues in the project undertaken here. The delineation of place can only be undertaken by a process that encompasses a variety of sightings from a number of conceptual 'landmarks' and that also undertakes a wide-ranging, criss-crossing set of journeys over the landscape at issue. It is only through such journeying, sighting, and re-sighting that place can be understood.

It should be emphasized, if it were not evident already, that this is not merely a methodological or epistemological point. What the practice of topographical surveying illustrates and exhibits is something about the very nature of place on which that practice depends. It shows place, and the appearing that place makes possible, to be itself essentially relational. What is being advanced is thus an ontological point that is also evident methodologically. What it also shows, if less directly, is that place does not operate here, nor in any other topographic analysis (including that of *philosophical* topography) as if it were some determinate, substantive, entity, or principle to which all else can be reduced or from which all else can be derived. Place is that bounded open region of possibility in which even space and time, as well as subjectivity and objectivity, first emerge. As such a region, it is fundamentally relational, and that relationality permeates everything that pertains to place, everything that belongs with it, everything that appears in its embrace. It might even be said that it is the relationality of place that underpins the idea of the essential human connection to place since that connection is itself a specific mode of the broader relationality that characterizes place as such, and so also characterizes what is in place.

In taking place as central, and in treating place as encompassing both the subjective and objective, the spatial and the temporal, it should not be thought that the concept of *space* (or time for that matter) is thereby neglected or abandoned. Indeed, in the analysis that appears in *Being and Time*, Heidegger's own refusal to countenance the necessary role of spatiality in the structure of *Dasein* gives rise to insuperable problems in his account. Heidegger's insistence on the separation of the spatiality proper to *Dasein* from the spatiality of objects is part of what leads Heidegger, in *Being and Time*, to treat spatiality as always secondary to, and derivative of, temporality. Even the 'existential spatiality' that is proper to *Dasein* is held to be derivative in this way – so much so that Heidegger seems almost to reduce existential spatiality to a form of temporality.[57] Yet if 'objective' spatiality alone is inadequate to the understanding of human being-in-the-world, so too must any purely temporal conception also fall short,[58] and the difficulties to which the Heideggerian analysis of spatiality gives rise undoubtedly contribute to the unfinished character of *Being and Time* itself.

As already made clear, the concept of place cannot be divorced from space, just as space cannot be divorced from time (and so place encompasses time no less than space[59]). But this does not mean that the concept of space can simply be assumed. Unless the recognition and re-evaluation of the significance of place also recognizes the connection between space and place, and so includes a re-evaluation of the concept of space itself, the result will simply be a replacement of one set of problems with another. A closer analysis of the concept of space, as well as of the concepts of subjectivity and objectivity, is indeed a central focus for the next chapter. Spatiality is shown to be, not a simple concept analysable only in terms of some notion of objective physical extension or location, but instead as involving both subjective and objective aspects. Indeed, the relation between space and place in standard treatments of these notions – according to which place, understood as a matter of simple location, is seen to be based on space as physical extension – will, to some extent, turn out to be reversed when these notions are understood in any richer sense. When we try to take account of the complexity of spatiality, as it arises in relation to a creature's involvement in the world, we are forced to look to a way of thinking about spatiality that sees it as embedded within the larger structure, not of a single space, but of a unitary and encompassing place. Moreover, as shall become evident in the following chapters, the exploration of that larger structure requires an elaboration, not merely of spatiality, but of the interconnection between notions of subjectivity, objectivity, and intersubjectivity, as well as of notions of agency and causality.

Notes

1 Albert Einstein, Foreword to *Concepts of Space: The History of Theories of Space in Physics*, by Max Jammer, 2nd ed. (Cambridge, MA: Harvard University Press, 1970), xii.

2 Elizabeth Grosz, *Space, Time and Perversion* (St Leonards, NSW: Allen and Unwin, 1995), 123.

3 Edward Casey, *The Fate of Place* (Berkeley, CA: University of California Press, 1996), passim, esp. 133ff. Sometimes Casey seems to assume rather than explicate this distinction and, in *The Fate of Place*, the interconnection of space and place is not something to which he devotes any especially detailed analysis. In a subsequent paper, Casey does indeed address the issue of the relation between place and space in a direct and intriguing manner that has some parallels with my own treatment – at least inasmuch as it emphasizes the necessary connection of place with space. See 'Smooth Spaces and Rough-edged Places: The Hidden History of Place', *Review of Metaphysics* 51 (1997): 267–296. See also Edward Casey, *Getting Back into Place* (Bloomington, IN: Indiana University Press, 1994). Casey's own background is strongly phenomenological, and it is perhaps within the phenomenological framework that the most extensive explorations of concepts of space and place (though the emphasis is often more on space as such) have been undertaken. See especially, Elisabeth Ströker, *Investigations in Philosophy of Space*, trans. Algis Mickunas (Athens, OH: Ohio University Press, 1987).

4 The French philosopher and social theorist Henri Lefebvre is another, rather like Foucault, who has been especially influential in the development of spatiality as a notion applicable in sociological and socio-geographical analyses. However, Lefebvre's analyses arise, in part, precisely out of dissatisfaction with what he sees as the indiscriminate employment of spatial concepts – see *The Production of Space*, trans. Donald Nicholson-Smith (Oxford: Blackwell, 1991) – and Lefebvre singles out Foucault as a notable offender in this regard – see ibid., 3–4. Lefebvre's approach is an important influence on Rob Shields, *Places on the Margin: Alternative Geographies of Modernity* (London: Routledge, 1991). In a way that bears comparison with aspects of my own approach, Shields emphasizes both the role of spatialization in the structuring of social practices, as well as the complex determination of spatialization itself. Amongst social theorists who have given attention to the concept of spatiality, the work of Pitirim Sorokin should also be noted. See Sorokin, *Sociocultural Causality, Space, Time* (New York: Russell & Russell, 1964), esp. 97–157. Neither Sorokin nor Shields or Lefebvre, however, attempt the sort of philosophical analysis of space and place, or the relations between them, attempted here.

5 Doreen Massey, 'Politics and Space/Time', in *Place and the Politics of Identity*, ed. Michael Keith and Steve Pile (London: Routledge, 1993), 141–142; see also Neil Smith and Cindi Katz, 'Grounding Metaphor: Towards a Spatialized Politics', in ibid., 67–83. While Massey's comments are echoed by other writers, part of her own concern over this matter derives from the view that the indiscriminate use of notions of space and spatiality threatens to deprive these notions of any political content, and this she views as problematic. It is notable that while Massey argues for clarification of the notion of space as it appears in political and sociological contexts, she also argues for the abandonment of the concept of place – or of a particular concept of place. In regard to the suspicion of place in contemporary geography and cultural theory, see also David Harvey, 'From Space to Place and Back Again: Reflections on the Condition of Postmodernity', in *Mapping the Futures*, ed. Jon Bird, Barry Curtis, Tim Putnam, George Robertson, and Lisa Tickner (London: Routledge, 1993). Both Harvey and Massey often employ a somewhat simplistic view of place, even while they appear to be reacting against some of the oversimplifications in the work of many humanistic geographers. For a useful and influential discussion of place in geography that focuses on the differences between Harvey and Massey, see Tim Cresswell, *Place: A Short Introduction* (Chichester: Wiley-Blackwell, 2004).

6 In this respect, it is interesting to note that while many English-speaking geographers, in particular, have adopted 'place' as a theoretical term, the term that one might take to correspond most closely to it in French (though see my comments on this in n.8 below), *lieu*, is used by French-speaking geographers, as Vincent Berdoulay points out, 'in an informal sense. As such it is generally not used as a research-inducing concept.' See Berdoulay, 'Place, Meaning and Discourse in French Language Geography', in *The Power of Place*, ed. John A. Agnew and James S. Duncan (Boston, MA: Unwin Hyman, 1989), 124.

7 Michel Foucault, 'Of Other Spaces', *Diacritics* 16 (1986): 22.

8 Place is a more restricted term in French than is the English 'place', usually referring to a specific location or even position. Although often translated as 'place', *lieu* also has a narrower set of senses, usually meaning just 'location' or even 'site' (although Poulet uses the term in his discussion of Proust referring, for instance, to the uniting of 'lieux et personnes' – Poulet, *L'espace proustien* [Paris: Gallimard, 1963], 42 – and, as noted above in n.6, it is also the term discussed by Berdoulay). There are other terms such as *pays* or *patrie* ('country') that can carry connotations of place, but again, without the breadth of the English 'place'.

9 *The Oxford English Dictionary*, 2nd ed., ed. J.A. Simpson and E.S.C. Weiner (Oxford: Clarendon Press, 1989), 11: 937.

10 All of these senses are included in *The Oxford English Dictionary*, s.v. 'place', although twenty-seven separate senses are actually listed there. The summary given here is an attempt to capture the most important and most basic meanings of the term.

11 See ibid., 937. It should be noted that, for the most part, those European terms (*place*, *piazza*, etc.) that have a similar etymology to the English 'place', nevertheless lack the breadth of meaning associated with the English term. See David E. Sopher, 'The Structuring of Space in Place Names and Words for Place', in *Humanistic Geography: Prospects and Problems*, ed. David Ley and Marwyn S. Samuels (London: Croom Helm, 1978), 262–263.

12 See *The Oxford English Dictionary*, 16:87; and also *A Latin Dictionary (Founded on Andrews' Edition of Freund's Latin Dictionary)*, rev. Charlton T. Lewis and Charles Short (Oxford: Clarendon Press, 1879), 1735.

13 The term was also used to refer to a racecourse, an area set aside for some purpose (as for dancing) or a walk or way (in, for instance, a garden) – see *A Greek–English Lexicon*, comp. Henry George Liddell and Robert Scott, rev. ed. (Oxford: Clarendon Press, 1968), 1631.

14 Heidegger uses *Zeitraum* to refer to the idea of time and space as a single conjoined structure in which neither component can be regarded as secondary to or derivable from the other. See Heidegger, *What is a Thing?*, trans. W.B. Barton Jr. and Vera Deutsch (Chicago, IL: Henry Regnery, 1967), 16. See also Theodore Schatzki's development of the idea of timespace in his *The Timespace of Human Activity: On Performance, Society, and History as Indeterminate Teleological Events* (Lanham, MD: Lexington Books, 2010).

15 See, for instance, Elizabeth Grosz's discussion, which draws on the work of Luce Irigaray in particular (Irigaray has taken up notions of both *chora* and *topos* at various places in her work), in *Space*,

Time and Perversion, 111–124. See also Jacques Derrida, *On the Name*, trans. T. Dutoit (Stanford, CA: Stanford University Press, 1995), originally published as *Khôra* (Paris: Galilée, 1993).

16 Aristotle, *Physics IV*, 208a30, *The Complete Works of Aristotle*, ed. Jonathan Barnes (Princeton, NJ: Princeton University Press, 1984), 1:354.

17 Aristotle, *Physics IV*, 5, 212a20, *The Complete Works of Aristotle*, 361. For a more detailed discussion of Aristotle on *topos*, see Keimpe Algra, *Concepts of Space in Greek Thought* (Leiden: E.J. Brill, 1995), 121–191. Casey also has an extensive discussion of Aristotle, as well as Plato, in *The Fate of Place*, 23–74.

18 Plato, *Timaeus*, 52b, in *The Collected Dialogues*, ed. Edith Hamilton and Huntington Cairns (Princeton, NJ: Princeton University Press, 1963), 1178–1179. The Platonic idea of the *chora* (often translated as the 'Receptacle') arises in the course of Plato's consideration of the way in which a thing comes into being, or in which one thing can change into something else. Such a process of becoming requires, according to Plato, three elements: that which becomes, that which is the model for becoming, and that which is the seat or place for such becoming (*Timaeus* 50c). The third element here is the *chora* – it is the place in which the qualities of the thing that comes into being appear. Since the *chora* is precisely that which allows qualities to appear, but which does not contribute any qualities of its own to such appearing, so Plato claims that the *chora* must itself be completely indeterminate (*Timaeus* 51a-51b).

19 Some commentators on Aristotle, for instance, treat him as sometimes using *topos* and *chora* in a way that allows the terms to be correlated with place and space respectively, and it is often assumed that *chora* names something close to space, understood as 'extension', while *topos* names something more like 'location'. In general, however, as Keimpe Algra notes, 'the Greek language did not have a terminological distinction matching the conceptual distinction between place and space' (Keimpe Algra, *Concepts of Space in Greek Thought*, 32, and the following discussion, 32–38). Of the two Greek terms at issue here, *chora* is probably the older and certainly the more concrete term, meaning, variously: space or room 'in which a thing is', place, spot, field, country, land, territory, estate, proper position (within, for instance, a social or military hierarchy). See Liddell and Scott, *A Greek–English Lexicon*, 2015. *Chora* may also be connected with the term *choris*, which in its adverbial form means 'separately', and in its noun form means 'a widow or one bereaved', and this may be taken to suggest a connection with the idea of a separated piece of land or allotment such as a piece of land that may be inherited. *Topos* seems to be originally the more abstract term (though this is clearly a matter of degree – *topos* retains a certain concreteness absent from some contemporary, yet otherwise similar, terms). Like *chora*, however, *topos* has a variety of senses including: place or position (and, in this sense, it can be used to designate place or position in a document or a passage in an author's work, as well as physical location), region, geographical position, site, burial-place, or an element in rhetoric (see Liddell and Scott, *A Greek–English Lexicon*, 1806). The connection of *topos* with a more abstract notion of location and of *chora* with a sense of particular locale is evident in early geographical writing and in Ptolemy. See F. Lukermann, 'The Concept of Location in Classical Geography', *Annals of the American Association of Geographers* 51 (1961), esp. 195–196. E.V. Walter, who also refers to the Ptolemaic use of the terms *chora* and *topos*, emphasizes the use of *topos* to signify objective location or position, and of *chora* as a more 'subjective' term appearing 'in emotional statements about places'. See Walter, *Placeways* (Chapel Hill, NC: University of North Carolina, 1988), 120. Walter notes that Plato's use of *topos* in the *Phaedrus* represents an exception to this. Walter also points out that, in general, 'writers were inclined to call a sacred place a *chora* instead of a *topos*' (Walter, *Placeways*, 120), although later, in Hellenistic Greek, *topos* came to be employed as the term for a holy place, while *chora* 'carried technical and administrative meanings'.

20 Salomon Bochner claims that the Greeks understood space only in terms of place as *topos* – see Bochner, 'Space', in *Dictionary of the History of Ideas* (New York: Charles Scribner's Sons, 1973), 295–307. Heidegger also claims that 'the Greeks had no word for "space". This is no accident; for they experienced the spatial on the basis not of extension but of place (*topos*); they experienced it as *chôra*, which signifies neither place nor space but that which is occupied by what stands there.' See Heidegger, *An Introduction to Metaphysics*, trans. Ralph Manheim (New Haven, CT: Yale University Press, 1959), 66). See also Nader El-Bizri, 'On Khôra: Situating Heidegger between the Sophist and the Timaeus', *Studia Phaenomenologica* 4 (2002): 73–98.

21 For more on *topos*, *chora*, and place, see my 'Five Theses on Place (and Some Associated Remarks): A Reply to Peter Gratton', Il Cannocchiale 62 (2017): 69–81.
22 See Keimpe Algra, *Concepts of Space in Greek Thought*, 38–70, 263ff.
23 See Edward Grant, *Much Ado About Nothing: Theories of Space and Vacuum from the Middle Ages to the Scientific Revolution* (Cambridge: Cambridge University Press, 1981).
24 See Einstein's use of a similar analogy in his foreword to Jammer, *Concepts of Space*, xiii). Of course, for many thinkers, both in the modern era and earlier, such a realm of pure spatial extension, while perhaps thinkable in abstraction from concepts of body, could nevertheless not exist apart from body. Descartes' treatment of space and bodily extension as one and the same, and his consequent rejection of the possibility of any actual void or vacuum, is one of the important points of difference between his view of space and that of Newton.
25 See Einstein's brief comments on this in the foreword to Jammer, *Concepts of Space*, xv; and also his discussion in Albert Einstein, 'The Problem of Space, Ether and the Field in Physics', in *Ideas and Opinions*, trans. Sonja Borgmann (New York: Crown, 1956), 276–285. In fact, the idea of containment probably contains remnants of what is essentially a richer place-based mode of thinking about space, but which, for precisely this reason, was certain to be superseded within physical theory by a more purely 'physicalist' conception.
26 Jammer, *Concepts of Space*, 1.
27 *The Encyclopedia of Philosophy*, ed. Paul Edwards (New York: Macmillan, 1967) – once the definitive reference work in English-speaking philosophy – contains a five-page entry on 'Space' (written by J.J.C. Smart) that focuses on a similar history of the concept to that dealt with in more detailed form by, for instance, Max Jammer, but contains no entry at all on 'place'. More contemporaneously, neither the *Routledge Encyclopedia of Philosophy*, www.rep.routledge.com/ – essentially the successor to the Edwards volume – nor the *Stanford Encyclopedia of Philosophy*, https://plato.stanford.edu/, contains an entry on 'place', even though both contain lengthy entries on 'Space' or 'Space and Time' (as well as various related entries).
28 Casey, *Getting Back into Place*, xiv.
29 René Descartes, *Principia Philosophiae* II:13 and 14, in *Oeuvres de Descartes*, ed. Charles Adams and Paul Tannery (Paris: Librairie Philosophique, J. Vrin, 1982), VIII-1, 47–48; translation from *The Philosophical Writings of Descartes*, vol. 1, trans. John Cottingham, Robert Stoothoff, and Dugald Murdoch (Cambridge: Cambridge University Press, 1985), 228–229.
30 Isaac Newton, 'Scholium to the Definitions', *Sir Isaac Newton's Mathematical Principles of Natural Philosophy and His System of the World*, vol. 1, trans. Andrew Motte, rev. Florian Cajori (Berkeley, CA: University of California Press, 1934), 6.
31 Richard Swinburne, *Space and Time* (London: Macmillan, 1968), 12–13.
32 Algra makes this explicit in *Concepts of Space in Greek Thought*, 20. See also Bruce Janz, ed., *Place, Space and Hermeneutics* (Dordrecht: Springer, 2017).
33 Once again, see Casey's discussion in *The Fate of Place*, ix–xi and 3–132.
34 Jammer, *Concepts of Space*, 7–8.
35 This is particularly true of many 'humanistic' approaches to the issue of place. Thus Yi-Fu Tuan, an important and pioneering figure within environmentalist discussions of place, who is otherwise remarkably sensitive to many of the issues at stake, often tends to treat place in a way that is suggestive of the concept as a purely psychological or experiential 'construct'. Much of Tuan's work is explicitly written from 'The perspective of experience', as the subtitle of his *Space and Place* has it, and experience is characterized by Tuan as 'a cover-all term for the various modes through which a person knows or constructs a reality'. See Tuan, *Space and Place: The Perspective of Experience* (Minneapolis, MN: University of Minnesota Press, 1977), 8. There is a certain equivocation in Tuan's work, common in much writing on place, between place or space as that which gives rise to experience on the one hand, and space or place as experiential construct on the other. Nevertheless, his work still largely operates within a view of place as essentially a psychological or affective notion. In another of his writings, Tuan characterizes his work in terms of the study of 'environmental perception, attitudes, and values'. See Tuan, *Topophilia* (New York: Columbia University Press, 1974), 245. There, Tuan is quite explicit about the nature of his work as an essay in environment psychology. He also makes clear that he is well aware of the disparity

in the materials and themes with which he is concerned and acknowledges that there is no 'single all-embracing concept' that guides his work (see *Topophilia*, 3).

36 See, for instance, Tuan, *Topophilia*, 113. 'The fact that images are taken from the environment does not, of course, mean that the environment has "determined" them; nor... need we believe that certain environments have the irresistible power to excite topophilic feelings. Environment may not be the direct cause of topophilia, but environment provides the sensory stimuli, which, as perceived images, lend shape to our joys and ideals.'

37 J. Nicholas Entrikin, *The Betweenness of Place* (Baltimore, MD: Johns Hopkins University Press, 1991), 14. Entrikin immediately goes on to suggest that 'a more modest, but not insignificant, goal is a better understanding of the narrative-like qualities that give structure to our attempts to capture the peculiar connections between people and places'. It is noteworthy that Entrikin explicitly takes up some of the issues relating to the conception of place as a purely mental or subjective construct and is explicitly concerned to encompass both 'objective' and 'subjective' aspects of place in his account (ibid., 6–26), but he attempts to do this by an appeal to the concept of narrative that he takes to somehow occupy a position 'between' subjective and objective (ibid., 132–134). In fact, Entrikin appears to retain a view of place as an essentially 'subjective' structure.

38 In *The Fate of Place*, Casey titles the chapter that deals with the Heideggerian appropriation of place 'Proceeding to Place by Indirection' – see *The Fate of Place*, 284, and, more generally, 243–284.

39 See Martin Heidegger, *Being and Time*, trans. John Macquarrie and Edward Robinson (New York: Harper & Row, 1962), H54; and Jeff Malpas, *Heidegger's Topology: Being, Place, World* (Cambridge, MA: MIT Press, 2006), chap. 3, 65–146.

40 Although, as we shall see later, the notion of containment is more complex that just that associated with physical containment – a point that Heidegger seems, in *Being and Time* at least, not properly to have appreciated.

41 See Charles Guignon, *Heidegger and the Problem of Knowledge* (Indianapolis, IN: Hackett Publishing, 1983), for a detailed analysis of Heidegger's position in relation to the traditional problems of epistemology. For the most part, what Heidegger means by 'subjectivism' is broader than the usual sense of the term. In his case, it refers to any thinking that looks to identify a fundamental underlying ground or 'substratum' (a *subjectum* in the original Latin meaning).

42 Martin Heidegger, 'Einleitung Zu: "Was ist Metaphysik"', in Wegmarken, *Gesamtausgabe*, vol. 9 (Frankfurt: Vittorio Klostermann, 1976), 373.

43 Once again, see my *Heidegger's Topology*, but also *Heidegger and the Thinking of Place: Explorations in the Topology of Being* (Cambridge, MA: MIT Press, 2012), for further clarification of this connection.

44 The rejection of reductive accounts – whether of ordinary language into some 'purer' language of physics, of the richness of place into the mere ordering of spatial location, or of the realm of mental life into the terms of neuropsychology – is a central feature of my account here. Various arguments in favour of the rejection of such reductionism are, in fact, developed in the course of the analysis over the following chapters, although, for the most part, the central focus is on the development of the positive account of place, rather than taking issue, in any detailed fashion, with the full range of alternative accounts.

45 See, for instance, David Harvey, *Justice, Nature and the Geography of Difference* (Cambridge, MA: Blackwell, 1996), 324; see also Sarah Menin, ed., *Constructing Place: Mind and Matter* (London: Routledge, 2003), the very title of which is indicative of the volume's constructionist construal as well as its treatment of place, as in so many writers, as a function of space plus subjectivity – see Menin, 'Introduction', in *Constructing Place: Mind and Matter*, 1–37.

46 In this respect, neither can the 'social' be seen as having any clear priority over the 'individual' – both arise within the same encompassing structure.

47 There are obvious affinities between this idea and the idea of 'the world' that Merleau-Ponty articulates in the *Phenomenology of Perception* (esp. 405–407), and of which he writes, at one point, that 'the world is the field of our experience, and... we are nothing but a view of the world' (ibid., 406). The very idea of the world as Merleau-Ponty employs it is, in fact, the idea of just such a topographical structure (a field or region) as that which I have set out here. This should also indicate the extent to which the task undertaken here has a certain 'transcendental' character – it is a matter of undertaking an analysis of the structure in which the very possibility of subjectivity and of objectivity, of experience and self, are grounded.

48 Objectivity and subjectivity are, on this account, correlative concepts. And while, generally speaking, one can characterize the 'subjective' as that which derives from the subject or is dependent on features of the subject's position in or experience of the world and the 'objective' as that which derives from the object alone, this need not imply that either of these terms have a sense that is completely independent of the other. What counts as pertaining to the object and what to the subject is, in fact, dependent on the frame within which a particular inquiry or practice is established. We can thus speak of 'objective' features of the social, or of mental life, as well as 'objective' features of the world. 'Objective' should not, in this respect, be taken to designate exclusively those features of the world as given within a purely physicalist analysis.

49 See note 48, immediately above.

50 The issue of metaphor, and especially of the 'metaphorical' sense that may be supposed to attach to topographical as well as spatial language outside of certain narrow physical contexts, is one that I have addressed elsewhere, most notably in '"The House of Being": Poetry, Language, Place', in *Heidegger's Later Thought*, ed. Günter Figal, Diego D'Angelo, Tobias Keiling, and Guang Yang (Bloomington, IN: Indiana University Press, forthcoming 2018). The metaphorization of the language of place is both widespread in philosophical thinking and, for the most part, almost entirely unthinking.

51 See my 'Place and Situation', in *Routledge Companion to Philosophical Hermeneutics*, ed. Jeff Malpas and Hans-Helmuth Gander (London: Routledge, 2015), 354–366; see also Bruce Janz, ed., *Place, Space and Hermeneutics* (Dordrecht: Springer, 2017).

52 Marcia Cavell, *The Psychoanalytic Mind: From Freud to Philosophy* (Cambridge, MA: Harvard University Press, 1993), 41.

53 Great Britain Ministry of Defence, *Textbook of Topographical Surveying*, 4th ed. (London: Her Majesty's Stationery Office, 1965), 1.

54 Is such a picture to be construed as a metaphor? That all depends on how metaphor is itself understood and whether metaphor is indeed imagistic or whether it operates in some other fashion. Heidegger, for instance, treats metaphor and image as distinct, rejecting metaphor, but employing the image – see my '"The House of Being": Poetry, Language, Place'. One might also say that what is at work in this topographical picture is an analogy, but again, much rides on exactly what is meant by this.

55 In this respect, the significance of the picture at issue here should not be misconstrued. The reference to the practice of topographical surveying does not mean that place is identical with what can be mapped or measured (indeed, place will always exceed any such mapping or measuring), nor does it mean that place is a concept uniquely tied to the practices of measuring and mapping (or the scientific modes of practice, and even the economic and political forms that may accompany them) that are part of topographical surveying. Topographical surveying depends on the character of place and so also shows that character, in spite of its many other associations.

56 Ludwig Wittgenstein, *Wittgenstein's Lectures on the Philosophy of Mathematics: Cambridge 1939*, ed. Cora Diamond (Hassocks: Harvester, 1976), 44. In *Analysis and Metaphysics* (Oxford: Oxford University Press, 1992), 2–3. P.F. Strawson also refers to the idea, which he attributes to Ryle, of philosophy as a form of 'conceptual geography or conceptual mapping or charting'. The idea is not given much development, however, and while Strawson acknowledges that the picture 'has merits' he nevertheless finds it to be 'uncomfortably metaphorical'. Perhaps I am less worried by the threat of metaphor than Strawson (although as I note above, the extent to which metaphor is indeed at work here is open to question), but certainly I think that the topographical conception of philosophy, which I outline here, is significant and methodologically instructive.

57 See Heidegger, *Being and Time*, §70, H367–H369; see also Malpas, *Heidegger's Topology*, chap. 3, esp. 96–146. The attempt to treat spatiality as secondary in this way is something that Heidegger later rejects, as he makes clear in 'Time and Being', in *On Time and Being*, trans. Joan Stambaugh (New York: Harper & Row, 1972), 23. In fact, as early as 1935 he already seems to have modified his position. See Heidegger, *What is a Thing?*, 16. See also Stuart Elden's discussion of the shift in Heidegger's thinking about space and place in the early Hölderlin in 'Heidegger's Hölderlin and the Importance of Place', *Journal of the British Society for Phenomenology* 30 (1999): 258–274.

58 For criticisms of Heidegger's prioritizing of temporality, see my *Heidegger's Topology*, chap. 3, 65–146. See also Maria Villela-Petit, 'Heidegger's Conception of Space', in *Critical Heidegger*, ed. Christopher Macann (London: Routledge, 1996), 134–157.

59 On this point, see Don Parkes and Nigel Thrift, 'Putting Time in its Place', in *Timing Space and Spacing Time*, ed. Tommy Carlstein, Don Parkes, and Nigel Thrift, vol. 1, Making Sense of Time (London: Edward Arnold, 1978), 119–129. See also my discussion in 'Timing Space – Spacing Time: On Transcendence, Performance, and Place', in *Performance and Temporalisation: Time Happens*, ed. Jodie McNeilly, Stuart Grant, and Maeva Veerapen (London: Palgrave Macmillan, 2015), 25–36; and also in '"Where are We When We Think?" Hannah Arendt and the Place of Thinking', *Philosophy Today*, forthcoming 2018.

Further reading

Algra, Keimpe. *Concepts of Space in Greek Thought*. Leiden: E.J. Brill, 1995.

Casey, Edward S. *The Fate of Place*. Berkeley, CA: University of California Press, 1996.

Cresswell, Tim. *Place: A Short Introduction*. Chichester: Wiley-Blackwell, 2004.

Entrikin, J. Nicholas. *The Betweenness of Place*. Baltimore, MD: Johns Hopkins University Press, 1991.

Jammer, Max. *Concepts of Space: The History of Theories of Space in Physics*, 2nd ed. Cambridge, MA: Harvard University Press, 1970.

Ströker, Elizabeth. *Investigations in Philosophy of Space*. Translated by Algis Mickunas. Athens, OH: Ohio University Press, 1987.

Tuan, Yi-Fu. *Space and Place: The Perspective of Experience*. Minneapolis, MN: University of Minnesota Press, 1977.

2 The structure of spatiality

> Any thinker who has an idea of an objective spatial world. . . must be able to think of his perception of the world as simultaneously due to his position in the world, and to the condition of the world at that position. The very idea of a perceivable, objective, spatial world brings with it the idea of the subject as being *in* the world with the course of his perceptions due to his changing position in the world and to the more-or-less stable way the world is.
>
> (Gareth Evans, *The Varieties of Reference*[1])

It is only when we begin to examine the way in which creatures like ourselves find themselves in the world, and organize their activities in that world, that the limitations of viewing space only in the terms in which it figures in physical theory, or as it is 'objectively' conceived, become clearly apparent. As Ernst Mach notes, in discussing the difference between 'physiological' and 'geometric' space: 'Of cardinal and greatest importance to animals are the *parts of their own body* and their relations to one another. . . *Geometric space* embraces only the relations of *physical bodies to one another*, and leaves the animal body in this connection altogether out of account.'[2] Understanding the way in which creatures, including both human and non-human animals, find themselves 'in' space, both in relation to their bodies and to one another, requires more than just a concept of space as articulated within physical theory. Moreover, since the concept of space is intertwined with the idea of place, so the restriction of focus that limits space to the physical and objective must also constitute a severe, indeed debilitating, restriction on any attempt to arrive at an adequate understanding of both space and place.

If we are to examine the questions at issue here in a more adequate fashion, then we need to consider the concept of space from a point of view that, as Mach suggests, includes the relation of space to those creatures who are 'in' space. This means that we must investigate space as it presents itself, not only in terms of physical extension or location, nor even merely as a space within which the perceptual presentation of objects is possible, but as a space for movement and activity. Such a focus brings with it a focus on creatures as *acting subjects*. This turn to the 'subject' in no way implies, however, that the approach adopted is a purely 'psychological' one, nor one given over to the simple prioritizing of the 'subjective'. What is at issue here is the possibility of *agency*, and what emerges is the dependency of such agency on a structure that encompasses concepts of both subjectivity and objectivity, and that cannot be accounted for solely in terms of features that are dependent on, or derived from, the subject alone. At the same time, the investigation of the structure at issue here, while it is informed by the findings of psychology along with other empirical sciences, is properly *ontological* in character, precisely because it does indeed concern itself with the structure within which agency, and more besides, is possible.

Agency involves a capacity for action and activity. Activity is, first of all, *movement*, and since movement presupposes space (as that in which movement occurs as well as that which allows for position and location), so to be capable of any sort of oriented or directed movement must also involve a capacity for orientation and direction with regard to space, and with respect to the parts of space – the latter including the capacity to distinguish between the space of one's own body, and its parts, and the space apart from the body. This point is not impugned by the fact that not all movement requires such orientation or direction on the part of that which moves or causes movement. The blowing of leaves in the wind, for instance, does not require orientation on the part of the wind or the leaves. The gathering of leaves by a human gardener, however, even one using a powered 'blower', is a different matter. The integrated activity the gardener exhibits is only possible because of the way in which the space in which the gardener moves, both the space of the garden and the space of the gardener's own body, is itself incorporated into that activity, is incorporated, in some sense, into the gardener. The agent is thus 'in' space, but space is also 'in' the agent.

It is because of the way space is necessarily implicated in agency that agency becomes an important route for the investigation of space – and so also of place – at the same time as space becomes important for the investigation of agency. Yet it is crucial to note that the way space is implicated in agency is not in in some merely causal fashion – as if being 'in' space were alone sufficient to also be 'in touch' with or to have a 'grasp' of space. To be spatially located or positioned is not, by that fact alone, to be spatially oriented and directed. Indeed, it is hard to see how it could be so, since to be in a space is only ever to be in relation to a part of that space at any one time. How could a space that extends beyond any immediately given location or position ever be accessible in such a way as to orient or direct activity or movement as that occurs in just that location or position? More generally, one might ask how orientation, which is a relation to the whole, ever be possible only on the basis of a relation to the part? The answer has to be that where a creature is spatially oriented and directed, it is so through having access, in its current location or position, to more than is given in that location or position alone – the whole space must thus be included within the part of space.

What this means is that the space in which a creature acts must be incorporated in the very activity of that creature, or as we may also say, in the creature itself – as the agent is embedded in space, so space is indeed embedded in the agent. This requires a certain duplication of the space in a form that is accessible to the creature in acting, and that can therefore be operative in its activity. The only way in which this would seem to be possible is if the creature or agent has some internalized grasp of space, that is, if the creature has access to some spatial framework that can orient and direct its activity and movement. This is just what is at issue in the idea that spatial orientation and direction is based in access to some spatial representation or 'cognitive map' in the brain.[3] It is also at issue, however, in those ordinary and familiar cases where conventional maps and models are used for spatial navigation and orientation – whether, for instance, a tourist using a printed guide to walk a city's streets or a driver following the instructions of a computerized satellite navigation system. It is precisely by means of such representations, maps, and models that the larger space is made accessible from – *through being included within* – the particular space of a creature's location or position. Acting or moving in a space in an oriented and directed fashion thus requires a grasp of the space in which such action of movement occurs and this requires, in turn, access to an appropriate spatial framework in the form of a representation or map.

One cannot avoid the implication that access to some form of spatial representation or mapping is necessary for spatial orientation and direction by arguing that that the embedding of the space 'in' the agent, in the creature that moves and acts, is a matter of the creature's tacit knowledge of the space or of its embodied engagement in space (the latter being the sort of account popularized by writers such as Hubert Dreyfus[4]). This is so for two reasons: first, because it runs afoul of exactly the problem mentioned in the discussion just above, namely, that orientation to a space as a whole cannot be on the basis merely of location in a part of that space, and one cannot assume that such location is already oriented since that is precisely what is in question (writers like Dreyfus typically assume such orientation even as they seek to explain it); and second, because all the invocation of tacit knowledge or embodied engagement does is to push back the question as to how such tacit knowledge or embodied engagement itself works – so taking us back to the further question, 'In what is such knowledge or engagement itself grounded?' – and if some writers (such as Dreyfus) seem to avoid this, it is only because, once again, the orientational capacities at issue are effectively assumed in the very idea of embodied engagement itself.

Alfred Korzybski famously pointed out that 'the territory is not the map'[5], and not only does this counsel against confusing representations with their objects, the territory with the map, but it also indicates something important about maps, namely, that they function as maps precisely because they are distinct from the territory. The same point also applies to spatial orientation and direction: the orientation and direction necessary for integrated activity and behaviour cannot be found in the space itself even though the structure of spatial orientation is a structure derived from the structure of the space. Thus, although location or position in a space is necessary for action or movement in that space (one cannot move or act at all unless one is first located or positioned), location or position in a space is not itself sufficient for action or movement in that space to be oriented and directed. Even so, recognizing the way the capacity for activity and movement in a space requires some internalized access to that space in the form of a representation or map does not mean that the access to space is solely by means of the representation or map. Indeed, the representation or map only gives access to space in conjunction with the location or position of the creature that has access to that representation or map (a point to which I shall return below). The role of spatial frameworks, representations, or maps in the possibility of agency does not imply, therefore, that what supports agency is a purely mediational or indirect access to space or, more generally, to the world. Agency draws on both the immediate and 'direct' access to space given in location or position and on the mediated or 'indirect' access given through the representation or map. The complex character of the spatiality that is already evident here as necessary for agency exemplifies a complexity that will appear throughout much of the investigation of space and of place as set out in the pages that follow: the structures at issue are not reducible to single elements, but typically involves the interplay within a duality or multiplicity of elements.

The fact that agency requires access to a larger space than is given in a creature's immediate location or position – access that is possible only by means of a representation or map – does not imply, however, that what is also required is access to the character of the representation or map *as a representation or map*. To have a grasp of space as required for agency, to have access to a spatial framework within which action is possible, to be able to make use of a representation or map, is not necessarily to have a grasp of the *idea* or *concept* of space or the *concept* of some spatial framework, representation, or map. As Davidson says, '[a] creature could construct a "map" of its world without having the idea that it was a *map* of anything'.[6] The rat that successfully runs a maze may thus be attributed with a grasp of the space of the maze, but there is no reason to attribute it with any grasp either of the maze *as a maze* or of the space *as a space*; the rat may navigate by means of an internal representation of the space – a cognitive or mental map – and yet it need not have any grasp of that representation *as a representation* or of the map *as a map*.

That having a grasp of space requires no fully-fledged capacity for conceptual thought is a significant point.[7] It not only means that it is possible to talk about a grasp of space even for creatures that lack any conceptual or linguistic capacity (and so also goes some way to addressing the intuitions that underlie the idea, advanced by Dreyfus and others, that agency is not based in any internalized representation), but it also requires distinguishing between the grasp of space that involves a grasp of the concept of space and the grasp of space that remains at the level only of certain behavioural capacities or dispositions. The latter case is one in which the spatial framework that orients and directs action will operate *in* action, but will not itself be able to made a focus *for* action (it will not be capable of explication or externalization).[8]

Both of these ways of grasping space play a role in the behaviour exhibited by human and non-human animals (and in any behaviour that is to count as an instance of genuine agency), and both will play a part in the discussion in the following pages. The primary focus of the inquiry here, however, is on place and on the essential inter-relation of place with *human* being (and here the 'human' should be understood as naming an *ontological* rather than primarily a *biological* category – it is indeed *a mode of being*[9]). This focus is not arbitrary. There is a connection between the mode of being that characterizes human being and the phenomenon of place that is not present in the case of other creatures and the modes of being proper to them. Only if place can be taken up *as place* – that is, as recognized conceptually and articulated linguistically (though how it is recognized and articulated will take multiple forms[10]) – can place operate in the rich and complex way that was sketched out in the introductory discussion with which this book began.

Language plays a key role here, although it is a role that has received relatively little attention in most discussions of place – at least outside of discussions explicitly concerned with the poetic.[11] Language exhibits, in fact, the same openness that is also characteristic of place itself – an openness that is tied to the character of utterance (which is where the reality of language is surely to be found, and which can take the forms of speech, gesture, or inscription) as always arising in specificity and yet as always extending beyond that specificity. In the language Martin Heidegger employs, one might say that language always arises in the midst of the 'there' or the 'here', and that language contributes to the holding open of that there/here. Thus Heidegger comments that 'only where there is language, is there world',[12] and elsewhere that 'language holds open the realm in which man, upon the earth and beneath the sky, inhabits the house of the world'.[13] Although it is fashionable to deride such claims as anthropocentric and as failing to attend to that which is 'more than human', the emphasis on language here derives from powerful considerations, both conceptual and empirical, concerning both the nature of language itself and of the human relation to language.[14] Moreover, far from implying an undue focus on the human as one mode of being to the exclusion of other modes, the focus on the special relation between language and the human actually involves attending to precisely that which differentiates the human from other modes of being, and so attending to the genuine character of both human *and* non-human modes of being, refusing any simple collapse of the one into the other, and acknowledging the distinctiveness of each as well as their similarities.[15]

Although there is indeed a special connection between place and the human, place is nevertheless distinct from the human – as *place* is distinct from *being-in-place* – and it is in and through place that both the human *and the non-human appear*. Place is thus not restricted to the human – place always involves that which goes beyond the human. Place is not determined by the human, and neither are individual places – or, at least, they are not determined by the human alone – and so, as noted earlier, place cannot be regarded as a function of the human or as constituted by it. Place encompasses the sensuous and the concrete, yet it cannot be grasped *as place* in the absence of some capacity for conceptuality and for language. Space too is not restricted just to that which operates below the level of conscious activity or as that is experienced bodily and experientially; space includes that which is engaged conceptually and abstractly. Just as the subjective and objective are tied together within the structure of place, as are the spaces correlated with these, so too are the concrete and the abstract, the behavioural and the conceptual, the felt and the thought similarly bound together within that same structure. Yet even if one took issue with my own focus on the human relation to place and on the role of conceptuality and representation in relation to place and space, that need not force the rejection of the entirety of the analysis offered here. That analysis extends across all forms of embodied agency, and even many of the structures that I argue are characteristic of those modes of (typically) human agency associated with explicit capacities for conceptualization, representation, and self-reflection can be seen as also having an expression in analogous structures (though usually operating in the absence of any awareness of them) that are at work in forms of non-human agency that involve no such explicit conceptual, representational, or reflective capacities. There is thus a degree of ambiguity in some of my analysis inasmuch as it can often be seen as applying, with appropriate adjustment, across a wide range of cases. Having made that concession, however, I would still argue that to refuse to recognize the particular relation between place and the human that is also at work in my explorations here would be to refuse to recognize a key element in the structure of place and in the character of human being.

The capacity for agency and the grasp of space are mutually dependent – to lack one is also to lack the other. Agency comes, however, in many different forms that reflect the differing capacities of acting creatures, and consequently the grasp of space associated with different forms of agency will also differ – and here the differences between human and non-human agency are indeed important to recognize. The way a creature grasps space, and so also, one might say, the manner in which space is represented or mapped such that the creature has access to it, will be directly keyed to the creature's own capacities for agency – for action and movement. So, for instance, the grasp of space that is operative in the behaviour of an octopus will be quite different from the grasp of space operative in the behaviour of a honeybee, or, indeed, in the case of an adult human being. In any particular case, a creature's grasp of space will be directly evident in the creature's capacity for oriented, directed action, and movement, and so also in the creature's capacity to orient and locate itself within the space in which it acts and moves. One corollary of this is that a creature cannot be said to have any grasp of space at all if it lacks the capacity to orient and locate itself in space, and so also lacks the capacity for oriented and directed activity and movement. Such a lack of capacity, if manifest as a persistent and long-standing lack, would not only count against the creature's having a grasp of space, but it would also count against it being properly an agent.[16]

The grasp of space implicated in the capacity for agency must be tied directly to the agent's capacities for activity and movement, but also to the agent's bodily and environmental awareness, and so to the agent's past and present experience, since it is only by means of features that enter into the agent's experience and awareness (even if it is sometimes, in the case of human agents especially, below the level of *conscious* awareness) that an agent can orient and locate itself or orient and direct its activities. On this basis one might say that the form of space that is operative in the immediate orientation and direction of agency – of an acting subject – is 'subjective' or 'egocentric' insofar as it is a space that is tied to the agent's capacities, and so to spatial features as presented in the agent's experience. We may even talk of such space as indeed an 'experiential' space as a way of marking the fact that an agent must have some experience of the feature or features that organize the space in which it is located if it is to have some grasp of that space. Such talk of 'experiential space' can be seen to indicate the way in which an agent's subjective space is precisely the space of that agent's own involvement with the world – the space of awareness within which it acts, and with respect to which its actions are oriented and located. For this reason, we might also characterize such a space in terms of the notion of perspectivity – a subjective space is an intrinsically perspectival space.[17] If the notion of perspective is to be employed in this way, however, it must be a notion of perspectivity that does not allow the reduction of perspectivity to a mere 'point'. Subjective space is perspectival, but also has a certain orientation and extension to it – it is a space that 'gives space' for action.

An agent's grasp of what I have called 'subjective' space is inseparable from the complex of sensory, cognitive, and motor capacities that the agent possesses – inseparable from its bodily and environmental awareness as well as its capacity to act on and to interact with aspects of that environment. It is those capacities that in large part, define the perspective with respect to which a particular subjective space is constituted. That perspective can be defined, in general terms, in relation to an agent's sensory, cognitive, and motor capacities; it can also be defined, more particularly, in relation to the specific capacities currently being exercised by the agent. The latter perspective will change, of course, as the agent's behavioural and sensory engagement changes, whereas the former perspective will remain more stable inasmuch as the agent's overall capacities remain stable over time. Yet whether considered in terms of an overall set of capacities – even if not currently being exercised – or with respect to just those capacities being exercised on any particular occasion, the perspective at issue in the constitution of subjective space is not merely a passive 'point of view', but is indeed a perspective of *active engagement*.[18] Consequently, an agent's grasp of subjective space involves, not merely perceptual acquaintance with the surrounding environment (although along Gibsonian lines, we may well take perceptual acquaintance itself to presuppose a practical grasp of environmental circumstance[19]), but also a grasp of the agent's own causal embedding in that environment. It will include a grasp of aspects of the agent's surroundings given in terms that relate those surroundings to the agent's capacities to act and to move, and so will include a grasp of how the agent must act in order to achieve certain practical outcomes.

This account of 'subjective' or egocentric space has some affinities with John Campbell's characterization of an egocentric spatial framework as one that is 'immediately used by the subject in directing action'.[20] There is, however, an ambiguity in Campbell's characterization that might be taken to render it problematic. Depending on what sense is given to the term 'immediately', the idea of a framework that is 'immediately used by the subject in directing action' could be taken to be applicable both to properly subjective *and* objective frameworks. One can, after all, use a map in directing action even where that map is a map of space as 'objectively' conceived. I may, for example, use a published road map to direct my travel from Sydney to Melbourne and yet the map I use is not therefore to be construed either as identical with or as representing a subjective or egocentric spatial framework. Using a map is precisely a matter of applying an objective framework, from within a local or subjective perspective, to the space, and the features of that space, as presented within that perspective – a point that was already evident, if put in slightly different terms, in the discussion above. With that, I will, for the moment, leave Campbell's characterization to one side.

Subjective space is a space structured by the causal properties of features evident within that space, and by the sensory, cognitive, and behavioural capacities to which those features are related. Thus, Gareth Evans, from whose work the epigraph to this chapter is taken, characterizes a subjective, or in his terms 'egocentric', space as existing 'only for an animal in which a complex network of connections exists between perceptual input and behavioural output'.[21] Since the precise nature of those connections and the degree of their complexity, together with the actual capacities possessed, may vary according to the species of animal, or, more generally, the type of agent, and may even vary from individual to individual, so the subjective space that exists for some agent, and is able to be grasped by it, will vary also. A difference in bodily and environmental awareness, or in the capacity to act in ways that are guided by such awareness, will correlate with a difference in the grasp of subjective space. Agents with, for instance, similar cognitive but only partially overlapping sensory capacities may inhabit subjective spaces that are structured quite differently from one another. Additionally, the more complex and sophisticated the agent's sensory awareness and cognitive and motor capacities, the more complex and sophisticated will be the subjective space it inhabits.

This conception of subjective or egocentric space differs from that usually found in the relevant psychological and philosophical literature. There, the notion of egocentric space, as applied to an agent's grasp of space, has usually been taken to involve a concept of space centred on that agent's body, and has been contrasted with a notion of allocentric space, understood as a space centred on or 'cued to' some aspect or feature of the agent's environment distinct from its body. It is tempting to think of the difference between egocentric and allocentric space as indeed just a difference in that on which these two forms of space are centred – on body or environment – but this can be a misleading way of understanding the difference at issue. If egocentric or subjective space is understood in the terms I have employed – as something like an experiential space that is also a space of activity – then the very way in which that space is 'centred' (if we are even to talk about 'centring' here at all) is itself rather different from the 'centring' associated with any putative allocentric space. Subjective space is centred 'on the body' only insofar as it is structured as the experiential space of the agent whose space it is, and in terms of the sensory, cognitive, and motor capacities of that agent – it is a space that the agent 'inhabits'. In this respect, however, talk of subjective space as being 'centred on the body' rather than on something else, as the distinguishing mark of that space, is indeed misleading. A subjective space is not constituted as the space that it is simply in virtue of a certain prioritization of one entity or feature rather than another. Instead, a subjective space exhibits a different character as a space altogether – it is indeed an experiential space possessing a perspectivity that is essential to it (a point partly captured in this idea that it is a space the agent 'inhabits'). Within that space, there is certainly a different centring, but the centring alone is not what makes the space. Spaces that are characterized as allocentric, in contrast, have none of the character of the experiential perspectivity associated with subjective space, and are constituted just through the prioritizing of a particular entity or feature (the shape of the space being determined by that prioritization).

Much of the discussion around the notion of allocentric space has tended to associate that notion with a concept of *objective* space – thus the introduction to an important volume on spatial representation refers to 'allocentric/detached/map-like/objective spatial representation'[22] – and in this way, the distinction between egocentric and allocentric is often assimilated to that between subjective and objective. Yet such assimilation is not entirely appropriate: allocentric space cannot be opposed to subjective space (even though it is different from it) and allocentric space cannot be simply identified with objective space (even though it is also connected to it). An agent's grasp of subjective space consists in a grasp of space that is directly tied to the agent's capacity for movement and activity whereas an allocentric space is a space organized around a salient feature or features of the environment. Any and every agent, if it is to be able to find its way around its environment, requires a grasp of an allocentric space as the means by which it can orient itself, from within its own subjective space, in relation to the objective space in which it is located. So, it is by taking some feature of my environment, to which I am subjectively oriented, that I am able to configure the larger space around me as that space extends beyond my immediate perceptual and agential capacities. The point is neatly illustrated by the commonplace experience of being momentarily lost, recognizing a familiar landmark, and then being reoriented as everything falls back into place. Through identifying the landmark, I am able to bring to bear my own prior knowledge of the way that landmark is related to other objects and locations, and so connect that knowledge, which is a knowledge of the space as objective, to my own subjective space.

In contrast to both subjective and allocentric space, however, the idea of objective space, pure and simple, is not organized around any subjective capacities or subjectively presented features of an agent's environment, and is rather the idea of an extended field that is independent of any particular agent operating within it and within which no single feature or location has any precedence over any other. Objective space is nonetheless important, even for some forms of agency, since objective space is that which is presupposed by the interconnectedness of subjective and allocentric space, and of different subjective and allocentric spaces. It is only by being oriented to certain features in its environment – by having a grasp of space as allocentrically configured – that an agent can have any grasp of objective space, and so allocentric space might be said to stand between subjective and objective space. The interconnection that is at issue here is something that will be the focus for further exploration in the discussion below (it will be particularly important in explicating the character of spatial representation and mapping). Yet although all three of these notions – subjective, allocentric, and objective – interconnect and are implicated with one another, they are nevertheless distinct. They thus form a triad whose elements can neither be simply identified nor opposed. Of course, although it is easy enough to understand the difference between objective and subjective space, within this triad, allocentric space appears as somewhat obscure, and this is just because it is connected differently to both the objective and the subjective. In part in can be said to stand between them, and yet one might also say that it stands differently in relation to each. One may even be led to say that the allocentric does not really name a *space* at all – or if it does, it is a purely notional space. Allocentricity is perhaps best understood as a feature of represented spaces – all such representation involves presenting objects and locations as they stand in certain relations to one another, and the very nature of such representation is that it operates by means of the prioritization of certain locations, objects, or orientations, in other words, by means of allocentricity. Perhaps the point at issue could be captured by saying that if the map is distinct from the territory, then this is partly because the map is allocentric and the territory is not, even though the map is a map of the territory.

In keeping with his own treatment of egocentric space as tied to action, John Campbell emphasizes the distinction between what he calls egocentric and 'absolute' space over that between egocentric and allocentric space.[23] Of the egocentric/absolute distinction, Campbell writes: 'Intuitively, the distinction is between thinking about space as a participant, as someone plunged into its center, as someone with things to do in that space, on the one hand, and, on the other hand, thinking about the space as a disengaged theorist.'[24] Although I have some qualms, already expressed in the discussion above, about the way in which Campbell characterizes egocentric space, his emphasis on the egocentric/absolute distinction over the egocentric/allocentric distinction is largely in accord with the approach I have adopted here. The same is true of his intuitive characterization of the egocentric/absolute distinction in terms of engagement and detachment. Perhaps, then, it is worth giving further thought to his treatment of an egocentric spatial framework as a framework that is 'immediately used by the subject in directing action'.

Inasmuch as maps are taken to be representations of objective space (even though there may well be a question about how they do this), so the use of a map in directing action should not be taken to impugn the objectivity of the map. If the map does indeed represent, then, irrespective of the form in which the map is encoded and assuming only that we can gain access to the manner of that encoding, we can always, at least in principle, 'read off' the space represented from the map itself (which is just what we do in the case of ordinary, printed maps). There is undoubtedly a difference, however, between cases where some spatial framework, as given in the form of a representation or map, has significance for an agent *only* insofar as it directs action in specific instances, and cases where the framework has significance *apart from* and *in addition to* its use in those instances. Thus, a rat may navigate a maze using some internalized 'cognitive map', but the map will not be available to the rat other than in this restricted navigational use. We might say that this is precisely the difference between a minimal behavioural grasp of space and a properly conceptual grasp. An important part of what distinguishes, for instance, my use of a topographical survey map in exploring the countryside around my home from the role played by some 'cognitive map' in a rat's navigating of a maze is that I grasp the map conceptually, *as* a map, and so *as* a representation of space. Insofar as the map is indeed grasped conceptually, and so is grasped as a representation, so it is already grasped as distinct from that which it represents (here is the very distinction to which Korzybski famously draws attention) and the map can thereby be used in an 'engaged' fashion, in relation to action, as well as in a more detached and even 'theoretical' mode.

On this account, Campbell's characterization of egocentric space, whatever other problems it may present, nevertheless serves to call attention to precisely those cases in which the operation of a spatial framework in directing action, even though it may operate by means of some spatial representation, does not depend on any conceptual grasp of the spatial framework or representation at issue. It will, in this respect, be as true of much human as well as of non-human animal behaviour that it is oriented and directed by a spatial grasp that does not depend on a conceptual grasp of the spatiality at issue – and this will be true, in the human case, even though some conceptual grasp may also be present. Thus, when I automatically take hold of a glass in order to drink the water within it, I can do so without having to call upon any conceptual understanding of the subjective space within which such 'taking-hold' operates, even though I can, in fact, conceptualize that space in a variety of different ways (such a line of thinking often underpins the appeal to the idea of non-conceptual content, but it seems to me unclear in what sense the 'content' at issue here is indeed non-conceptual, and the point at issue can be just as well put without reference to that idea at all).

It might be argued, however that to talk, as Campbell does, of a spatial framework being *used by the subject* in directing action, or, as I have done, of an agent having access to some spatial framework, is problematic in those cases where the agent seemingly lacks any conceptual capacity, and when it seems more as if the framework is itself immediately directing action rather than being 'used by' or 'accessible to' the agent. Similarly, the very character of maps as representational may lead to the view that it is mistaken to treat agents who lack a capacity for conceptualization as capable of using spatial frameworks or maps in the directing and controlling of their behaviour – where space is grasped without recourse to concepts, it might be argued that the grasp of space must be *non-representational* as well as non-conceptual. Part of what is at issue here is surely what counts as a representation – or, indeed, what counts as a map. Can something count as a representation or a map only if it is used or intended to be used as such? In fact, there is good reason, as indicated in the discussion above, to think that agency requires a capacity for some grasp of space, regardless of whether the agency at issue is associated with a capacity to grasp things conceptually or representationally, and that such a grasp must be realized through some sort of access to an internalized form of the space in which the agent acts and moves – through access, in other words, to a spatial representation or map. Here access may indeed take the form of a conceptual or non-conceptual (i.e. purely behavioural) grasp, but what is grasped must itself *be* representational even if it is not grasped *as* representational. There is no good reason, however, to suppose that a representation or map only is a representation or map if it is explicitly or conceptually grasped as such, or that it can operate as a representation or map only if it does so by means of such an explicit or conceptual grasp. A hammer is a hammer (even though it may also be other things as well) regardless of whether its character as a hammer is currently being made use of, and a hammer may be used as a hammer even in the absence of any explicit understanding of its being so used or of its character as a hammer. Yet although the role, not only of some grasp of space, but also of that specific grasp of space that involves spatial representation, in the possibility of agency should be clear, there is more to be said concerning the nature of spatial representation, including the representational character of maps, and the relation between such representation and the different modes of space. This is, in fact, just what had started to come to the fore in the discussion above concerning the relation between subjective, objective, and allocentric spaces.

If something is indeed a map, then there is no in-principle reason why any agent with the appropriate capacities, who understands the manner of the map's encoding and is capable of orientation within the space that the map represented, should not be able to make use of the map as a map, that is, to read off the space represented from the map itself. This demonstrates something important about, not just maps, but also representations in general: because a representation is already abstracted from that which it represents, so every representation is already objective – which is to say that it is accessible from outside of the particular subjective framework in which it was originally embedded.[25] As a consequence, even a map that consists only in a set of directions to get from one's present location to some other location can nevertheless also be used to get from that other location to one's present location, or, indeed, from any location that figures within that set of directions to any other such location. The map is thus the paradigmatic *representation* of an objective space, for even the map that attempts to capture a particular subjective ordering of space must represent that space in what are primarily *objective* terms. In other words, what the map presents is an ordering of space, and objects or locations within it, that is accessible from different subjective spaces and so captures something that is common across those spaces (which means it is also *intersubjective*). Since the map plots the arrangement of objects and locations in relation *to one another* rather than in their relation *to an acting creature*, one may be tempted to say that an objective ordering of space as represented in the map is *independent* of any subjective space – except that (and this is a point discussed further below) if the map is to be readable as a map, then the map has to be able to be connected with the subjective spatiality of a potential reader or readers. This means that the map cannot be wholly independent of any subjective space at all (see figures 4.1–4.4).

The *objective* character of maps, in the sense employed here, is rather nicely illustrated by consideration of the case of fictional maps. Such maps – even the maps of a completely imaginary realm, such as the hand-drawn maps that accompany Tolkien's fantasies *The Hobbit* and *The Lord of the Rings*[26] – do not provide a counter-instance to the 'objective' character of maps. In fact, such maps gain part of their attraction and intrigue from the manner in which they present the fictional as nevertheless almost tangibly real. Thus, we can trace – here on the map – the journeys that are also detailed in prose, and we can 'see' the relation between the imagined places we have visited in our reading, just as we can see the relation between actual places in a standard atlas. In the case of maps that combine imagined and real elements, and where the difference between real and imagined landscape is almost non-existent, those maps further enable the transposition of the fictional into the realm of the real. Much of the interest and romance of such fictional maps lies precisely in this juxtaposition of the imagined with the real – in the subtle blurring of boundaries between the two. In the maps of Thomas Hardy's Wessex, for example (see Figure 5 on p.65), an imaginary country is portrayed that almost exactly resembles the real landscape of a part of southern England.[27]

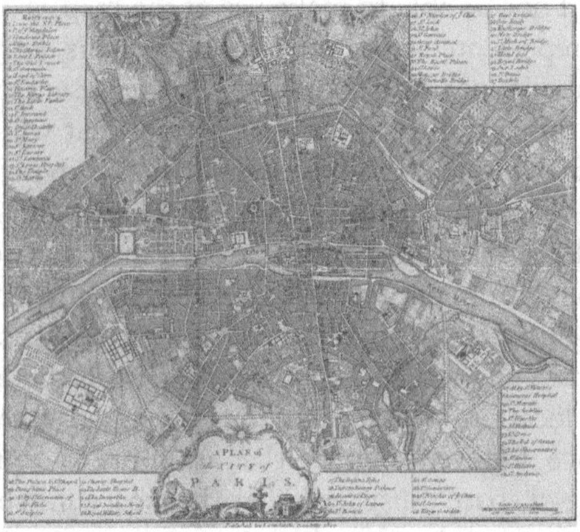

Figure 4.1 Plan of Paris (published 1800) from www.oldmapsofparis.com/map/1800 (accessed 28 August 2017). The Place de la Concorde (prior to 1795, referred to, in English, as 'Lewis the XV Place' or in French as 'Place de Louis XV') appears at the centre-left of this map (marked with the numeral 1) as one part of a complex spatial network. Here is a representation of an objective space that nevertheless appears within an allocentric frame – in this case, in terms of an array of roadways and built sites as intersected by the River Seine and presented according to the mapping conventions of the late eighteenth and early nineteenth centuries. The allocentric character of the representation (which is a feature of all maps) does not impugn the objectivity of what is represented. This is a representation of an objective space even though the representation is allocentric (and even though it can be seen as a view 'from above').

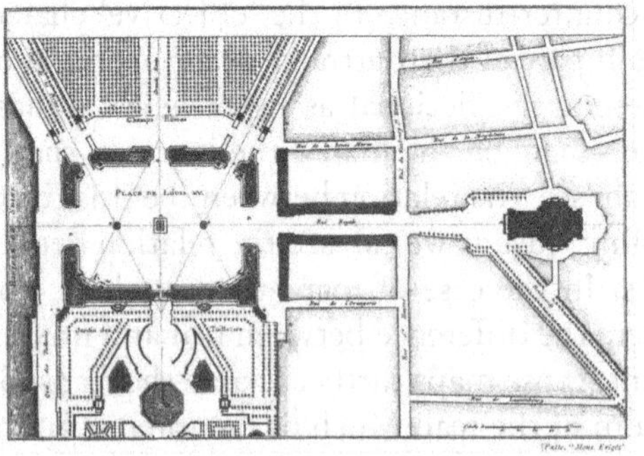

Figure 4.2 Detail (rotated for consistent orientation) from Ange-Jacques Gabriel, Plan of Place Louis XV (today, de la Concorde), Paris (1753), in Reginald A. Blomfield, *History of French Architecture, 1661–1774* (London: G. Bell and Sons, 1921), 124. Again, this map objectively represents the Place de la Concorde but at a larger scale and with respect to a slightly different set of representational conventions – a different allocentric frame.

Figure 4.3 Bird's-eye view, Place de la Concorde, 1855, engraving, in *Guide dans la monuments de Paris* (Paris: Paulin et Le Chevalier, 1855). Here the representation remains objective – one could read off from this image a partial mapping of the relations between the objects and locations portrayed – but the particularity of its orientational structure is much more salient. In this latter respect, the representation seems to move us more towards a subjective mode of appearance.

Figure 4.4 Alfred Smith, *L'Averse (Place de la Concorde)*, oil on canvas, 1888, Musée des Beaux-Arts de Pau. Here the Place de la Concorde is shown in a very different way. Not a map (even though it could be read as a certain kind of mapping), what this painting attempts to provide is a sense of the place as it might subjectively be experienced from within a particular circumstance – something that is a characteristic feature of the impressionistic style of painting, of which Smith's work is an example. Yet precisely because it is a representation, even a painting such as this must render what is represented in a way that is accessible to more than just one subjective view.

Maps represent space in a way that already assumes a particular orientation within that space. When we look to medieval European maps of the world – *mappa mundi* – we find that they are typically organized in a 'Y' or 'T' form with Jerusalem at the centre (see Figure 6). When we look to modern maps of the world, many place the Northern Hemisphere at the top with Europe, and often Britain, positioned top-centre. Australians and New Zealanders are familiar with maps that reverse this 'colonialist' orientation and position Europe and Britain 'down-under' – and similar shifts in cartographic orientation can be seen in other maps with different regional or national origins. Yet if a map is indeed to be useful as a map, then it must represent space, and the features located within it, in ways that are accessible to the user of the map, both in terms of employing a method of representation to which the user has access, and in terms of providing a method by which the features represented can be matched with features in the user's own subjective experience of space. The use of compass directions and a coordinate system, for instance, as well as the identification of certain key points, enables users of a topographic survey map to use that map in directing their movements, since it allows them to orient and locate their own subjective space in relation to the objective space represented by the map. Thus, rather than providing instances of unfortunate cartographic bias, the sort of examples just mentioned – medieval maps centred on Jerusalem or modern maps oriented to Europe – exhibit something that is common to any and every map, namely, that maps are inevitably constructed in ways that reflect the prior interests and orientations of the map-maker and the map-user. Another way of putting this (as noted briefly above), is to say that maps must always employ some *allocentric* frame – a frame keyed to certain particular features of the map-user's environment – in their representation of *objective* space. That this is so should not, however, be allowed to obscure the fact that to have a map is already to have a representation of space in objective terms. A map that does not employ appropriate methods of representation, or that fails to map out features relevant to the likely users of the map, would simply not be useable as a map. Thus, a street map intended for English-speaking Australians is unlikely to employ only Chinese characters, or to assume a method of identifying street systems that is based around concentrations of air-borne pollutants. Maps are, for the most part, conventional and purpose-specific, and their presentation of objective space is similarly bound by convention and purpose. Maps represent objective space, but they represent it in a manner that allows it to be grasped by particular agents from within their own subjective spaces precisely by means of the allocentric character of the representation – and this also means that such allocentricity underpins the inter-subjectivity of spatial representation (again, see Figures 4.1–4.4).

While a map must always employ modes of representation keyed to the capacities and interests of the agents who are its likely or intended

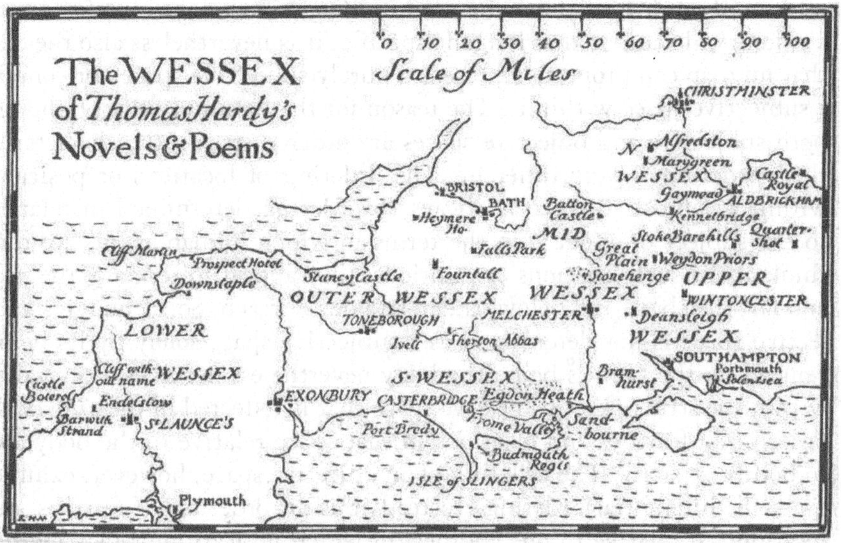

Figure 5 Thomas Hardy's Wessex, by Hermann Lea from *Thomas Hardy's Wessex* (1913; repr. London: Macmillan, 1977).

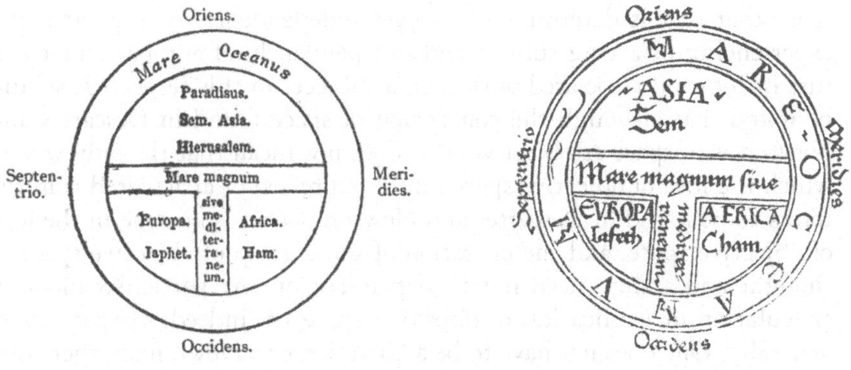

Figure 6 *Left*: Idealized form of medieval world map from *Meyers Konversations-Lexikon. Ein Nachschlagewerk des allgemeinen Wissens* (Leipzig und Wien: Bibliographisches Institut, 1895–1898).

Right: T-O map of world by Gunther Zainer of Augsburg, Germany, included in his publication of the *Etymologiae of Isidore of Seville* (1472), often said to be the first printed map.

users, and while a map may be used to identify locations by reference to a system of locations that is agent-specific, it is nevertheless also the case that no map can properly represent a purely subjective space nor contain a subjective space within it. The reason for this is simply that, although both subjective and objective spaces are ordered spaces, the character of their ordering is very different. The ordering of locations or positions within a subjective space is always an ordering determined in relation to the subject or agent – in the terms in which human agents we may think about such locations or positions, they appear in terms of the near and far, the above and below, the in and out of reach. So, although a subjective space is not determined as a subjective space solely by its being centred on the agent's body, the body nevertheless occupies a centrality within the structure of subjective space that is reflected in the *differential* ordering of features and locations in that space relative to the body and to bodily capacity. The ordering of an objective space, however, exhibits no such differential ordering. Instead it is an ordering of features and locations co-relative to one another, in which no feature or location has any priority over any other, and in which there is, therefore, no centre or focus. It should be emphasized that this difference in the ordering of subjective as against objective spaces means that no *experiential* space, which is itself a subjective space, can properly be said to be an objective space. The representation of objective space may require taking account of the capacities and interests of subjects or agents, but an objective space is a space that that is determined *as a space* independently of any particular experiencing or acting subject and independently of any particular feature or location associated with such a subject. In this respect, it should be noted that although the conception of space found in Descartes and Newton is of space as objective, this does not mean that the only way in which the idea of objective space can be expressed or articulated is in the terms to be found in Descartes and Newton. What is at issue in the idea of objective space, and the operation of some grasp of objective space in thought and action, need not be dependent on any particular mode of articulation or explication of objective space or, indeed, of space more generally. One does not have to be a Cartesian or a Newtonian, therefore, to be able to grasp what is at issue in the idea of objective space or even to have some grasp of the concept.[28]

Any agent, whether capable of conceptualization or not, must, if it is to be able to orient itself spatially, possess a minimal grasp of objective space, at least in the sense that ties space to real features of the agent's environment, even if those features are only grasped from the perspective of the agent itself. In this manner, objective space can be grasped through an allocentric (and, so, a subjectively presented) framework – including through an internal spatial representation or cognitive map. The manner in which the objective space is encoded or represented is thus not a barrier to the space that is grasped being properly objective. If one takes the view that the grasp of objective space must indeed be internally represented, then, provided that the internal representation is read in conjunction with the capacities of the agent in whom it is internalized, such representation could be seen as able to yield, or even to consist in, an objective mapping of space or of some portion of space. Of course, as the agent concerned may have no *conceptual* grasp of the space mapped in this way, so it may also have no concept of the map internally represented within it (that being the gist of the Davidsonian quotation mentioned earlier in this chapter). Yet, if having a grasp of objective space is taken to mean having a *conceptual* grasp of such a space (and I think Campbell sometimes comes close to such a view[29]), then an agent that has no grasp of the concept of objective space would have no grasp of objective space at all, even though any explanation of the agent's capacity for movement requires reference to just such a grasp.

On the assumption, however, that an agent can indeed have a grasp of objective space without grasping the concept of such a space, then to what extent might a grasp of objective space depend upon a grasp of subjective space? Moreover, to what extent is there *conceptual* dependence of objective on subjective space – that is to say, to what extent is it the case that to have the one concept one must also have the other? Certainly, for an agent that has a grasp of objective space, that grasp of space may well be causally dependent upon, may even be said to derive from, the agent's present and past experience (even though there may also be some pre-determined or 'innate' component). However, contrary to some commonly held views to the contrary, the *concept* of objective space cannot be generated from the idea of subjective space alone.[30] Objective space is not to be derived, for instance, from a mere concatenation of subjective spaces. Indeed, the very idea of such a concatenation presupposes the idea of objective space, for to conceive of a plurality of subjective spaces that can be located in respect of one another already presupposes the concept of a single space within which such location can be made. Such a space is thus not derived from the combination of subjective spaces, but is presupposed by the idea of such a combined plurality.[31]

In *The View from Nowhere*, Thomas Nagel characterizes objectivity in general such that 'a view or form of thought is more objective than another if it relies less on the specifics of the individual's makeup and position in the world, or on the character of the particular type of creature he is'.[32] An objective view, whether more or less so, is said by Nagel to arise out of 'a process of gradual detachment. . . An objective standpoint is achieved by leaving a more subjective, individual or even just human perspective behind.'[33] We are, indeed, able to move between different perspectives or standpoints – and sometimes this may be understood as a movement between subjective and objective points of view. It would, however, be mistaken to suppose that an objective view – or an objective space – can be arrived at merely through a process of detachment or abstraction, and this is so for at least two reasons. The first reason is that the process of detachment – that of getting 'outside ourselves', in Nagel's terms – already depends on a grasp of something like an objective space as that which originally enables that very detachment or abstraction. This is clearest if we look to the movement from the concept of the subjective to that of the objective. The very move presupposes a grasp of the objective as that which enables the move between concepts, and one might even argue that such objectivity is already part of the very capacity for conceptuality. A similar argument is made by Bergson, who emphasizes that one cannot ground the concept of space in the capacity for abstraction, because the situation is quite the reverse. 'Instead of saying that animals have a special sense of direction,' he writes, 'we may as well say that men have a special faculty of perceiving or conceiving a space without quality. This faculty is not the faculty of abstraction: indeed, if we notice that abstraction assumes clear-cut distinctions and a kind of externality of the concepts or their symbols with regard to one another, we shall find that the faculty of abstraction already implies the intuition of a homogenous medium. . . namely space.'[34] The second reason is that the notion of detachment misrepresents the idea of subjective space, which is defined by its dependence on a particular agent's experience or awareness. One can perhaps generalize from a particular case by abstracting from the particular features of that case – from that which constitutes its 'perspectivity' – to arrive at a more general concept of subjective space. To so abstract from *all* subjective features of a space is to be left, however, not with a purely objective space, but with no space at all. There is nothing 'left over', as it were, from some particular subjective space when one abstracts from the experiential perspectivity of that space. Remove the orienting features that establish the space and one is left, not with a field of open and un-centred spatiality, but with no spatial field at all. In the case of subjective space, then, to remove perspectivity is to remove the space. In this respect, one might say of Nagel's 'view from nowhere' that it involves less a purely objective conception of things, than a particular view that has been so nearly emptied of specific experiential content that it is consistent with as wide a range of subjective views as possible.

What gives the impression of being able to move from the grasp of subjective space, or from some particular instance of subjective space to the idea of space as objective is that our grasp of the concept of subjective space is already intertwined with a grasp of objective space. Indeed, it is precisely because we can grasp the larger space, within which a particular agent is located (and on whom a particular subjective space is centred), that we can engage in any detachment from our own subjective space. There is no necessary connection between different subjective spaces that could enable us to move from the grasp of one such space to another. What enables our detachment from particular subjective spaces is the idea of objective space as that which is independent of any particular experience, and yet which provides a framework within which particular agents can be located and the particularities of experience explained. The capacity to conceptually 'detach' ourselves from the subjective space of our experience (a subjective space that, in our own case, never arises other than in connection with a grasp of objective space) is thus indicative, not of the derivation of objective from subjective space, but of the prior grasp of objective space that enables such conceptual detachment. As Bergson has it, 'the faculty of abstraction already implies the intuition of a homogenous medium. . . namely space'. Consequently, an agent whose grasp of space enables it to conceptually detach from the immediate space of its own subjectivity is an agent that already possesses a grasp of the concepts both of objective and of subjective space. Thus, while the ideas of 'detachment' or 'abstraction' may be used to describe the shift from subjective to objective, they do not establish any simple conceptual dependence of objective on subjective space, even though they do demonstrate the fact that, in terms of human experience, these concepts are invariably tied together.

I have emphasized the fact that objective space cannot be derived from subjective space. But we should not suppose that subjective space can be derived from objective space either – as if subjective space were merely some narrow portion of objective space. Essential to the idea of subjective space is the idea of an experiential viewpoint, and what is absent from the concept of objective space is precisely the notion of a 'view'. Nagel's talk of the 'view from nowhere' is misleading in this respect, since whatever else Nagel intends by it, the phrase suggests that objectivity is indeed a view that can be correlated with another sort of view – a 'view from somewhere' – as if the difference between these views was merely a difference in 'point of view'. A 'view from nowhere', however, cannot properly be a view at all. The very idea of a view cannot be separated from the idea of perspectivity and location, and so cannot be separated from the idea of subjective space. Although one may identify a point within objective space and take it as the point from which a particular view opens up, this presupposes a grasp of orientation and perspectivity, and, more importantly, it presupposes an agent who is positioned at that point. Yet the sort of 'immersion in location' that is required here does not have any basis in objective space as such. Indeed, the only sort of location that objectivity provides is the location of a single point, but such a point lacks any directionality – distance aside, any point within an objective space is equally related to any and every other point.

Still, one might reasonably suppose that objective and subjective space have *something* in common, at least in the sense that both seem to involve a notion of extension within a region – a notion that makes for the possibility of movement. This idea is expressed in one sense of the word 'space' – a sense captured in the idea of idea of 'room' (particularly in the German *Raum*[35]). Yet even the idea of 'room' differs according to whether the space at issue is objective or subjective. Objective space possesses no constrictions, at least none that can be represented in its own terms. Consequently, the notion of 'room' associated with objective space is one that allows unrestricted movement, and its region of extension is one that has no limits. In contrast, the region of subjective space is a region of limited extent. As it is tied to a particular agent's bodily and environmental awareness, so subjective space is tied to a particular set of orientational and motor capacities that define the 'room' of subjective space, and thus limit it. One could not, moreover, move from a concept of subjective space, defined in terms of some set of capacities for movement or action, to an 'objective' space merely by expanding the set of capacities or removing any limitation upon them. Already to have some capacities rather than others, is for capacities to be limited, and the idea of a complete removal of restriction, for an agent that nevertheless remains embodied and located, is so obscure as to verge on the meaningless. Equally capacities cannot themselves be extended limitlessly, without losing all sense of them *as capacities* (or as capacities associated with particular bodies and agents), since, by definition, they are essentially limited and finite, and that is precisely how they define the particular space that belongs to the body and the agent.

The difference between subjective and objective spaces is that the former is tied to the experiencing agent while the latter is not, and for just this reason one cannot generate a notion of subjective space from objective space alone nor can one generate an objective space from a subjective space. The notions of subjective and objective space are thus irreducibly distinct. Yet notwithstanding the absolute nature of this distinction, we should not suppose that subjective and objective space are therefore also completely independent notions. If we focus on the grasp of concepts, there exists an important interdependence between subjective and objective, not in the sense of conceptual derivation, but in the sense that for an agent to have a concept of subjective space, it must also possess a grasp of the concept of objective space – and vice versa.[36] The connection between objective and subjective space is, in fact, already suggested by the way in which our capacity to detach from the subjective space of our experience is dependent on a grasp of space as objective. It is partly this entanglement of the concept of subjective space with the concept of objective space, as it occurs within the structure of conceptuality as instantiated in the conceptual grasp of agents, that gives the impression that an objective 'view from nowhere' can be arrived at through a progressive 'stripping away' of the perspectival or subjective elements from some particular subjective view. The very possibility of conceiving of a subjective space as such depends upon being able also grasp both the idea of the agent (whose subjective space it is) and the objective space within which the agent is located (and to which the agent gains access, in part, through that subjective space). Only if one has recourse to the concept of objective space can one begin to explain how a particular orientation and a particular set of behavioural and experiential capacities can give rise to a particular grasp of spatiality. Indeed, as soon as one understands the possibility of there being a view of space that may differ from one agent to another as capacities and location may differ, so one also possesses a grasp of objective space by means of which such changes in subjective space can be plotted.

The concept of objective space is necessary for any grasp of the concept of subjective space as such, but additionally, only insofar as we can make use of the notion of objective space in relation to particular subjective spaces – that is, in relation to our own capacities and surroundings – can we be said to have any grasp of objective space. An agent cannot be said to have a grasp of objective space if it lacks any capacity to relate it to any subjective space. Moreover, as was established earlier, although the concept of objective space is indeed conceptually distinct from that of subjective space, the grasp of the concepts of subjective and objective space are nevertheless mutually interdependent – each requires the other. Thus, as Gareth Evans argues, our conception of ourselves is necessarily tied to our ability to locate ourselves within an objective spatio-temporal framework, while our grasp of the concept of the objective order is in turn dependent on our grasp of our position within that order: 'For no one can be credited with an "objective" model of the world if he does not grasp that he is modelling the world he is in – that he has a location somewhere in the model, as do the things that he can see. Nothing can be a cognitive map unless it can be used as a map – unless the world as perceived, and the world as mapped, can be identified.'[37] To have a grasp of objective space, then, is to have a perspective to which that space can be related; and to have a grasp of some perspective is to have a grasp of the objective space, and the location of the agent whose perspective it is within that space, in relation to which such perspectivity is established. For these reasons, if for no others, perspectival notions are ill-suited to those relativistic approaches that promote the rejection of the very idea of objectivity – the notion of perspectivity is itself implicated with, even if it cannot be reduced to, that which is non-perspectival and objective.

Inasmuch as the grasp of objective space, although requiring a grasp of one's own perspective and location, is nevertheless a grasp of space as that space is itself constituted independently of any particular perspective or on any particular location, so it is a grasp of space that stretches beyond one's current perceptions – beyond one's immediate sensory awareness of the world. Yet it is a grasp of space that must also extend beyond any past and future experiences of that space whether of one's own or of any other agent (about this latter point I shall have more to say in Chapters 5 and 6). The grasp of objective space is, in other words, a grasp of space that is *non-experiential*. It is not a grasp of space as it is or might be experienced, but precisely a grasp of space that goes beyond and, in this sense, is strictly distinct from any particular experience of space.

This is not to say, however, that objective space is somehow a space severed from experience. Clearly, an agent's grasp of objective space is effective in structuring aspects of the agent's activity and so aspects of its engagement with the world. For an agent lacking any capacity for conceptualization, such structuring consists simply in the way in which objective features exert a directing influence (by whatever internal mechanism or system) on the agent's behaviour.[38] For an agent that has a conceptual grasp of objective space, the situation is a little more complex, since not only will objective features determine that agent's experience in various ways, but the agent will also possess a capacity to represent portions of objective space, and so to express the concept of such a space in experiential terms, that is, in terms of maps, drawings, diagrams and descriptions. This may be thought to provide an instance of objective space as somehow brought within the realm of the experiential. Yet although one could describe matters in this way, such an 'experiential' grasp of objective space (the grasp that is enabled through the map or drawing) is actually nothing other than a grasp of objective space as presented from within a certain spatial orientation as keyed to some representable feature or features – it is, in other words, a way of grasping objective space as that space is given *allocentrically*. We can, then, retain a sense of the strictly non-experiential character of objective space, while acknowledging both its role in the structuring *of experience* (as objective space has a role in the determination of subjective space) and the possibility of its allocentric presentation *in experience* (as objective space is given in the spatiality of the map or drawing).

The idea of objective space as a space that is 'non-experiential' can be seen to be implicit in Colin McGinn's discussion of what he calls the 'subjective view'. McGinn considers the way in which, through the indexical character of certain thoughts and the experience of secondary qualities, the world is viewed in a way that is subjectively determined. In relation to this, McGinn writes:

> When an aspect of our means of representing the world has been shown to have a subjective source it is natural to ask whether that aspect is eliminable. The thought is that if a way in which things are represented is contributed by the mind it ought to be possible to envisage a form of mental representation in which this subjective contribution is absent, a form which is purely objective in its representational content.[39]

An alternative way of putting the matter, which can arise in relation either to perception or to conception, is to ask whether it is possible for primary qualities to be presented without being conjoined with certain secondary qualities. What McGinn terms the 'inseparability thesis' consists in the claim that primary qualities cannot be so presented. Extension, then, cannot be presented other than as conjoined with, say, colour or some other sensible secondary quality.[40] McGinn further claims that the inseparability of primary from secondary qualities, and so the ineliminability of the subjective view, applies to the *perception* but not the *conception* of things. He writes: 'My own view is that we should reject this inseparability for conception but admit it for perception. To take this divided attitude is to commit oneself to a radical discontinuity between perception and conception: we cannot any longer regard conception as a kind of "faint copy" of perception; it is not explicable in terms of an imagined perceptual point of view, indeed it is not strictly a point of *view* at all.'[41] In conception, McGinn suggests, we can indeed arrive at an objective understanding of things, but such an understanding should not be considered as constituting an objective view, since it is precisely the fact that it is not a view that makes it possible for conception to achieve any sort of objectivity.

McGinn gives, in his analysis, no special attention to spatiality, nor does he consider how his account might relate, for instance, to diagrammatic or map-like representations of space, or, more generally, to perceptual presentations of concepts or conceptual structures. McGinn's concern is solely with 'mental representations'. It seems clear, however, that McGinn would view the 'inseparability thesis' as applicable to any perceptual presentation – including any perceptual presentation of what would otherwise be understood as 'abstract' or conceptual. McGinn's account does not, moreover, rule out the possibility of a concrete presentation of objective space in some form. His emphasis on the way in which any concrete or perceptual presentation of things is always in terms of a particular subjective view or perspective on the world can be seen as simply another way of putting the point made earlier concerning the necessarily allocentric character of any concrete presentation of objective space.

There is still a good deal more that must be examined in relation to the interconnection of spatial structures. What should be clear already, however, is that the idea of spatiality actually conceals a number of irreducibly distinct but nevertheless interconnected elements. Understanding the way in which a particular agent has a grasp of space is not a matter a delineating only one of these elements, but of uncovering the larger, unitary structure in which those are embedded. This larger structure is necessarily complex, since it must encompass both the subjective space that is tied to a particular agent's capacities as realized in a surrounding environment and the objective space within which the agent and its surroundings can be located. We may be tempted to describe the grasp of this unitary, but complex structure as the grasp of a just a single 'space' – and there is *a sense* in which this is true – but this also overlooks the way in which the structure actually encompasses both subjective and objective components.

Indeed, if we were to describe the structure this way – as we might be led to do by the unitary character of the structure – then we would be unable to give any content to the idea of the 'space' that is so described. Since the structure necessarily encompasses irreducibly distinct, though interdependent spatial structures within it, so no single form of spatiality will be adequate as a means to characterize the structure as a whole (and to try to address this point by responding that that the one space has to be described by reference to *both* subjective and objective spaces would be to undermine the very emphasis on the idea that is indeed a single space).[42]

It is, in fact, precisely the complex, yet unitary structure that appears here that was already at issue in the concept of place as initially sketched out in Chapter 1. The 'topographical' structure of place is such that it encompasses a number of distinct but inter-related components: place itself brings a certain ordering of the world, a certain perspectivity (which can be understood in both subjective and allocentric terms), *and*, inasmuch as every place opens out into other places, every place also stands within a larger network of places in a way that itself moves beyond the perspectival, towards the objective. The idea of place thus provides the framework within which the complex interconnection of notions of *both* subjective and objective spatiality can be understood. Although place cannot be severed from ideas of space, neither can space – in any sense rich enough to do justice to the spatial involvements of acting beings – be severed from the concept of place.[43]

The concepts of subjective and objective space that have been the focus for the discussion throughout much of this chapter are, of course, specific instances of the more general concepts of subjectivity and objectivity (it is the more general concepts that appear in Nagel and McGinn), and the interconnection between subjective and objective spaces mirrors the interconnection between the concepts of subjective and objective in general. Consequently, the way in which subjective and objective space are interconnected elements within the structure of place is also indicative of the way place encompasses both subjectivity and objectivity understood more generally. The structure of place at issue here – since it is a structure in which the different elements are seen to be necessarily interconnected and, in certain respects, interdependent – is not a structure that can be reduced to any single element within that structure. Neither subjectivity nor objectivity alone is adequate to ground the other or to provide a basis from which the other could be derived – and the same is true of subjective and objective space. The same point applies to the relation between these concepts and the concept of place: neither subjectivity nor subjectivity alone can be adequate to ground or to provide a basis from which place could be derived. Indeed, if anything, it is from out of place that both subjectivity and objectivity, both subjective and objective space, must come.

In discussing the idea of place as a central concept in geographical studies, J. Nicholas Entrikin writes:

> The apparent insignificance of place in modern life and the concomitant insignificance of the study of place are related to the confidence that moderns have in the objective view of the theoretical scientist. Our technological control of nature emphasizes the global, the universal and the objective, and the success in the manipulation of nature has led to the application of the same perspective to human society. Such a view is unable to capture the importance of the moral uniqueness of the individual agent and the source of agency in the local, the particular and the subjective. The narratives of place help to redress this imbalance, without camouflaging the underlying tensions between the subjective and objective and between individual agents and the circumstances within which agents act.[44]

Entrikin is correct in pointing to the problematic character of certain reductive modes of analysis and in his suggestion that a concept of place, encompassing both subjectivity and objectivity, provides an important counter to such reductive approaches. Where Entrikin's position differs from mine, and where his approach may become problematic, is in supposing that the contrast between subjective and objective is to be taken account of by somehow finding a position 'between' the two poles of this contrast, a position 'that leads us into the vast realm of narrative forms'.[45] It is not altogether clear how 'narrative forms' enable us to take account of both subjectivity and objectivity,[46] but what is clear is that, for Entrikin, place largely remains a subjective concept (as it is for many contemporary thinkers, especially within geography[47]). It is thus the *experience* of place that concerns Entrikin, and more particularly, the problem of how to incorporate this experience into a scientific geography. My interest is also in experience (although, once again, I would emphasize my non-technical use of this term). To reiterate an earlier point, however, it is an interest not so much in place *as* experienced, but rather in place as a structure *within which* experience (as well as action, thought, and judgment) is possible. With this in mind, we need to look more closely at the concepts of subjectivity and objectivity. It is the notion of subjectivity, and its associated notion of subjective space, that I will consider first, but as might be expected, such exploration inevitably leads back to the concepts of objectivity and objective space.

Notes

1 Gareth Evans, *The Varieties of Reference*, ed. John McDowell (Oxford: Clarendon Press, 1982), 221.

2 Ernst Mach, *Space and Geometry in the Light of Physiological, Psychological and Physical Inquiry* (Chicago, IL: Open Court, 1906), 32.

3 Work on cognitive maps began with Edward C. Tolman, 'Cognitive Maps in Rats and Men', *Psychological Review* 55 (1948): 189–208, and was developed further in work by John O'Keefe, for example, John O'Keefe and Lynn Nadel, *The Hippocampus as a Cognitive Map* (Oxford: Oxford University Press, 1978). Over recent decades, work in this area has advanced considerably, leading to O'Keefe's award of the 2014 Nobel Prize in Physiology or Medicine, jointly with May-Britt Moser and Edvard I. Moser, 'for their discoveries of cells that constitute a positioning system in

the brain' (see The Nobel Assembly at Korlinska Institutet, Press Release, 6 October 2014, www.nobelprize.org/nobel_prizes/medicine/laureates/2014/press.html).

4 Although Dreyfus never explicitly addresses the issue of space and the body at any length, it is clear that his emphasis on 'absorbed coping' as non-representational is generally opposed to those other accounts that take some form of internalized 'map' as a necessary element in the possibility of embodied agency and movement. See Peter Godfrey-Smith's discussion of Dreyfus's position – as set out in Hubert Dreyfus and Charles Taylor, *Retrieving Realism* (Cambridge, MA: Harvard University Press, 2015) – in Godfrey-Smith, 'Finding Your Way Home', *Boston Review*, 14 September 2015, http://bostonreview.net/books-ideas/peter-godfrey-smith-dreyfus-taylor-retrieving-realism.

5 See Alfred Korzybski, 'A Non-Aristotelian System and its Necessity for Rigour in Mathematics and Physics', in *Science and Sanity: An Introduction to Non-Aristotelian Systems and General Semantics* (Lancaster: International Non-Aristotelian Library Publishing Company/Science Press Printing Company, 1933), 747–761.

6 Donald Davidson, 'The Problem of Objectivity', *Tijdschrift Voor Filosofie* 57 (1995): 209.

7 That a being can have a grasp of space without having a grasp of the concept of space might be taken to mean that the grasp of space at issue in such a case involves a grasp of some spatial content that is non-conceptual (a position close to that of Gareth Evans's, as set out in *The Varieties of Reference*). There are two points I would note here in relation to my own position. First, the contrast between content that is conceptual and content that is non-conceptual is usually intended as a contrast between types of content rather than merely between types of behaviour, but I do not use the conceptual/non-conceptual distinction as a distinction between types of content. Second, while it is often claimed that human experience is such as to have a significant non-conceptual component, I am not convinced as to the usefulness of the idea of non-conceptual content when applied to the sort of grasp of the world (even if it is just the grasp associated with perceptual experience alone) that is characteristic of human beings. This is not because I take all human experience to be such that it can be fully captured in conceptual or propositional terms (it is clear that it cannot be so captured), but rather because I think the notion of content employed here remains obscure, and because I take the capacity to employ concepts to transform human experience in its entirety. On this latter point, I am in sympathy with much (though not all) of what John McDowell has to say about the idea of non-conceptual content in *Mind and World* (Cambridge, MA: Harvard University Press, 1994), 46ff. However, since the issue of conceptual versus non-conceptual content is, while not irrelevant, nevertheless only obliquely related to my main interests, it is not an issue that will receive any detailed discussion here.

8 The distinction I draw here between an acting being that has a conceptual grasp of the space in which it acts and a being that, while it has some 'grasp' of its surroundings that can be expressed in behavioural terms (even though it may also be underlain by some representational structures), has no conceptual grasp, seems analogous to a distinction drawn by McDowell between creatures that 'live in the world' and those that live merely 'in an environment'. Drawing on H.-G. Gadamer's distinction between 'environment' (*Umwelt*) and 'world' (*Welt*), McDowell claims that animals lacking a capacity to employ concepts lack any orientation to the world as such even though they can respond to features of their environment – consequently they live in an environment, but do not live in the world. See McDowell, *Mind and World*, 116–117.

9 As such, a creature could well be counted as human even though it did not share the same evolutionary history as the species *homo sapiens*. The question of humanity is not settled by reference to biological history or even material constitution – more relevant are exactly the sorts of considerations at issue in the discussion of place here, namely, behavioural, cognitive, affective, and responsive capacity. Although the distinction of the human from the non-human is not an ethically neutral distinction – it is tied to different attributions of ethical responsibility and obligation, and sometimes to different judgments when it comes to the weighing of interests – the mere fact of such a distinction provides no warrant for the mistreatment or neglect of the non-human. Indeed, recognition of the different ethical status of the human ought to bring with it a heightened awareness of the ethical responsibility of the human in respect of the non-human. It is only in the space that is opened up by the possibilities of human being that the question of the ethical emerges as a question – only in that space does the issue of the ethical responsibility that may be owed to the human or the non-human even appear.

10 The grasp of space required for agency, even for agency that is conceptually articulate, need not involve a grasp of any particular theory of space or any specific term used to refer to space. If this were not so, we would be forced to posit, for example, that neither Aboriginal Australians, in the time before European contact, nor the Classical Greeks, had any conceptual grasp of space. Although it may be true that neither had a theory of space that matches the modern understanding of that notion, their possession of complex spatial and topographic vocabularies unquestionably demonstrates a clear conceptual grasp of spatial and topographic frameworks. See Marwyn S. Samuels, 'Existential and Human Geography', in *Humanistic Geography: Prospects and Problems*, ed. David Ley and Marwyb S. Samuels (London: Croom Helm, 1978), 29. This is an important point in the ensuing discussion, since one of the claims I advance is that a grasp of the concept of space is necessary for the sort of understanding of the world that characterizes human experience and thought, but by this, I do not mean a grasp of any particular theoretical concept of space. It would be grossly mistaken to suppose that a failure to articulate spatial understanding in the terms of modern, post-Cartesian philosophy, for instance, is indicative of a lack of spatial understanding.

11 Bachelard touches on this issue in his *Poetics of Space*, trans. Maria Jolas (Boston, MA: Beacon Press, 1969), as does Martin Heidegger at several places in his work – see, for example, Heidegger, 'Hebel – Friend of the House', trans. Bruce V. Foltz and Michael Heim, *Contemporary German Philosophy* 3 (1983): 100–101; and Heidegger, 'The Nature of Language', in *On the Way to Language*, trans. Peter D. Hertz (New York: Harper and Row, 1971), 107. On this, see my '"The House of Being": Poetry, Language, Place', in *Heidegger's Later Thought*, ed. Günter Figal, Diego D'Angelo, Tobias Keiling, and Guang Yang (Bloomington, IN: Indiana University Press, forthcoming 2017), and also 'The Beckoning of Language: Heidegger's Hermeneutic Transformation of Thinking', in *Hermeneutical Heidegger*, ed. Ingo Farin and Michael Bowler (Evanston, IL: Northwestern University Press, 2016), 203–221. The relation between poetry and place, or poetry and world, is a key theme in Kenneth White's work and his idea of 'geopoetics' – see especially the essays in White, *On Scottish Ground* (Edinburgh: Polygon, 1998).

12 Martin Heidegger, 'Hölderlin and the Essence of Poetry', in *Elucidations of Hölderlin's Poetry*, trans. Keith Hoeller (New York: Humanity Books, 2000), 56.

13 Heidegger, 'Hebel – Friend of the House', 100–101.

14 As Louise Röska-Hardy writes in the introduction to *Learning from Animals? Explaining the Nature of Human Uniqueness* (a volume that provides an excellent overview of research in the comparative study of the human and non-human): 'Anyone seeking to understand humans' place in nature is faced with an explanatory challenge where human language, cognition, and culture are concerned, especially within an evolutionary perspective. These human capacities are not just distinctive; they are profoundly unparalleled in the animal kingdom. No other known species communicates by means of a system with the features of human language. Language enables us to produce novel utterances that others can understand and lets us offload information onto artifacts like note paper and computers. It allows us to talk about the past and the future, to refer to things that are physically distant and to things that do not exist. Importantly, language allows humans to influence and affect the cognition and the culture of other humans by symbolic means – a feat unequalled among other animals.' See Louise Röska-Hardy, 'Introduction – Issues and Themes in Comparative Studies: Language, Cognition, and Culture', in *Learning from Animals? Explaining the Nature of Human Uniqueness*, ed. Röska-Hardy and Eva M. Neumann-Held (Hove: Psychology Press, 2009), 1. For a useful overview and discussion of a range of issues relating to the understanding of language, especially in a comparative evolutionary context, see Marc D. Hauser, Noam Chomsky, and W. Tecumseh Fitch, 'The Faculty of Language: What Is It, Who Has It, and How Did It Evolve?', *Science*, New Series 298, no. 5598 (2002): 1569–1579.

15 Although much of the contemporary literature around place draws on notions that implicate language – especially notions of narrative and narrativity as exemplified in Entrikin's work (referred to at the close of Chapter 1) – there is very little attention given in most discussions to language, or to issues of representation and conceptuality, and the way these relate to the understanding of place (Edward Casey's work is a notable exception). Part of the aim of this volume is to rectify that omission, and so to ground the understanding of place in a more developed philosophical framework, thereby exhibiting the interconnection between place and other key concepts, and also enabling a better understanding of the structure of place as well as its philosophical significance.

16 This is not to say that an agent that is paralysed, anesthetized, or otherwise disabled is thereby deprived of its being as an agent or that it is also deprived of any grasp of space. A capacity, once developed, may be retained even when it is not able to be realized or when some other capacity on which it depends has been lost. So, a human being who suffers paraplegia as a result of an accident may still have a grasp of space that goes beyond their capacity for bodily movement or activity. The retention of the grasp of space, and especially of the space that belongs to one's own body (often referred to in terms of body-schema), even in the face of the loss of bodily capacity, may be part of what underlies the phantom limb phenomenon in the case of human amputees.

17 Bertrand Russell makes extensive use of the idea of the perspectivity of an individual's grasp of space in *Our Knowledge of the External World* (London: George Allen & Unwin, 1926), 94ff.

18 Thus, we may think of the subjective space at issue here as, to use Elisabeth Ströker's phrase, a 'space of action' – see Ströker, *Investigations in Philosophy of Space*, trans. Algis Mickunas (Athens, OH: Ohio University Press, 1987), 48ff. As Ströker writes, 'the space of action... is a space constituted in the project of activity, a space whose being is relative to the situation of the acting subject' (ibid., 62). As will become clearer below, however, the way in which the 'space of action' depends upon the acting subject is not such as to provide any basis for the idea of the subject as prior to or independent of the space of action – instead the two are defined co-relatively to one another.

19 See J.J. Gibson, *The Ecological Approach to Visual Perception* (Boston, MA: Houghton Mifflin, 1979).

20 John Campbell, *Past, Space, and Self* (Cambridge, MA: MIT Press, 1994), 14. Campbell also discusses the way in which our grasp of our environment depends on a grasp of a 'primitive physics' that involves a grasp of 'causally indexical' concepts (concepts such as 'is it a weight I can easily lift', the grasp of which consists in a grasp of one's own causal capacities), as well as what Campbell calls 'working concepts' (concepts the grasp of which consists in a practical grasp of certain causal features of the environment – see ibid., 43–46).

21 Evans, *The Varieties of Reference*, 154.

22 Naomi Eilan, Rosaleen McCarthy, and Bill Brewer, 'General Introduction', in *Spatial Representation: Problems in Philosophy and Psychology*, ed. Naomi Eilan et al. (Oxford: Blackwell, 1993), 10.

23 See Campbell, *Past, Space, and Self*, 5–33.

24 Ibid., 5.

25 Indeed, a significant feature of maps is that, while they represent, they do not depict. By this, I mean that maps are not pictures (though they may include pictures) and so do not present any particular 'view' of things even though they do employ certain modes of representation. The non-pictorial character of maps is perhaps clearer when one considers the highly schematic nature of some medieval maps (as well as modern examples such as the famous and much copied map of the London Underground) – see Evelyn Edson, *Mapping Space and Time: How Medieval Mapmakers Viewed Their World* (London: British Library, 1977) for an excellent account of medieval maps and the differences between modern and medieval cartography.

26 J.R.R. Tolkien, *The Hobbit* (London: George Allen and Unwin, 1937), and *The Lord of the Rings*, 3 vols. (London: George Allen and Unwin, 1955). There is a proliferation of maps associated with these volumes, especially *The Lord of the Rings*, not merely in the various maps of the imaginary realm of 'Middle-Earth' that Tolkien himself drew up, but in a proliferation of maps produced by others.

27 Of particular interest in this respect is the illustrated guidebook produced by the photographer Hermann Lea, *Thomas Hardy's Wessex* (London: Macmillan, 1977, original publication 1913); see also Dennis Kay-Robinson, *The Landscapes of Thomas Hardy* (Exeter: Webb & Bower, 1984). William Faulkner is another notable writer whose imagined literary landscape – Yoknapatawpha County – is drawn onto a real stretch of country – the area around Oxford, Mississippi, USA (see especially the collection of writings in *The Portable Faulkner*, rev. ed., ed. Malcolm Lowry [New York: Viking Press, 1967]). In both Hardy and Faulkner, the fictional landscape differs in certain ways from the real – especially in the names of towns and in aspects of the topographical layout – although mirroring it closely in many other respects.

28 In part, the point at issue here is a basic one that applies to all concepts – concepts are always amenable to multiple forms of expression and articulation. When it comes to the idea of objective space, however, it is not just that the concept may be variously expressed, but also what is at issue in the concept plays such a fundamental role within a larger structure of conceptuality that it

cannot be absent from conceptuality as such. What is at issue in the idea of objective space can thus be operative in thought and action even in the absence of any explicit concept of the experiencing subject or, indeed, of a clear concept of space as distinct from place.

29 Indeed, inasmuch as it is Campbell's particular characterization of the nature of egocentricity (in terms of the direction of action) that might be seen to lead to such a view, so this characterization is likely to be one that must, on my account, remain unacceptable.

30 Campbell also rejects the idea that objective space can be derived from egocentric space (see Campbell, *Past, Space, and Self*, 9–33), as do O'Keefe and Nadel, *The Hippocampus as a Cognitive Map*, 1–2. Kant argues that the grasp of space (by this he means, in the terms used here, objective space) cannot be 'connate' and yet neither is it derived from experience. See Kant's inaugural dissertation of 1770: 'Dissertation on the Form and Principles of the Sensible and Intelligible World', §15E (Corollary), in *Kant's Inaugural Dissertation and Early Writings on Space*, trans. John Handyside (Chicago, IL: Open Court, 1928), 65.

31 Here we can perhaps see some hint of the reasoning that lies behind Kant's emphasis on the unity of space in the *Critique of Pure Reason* A25/B39. The account of space developed here obviously differs in important respects from that offered by Kant in the *First Critique*. Nevertheless, in giving a central role of spatial and topographic concepts, the broad thrust of this book can be seen to be consistent with certain Kantian themes also – see, for instance, the discussion of space and embodiment in Kant in the works referred to in the introduction to this book, n.46.

32 Nagel, *The View from Nowhere* (Oxford: Oxford University Press, 1986), 5.

33 Ibid., 7. Note that even this characterization retains the correlation of objectivity with subjectivity that I noted earlier (see Chapter 1, n47) as well as the ambiguity that consequently attaches to the notion.

34 Henri Bergson, *Time and Free Will*, trans. F.L. Pogson (London: George Allen and Unwin, 1910), 97 and, more generally, 96–97.

35 As Mill noted: 'The sensation of muscular motion unimpeded constitutes our notion of empty space, and the sensation of muscular motion impeded constitutes that of filled space. Space is Room – room for movement; which its German name, *Raum*, distinctly confirms.' See John Stuart Mill, *An Examination of Sir William Hamilton's Philosophy*, ed. J.M. Robson (Toronto: University of Toronto Press, 1979), 221.

36 Elisabeth Ströker also emphasizes the interconnection between different concepts of space: 'We recognize that in his activity the subject employs something other besides his own corporeal functions in his modes of comportment toward the world. Thus, his space of action can only be conceived from the possibility of another space, the mathematical space. This is valid independently of whether the acting body is cognizant of it or not... the space of action reveals the presence of another space that is yet to be investigated. The subject of the space of action always has it at his back, and his space of action is co-determined by it from the outset.' See Ströker, *Investigations in Philosophy of Space*, 61.

37 Evans, *The Varieties of Reference* (Oxford: Clarendon Press, 1982), 212. And Evans adds that 'the gulf between the "subjective" and "objective" modes of thought which Nagel tries to set up is spurious. Each is indispensably bound up with the other.' The gulf referred to here is that which figures in Nagel's claim, in *The Possibility of Altruism* (Oxford: Clarendon Press, 1970), 103, that, as Evans puts it: 'We do not really understand what it is for us to be identical with objects conceived to be parts of the objective spatio-temporal framework.'

38 It is, indeed, only in this minimal sense that the agent will have any 'grasp' of objective space. Such a grasp of objective space will, of course, be a grasp of objective space achieved through a grasp of allocentric space – through certain environmental features. Such an allocentric grasp of objective space will not imply, however, that the agent concerned has any access, within the perspective of its own experience of the world (and using the terms of the discussion immediately below), to some allocentric presentation of space. One might claim (as Campbell seems to) that the minimal sense in which an agent whose behaviour is somehow determined by environmental features, but who has no capacity to grasp those features conceptually, is too minimal to count as a grasp of objective space at all. This seems to me a plausible view, but a view that ought also to entail a parallel rejection of the idea that such agents have any grasp of an allocentric space.

39 Colin McGinn, *The Subjective View* (Oxford: Clarendon Press, 1983), 73.

40 McGinn, *The Subjective View*, 80, cites Berkeley, as well as F.H. Bradley, as holding such an inseparability thesis, and quotes from Berkeley's *Of the Principles of Human Knowledge*: 'I see evidently that it is not in my power to frame an idea of a body extended and moving, but I must withal give it some colour or other sensible quality which is acknowledged to exist in the mind. In short, extension, figure, and motion, abstracted from all other qualities, are inconceivable.' See George Berkeley, *Of the Principles of Human Knowledge*, part 1, §10, in *Philosophical Works, Including the Works on Vision*, ed. M. Ayers, vol. 2 (London: Dent, 1975), 79.

41 McGinn, *The Subjective View*, 80–81.

42 The distinction between space and spatiality might be seen as a possible solution here: there is a single space, but two modes of spatiality. The trouble with this, however, is in giving real content to the single space as single, and, associated with this, the almost inevitable tendency for the space as single to be identified with space as objective (subjective space then being seen as somehow a subsidiary mode of spatiality occurring within objective space). Maintaining a proper sense of the complexity of the structure at issue thus seems to require resisting the tendency to think of the structure as a single space no matter how that is explicated.

43 Notice that one cannot here appeal to our ordinary experience of space as somehow an experience of space simply as 'physical' or objective, and so argue that all our ideas of spatiality are really drawn from some experience of an objective space of pure extension. Our experience of space is 'always already' structured in complex ways that go beyond the structure of any objective or physical space alone. Put simply, we cannot and do not experience space purely as physical extendedness.

44 J. Nicholas Entrikin, *The Betweenness of Place* (Baltimore, MD: Johns Hopkins University Press, 1991), 126.

45 Ibid., 134.

46 Although I suspect Entrikin, who draws explicitly on the work of Paul Ricoeur, may well have in mind something like Ricoeur's conception of the way in which the turn to narrative overcomes the problematic character of temporality – see Ricoeur, *Time and Narrative*, trans. Kathleen McLaughlin and David Pellauer, 3 vols. (Chicago, IL: University of Chicago Press, 1984–1988). I agree with Entrikin that narrative is indeed central to an understanding of place, but it remains place, rather than narrative that is the fundamental notion here. See, however, Entrikin, *The Betweenness of Place*, 109–131.

47 See Chapter 1, n34 and n36.

Further reading

Campbell, John. *Past, Space, and Self*. Cambridge, MA: MIT Press, 1994.

Eilan, Naomi, Rosaleen McCarthy, and Bill Brewer, eds. *Spatial Representation*. Oxford: Blackwell, 1993.

Mach, Ernst. *Space and Geometry in the Light of Physiological, Psychological, and Physical Inquiry*. Chicago, IL: Open Court, 1906.

McGinn, Colin. *The Subjective View*. Oxford: Clarendon Press, 1983.

Nagel, Thomas. *The View from Nowhere*. Oxford: Oxford University Press, 1986.

O'Keefe, John, and Lynn Nadel. *The Hippocampus as a Cognitive Map*. Oxford: Oxford University Press, 1978.

3 Holism, content, and self

> There must be, then, corresponding to the open unity of the world, an open and indefinite unity of subjectivity. Like the world's unity, that of the I is invoked rather than experienced each time I perform an act of perception, each time I reach a self-evident truth, and the universal *I* is the background against which these effulgent forms stand out: it is through one present thought that I achieve the unity of all my thoughts... The primary truth is indeed 'I think', but only provided that we understand thereby 'I belong to myself' while belonging to the world.
>
> (Maurice Merleau-Ponty, *The Phenomenology of Perception*[1])

The idea of subjective space is tied to the idea of an experiencing creature around which such a space is organized. For a creature that has a grasp of the concept of subjective space (itself necessary for the grasp of the concept of objective space) the grasp of that concept must also be tied to the creature's grasp of its own self-identity, and to the creature's own self-conception. Yet what exactly is the relation between the concept of self or of subjectivity that is involved in a creature's grasp of subjective space and the idea of spatiality? More generally, what is the relation between the ideas of space and spatiality, and the concepts of subjectivity and objectivity? Since it might seem, superficially at least, that there is no need for recourse to ideas of space and spatiality in understanding these latter concepts, it might seem that the concepts of subjective and objective space are simply specific applications of the more basic notions of subjectivity and objectivity, and are therefore derivable from them. Indeed, such a view might appear to cast doubt on any attempt to treat space and place as having a central role in the possibility of thought and experience – making it seem as if it is subjectivity and objectivity, understood as autonomous notions, rather than either space or place, which are actually fundamental.

The notion of subjectivity is a particularly important focus here, since it is precisely the consideration of the way subjects find themselves in space, and the way space enters into the activities of subjects, that leads to the more complex analysis of space and spatiality developed in Chapter 2, and that is itself encompassed in the structure of place. A key question here is whether the concept of the subject that seems to underlie the idea of subjective space is really independent of that notion, and, more generally, whether subjectivity can be seen as prior to, and so as standing apart from, ideas of space or, indeed, of place. Consequently, if we are to explore further the concept of subjective space, as well as the network of concepts – including that of objective space – within which the idea of subjective space is located, then we must also explore the very concepts of self and of subjectivity. In what does the grasp of self or of subjectivity that is implied by the grasp of subjective space consist? And what exactly is the 'self' that is at issue here? Such questions, and others like them, will be the focus of this chapter and the chapter immediately following. Addressing these questions will not only enable a better understanding of the structure of subjectivity and its relation to spatiality, but will also return us to the idea of objectivity and its own relation to spatiality – the latter explicitly taken up in Chapter 5. Place itself, it should be noted, is not directly taken up in this discussion (as it was also not directly taken up in Chapter 2), and the reason is simply that the analysis of these concepts – space, self, subjectivity, objectivity, and so on – provides the necessary pathway that leads on to the larger account of place that is arrived at in Chapters 7 and 8, and is central to Chapter 9.

One way of understanding the idea of subjectivity and the sort of self-conceptualization at issue in the idea of subjective space is in terms of a grasp of self that is foundational and given independently of and prior to the grasp of any other concept, experience, or thought. Understood in this way, the ability of a creature to identify its experiences and thoughts as its own, and to grasp the subjective space of experience as a space that belongs to it (as indeed the space of its own experience), would have to be based in the creature's more primitive grasp of its own *self-identity*. Similarly, the ability to attribute a subjective space to a particular subject, viewed externally to it, would, on such an understanding, be possible only on the basis of having already identified the subject in question *as a subject*. Such a way of thinking takes subjective space to be secondary to and dependent upon the existence of the subject, so that the existence of the subject underlies (in the literal and original sense of subject that derives from the Latin subjectum) the space of subjectivity. Some such account – or an analogue of it – might be thought to be present in Descartes and in the founding role given to the *cogito* in Cartesian thought. In a more general sense, it might also be seen to underlie the understanding of place that was encountered in Chapter 1, according to which place is a function of subjective attitudes or experiences. On such an account, subjectivity is prior to place, and place is grasped as something imposed *on* space *by* subjects. In one sense, of course, it is surely correct to say that a particular subjective space is identified by reference to the agent around which that space is ordered, but this is to say no more than that a particular subjective space is indeed constituted in terms of a particular 'view' of the world from the perspective of a particular location within the world.

It does not commit us to any idea of the 'self' as foundational or as the primitive basis for the notion of subjective space.

The idea of a primitive subjectivity as somehow providing an independent ground that is prior to any particular set of thoughts or experiences, and on which such thought or experience depends, would seem to imply a particular view of the relation between the subject and the thoughts and experiences – and, in general, the mental states – that are attributable to that subject. The subject would, on such a view, be independent of any mental states that may be attributable to it – it would be precisely that which underlies those states as their ground, just as it would also underlie a particular subjective space. Consequently, the fact that that certain states can be attributed to a subject would be dependent on the subject rather than on the mental states themselves, and the 'ownership' of mental states by a subject would derive from some activity or operation of the subject whereby it made those states its own. Such a view is problematic, however, since if mental states are conceived as distinct from the subject to whom they nevertheless belong, and if that belonging is therefore dependent on some subjective activity or operation by the subject, then mental states will lack any *intrinsic* relation to the subject. Mental states will belong to a particular subject, not in virtue of any feature internal to the states themselves, but rather through their being 'appropriated' by the subject. That means too that the mental states that belong to a subject need not possess any intrinsic relation *to each other*, since if the possession of a mental state – a belief, a desire, a memory – is dependent on appropriation by the subject, then its possession by a subject will be independent of any relation it may have to any other state.

The conception of the relation between the subject and the states belonging to it draws upon a more or less familiar sense of belonging – the sense in which, for instance, my hat may be said to belong to me, or even, to use the sort of example common in Greek philosophical texts, the sense in which Socrates's snubnosedness belongs to Socrates. Yet familiar though it may be, such a way of thinking conflicts with the character of mental states, and of contentful states generally, as 'holistic', which is to say that such states never appear singly, but always as part of larger constellations of states (one cannot have just *one* belief, for instance, since beliefs are always enmeshed with many other beliefs). Such holism will figure at various points in the discussion to come, and it is important to note the way in which the fact of such holism already renders inadequate any account of mental states that treats them as if they were items that a subject may or may not take up as their own – which is what is required by the view that mental states belong to the subject in virtue of some act of appropriation by the subject. What this indicates, however, is that what is at issue here is not just a question concerning the relation *between* mental states and subjects, but the very nature of mental states *as such*, and, indeed, the very nature of the subject.

We are thus brought from the question of subjective space to the question of the nature of subjectivity, and so also to the question of the nature of mental states and mental content.

Although it may be tempting to think of thoughts and experiences as separate from the subjects whose thoughts and experiences they are – tempting, perhaps, because our own thoughts and experiences do seem to have a content that is not entirely dependent on us – such an idea is inconsistent, not only with the holistic character of states, but also with the manner in which mental states actually present themselves. In fact, if one has a thought or an experience, one can hardly doubt that it is one's own, since ownership comes with the very 'having' of such a state. We sometimes talk as if we could encounter mental states that are not really our own (the notion certainly appears in literature and film), but such talk, if made explicit, most often relates to a concern about the veridicality of those states, their reliability and provenance, or perhaps our *identification* of them (what sort of states they might be), rather than properly to our *ownership* of those states. Thus, although we can certainly wonder whether some memory we have now is actually the remembrance of a real event in our past (whether it really is a *re*membering), this is not the same as wondering if the memory is ours, in the sense of being something that is present to *our* thoughts. Even were it possible to somehow 'transplant' specific memories into one person from another – to give them 'false' memories, along the lines suggested, for instance, in the Ridley Scott film *Blade Runner*[2] – this would not demonstrate that someone could have memories that were not, in the relevant sense, her or his own. A memory may indeed be false in that it is not what it seems to be, and could perhaps even be a memory of someone else's experience (somehow caused to arise in us), but the memory is nonetheless our own just in virtue of being present to us as something *we* recollect.

There is, of course, no need for science fiction examples to see how memory can simply play us false. Harold Nicolson provides an amusing and instructive instance of the unreliability of memory in real life. He describes, in vivid detail, the scene of a railway accident in Russia – clearly identified with a particular landscape and locale – which 'until recently, was the first thing that I remembered'. Continuing, he writes:

> Stamped upon my mind was the picture of our train brought to a standstill in the open steppe: a snow-bound horizon glimmering like a large white plate under the stars: the engine in front upwardly belching sparks: the carriage at the back, which was the cause of our stoppage, crackling into little scarlet flames; and myself a supine bundle being lifted down from some great height to many hands stretched up towards me. . . That picture, so vivid to me and so sincere, became a cherished mental possession.[3]

On recounting this memory to his mother, however, Nicolson is disappointed to discover that he had 'got it all wrong'. In fact, some of the incident his mother confirms – primarily the fact of the accident itself – but the vivid details turn out to be completely false, and the baby Nicolson apparently slept on, seemingly oblivious to what was going on around him, through the entire event.

Nicolson's story illustrates the manner in which memories may combine both true and false elements into a single recollection. It also evinces a memory that is probably constructed from other elements – perhaps from Nicolson's hearing a version of the story of the accident from someone when a child and embellishing it with further details from his own imagination. We undoubtedly do construct memories in this way,[4] and it is often difficult to determine whether some recollection is of an event actually witnessed or, rather, of something imagined, read, or seen in a movie. Indeed, recent work on the relation between memory and language indicates that memories are less reliable the more they are recalled as part of an articulate narrative, and Freud famously claimed that almost all childhood memories are probably constructions, 'screens' whose real meaning is hidden.[5] Recognizing the falsity of a memory, however, does not mean that it is any less a part of our own mental life. Nicolson's 'memory' of the Russian rail scene was no less a part of his autobiography for being false – it merely came to occupy a different place within that autobiography. In judging the accuracy of memory, and of other experiences or mental presentations, it is not a matter of judging whether certain memories are our own, but of determining how those memories are integrated into the overall pattern of our lives. From the standpoint of our own experience of ourselves, we can wonder about the *accuracy* of what we recollect, but we cannot wonder about whether the recollections are *ours*. Similarly, we can wonder about the accuracy of our vision or hearing – about whether we might be hallucinating or daydreaming – but we cannot doubt that our seeing and hearing now (or remembering or thinking or whatever) is really *our* seeing and hearing rather than someone else's. What this illustrates, in fact, is just the way in which all thought and experience is already given within a certain subjective space. To ask what marks certain experiences as 'ours' is no different from asking what marks the subjective space in which our experiences arise as our own. If we do not grasp certain experiences as our own, then we cannot question whether they are own; and if they are not our own, then we cannot grasp them as our own.

If the question of the ownership of mental states makes little sense from a first-person point of view (whether plural or singular), it is no easier to formulate in the third person. One can certainly ask whether a person has had an experience of a certain sort or whether they have had a particular thought. Yet experiences do not come 'detached' from the subjects whose experiences they are, and so as soon as one is presented with some particular and concrete experience, one is thereby also presented with an experiencing subject to whom the experience 'belongs' as well as a particular subjective space within which the experience arises. Similarly, when presented with some particular instance of thinking – some particular mental state such as a concrete instance of believing, desiring, hoping, or whatever – what is thereby also presented is a subject, or the idea of a subject, to whom that state can be attributed. Put in a way that will be made more perspicuous below, the identification of a particular experience or thought already presupposes a *system* of experiences and thoughts within which that experience or thought is embedded – like the structure of mental content, experience and thought is thus *holistic*. To presuppose such a holistic or systematic embedding of experiences and thoughts is, however, already to presuppose a particular subject – and therefore a particular subjective space and a particular 'perspective' – to which the experiences and thoughts in question belong.[6] Since thoughts and experiences never come 'unowned', but always as belonging to an experiencing and thinking subject, ownership cannot be something conferred upon such states through any operation carried out by the subject. Inasmuch as we identify our experiences and thoughts as 'our own', this cannot be by means of some knowledge of a self that precedes those thoughts and experiences. Such a solution would be absurd, suggesting that thoughts and experiences are things from which we can pick or choose, and that the relation between a subject and the states that belong to it can be understood in terms of ordinary 'possession'.

There is, however, still a problem here. Although there is no genuine sense in which the 'ownership' of any particular mental state or states could properly be put into question, this does little to elucidate the nature of the ownership that pertains to such states. One cannot explain the difference between my mental states and yours by saying that mine are mine just in virtue of being presented as mine within the subjective space of my experience, whereas yours are yours in virtue of being presented as yours within the subjective space of your experience. Such an approach begs the very questions at issue. In what does a grasp of some thought or experience as 'mine' consist and what is involved in the self-understanding that is tied to my grasp of subjective space? What makes 'my' subjective space 'mine', and what makes 'your' space 'yours'? These questions, which concern the very structure of subjectivity and the unity in which it consists, still remain – and it is just these questions to which the issue of the 'ownership' of states directs us. Addressing these questions requires a more detailed consideration of the ways in which mental states are related to one another and to the subjects whose mental states they are – it requires, in other words, more detailed consideration of the structure and possibility of mental content. Such consideration will enable us better to understand why there can be no appeal to a concept of subjectivity as somehow more fundamental than the concepts of space or place.[7]

Our grasp of particular thoughts and experiences, and of the contents of particular experiential and cognitive states, depends upon the way in which the different elements within them are related. Indeed, the holistic character of mental states means that such states are organized, and their content determined, through their embeddedness within larger systems of mental states. Memories, for instance, do not have content or significance independent of the wider context into which they fit. Thus, in realizing the inaccuracy of his childhood recollection, Nicolson's memories, and his vivid impressions of the Russian rail accident, are relocated and repositioned in relation to his other beliefs and memories. In this fashion, not only does Nicolson adjust his judgment of the images and impressions to which he has access, but his conception of himself is also adjusted, even if in relatively small details. It is characteristic, in fact, both of particular thoughts and experiences, and of our own conceptions of our selves, that they exhibit just this sort of interdependence. Our self-identity is dependent upon the overall configuration of our mental lives and of the states they comprise, even as the character and identity of particular mental states (at least so far as their content is concerned) is dependent upon the manner in which those states are integrated as part of a larger network of experiences, thoughts, and attitudes in general.[8]

Although it is seldom put in just these terms, the holistic feature of mental states is notably and quite specifically evident in autobiography – both the autobiographies we each construct as part of our ongoing self-image, and those that are constructed within the literary genre of autobiographical writing. Any recounting of the story of a life must look, not only to a recounting of a sequence of events, but also to the unity of those events in the life at issue and, so to the way in which those events come together for the individual concerned. It must look, in other words, to the individual's own grasp of events and to the integrity of the individual's attitudes and behaviour over time. The unity of a life – imperfect though it may be – that is exhibited and even partially articulated through the telling of the story of that life is exactly parallel to the unity that is a precondition of the possibility of mental content. It is true, of course, that we are seldom the most reliable tellers of our own tales – autobiographies typically omit and sometimes falsify. Such falsification need not be regarded, however, as necessarily a failure of consistency, as a deliberate attempt to mislead, nor even as some unconscious attempt to conceal (even though such possibilities cannot always be ruled out either). Instead, falsification and omission can be seen as concomitant with the project of construing a life as having a certain unity and consistency that is necessary to the very idea of such a life; a unity and consistency that must be articulated in the very course of that life.

The continuing construction and reconstruction of one's life – which, by its very continuing character, cannot be immune from error or omission – should be seen as part of a larger attempt to grasp a life as a whole to which we are committed, not merely by the demands of a literary form, but by the demands of our own self-understanding.

Only by grasping our lives as having some such unity and consistency – through being able to fit together the parts of our lives – can our lives be constituted *as lives*, and only thus can the beliefs, actions, desires, hopes, and memories that make up our lives have the content they do. The construction and reconstruction of our selves in the stories we tell to ourselves and to others, and with respect to our pasts and our futures, is integral to the very content and identity of our attitudes and actions. Often, coming to understand how and what we believe, and who and what we are, is just a matter of coming to configure and reconfigure our lives in ways that enable them to be more adequately integrated and interconnected. This suggests a central role for narrative in the sort of life of which human beings are capable – the interconnectedness that makes for mental content and self-identity would seem to be the sort of interconnection achieved, in a certain paradigmatic fashion, by means of narrative and story (though it is certainly not the only form in which such interconnection may obtain). As Alasdair MacIntyre emphasizes, 'narrative history of a certain kind turns out to be the basic and essential genre for the characterisation of human actions',[9] and as for actions so also for attitudes and mental content in general. Through narrative, whether explicitly formulated or merely implicitly presupposed, one is able to interconnect elements within a larger structure in a way that 'makes sense' of those elements and gives them a certain thematic unity.[10]

The concept of 'narrative' to which I am appealing is quite broad, and inevitably so. A narrative is a telling or recounting, and as such, it is, like the map, a form of representation. Like the map, and like all representations, a narrative presents a set of elements as unified or connected in a certain way, but there are many ways in which a narrative can do this, and so there are many forms that a narrative can take. There is a minimal sense in which the presentation of any temporally ordered series may count as a narrative – this happened, and then that happened, and then something else happened. Yet such minimal narratives are indeed just that, precisely because they are so minimally unified. In the fullest sense, a narrative involves the connecting of events in a way that draws on features that belong to the character of the events themselves – the narrative thus exhibits those events as 'belonging' to one another. Narratives may be simple or complex. They may take the form of basic means–end connections (even seemingly nonsensical ones): 'Why did the old lady swallow a spider? Why, she swallowed the spider to catch the fly.' Or, they may follow an entire journey, whether from one place to another, or from one end of a life to another (the latter also being typically a journey between places).[11] Most of the narratives or stories we tell about ourselves relate only to parts of our lives rather than encompassing our lives in their entirety. They are indeed stories that locate particular happenings and actions in the midst of other happenings and actions, and in relation to particular hopes, loves, hates, dreams, fears, desires, and beliefs, and that function, again rather like maps, to orient us in the world.

The fact that the narratives or stories that structure our lives are indeed often partial, and are also typically in the process of constant reconfiguration (constant telling and retelling), does not undermine their character as narratives or stories, nor their efficacy in orienting and locating us. The endings and beginnings that those narratives and stories may project (every story projects a beginning backwards just as it projects an ending forwards) may take the form of anticipations and reconstructions whose accuracy is often beyond our ability to ascertain, but accuracy is not what good storytelling is most about, nor is it always what matters most in the configuration of a life. Many of the ordering narratives in a life draw on stereotypical or exemplary narratives and figures, rather than on any direct grasp of a specific series of events the Christian idea of a life lived on the model of Jesus provides a powerful version of the way such an exemplary narrative might order a life in the very living of that life.) In this latter respect, especially, what forms of narrative might be at work in the ordering of a life (like the forms of the maps we use), and whether there is any explicit recognition of the relation between self and narrativity, will naturally depend on the cultural-historical context of the time.[12] Since narratives are part of the unifying structure of a life, and of the content of a life, by which the very identity and character of the life is articulated, one cannot treat narratives, in general, as if they were impositions onto a life. There are some narratives that may be impositions in this way – like the 'rationalisations' we may impose onto actions *after the fact* – and that therefore have no real relation to the lives into which they are read, but the narratives that properly belong to a life are narratives that function in the very constitution of that life as such.[13]

The interdependence of states that is evident when we reflect on the narrative structure of human self-constitution and self-understanding, or on the character of autobiographical memory, exemplifies, as noted above, a general and quite basic feature of mental states and their content, as holistically structured. That is, the identity of particular states depends on how those states are located in relation to other states, which, in turn, is primarily a matter of the relations of implication that obtain between states (or, one might also say, between the sentences in terms of which those states are characterized). Thus, on the one hand, to believe that I spent time in Russia when a child would ordinarily rule out certain other beliefs; for instance, the belief that I lived my whole life in the East End of London. On the other hand, it may also imply other beliefs – perhaps beliefs about Russia, about childhood, or about other aspects of my own identity (where I went to school, what language I grew up with, what holidays I celebrate).[14] It is, in large part, the holistic character of mental states, and of mental life in general, that makes narrative so important in the structuring of human life and identity, and in the understanding of human attitudes and behaviour. Of course, with respect to any belief, there is no way of specifying all of the other beliefs and attitudes that are implicated with that belief. Epistemic or 'doxastic' connections are multiple, and just as one belief may implicate another, so may that belief implicate still further beliefs. As there are, in addition, no clear identity criteria for beliefs (how does one count beliefs? – is my belief that echidnas are oviparous mammals a single belief or a complex of beliefs?), so there is no single way of specifying the relations between beliefs or even the contents of beliefs. There is always more than one way of stating what it is we or others hold to be true, and such indeterminacy is itself a direct consequence of the holistic character of mental states and of content as such. In this respect, one should perhaps treat the idea of a single belief as merely an abstraction from the larger holistic structure that makes up the life of the subject – a structure that can be given multiple descriptions or, to give a slightly different emphasis, that can be articulated through multiple narratives.[15]

Given some particular belief, it is almost always possible to find a holistic pattern of beliefs – a story of some sort – within which that belief can cohere with other apparently incompatible beliefs. I may believe, for example, that during the 1960s I did indeed live for a time in Russia, and, in such a case, it seems to follow that I also believe that I spent a portion of my life in what was the Soviet Union, but one can readily conceive of a situation in which such beliefs might not be consistently held. The only requisite would be appropriate adjustments to other beliefs that I also hold: perhaps a belief that not all of Russia was part of the Soviet Union, or some belief arising from a general ignorance of twentieth-century Russian history (I never thought that Russia and the Soviet Union might be the same country). Relatively clear and unequivocal cases of contradiction among beliefs and attitudes can and do arise. Yet inasmuch as such contradiction undermines the connections between attitudes, so the existence of such contradiction is a *prima facie* threat to the existence of those attitudes. As a consequence, when such contradiction between one's attitudes comes to light, there are strong pressures to resolve that contradiction in some way or other – either by modifying one's beliefs or by revising one's understanding of those beliefs (that is, revising what one means by the sentences that one holds true).[16]

Our thoughts, memories, and experiences are thus constrained by certain basic principles of consistency and rationality – and these constraints are expressed in one particularly important form: the integration of mental life over time that is achieved through the structure of narrative. This is not to say, however, that each of one's experiences, memories, or thoughts must be rationally connected with every other such experience, memory, or thought. We do have memories that conflict with other memories. We make judgments that are sometimes inconsistent. We see, hear, and feel things that do not fit with other things we see, hear, and feel. The existence of various forms of 'irrationality' and incompatibly can be seen as largely due to the complex and ramified character of mental life, and to the impossibility of simultaneously grasping all of one's thoughts and experiences in order to somehow render them consistent in one fell swoop. Even were it possible to achieve such a grasp at any *one* time, the fact that our mental lives are spread out *over* time would result in the gradual erosion of such perfect consistency as new thoughts and experiences arose in the face of new circumstances. Of course, as noted earlier, the very attempt to grasp actions and attitudes – and the whole of a life – as being consistent and unitary, will almost invariably lead not only to a certain degree of falsification, but also to the creation of some degree of inconsistency, according to the manner in which such unity is achieved and as certain features are emphasized at the expense of others. Additionally, inconsistency among mental states can be viewed as arising, in part, simply from the way in which those states stand, not only in *rational*, but also *causal* relation to other states and events – even rational subjects are also causally embedded subjects (all the more obviously so when they are understood as also *agents*).[17]

The causal underpinnings of our thoughts and experiences include other thoughts and experiences, but also occurrences and states that have no rational connection with any thought or experience at all – something of which the casebooks of clinical neurophysiologists provide some especially striking examples. Oliver Sacks, for instance, writes of a patient who presented with symptoms that consisted in her hearing – with vivid clarity, as if from a nearby radio – popular songs from her childhood; sounds only she could hear.[18] The music was, in fact, a causal consequence of a form of epilepsy. The stimulations produced by the epileptic seizures provoked memories of music from the patient's childhood, which brought with it feelings of nostalgia and happiness, along with images and impressions of childhood scenes. The patient's hearing of the music was nevertheless inconsistent with other features of her experience, as demonstrated by the absence of any device that might be the source of the music, and the fact that the sounds could not be heard by anyone else.

In fact, we do not need to look to exotic cases from neuropsychology for examples of this. Every instance of perception is an instance in which some non-mental event gives rise to a mental event, and in which the connection between the two is causal and non-rational. For the most part, the fact that the causal influences upon us reflect our integrated location and operation in the world (something to which I shall return later) means that our experiences and thoughts are similarly integrated and consistent, but this is not always the case. Just as anomalies can arise affecting our physical integration, and causal influences can impinge on our senses and upon our brains in unusual ways, so, too, can anomalies arise in our experience of us and the world. The simplest examples of the latter are perhaps visual illusions (where certain special circumstances result in our seeing some feature that is not actually present) or false 'memories' that neither cohere with other recollections nor even with the knowledge of our own past histories. Even in these cases, however, there is enormous pressure to try to integrate such experiences with the rest of our experience. Where we cannot reconcile our perceptions or memories with the rest of our thoughts and experiences we rightly suspect that something has gone awry. So, to generalize from the case Sacks presents, someone who begins to hear vivid music continually playing around them, but cannot find any orchestra, radio, or other likely source of the sound anywhere in the vicinity, may well visit their doctor and perhaps, ultimately, a neuropsychologist for diagnosis and explanation. They may still continue to hear the music, but the inconsistency in their experience will be resolved through the physiological explanation of the phenomenon – and the availability of that explanation will allow the belief that they are experiencing certain auditory stimulation to be rendered consistent with the belief that there is no external source for such stimulation.

Cases of false memory or visual illusion, particularly where we recognize them as such, may well be taken as obvious instances of mental states that fail to exhibit appropriate integration with other states. Nonetheless, the failure of integration in such cases is never complete. Consider the case of a memory I may have that is inconsistent with other memories, inasmuch as I cannot affirm the accuracy of the combined set of memories on pain of contradiction. I may have a 'memory' that locates me in some childhood Russian setting, but since I hold another belief that, for example, I have never been outside of Tasmania (a belief that may be confirmed by an overwhelming number of other beliefs, memories, and experiences), I may be unable to affirm that I was in Russia as a child. Yet even such an inconsistent 'memory' must fit with my other thoughts and experiences in certain respects, most importantly, perhaps, inasmuch as the concepts on which the memory draws must be consistent with those concepts as they figure elsewhere in my thoughts and experience. My memory of a railway accident, as in Nicolson's story, must thus include features that are consistent with my grasp of the concepts relating to railways, accidents, and the like as they figure in other of my memories and attitudes – *and this remains so even if the original memory is false*. In this way, the content of experience and thought always possesses *some* consistency, even when there is inconsistency in respect of specific affirmations or judgments. Such consistency reflects the way in which content, at least content that can be given specifiable characterization, is dependent on the mastery of a set of concepts and a language (indeed, it is language, and the high level of discrimination it enables, that makes possible consistency inasmuch as it goes beyond the mere integration and coordination of basic forms of behavioural response). The need for memories and attitudes to be embedded within a larger context of memory, attitude, and behaviour is also exemplary of the narrativity that I have noted as a characteristic feature of mental life, and of the understanding appropriate to it.[19]

The embedded character of memories and attitudes, as well as the role of narrative here, draws attention, once again, to the holistic character of mental life and of mental content. Such holism can be expressed in a variety of ways, but when understood in relation to mental states, it consists essentially, as was seen earlier, in the idea that such states are not given singly, but only as they are interconnected elements within a larger system of such states – only as they form part of the whole. Some care is needed, however, in the understanding of such holism: it does not imply any single unity that stands apart from the multiplicity of states themselves, but refers instead to the way, with respect to any particular state, that state must be integrated with a large number of other states if it is even to be a state at all. It is just such integration of states that was at issue in the immediately preceding discussion, except that the point now is not merely whether some state can properly be counted as a true or a false memory, but rather whether the state has *any* content such that it could be a memory or a false memory *or any other sort of state*.

The possibility that some putative state may turn out, under closer examination, not to be a state is not an outcome that we are likely to experience in the first person. We may decide that what we thought was a memory is actually some imagining based on a picture we have seen or a story we have heard, but that recognition does not mean that we thereby lose any and all sense of the content of what we thought we remembered. Indeed, Nicolson's own seemingly false memory is still vivid and rich in content for all that he comes to realize its falsity as something remembered. However, in cases of third-person attributions, we may well be mistaken, not only about the character of the attitude or state at issue (whether for instance it is a memory or an imagining, whether it is true or false), but even whether there is any attitude or state, any content, to be attributed. Alan Turing's famous proposed test to determine whether a machine can be attributed with the capacity for intelligent behaviour can be used to illustrate the point at issue, since the test make use of exactly the requirement of integration between states (here evident in the integration and consistency of verbal responses) as the means to determine the capacity in question.[20] In the Turing example, we are faced with sets of responses that, at least initially, may well appear explicable by the attribution of appropriate beliefs and other attitudes to each of the putative 'speakers' (the interlocutors responding via the remote terminals). Yet although this may be true of the initial responses, and even of individual responses taken apart from the rest, further engagement (and so the connecting of responses with one another and with the larger conversation) may lead to the conclusion that one of the sets of responses are not explicable in this way, and that therefore the responses are not the result, nor indicative, of any mental states at all. One can easily imagine other cases in which the initial supposition that an entity is genuinely uttering meaningful sentences, and has beliefs and other attitudes consistent with this, turns out to be impossible to maintain in the face of growing evidence of lack of consistency and integration. Being able to attribute mental states requires also being able to find a certain degree of integration among the states so attributed – a failure to integrate implies an inability to attribute, and where we cannot attribute such states we have no reason to suppose that any such states exist (the point here is that there is a conceptual link between the having of states and the integration of states, and it is on this that the capacity to attribute states depends).[21] Since the ability to attribute states is also a condition for being able to identify a creature *as a subject*, that is, as having a mental life of its own, so the integration of states is a prerequisite for such identification and, *ipso facto*, for being a subject – to be a subject is to have an more or less integrated mental life.

Accepting the need for the integration of states, it may nevertheless be thought that such integration is itself something brought about by the subject – that the subject somehow acts upon states so as to integrate those states and that this is also the basis on which states may be said to 'belong to' a subject (the act of integrating states and appropriating them may be one and the same). On such an account, the integration of states would be a consequence of the prior unity of the subject or 'self' as it is independent of the states that belong to it, and so, although the states would be determined holistically or 'relationally' (the two being here more or less the same), the subject or self would be atomistic (a single independent unity) and non-relational. Such a notion is, however, untenable. One reason for this is that the integration of states must be intrinsic and not extrinsic to the states at issue. That is, it must be in virtue of the very *content* of the states, and the nature of the attitudes involved, that those states connect up with one another. States are identified only in virtue of their connections with other states, so the connections between states cannot be imposed on states from without. In addition, the idea that the unity of states that makes for content can be grounded in some self that is independent of those states – a self that is atomistic and non-relational – merely shifts the question of the unity of states onto the question of the unity of that which unifies those states. The question of the unity of content thus becomes a question concerning the unity of the self. Yet, it is not at all obvious that any clear sense can be attached to the idea of a self or subject whose existence is itself independent of its own mental life – and thereby independent a certain complex system of mental states – such that the unity of the subject could be separated, even in principle, from the unity of states that makes for content. In fact, it may well be that the idea of the unity of subjectivity is identical with the idea of the unity of states that are attributable to the subject. In the absence of any separation between the unity of states and the unity of the subject, there can be no possibility of appealing to the subject as a ground for the unity of mental states.

These considerations apply not only to the idea that the unity of mental states might be grounded in the unity of an underlying self, but also to the idea that mental unity can be grounded in the unifying operation of some 'sub-personal' (to use Daniel Dennett's phrase[22]) mechanism or module within the brain. The existence of our experiences, memories, and thoughts is, of course, dependent on certain causal processes. But understanding the unity and ordering of mental states, at the level at which those states have content, is just a matter of understanding how those states are themselves related in terms of their content, not how those states are causally produced or physically realized (a matter that was central to the earlier discussion of irrationality). It is here that some of the considerations motivating Davidsonian anomalous monism, as well as Davidson's rejection of certain elements of empiricist epistemology, come to the fore. Although mental events are identical with physical events, mental events cannot be simply reduced (via any one-to-one correlation) to physical events, and there are no strict psycho-physical laws. The physical causes of mental states, as given under a physical description, cannot provide any rational ground for those states nor shed light on the rational connections – the connections at the level of content – that obtain between them and are constitutive of them.[23]

To reiterate: the integration of states cannot be attributed to the operations of some self, independent of and prior to the states that are integrated. As Merleau-Ponty notes, 'I am not myself a succession of "psychic" acts, nor for that matter a nuclear "*I*" who brings them together into a synthetic unity, but one single experience inseparable from itself, one single "living cohesion".'[24] Indeed, if the relation between the self and the states belonging to it is not to be an arbitrary and accidental relation – if it is to be a relation such that the 'ownership' of states is given with the states themselves – then this can only be because both the identity of states and the ownership of states by a particular subject are both tied together; that is, the unifying of both content and of self in the same unitary structure, the same experience. In this respect one might well say that the integrating of states that makes for the 'contentual' identity of states (and such contentual identity is what matters here[25]) is the same as that which makes for the ownership of those states by a particular subject. Moreover, because the sense of self-identity is given with the sense of ownership of one's own mental states, so too must the sense of self-identity be tied to the very integration of states, rather than being something additional to it. To have a grasp of oneself, then, is just for one's thoughts and experiences to exhibit the requisite degree of integration that is necessary for the constitution of those states, and this is indeed sufficient for having a grasp of one's thoughts and experiences as one's own.

If my mental states are always presented as 'mine', then it might seem that I cannot be mistaken about the mental states that are mine, and therefore cannot be mistaken in my own self-attribution of mental states – but this does not, in fact, follow. Any thought or experience I have is indubitably 'mine', and yet the infallibility that obtains here does not mean that I cannot sometimes doubt whether I have properly identified the *contents* of my thoughts and experiences. I can certainly discover, on particular occasions, that I have been mistaken in the beliefs, desires, or other attitudes I have taken myself to hold or in the meanings to be attached to my utterances. The 'mine-ness' that accompanies my thoughts and experiences – which renders it impossible for me to be mistaken in my identification of those thoughts and experiences as 'mine' – might then be said to be a purely 'formal' feature of those thoughts and experiences. It simply reflects the way in which thoughts and experiences are always combined within a network of other such thoughts and experiences.

Just as mental states are constrained by certain general principles of rationality and consistency, so analogous constraints also apply to an agent's own self-knowledge. The idea of a state as having content presupposes a subject to whom that state can be attributed – a point given particular expression in the fact that subjects must be held, in general, to know what they believe, hope, desire, mean, and so forth. None of this implies that subjects cannot sometimes be wrong in their *self-interpretation*, since, as interpreters, subjects are in much the same boat with regard to their own states as with regard to the states of others. It does, however, imply that in believing, meaning, hoping, and fearing, subjects must be held to know what it is that is believed, meant, hoped, and feared. The failure of this presumption would disrupt the integrity of states in such a way that the attribution of the states would itself be rendered dubious. In this respect, the idea of 'first-person authority' (the idea that speakers must always be assumed to have knowledge of their own attitudes and the meanings of their utterances) is a direct consequence of the holistically interconnected character of mental states and the requirements of integration and consistency that follow from such interconnection.[26]

The idea of subjectivity cannot, then, be understood in terms of some simple and independently existing 'self' or subject that somehow underlies and thereby unifies a complex of mental states. Just as mental states are themselves constituted through the inter-relation of such states, so is subjectivity itself a structure whose unity is established and articulated only in terms of a certain interconnection of thoughts and experience. Moreover, just as the idea of the unitary subject cannot be understood independently of the unity of mental states – the unity that makes for content is identical with the unity that makes for subjectivity – neither can it provide any unifying principle or ground for the unity of subjective space. Indeed, it is not that any one of these concepts somehow 'grounds' the others, but rather that they must be understood only in inter-relation to each other. Understanding the nature of that inter-relation, however, is not merely a matter of understanding, in some general sense, the holistic character of mental content or the unitary structure of subjective space, but of understanding that structure in relation to more specific concepts of agency, narrativity, and memory. It is the further analysis of this structure, and the unity that belongs to it, that is the focus of the next chapter. Such analysis is fundamental to the exploration and elaboration of place, since what that analysis shows is both the necessary implication of place in the very structure of subjectivity (so that persons are indeed tied to places), but also the impossibility of any reductive decomposition of place into some more basic notion either of subjectivity or of spatiality.

Notes

1 Maurice Merleau-Ponty, *Phenomenology of Perception*, trans. Colin Smith (London: Routledge & Kegan Paul, 1962), 406–407.

2 Made in 1982, directed by Ridley Scott and starring Harrison Ford, this science-fiction movie centres on Ford's hunt for a group of artificially engineered humans ('replicants') of abruptly limited lifespans. A central theme of the movie is the relation between memory and identity – the identity of one of the main characters is apparently constructed around a set of false memories that have been artificially implanted, and in the director's original version (released some time after the first commercial release), the audience is led to wonder whether this might not also be true of the Harrison Ford character himself.

3 Harold Nicolson, *Some People* (London: Pan Books, 1947), 9.

4 The nature and possibility of 'false memory' was a hotly contested issue in relation to so-called 'repressed memory syndrome' in the 1980s and 1990s. See Daniel L. Schachter, *Searching for Memory* (New York: HarperCollins, 1996), 248–279, for a discussion of some of the difficult issues involved here.

5 As Freud comments: 'It may indeed be questioned whether we have any memories at all from our childhood: memories relating to our childhood may be all that we possess. Our childhood memories show us our earliest years not as they were but as they appeared to us at the later periods when the memories were aroused.' See Freud, 'Screen Memories', in *The Complete Psychological*

Works, vol. 3, 1893–99, trans. James Strachey (London: Hogarth Press, 1966), 322. Donald P. Spence echoes this Freudian claim when he writes that 'whenever we hear reports of incidents that are supposed to happen before age 4 years, I would suspect that we may be in the presence of some kind of substitution'. See Spence, 'Passive Remembering', in *Remembering Reconsidered*, ed. Ulric Neisser and Eugene Winograd (Cambridge: Cambridge University Press, 1988), 317. Autobiographical literature provides numerous examples, like Nicolson's, of quite vivid, but false, childhood memories.

6 The idea of a state as having content thus presupposes the idea of a subject to whom that state can be attributed. Moreover, this idea is reflected in the fact that a certain 'authority' must attach to the subject to whom states are attributed in relation to the content of those states. The subject must be held, in general, to know what she or he believes, hopes, desires, means, and so forth, simply as a consequence of the holistic character of those states. This does not imply that subjects cannot sometimes be wrong in their self-interpretation, since, as interpreters, subjects are in much the same interpretive situation in regard even to their own states as with regard to the states of others, but it does imply that, in believing, in meaning, in hoping, and in fearing, subjects must be held to know what it is that is believed, meant, hoped, and feared. The failure of this presumption would disrupt the integrity of states in such a way that the attribution of the states would itself be rendered dubious. See the more detailed discussion of this point in my 'Self-knowledge and Scepticism', *Erkenntnis* 40 (1994): 165–184; and also my 'Constituting the Mind: Kant, Davidson and the Unity of Consciousness', *International Journal of Philosophical Studies* 7 (1999): 1–30.

7 As becomes evident in the pages below, the nature of mental content, and of mental life in general, is such that there can be no room for a notion of subjectivity that could provide a basic ground in which concepts of space or place might be founded. Indeed, the holistic character of mental content can itself be seen to lead to a concept of mental organization that gives a central role to embodied, spatialized agency. The holistic character of mental content is thus an important element in the larger argument concerning the necessary interconnection of subjectivity with space, and also with place.

8 As Ulric Neisser points out, the unitary self is a complex and not wholly coherent structure that can even be conceived as comprising several different 'selves' Neisser distinguishes five such: the ecological, interpersonal, extended, private, and conceptual selves. See Neisser, 'Five Kinds of Self-knowledge', *Philosophical Psychology* 1 (1988): 36. Neisser's discussion indicates the extent to which the idea of the self exhibits a similar complexity to the complexity – and interconnection – also exhibited by ideas of spatiality. As Neisser suggests, however, it is the 'conceptual self' that offers the most encompassing sense of self 'providing a roughly coherent account of ourselves as persons in interaction with our neighbours, an account that is almost always similar in structure, though different in detail, from the one that our neighbours would give of us' (ibid., 55), while 'each of the other four kinds of self-knowledge is also represented in the conceptual self' (ibid., 54). On this basis, much of my own discussion of self and self-identity can be taken as primarily concerned with the 'conceptual self', as explicated by Neisser. Neisser's distinction between different kinds of self-knowledge clearly has interesting implications for discussions of self, especially of self-identity and self-recognition, in relation to non-human animals. See, for instance, Sue Taylor Parker, Robert W. Mitchell, and Maria L. Boccia, eds., *Self-awareness in Animals and Humans: Developmental Perspectives* (Cambridge: Cambridge University Press, 1994). But while some of the different senses of self-explicated by Neisser seem implicit in such discussions, Neisser's work seems not to be explicitly drawn upon. Undoubtedly, much of the obscurity that surrounds discussions of these matters derives from a certain lack of clarity surrounding the basic concepts at issue.

9 MacIntyre, *After Virtue: A Study in Moral Theory* (London: Duckworth, 1981), 194.

10 MacIntyre's discussion of the role of narrative in *After Virtue*, 190–209, is particularly relevant here, but see also Paul Ricoeur's exploration of the connection between narrative and personal identity in Ricoeur, *Oneself as Another*, trans. Kathleen Blamey (Chicago, IL: University of Chicago Press, 1992), 113–168; and in Ricoeur, 'Life in Quest of Narrative', in *On Paul Ricoeur: Narrative and Interpretation*, ed. David Wood (London: Routledge, 1991), 20–33. Also containing an extensive investigation of these and related issues is Ricoeur, *Time and Narrative*, trans. Kathleen McLaughlin and David Pellauer, 3 vols. (Chicago, IL: University of Chicago Press, 1984–1988). For a discussion of

the role of narrative in the constitution of self through memory, see Craig R. Barclay, 'Remembering Ourselves', in *Memory in Everyday Life*, ed. G.M. Davies and R.H. Logie (Amsterdam: Elsevier, 1993), 285–309. Barclay views the self as something composed and recomposed through a process of remembering in which narrative and interpersonal interaction play a central role.

11 Once again, see MacIntyre, *After Virtue*, 190–209.

12 Indeed, for MacIntyre, tradition and community have a central role to play here (ibid., 205–207). It should be noted that, although the idea of the narrativity of life, and with it, the idea of autobiography, seems to have a particular historical origin – see, for instance, Patricia Meyer Spacks, *Imagining a Self* (Cambridge, MA: Harvard University Press, 1976), which suggests that the rise of the idea of a life as a story, and a personal story at that, seems to correspond, at least in European thought, to the rise of the novel as a dominant literary form – this does not detract from the idea that narrative structures, in one form or another, have always been central to the ordering of mental life.

13 Louis Mink famously claims that 'stories are not lived but told' – see Louis O. Mink, 'History and Fiction as Modes of Comprehension', *New Literary History* 1 (1969–70), 557 – but Mink's argument seems largely to ignore the sorts of considerations at issue here. In contrast to Mink, see David Carr, 'Narrative and the Real World: An Argument for Continuity', *History and Theory* 25 (1986): 117–131. There is now a very large philosophical and psychological literature on the role of narrative in the formation of identity. See, for instance, Jens Brockmeier and Donal A. Carbaugh, eds., *Narrative and Identity: Studies in Autobiography, Self and Culture* (Amsterdam: John Benjamins Publishing, 2001); Daniel D. Hutto, ed., *Narrative and Understanding Persons*, Royal Institute of Philosophy Supplement 60 (Cambridge: Cambridge University Press, 2007); Kim Atkins, ed., *Narrative Identity and Moral Identity: A Practical Perspective* (London: Routledge, 2008); Julia Vassilieva, *Narrative Psychology: Identity, Transformation and Ethics* (Dordrecht: Springer, 2016).

14 I say that such beliefs 'ordinarily' rule out certain others, but extremely bizarre cases can certainly arise, especially in cases of schizophrenia – see, for instance, Alan Baddeley, Andrew Thornton, Siew Eng Chua, and Peter McKenna, 'Schizophrenic Delusions and the Construction of Autobiographical Memory', in *Remembering Our Past*, ed. David Rubin (Cambridge: Cambridge University Press, 1996), 384–428.

15 The multiplicity of possible descriptions or narratives that may attach to any system of mental states – what may be termed the 'indeterminacy' of the mental – suggests that, inasmuch as self-identity may be tied to such systems of states, such self-identity is also capable of multiple description and narration. This might be thought to present problems for such a conception of self-identity, since it seems to render self-identity unstable. Indeed, Paul Ricoeur's emphasis on the identity of a life as tied to narrative can be taken to suggest just such a problem (see, for instance, the discussion of this point in David Wood, introduction to *On Paul Riceour: Narrative and Interpretation*, 4). Rather like Ricoeur, however, I do not regard such 'indeterminacy' as an objection to holistic or narrativist conceptions of mental content or self-identity (nor do I regard it, as Wood suggests we might regard these problems in Ricoeur – see ibid., 5 – as a sort of 'return of the repressed') but instead as indicating one of the limits within which those notions operate. Moreover, it is not clear why we should expect, or even whether it is legitimate to expect, any greater determinacy or 'stability' here. Moreover, the fact that mental content or even self-identity is 'indeterminate' does not undermine the reality of such content – a multiplicity of true descriptions does not imply the unreality of what is described and neither does a multiplicity of descriptions of the same object imply the necessary falsity of those descriptions. For a discussion and defence of indeterminacy in relation to mental content, see Malpas, *Donald Davidson and the Mirror of Meaning* (Cambridge: Cambridge University Press, 1992), 104ff.

16 There is a connection here with Kripke's famous puzzle about belief. See Saul Kripke, 'A Puzzle About Belief', in *Meaning and Use*, ed. A. Margalit (Dordrecht: Reidel, 1979). Pierre, brought up in France, is taught by his Anglophone nanny that 'Londres est jolie.' In later life, Pierre goes to live in a drab part of London and acquires the belief that 'London is not pretty.' But Pierre does not realize that Londres is London, and so he continues to hold both that 'Londres est jolie' and 'London is not pretty.' Do we attribute two separate beliefs to Pierre? Do we take these beliefs to be inconsistent? We can avoid inconsistency only at the risk, it would seem, of depriving 'Londres' of its reference to London and by ignoring the causal/historical chain that connects Pierre's 'Londres'

with London. For further discussion of the Kripkean problem as it arises within a holistic theory of content, see Akeel Bilgrami, *Belief and Meaning* (Cambridge, MA: Blackwell, 1992), 16–19 and 56–60.

17 As Davidson points out: 'In standard reason explanations...not only do the propositional contents of various beliefs and desires bear appropriate logical relations to one another and to the contents of the belief, attitude or intention they help to explain; the actual states of belief and desire cause the explained state or event. In the case of irrationality, the causal relation remains, while the logical relation is missing or distorted.' See Davidson, 'Paradoxes of Irrationality', in *Problems of Rationality* (Oxford: Clarendon Press, 2004), 179. A breakdown in the interconnected character of the mental may arise along the lines Davidson considers here, where a causal relation obtains between two mental states in the absence of any rational connection, as well as in the way suggested by the Sacks case, considered below, in which some particular physical event 'intrudes', as it were, on the normal causal processes in a subject's body, thereby giving rise to a set of mental events that lacks any proper rational connection with the rest of the subject's mental life. There is, of course, an important difference between these two cases: in the Davidson case we have sets of contentful states that are causally but not rationally connected, while in the Sacks case we have a non-rational cause that gives rise to a set of contentful states that are rationally disconnected from other states. Davidson would treat only the former as a case of irrationality (see 'Two Paradoxes of Irrationality', in ibid., 180).

18 See Oliver Sacks, *The Man Who Mistook His Wife for a Hat* (London: Pan Books, 1985), 125–142.

19 It can also be seen as a way of understanding the Davidsonian idea of the partitioning of the mental – see n17 above.

20 The test (Turing originally referred to it as the 'imitation game') involves connecting one person and one computer, via remote terminals, to another person whose task is to determine which of the two is the computer and which the human on the basis only of verbal responses elicited via the terminals. If the accuracy is less than 50 per cent, then the computer is judged to be capable of intelligent behaviour or an imitation thereof. See Turing, 'Computing Machinery and Intelligence', *Mind* 59 (1950), 433–460. The fact that the test is too limited as a genuine test of the capacity for thought does not affect its relevance here.

21 It might be said that the argument here is verificationist – that it conflates the conditions that are required for a certain attribution or identification with the conditions that must obtain for the state or condition being attributed to obtain. It is, of course, always possible that, in any particular case, the conclusion that is reached regarding the attribution or identification in question turns out to be false (the creature is quite rational, but was, for instance, intentionally misleading us). Yet what is at issue here is not the accuracy or not of some attribution or identification, but rather the underlying conceptual connection on which attribution or identification depends, and which themselves express deeper ontological connections – the epistemology must thus, as it were, recapitulate the ontology.

22 See Daniel C. Dennett, *Content and Consciousness* (London: Routledge, 1993), 93–94. Dennett points out that shifting to the sub-personal level involves abandoning the personal level, and so, in the case of pain, for instance, 'abandoning the personal level of explanation is just that: abandoning the pains and not bringing them along to identify with some physical event' (ibid., 94).

23 See Davidson, 'Thinking Causes', in *Truth, Language, and History* (Oxford: Clarendon Press, 2005), 185–200; the classic statement of the position is in Davidson, 'Mental Events', in *Essays on Actions and Events* (Oxford: Clarendon Press, 1980), 207–224. Anomalous monism has been subjected to a range of criticisms – see L.E. Hahn, ed., *The Philosophy of Donald Davidson*, Library of Living Philosophers XXVII (Chicago, IL: Open Court Press, 1999), for various discussions of the issue. On Davidson's rejection of empiricist foundationalism, see Davidson, 'A Coherence Theory of Truth and Knowledge', in *Subjective, Intersubjective, Objective* (Oxford: Clarendon Press, 2001), 137–153.

24 Merleau-Ponty, *Phenomenology of Perception*, 407.

25 One might argue, especially from a Davidsonian perspective, that the identity of states is just a matter of their causal connections with other states. However, it is not the causal connections between states that directly determine their content, but rather their rational connections.

26 See the more detailed discussion of this point in my 'Self-knowledge and Scepticism' and also my 'Constituting the Mind: Kant, Davidson, and the Unity of Consciousness'; see also Davidson,

'First-Person Authority' and 'Knowing One's Own Mind', in *Subjective, Intersubjective, Objective*, 3–38. Marcia Cavell provides a useful discussion of this issue (as well as giving an excellent summary of the Davidsonian position in relation to the general points at issue here) in the first chapter of *The Psychoanalytic Mind* (Cambridge, MA: Harvard University Press, 1993), 9–41.

Further reading

Davidson, Donald. *Problems of Rationality*. Oxford: Clarendon Press, 2004.

Malpas, Jeff. *Donald Davidson and the Mirror of Meaning*. Cambridge, UK: Cambridge University Press, 1992.

MacIntyre, Alasdair. *After Virtue: A Study in Moral Theory*. London: Duckworth, 1981.

Neisser, Ulric, and Eugene Winograd, eds. *Remembering Reconsidered*. Cambridge, UK: Cambridge University Press, 1988.

Ricoeur, Paul. *Oneself as Another*. Translated by Kathleen Blamey. Chicago, IL: University of Chicago Press, 1992.

Rubin, David, ed. *Remembering Our Past*. Cambridge, UK: Cambridge University Press, 1996.

4 Unity, locality, and agency

> It is only when we turn to consider our practical experience as agents, and not our theoretical experience as thinkers, that we discover the true nature of reason.
>
> (John MacMurray, *The Self as Agent*[1])

The holistic character of subjectivity – including the holistic character of mental states and content – has the important consequence that the unity of subjectivity cannot derive from some more primordial unity that lies within the overall structure. The unity of subjectivity thus cannot be like the unity of a planetary system with the 'subject' or self in the role of the sun, and holding all other bodies in systematic relation through the force it exerts upon them. Instead, the unity of subjectivity is a dynamic unity that operates through the constant articulation and re-articulation of the interconnection between mental states – interconnections that belong or are 'internal' to those states. Moreover, the interconnection of mental states that is at issue here encompasses not only mental states such as beliefs and desires, and any and every other such state (intentions, hopes, fears, anxieties, anticipations, and so forth), but also *actions*. That actions are indeed implicated was already evident in the discussion in previous chapters, and most obviously so through the focus on agency as well as the way linguistic behaviour (itself a particular form of action) stands in an essential relation to the possession of attitudes. The very concept of an attitude (whether understood as a state or a disposition) is tied to the role those states play in giving sense to behaviour – linguistic and non-linguistic, directly and indirectly.[2]

The close connection between mental states and behaviour is evident in C.S. Peirce's treatment of belief, in particular, as a form of behavioural disposition. He writes that 'the essence of belief is the establishment of a habit; and different beliefs are distinguished by the different modes of action to which they give rise'.[3] It is clear that mental states cannot be treated in separation from action, since every mental state implies certain behavioural expressions, even if not always realized and even if realized only linguistically (for instance, in the avowal of that state). Action, moreover, can only be explained as action – rather than as mere 'behaviour' – inasmuch as it is related to some set of beliefs, desires, and other attitudes, as well as to other actions and propensities to action. Put simply, for an item of behaviour to count as action is for it to be explicable in terms of reasons attributable to the agent. Behaviour that cannot be explained in this way may well be caused by states internal to an agent's body or brain, but the absence of any rational connection with states of the agent means that such behaviour cannot be viewed as action.[4] My flicking of the light switch with the aim of illuminating the room is an example of an action that is seen as such in virtue of the connecting of the behaviour with an appropriate set of attitudes, whereas my flicking the switch as a result of my being jostled against the wall is not, since it lacks any such attitudinal connection or integration. Behaviour is thus constituted as *action* through being understood as *rational*; that is, through being related to some intention or purpose that is additional to the mere behaviour. A familiar way of capturing this point is to say that behaviour is intentional, and therefore counts as action, only 'under a description', where the description enables the behaviour to be grasped in a form that integrates or connects it with some complex of attitudes – locates it within a larger structure of subjectivity – that 'makes sense' of the behaviour, or that provides a framework within which it can be grasped as rational.[5]

The way description works here connects directly with the role of narrative in enabling a similar, if more developed, form of integration. Indeed, one might argue that descriptions themselves typically rely on larger narrative structures, albeit usually multiple and indeterminate, from which they get their meaning. Even a minimal description of an action, such as 'I turned on the light', depends on narratives about actors, lighting, darkness, and so forth, no one of which is immediately marked out as relevant by the description alone, but many of which might be so. The focus on description thus draws attention back to the idea of narrative, or story, as a key element in the integration of states that makes for subjectivity, and thereby also connects the capacity for narration with the capacity for complex forms of action. The purposeful character of action, as well as its coordination with a larger situational context, depends on being able to orient the agent and the action in a way that gives some sense of a past and future trajectory of activity, thereby allowing one action to relate to others, and to other elements in the life of the agent. As was seen earlier, narratives vary enormously – from the simple to the complex, the conventional to the idiosyncratic – and this variation reflects the complexity and richness, not only of action and of narrative, but of situational context and of the lives of agents. Yet whatever their character, it is through such narratives that agents are able to project their lives from the past and present into the future, and, in so doing, are able to explore and map out future possibilities for action. Purposeful behaviour, of any complex sort, would seem to depend on just such a capacity to play out possibilities aside from their realization, and thereby adjust actions to perceived situations. At a certain point then, the capacity for action comes to depend crucially on a capacity to construct narratives and understand them.[6] One might argue, in addition, that this is precisely what is at issue in the idea of action as *free* – not in virtue of any release from the constraints of causality (since without causality even rationality disappears), but rather through release into the domain of narrative possibility.[7]

Recognition of the connection between mental states, or attitudes, and action should lead to the further recognition that, although mental states and actions form a single interconnected system, that system possesses a directedness or orientation derivable from the directedness or orientation that is a necessary feature of action itself. Action is the attempt to bring something about, and thus requires a quite specific orientation in relation to the objects, locations, and events with which the agent is involved (cases of forbearance can be viewed as instances where what is to be brought about is the non-occurrence of some event or one's non-involvement in that occurrence). It is not merely that the agent must stand in relation to things in the right way in order to be successful in bringing something about, but that the very ability to act – successfully or unsuccessfully – requires that the agent grasp her or himself as standing in relation to things in a way consistent with the agent's intentions (which does not imply that the agent always grasps the situation correctly, only that there must be consistency between the agent's intentions and situational grasp). This partly reflects the need for action to cohere with the rest of an agent's attitudes as well as the way in which action is itself a form of oriented, directed behaviour. In this respect, it also reflects the oriented and directed character of the subjective space to which action is tied.

The way in which mental states interconnect with action is indicative of the way in which the unity of mental states, is always organized in relation to action – not merely to the array of possible actions that might lie before an agent, but also to the actions in which the agent is currently engaged and to the ongoing activities of the agent to which those actions contribute. The ordering of mental states in relation to action thus mirrors the ordering of subjective space in relation to the agent's active engagement with the world, as discussed in Chapter 2. Moreover, it is not only that subjective space and the 'mental space' of beliefs, desires, and other attitudes are both organized in relation to action and capacities for agency, but since action is defined in relation to certain objects and the bringing about of certain events, mental states are, to a large extent, also defined and individuated in relation to the objects and events to which they are directed. This is part of the familiar idea that mental states are defined and individuated in terms of their 'intentionality'.[8] In the present context, however, 'intentionality' can be viewed as a feature of the way in which *both* mental states *and* actions are defined and individuated (although it is more usual to distinguish these two senses of intentionality, of more interest here is the similarity that obtains between them). Treating the intentionality of mental states and of actions as analogous gives rise to an important outcome: rather than involving some sort of occult relation to objects, the intentionality of mental states is seen as grounded in the same sort of spatial orientation and causal involvement that is characteristically a feature of the engagement with objects in action.

Understanding an agent (including oneself) as being engaged in some activity has two aspects: understanding the agent as standing in certain causal and spatial relations to objects and grasping the agent as having certain relevant attitudes towards the objects concerned. Indeed, even being able to understand an agent as having certain attitudes is inseparable from being able to identify the objects of those attitudes that itself depends on the ability to understand the agent's spatial and causal involvement in the world. In Davidson's work, this idea is partially captured in the idea that identifying the contents of an agent's attitudes depends on identifying the causes of those attitudes. The causes are not the immediate, 'proximal' causes of belief – certain events in the brain, say, or impacts at the sensory surfaces – but instead the 'distal' causes of those beliefs, namely, certain worldly objects and events. Indeed, it is only beliefs about those 'distal' objects that, under certain descriptions, are rationally connected with other attitudes held by and attributed to agents.[9] The content of an agent's attitudes depends on the causal connections between those attitudes and their objects, as well as on the rational connections between attitudes themselves. Furthermore, just as action requires something independent of the agent on or with respect to which the agent acts, so must the objects of an agent's attitudes be, at least in the most basic cases, separate from the agent. Thus, the very possibility of content presupposes the idea of an external space and an objective world within which the agent moves and is located. I shall have more to say about this point in the next chapter, but for now it is worth noting that the having of attitudes by an agent depends on the agent's relation to objects that are distinct from the agent, and that this can be seen to derive, at least in part, from the interconnection of attitudinal content with action.

Inasmuch as mental states are organized in relation to the agent's actions and capacities for action, such organization is, as noted above, analogous to the ordering of subjective space. Moreover, since subjective space can be characterized though the idea of 'perspectivity', and therefore as having a certain directionality or focus that derives from the nature of the agent's current activity or capacities in general, something similar is also true of the system of mental states. Indeed, if we view mental states as forming a 'web' in which each state is connected with many other states, then it is a web that is always being pulled in some particular direction. Like a spider's web in which a fly has been caught, and in which all the threads are under stress from a single point, mental states are similarly organized in relation to, or 'pulled towards', the current activity of the agent – and, just as some parts of such a web will be stretched more than others, some states will be 'pulled' more than others. Consequently, the unitary system of mental states always has a certain focus, and this focus provides a certain ordering of mental states – beliefs, desires, and the like – that allows for differing degrees of integration among them.[10] Thus, the more directly states are connected to a specific action in which the agent is currently involved, or to the overall activity to which that action contributes, the higher the degree of consistency and coherence those states will require in relation to one another and to the action in question. As for states that are further removed from the current action or activity, a higher degree of inconsistency or lack of coherence may be tolerated. The unity and integration of states must therefore be understood as continuous with the unity and integration of an agent's activities. Importantly, however, the integration of these mental states is tied, first and foremost, to the integration of *action*, not mere behaviour. Nonetheless, there is an important connection with behaviour, inasmuch as behaviour must, in general, fit with the action the agent intends to perform, with the caveat that poor motor coordination or lack of skill in performance do not count as evidence of a lack of mental integration.

The idea that mental states are ordered in relation to action can, in most cases, be seen as an inevitable consequence of the idea that mental states are holistically determined. Indeed, it is partly the need to deal with certain problems arising from the holistic character of mental content that leads Akeel Bilgrami to tie mental content to action.[11] Bilgrami treats attributions of content as constrained by a requirement of consistency, but he acknowledges that this constraint cannot be applied to the entirety of an agent's concepts (what he terms the aggregative or 'meaning-theoretic' level), since this would make any attribution of concepts impossible, in that it seems to require, amongst other things, the simultaneous fixing of all of an agent's beliefs.[12] Consequently, Bilgrami insists that the attribution of concepts must be constrained both by a principle of unity *and* of locality, where the notion of locality is itself understood by reference to particular *actions* as a focus for explanation and, thereby, for concept attribution.[13] So, if we wish to attribute beliefs that will explain someone's grabbing an umbrella on the way out to the street, we do not need to look to beliefs about European geography or human anatomy and disease. Instead, we need to ensure that whatever beliefs are ascribed are consistent with, for instance, the agent's beliefs about the likelihood of rain and the usefulness of the object grasped as protection against the weather. It is precisely because we can focus on particular actions, and therefore on particular *contexts* for action (which we are required to do if we are to explain or understand the agent's behaviour), that we are able to focus on a certain range of beliefs and not on the agent's beliefs in their entirety. Our mental lives are indeed organized and defined only in relation to action. Our actions are thus not merely indicative of the attitudes we hold, but it is in and through our actions that our attitudes are constituted and the interconnection between attitudes is made apparent. Particular actions establish a context within which specific features of the world, and specific features of the agent's own conceptual repertoire, come into play, thereby providing a focus, not only by means of which we can understand and orient ourselves, but also by means of which we can make specific attributions of content.

It is in relation to the 'locality' established in action that the unity and integration of mental states is itself established and maintained. The unity of states in relation to action obtains, moreover, both at a time and also over time. Over time, an agent's behaviour will change as the agent's activities change; an agent will likely engage in many different activities; and as the activities vary, so too will the agent's physical location. The unity that is a prerequisite for the attribution of mental states – for the identification of actions and for the existence of an agent – will thus be a necessarily complex unity ranging over a great many different activities, states, occasions, and locations. This suggests that a certain degree of disunity will be a persistent feature in the life of any agent, simply in virtue of the shifting character of the agent's situation. It also shows how irrationality can arise, and sometimes remain, without significantly compromising the unity of the agent as a direct consequence of the ordering of mental life in relation to action, and so to different locations, occasions, and kinds of action.

One way of treating irrationality – particularly cases of weakness of will – has been to view irrationality as arising on the basis of a certain 'partitioning' of the mind. This is, in fact, the approach adopted by Davidson.[14] Problematic in this sort of approach, however, is the issue as to how such partitioning might occur. Yet, once we grasp the rationality of mental states as tied to action, and action as tied to embodiment and location, we can see a simple way of understanding such partitioning. It arises in the notion that different actions require a different orientation on the part of the agent; the latter involving a difference in the orientation of the body and its parts, as well as a difference in the orientation and ordering of mental states. This 'partitioning' of the mind, which can be viewed as making possible the possession of otherwise incompatible attitudes by a single agent, can be understood as arising through, and grounded in, the differing spatial orientations and locations associated with distinct actions and activities. There is, of course, still a need to understand those actions and activities as somehow related through their being the actions and activities of a single agent. Too much fragmentation in the activities of the agent will imply a fragmentation in the agent's mental life that may render dubious the supposition of agency (or of a *single* agent), but the concept of mental 'partitioning' nonetheless explains how a certain limited incompatibility in attitudes or behaviour could arise. The idea that such partitioning might be tied to differences in spatial orientation and location offers some explanation of the means by which such partitioning might itself operate.

The structuring of mental content (or, indeed, of the mind) in relation to action suggests that one cannot understand subjectivity as independent of the concept of agency. The possibility of agency, however, is itself tied to the idea of a particular subjective space – such a space defined largely in terms of certain capacities for action. The ordering of subjective spatiality, then, is an ordering in relation to action, and, inasmuch as mental states are also ordered in this way, the ordering of subjective space and the ordering of an agent's thoughts and experiences are closely interconnected. Yet, as evident in Chapter 2, the grasp of subjective space cannot be completely independent of the grasp of objective space. So, in establishing the necessary interconnection of self and content with spatiality and agency, a connection is also indicated between these concepts and the concept of objective space – and, more generally, with the idea of objectivity. Here a structure starts to appear in which subjective and objective elements are interconnected and interdependent. It is on the basis of this structure that thought and experience are possible; and it is through the delineation of this structure – more specifically, through the sightings taken in this and the previous chapter, as well as in those that follow – that the structure of place is itself revealed.

If the structure of subjectivity cannot be understood apart from the structure of agency, then neither can be severed from the structure of the world in which the subject is necessarily located. This is partly a consequence, as already seen, of the need to look to the autonomous objects to which subjects are causally related in order to identify the contents of attitudes. It is also a consequence of the structuring of mental content in relation to agency. There is, through a further connection that reinforces the necessary 'spatialization' of the mind and mental content; one that arises when we focus more specifically on the character of *memory*. In most discussions of mental content – at least those presented in philosophical literature – memory is perhaps accorded rather less attention than it properly deserves. Similarly, under-recognized is the importance of maintaining consistency and integration in memory as a prerequisite for the possibility of contentful thought and experience. Philosophers (it is perhaps less the case in disciplines outside philosophy) thus tend to focus on attitudes, particularly epistemic attitudes like belief, as if the content of those attitudes were primarily dependent on some simultaneous connection with other attitudinal contents, abstractly or generically conceived. It is commonplace to find talk (and I have put matters this way) of how the belief that snow is white, for instance, requires a large number of other beliefs about the nature of snow, whiteness, and so on. Yet such connections obtain at a number of different levels between different sorts of beliefs – for instance, personal beliefs pertaining to oneself and one's life, beliefs about the conventions that prevail in one's society, beliefs of a quite general character about the nature of the world and things within it – and are typically organized only in relation to a wide range of different memories. Beliefs about the whiteness of snow, to continue the example, may well be inseparable from memories of certain quite particular experiences of snow. The emphasis on memory rather than belief (and this is indeed more a matter of emphasis than anything else, since one cannot, certainly not in more complex cases, easily separate memory from belief) is not simply a matter of subjective semantic preference. To think of the ordering of mental life as largely dependent on the ordering of *memory*, rather than merely the ordering of atemporal beliefs or other attitudes, is to think of mental life in a way that highlights the necessarily temporal character of mental life, and this suggests connections with the role of narrative structure in the organization of mental content as well as bringing to the fore notions of spatiality – and place.

One of the features of memory, to which Ulric Neisser has given special attention, is its 'nested' character. Events – and so also the memories of events – can be understood both as being constituents of larger event structures and as composed of smaller constituent events. Neisser takes the concept of nesting from J.J. Gibson's ecological approach to psychology (an approach concerned with the subject's embeddedness in its environment), which emphasizes the way in which nesting is a ubiquitous feature of the world:

> Physical reality has structure at all levels of metric size from atoms to galaxies. The smaller units are embedded in the larger units by what I will call *nesting*. For example, canyons are nested within mountains; trees are nested within canyons; leaves are nested within trees; and cells are nested within trees. There are forms within forms both up and down the scale of size. Units are nested within larger units. Things are components of other things. They would compose a hierarchy except that this hierarchy is not categorical but full of transitions and overlaps.[15]

Neisser treats the nested character of things in the world, and of events,[16] as reflected in the nested structure of memory. Thus, just as the event of typing one letter or sentence, to use one of Neisser's examples, is nested within the larger event of the writing of a paper or book, my experience and memory of that event are similarly nested within the experience and memory of the larger event.

Neisser is emphatic that the nested structure of events and, especially, the nesting of particular occurrences within larger and often discontinuous processes, is not something arbitrary or merely imposed. He writes:

> It is frequently suggested that events like these have no objective reality – that they are brought into existence only by the way we perceive and talk about them. On that solipsistic assumption, nothing in the world is real until we make it so. To make such an assumption is to confuse selection with invention, flexibility with arbitrariness. The world is rich enough to support an indefinite number of descriptions, but not all descriptions are correct. 'Writing a chapter' is only one of many possible descriptions of what I am doing now, but it is certainly true; to say that I was riding a bicycle would be false.[17]

Such multiplicity of description is, as noted earlier, also a central feature of our mental lives. Connections between attitudes, and between experiences and memories, are multiple, and so there is always more than one way to order those attitudes, experiences and memories; more than one narrative within which they can be embedded.

The nested structure of memory, to which Neisser draws attention, can indeed be viewed as a central feature of mental states; and the holistic interconnection of mental states can, in turn, be treated as largely a matter of the nesting of states within other states. The idea of the mental as having such a nested structure is particularly useful in allowing a conception of the mental as a system composed of multiple and overlapping connections, which cannot be reduced to any simpler, completely consistent, logical ordering, and which always allows the possibility of re-description and reconfiguration. Indeed, given the characterization of mental unity in terms of the sort of unity paradigmatically associated with narrative, it is significant that the nested structure of memory is also, perhaps unsurprisingly, a characteristic feature of narrative. Narrative can be seen as a device by means of which a particular ordering of events is shaped by nesting events within a larger event structure. Of special significance for the present discussion, however, is the way in which Neisser suggests a connection between the nested structure of memory (and so, on my account, of mental life) and the nested structure of places. He notes that 'the nesting of events is very similar to the nesting of places. Events are "located" by inclusion in larger events, just as places are located with reference to larger places',[18] and, on this point, he again refers to Gibson: 'A place is a location in the environment as contrasted with a point in space. . . Whereas a point must be located with reference to a larger coordinate system, a place can be located by its inclusion in a larger place (for example, the fireplace in the cabin by the bend of the river in the Great Plains).'[19] In a number of discussions, Neisser then goes on to advance the hypothesis that personal memory is, in fact, closely tied to spatial understanding and that the part of the brain (centred on the hippocampus) devoted to spatial cognition 'may be the principal vehicle of personal memory'.[20]

Neisser bases this hypothesis on a number of considerations, many of which provide grounds for the general thesis that personal memory and spatial understanding are related quite apart from any more specific claim about their common neurophysiological basis. He summarizes these considerations as follows:

> The spatial cognitive system, then, has several intriguing characteristics. First, it operates on a domain that has a clearly nested structure. . . Second the system stores information about the spatial domain in a way that captures the hierarchical structure very effectively. Common experience suggests. . . that one can remember spatial information in considerable detail and for long periods of time. Third, the system enables us to 'mentally revisit' places that we have once encountered without actually returning to them. Indeed, it even allows us to rearrange the furniture of those places in our imaginations. All these features of the spatial module are equally characteristic of autobiographical memory. Our memories of our own past are also organised in terms of nested units. . . they also preserve information for very long periods and with great richness of detail. Autobiographical memory enables us to 'revisit' previously visited places, and perhaps even to rearrange some of their details.[21]

In addition, Neisser cites other theoretical and empirical considerations that appear to add weight to the hypothesis that personal memory and spatial cognition are closely connected. Yet not all of these considerations appear equally strong. In particular, Neisser's focus on the 'nested' character of both memories and places could be read as making too much of what might well be a superficial and coincidental similarity. Neisser's observations on this point become more significant, however, when one attends more explicitly to the way in which the very idea of such 'nesting' calls upon spatial or, better, place-related (topographical or topological) concepts.

The way in which one memory may be nested in another invariably depends, at least in the case of personal memory, on a nesting of the actual event or object concerned in another event or object. How should such nesting of event or object be understood? Fundamentally, it cannot be understood as independent of some notion of spatiality, because it is essentially a notion of *containment*, and this is so even in relation to the nesting of one event in another.[22] Moreover, if nested structures are always spatial (or spatio-temporal) structures, then the fact that memory is also characterized by such a structure will be indicative of the necessary dependence of memory on some form of spatial ordering. Of course, the spatiality at issue here is not simply that of physical extendedness. The character of a space as enclosing, while also being itself enclosed, is indicative of a 'space' that can be grasped as having both a within and without, as capable of being turned in towards its centre or out towards its periphery. It is a 'space' closer to the *topos* or *chora* of Aristotle and Plato than to the empty and isotropic space of Newton. The 'space' at issue is indeed better understood in terms of a place rather than any mere space (though a place gives space within it) – and it is places, rather than mere spaces, that 'nest' in the way identified by Gibson and Neisser.

The way in which such a spatial or place-based ordering allows for the nesting of things in relation to other things, and places within other places, indicates something of the way in which such ordering also allows for a unifying of diverse elements within a single structure. As Gibson points out, places are indeed located through being nested within other places and this means that one can specify a location in particular terms, without having to specify an entire coordinate system at the same time. Consequently, a place-based system of location is one in which objects can be located through reference to a place, rather than to some set of abstract coordinates. Use of such a nested, place-based system of location is characteristic of the way in which creatures like us – creatures capable of a conceptual grasp of both themselves and their surroundings – can make sense of the interconnected and unitary character of some spatially extended region. Places contain sets of interconnected locations that are nested within those places such that, depending on how broadly I think of the place in which I now find myself (for instance, the room in which I sit, the house where I live, the town where I reside – see Figure 9 in Chapter 7), I can grasp the interconnected character of a variety of locations within my current location. Places also open out to other places through being nested, along with those other places, within a larger spatial structure or framework of activity – some broader place. Thus, in being acquainted with a single place, one is also acquainted with a larger network of places.

The nested character of places enables us to see how the spatiality, or dimensionality, that is tied to the concept of place makes possible a particular form of differentiated unity – a unity that would seem to play a particularly important role in the organization of memory. More generally, however, one might say that inasmuch as the ordering of memories is dependent on the ordering of the *objects* of memory, the ordering of memory must always be an ordering that is spatial as well as temporal. This will apply both to instances of personal memory (since remembered experiences are typically within particular settings or locations) and to cases involving more general and impersonal forms of memory. Such will obviously be the case where the memory is of some aspect of spatial structure or of some general feature of the world or the objects in it that is tied to spatial location or position.

Nonetheless, wherever one is called upon to remember some complex and differentiated structure, one will invariably call upon spatial ideas and images of some sort, and this is because, as may become clearer in Chapter 5, spatiality is, in general, a form of dimensionality that allows the simultaneous presentation (the 'co-presence') of distinct elements. The spatial ordering of things is therefore fundamental to the possibility of any complex ordering at a time, as opposed to the ordering of things over time. One might add that the role played by spatial, and more broadly topographical ordering, evident in relation to memory can be seen as characteristic, not only of memory, but of mental life in general – of all thought and experience. It is not just memory that has a 'nested' structure, but the mind.[23]

If we think of memory, in particular, as closely connected with place and space in this way, then perhaps we can better understand the effectiveness of the classical method of *loci* that is part of the traditional art of memory that begins with the Greeks and Romans and continues into Medieval and Renaissance times (a tradition given special attention by Frances Yates in her *The Art of Memory*,[24] and noted in Neisser's discussion of the connection between memory and space[25]). The method of *loci* provides a memory system that operates through the association of particular memories with particular 'places', or 'loci', within a system of such places. Cicero describes the system, supposedly first devised by the poet Simonides: 'Persons desiring to train this faculty (of memory) must select localities and form mental images of the things they wish to remember and store those images in the localities, so that the arrangement of the localities will preserve the order of the things.'[26] In the 'method of loci' then, we have a system that draws directly on the characteristically nested character of place, and the spaces arising therein, as the basis for an explicit ordering of memory.[27]

We often think of memory only in connection with the dimensionality that belongs to time. Yet, it seems that memory is, in fact, as much tied to the topological and the spatial as it is to the temporal. Thus, Edward Casey draws attention to an affinity between memory and place, writing that 'not only is each suited to the other; each calls for the other. What is contained in place is on its way to being well remembered. What is remembered is well-grounded if it is remembered as being in a particular place – a place that may well take precedence over the time of its occurrence.'[28] Memory requires a grasp of the successiveness of events, but it also requires a grasp of the spatial and topographic ordering of events and objects (since events are 'in' space no less than are objects), including relations not only of proximity and distance, but also of the spatial nesting of events and objects in relation to other events and objects. In coming to see how important both temporality and spatiality are to the structure of memory, we can also begin to see the centrality of both temporality and spatiality in the organization of mental life. Moreover, as Casey emphasizes,[29] the connection between memory and place is also indicative of the close interconnection between memory and the body, and, we might therefore say, between embodiment and the possibility of mental content. The importance of spatiality *and* temporality, and so too of embodiment, is something that can easily be missed by a focus on beliefs or attitudes as the primary constituents of mental life. Yet the idea that mental life is fundamentally a matter of the integration of a self with respect to both space and time, and so with respect to a temporally and spatially extended *place* – a place in which it is possible to *act* – is central to any proper understanding of the possibility of thought or experience. The argument for this conclusion is, however, still to be fully realized, and forms a central theme of Chapters 5 and 6.

Notwithstanding the larger argument yet to be pursued, the more particular considerations concerning the nature of subjectivity, broached at the beginning of Chapter 3, have now been brought to a conclusion. Subjective spatiality cannot be seen as grounded in some simple and underlying subject or self. The subject is constituted in a way that already draws upon spatiality, rather than being independent of it. Consequently, although the analysis of subjectivity that has been developed in this and the preceding chapter has led to recognition of the central role of agency and spatiality in the structuring of subjectivity, it has not thereby rehabilitated the idea of an independent, underlying subject through some idea of the subject *as agent*. If we think of subjective space as a unitary structure whose unity depends, in large part, on a certain unity of agency, then the unity of mental states that makes for the possibility of content would also seem to be grounded in the same unity of agency. As evident from the analysis in Chapter 3, however, the unity at issue here is not that derived from the *agent* considered as a subject underlying the possibility of action. The unity of agency is just the unity generated and maintained in and through the inter-relation of different elements – a particular body, particular objects, a particular environment, particular capacities. In turn, the unifying that is at work in the possibility of a self, of mental content, or indeed of subjective space, is therefore nothing over and above activity itself, and is not grounded in the prior existence of an agent. Consequently, the problem concerning the need for a subject that produces unity among mental states or that produces the unity of a space, and to which particular states or a particular space belong, largely disappears, simply because no such unifying subject is required. Given a particular set of mental states, or a particular subjective space, one is thereby also given a particular subject to whom those states can be attributed and on which that space can be understood as focused.

The idea that the overall structure of subjectivity is organized around the structure of action can be seen to be presupposed in the original notion of subjective space as organized around, and in relation to, the behavioural and cognitive capacities of the subject. Yet, in taking action to have such an important role in structuring subjectivity, and in assuming a notion of subjective space that is structured according to the behavioural and cognitive capacities of the creature whose space it is, it may seem that I have predisposed my account towards a very specific conception of thought and experience – that I have predisposed the account towards one in which spatial and topographic notions will indeed have a central role.

Moreover, although I have so far argued that an understanding of the unity of subjectivity, and of cognitive and experiential states, requires an understanding of the interconnected character of states themselves as organized around concrete actions and ongoing activities, I have not yet explained why such unity should be tied, as implicitly supposed, not merely to action but to embodied action within a physical space. If action and agency provide the necessary foci around which thought and experience are unified, why could not such action take place in a non-spatial realm – for instance, in the purely 'auditory' realm of Peter Strawson's 'No-Space World', from *Individuals* (discussed further in Chapter 5)[30] – and why could not the required agency be seen as the agency of a creature that understands itself in non-spatial terms? Answers to these questions will enable a clearer view of the structure in which subjectivity is based and the role of agency within that structure. In this way, they will also advance our understanding of the complex structure of place.

Notes

1 John MacMurray, *The Self as Agent* (London: Faber & Faber, 1957), 54.

2 So, the holding of one belief, although it may remain largely unacted upon, may nevertheless incline us towards the holding of some other belief or complex of beliefs, or some desire, that is indeed immediately effective in relation to action.

3 C.S. Peirce, 'How to Make Our Ideas Clear', in *Collected Papers of Charles Sanders Peirce, vol. 5, Pragmatism and Pragmaticism* (Cambridge, MA: The Belknap Press, 1935), 397. In 'Objectivity, Causality and Agency', Thomas Baldwin refers to the 'classical pragmatist thesis... that only an agent can perceive' – in *The Body and the Self*, ed. José Luis Bermudez, Anthony Marcel, and Naomi Eilan (Cambridge, MA: MIT Press. 1995), 107 – and to the 'pragmatist theory of belief according to which the content of a belief can be defined in terms of its role in helping to bring about actions that would satisfy the subject's desires if the belief were true' ('Objectivity, Causality and Agency', 108).

4 Even if one is critical of the belief-desire model of action that is implied here, the point concerning the holistic character of action remains. Opponents of the belief-desire model may talk instead, for instance, of the way behaviour fits into some overall pattern of meaningfulness or intelligibility.

5 The classic statement of such a view of the nature of action, a view that has a largely Wittgensteinian pedigree, is Davidson's 'Actions, Reasons and Causes', in *Essays on Actions and Events* (repr.,

Oxford: Clarendon Press, 1980), 3–20. Davidson's own adjustment to the view is to claim that the reasons must, if they are properly to be the reasons for the action, be the causes of the action. For an excellent discussion of the Davidsonian position and especially its relation to the Wittgensteinian, see Fred Stoutland, 'Interpreting Davidson on Intentional Action', in *Dialogues with Davidson: Acting, Interpreting, Understanding*, ed. Jeff Malpas (Cambridge, MA: MIT Press, 2011), 297–324.

6 Ricoeur's work is important, once again, in exemplifying a position that takes narrative to be crucial, not only to the constitution and definition of the self, but also to the structure and possibility of action. See Ricoeur, *Oneself as Another*, trans. Kathleen Blamey (Chicago, IL: University of Chicago Press, 1992), esp. 88–163.

7 Just as the lack of any conceptual capacity on the part of a creature diminishes the sense in which notions of action and purpose can be applied to that creature's behaviour, it follows that the lack of any capacity for narrativity or narration will similarly diminish the sense in which behaviour can be regarded as action or as purposeful – and so also the sense in which notions of freedom may properly be applied to such behaviour. This does not mean that there is no sense in which concepts of action, purpose, and perhaps even freedom, may be deployed in relation to such behaviour, but it will indeed be a diminished or curtailed sense (and, one might also argue, a correspondingly more equivocal sense).

8 Understood as referring to the directness of thoughts, or mental states generally, towards an object, intentionality first appears in modern philosophy in the work of Franz Brentano. See his *Psychology from an Empirical Standpoint* (1874; London: Routledge and Kegan Paul, 1973), 88–89. Following Brentano, the term becomes central to the phenomenological tradition inaugurated by Edmund Husserl, and continued by, among others, Maurice Merleau-Ponty and Martin Heidegger.

9 The importance of the identification of the objects of belief in determining the content of belief is one reason why we can take the possession of attitudes to be tied closely to the capacity for language (on this latter point see also Chapter 2, 52–53). On a Davidsonian account, in particular, what belief is attributed to a speaker depends on identifying the object of belief through identifying the cause of belief, but since beliefs must also cohere with other attitudes, so the identification of beliefs also depends on identifying the objects of belief under descriptions that fit with other beliefs and attitudes attributed to the speaker. A creature that lacks a capacity for language will be a creature that is unable to discriminate between the same object under different descriptions and, as a consequence, will be a creature whose attitudes cannot be given any detailed or precise specification. On this point, see Davidson, 'Reply to Suppes', in *Essays on Davidson: Actions and Events*, ed. Bruce Vermazen and Jaakko Hintikka (Oxford: Clarendon Press, 1986), 252.

10 This idea is one that I have developed elsewhere (though to a lesser extent and in a slightly different fashion) around the notion of a 'project' – see my *Donald Davidson and the Mirror of Meaning* (Cambridge: Cambridge University Press, 1992), 78–79 and 127–138.

11 See Akeel Bilgrami, *Belief and Meaning* (Cambridge, MA: Blackwell, 1992). It seems that recognition of the importance of action in relation to mental content may be, for Bilgrami, also a consequence of certain ethical considerations – certainly such considerations are central to his brief discussion of self-knowledge in the appendix to *Belief and Meaning*, 250.

12 See ibid., 10–12 and 141–150. Bilgrami is particularly concerned to defend the unity of content thesis against the objections of Jerry Fodor. Fodor views holism – or, at least, what he calls 'Meaning Holism' – as 'a crazy doctrine'. See Fodor, *Psychosemantics* (Cambridge, MA: MIT Press, 1987), 60. Written in conjunction with Ernest Lepore, *Fodor's Holism: A Shopper's Guide* (Oxford: Blackwell, 1992) attacks a variety of holistic approaches in the work of philosophers such as Quine, Dummett, and Davidson. For a discussion of Fodor's position, see Akeel Bilgrami's review of two of Fodor's books (including *Holism: A Shopper's Guide*) in *Journal of Philosophy* 92 (1995): 330–344; see also the papers in *Holism: A Consumer Update*, ed. Jerry Fodor and Ernest LePore (Amsterdam: Rodopi, 1993). I do not attempt any detailed defence of the holism thesis against the objections of those such as Fodor (holism is not, as such, the main focus of discussion), although my emphasis on the way in which action provides a 'localized' context in relation to which mental states are organized can be seen as pre-empting certain objections of the sort found in Fodor.

Holism is something I discuss at greater length, and which I also defend, in *Donald Davidson and the Mirror of Meaning*.

13 See, for instance, Bilgrami, *Belief and Meaning*, 11.

14 See 'Paradoxes of Irrationality', in *Problems of Rationality* (Oxford: Clarendon Press, 2004), 169–188; and also 'Deception and Division', in ibid., 199–213.

15 J.J. Gibson, *The Ecological Approach to Visual Perception* (Boston, MA: Houghton Mifflin, 1979), 9.

16 See Ulric Neisser, 'Nested Structure in Autobiographical Memory', in *Autobiographical Memory*, ed. David C. Rubin (Cambridge: Cambridge University Press, 1986), 73–75.

17 Ibid., 73–74.

18 Ibid., 73.

19 J.J. Gibson, *The Ecological Approach to Visual Perception*, 34; as quoted by Neisser in 'Nested Structure in Autobiographical Memory', 73, and in a number of other papers.

20 See Ulric Neisser, 'What is Ordinary Memory the Memory Of?', in *Remembering Reconsidered*, ed. Ulric Neisser and Eugene Winograd (Cambridge: Cambridge University Press, 1988), 369. The localization of memory in the hippocampus is central to the work of John O'Keefe – see John O'Keefe and Lynn Nadel, *The Hippocampus as a Cognitive Map* (Oxford: Clarendon Press, 1978). It now appears that the hippocampus not only plays a role in relation to the grasp of space, but to the grasp of time also (as might be expected given the argument, advanced earlier, that space and time are not independent of one another) – see for instance, C. Ranganath and L.-T. Hsieh, 'The Hippocampus: A Special Place for Time', *Annals of the New York Academy of Science* 1369 (2016): 93–110.

21 Neisser, 'What is Ordinary Memory the Memory Of?', 369.

22 Even if we cavil at the idea that every event might have a spatio-temporal location that would enable us to provide a straightforward sense in which one event may be spatio-temporally included within another, we can always look to the objects that are involved in events and the spatial relations between those objects, other objects, and parts of objects as a basis on which to begin to explicate the nested structure that can be found in the ordering of events and objects.

23 See my 'Place and Hermeneutics: Towards a Topology of Understanding', in *Inheriting Gadamer: New Directions in Philosophical Hermeneutics*, ed. Georgia Warnke (Edinburgh: Edinburgh University Press, 2016), 143–160.

24 Frances Yates, *The Art of Memory* (London: Routledge & Kegan Paul, 1966).

25 See Neisser, 'What is Ordinary Memory the Memory Of?', 369; and also 'Domains of Memory', in *Memory: Interdisciplinary Approaches*, ed. P. Solomon, G.R. Goethals, C.M. Kelley, and B.R. Stephens (New York: Springer-Verlag, 1989), 78–79.

26 Cicero, *De oratore, II*, lxxxvi, 354, Loeb ed., trans. E.W. Sutton and H. Rackham (Cambridge, MA: Harvard University Press, 1942), 466–467. Cicero's Antonius also refers to Charmades at Athens and Metrodorus of Scepsis in Asia who 'each used to say that he wrote down things he wanted to remember in certain "localities" in his possession by means of images, just as if he were inscribing letters in wax' (*De Oratore, II*, lxxxviii, 360, Loeb ed., 472–473).

27 Although one also has to be careful not to read too much into the way in which, in the method of loci, place appears to enable memory (especially the idea that it does so by somehow giving to memory a fixity that it would otherwise lack) – see my comments on this in 'The Remembrance of Place', in *The Voice of Place: Essays and Interviews Exploring the Work of Edward S. Casey*, ed. Azucena Cruz-Pierre and Don Landes (London: Bloomsbury, 2013), 63–72.

28 Edward S. Casey, *Remembering: A Phenomenological Study* (Bloomington, IN: Indiana University Press, 1987), 214–215. Casey's focus on place in his subsequent work (and much of the discussion in the chapter on place memory here seems to adumbrate, though in much more summary form, ideas developed in Casey's work on place as such) seems to have arisen out of his inquiries into the relation between place and memory. On the connection between memory and place, see also Janet Donohoe, *Remembering Places: A Phenomenological Study of the Relationship Between Memory and Place* (Lanham, MD: Lexington Books, 2014).

29 Casey, *Remembering*, 189ff.

30 Strawson, chap. 2 in *Individuals*, 59–86.

Further reading

Bermudez, José Luis, Anthony Marcel, and Naomi Eilan, eds. *The Body and the Self*. Cambridge, MA: MIT Press, 1995.
Casey, Edward S. *Remembering: A Phenomenological Study*. Bloomington, IN: Indiana University Press, 1987.
Davidson, Donald. *Essays on Actions and Events*. Oxford: Clarendon Press, 1980.
Donohoe, Janet. *Remembering Places: A Phenomenological Study of the Relationship Between Memory and Place*. Lanham, MD: Lexington Books, 2014.
Rubin, David C., ed. *Autobiographical Memory*. Cambridge: Cambridge University Press, 1986.
Yates, Frances. *The Art of Memory*. London: Routledge & Kegan Paul, 1966.

5 Agency and objectivity

> Only a creature whose structure affords it the possibility of movement can be a sensing being.
>
> (Erwin Strauss, *The Primary World of the Senses*[1])

The primary concern in this investigation is with the sort of 'conceptualized' experience that is characteristically human, and with thought as it is associated with judgment and conceptuality, but related to that concern, there are many connections of special interest that obtain between spatiality, agency, and experience, and which arise at a primitive level. Earlier, I noted that any creature capable of directed movement, either of its whole body or of parts of its body, must not only be located within some space in which such movement is possible, but must also possess a grasp of that space (although not necessarily a conceptual grasp) both as subjectively presented and as independent of any particular perspective within it. Furthermore, this must apply to any creature, with or without a capacity to think conceptually. Likewise, the capacity for organized and directed behaviour – for action – is crucial in enabling the organization and integration of mental life in general, irrespective of the conceptual abilities of the creature concerned. Indeed, a creature lacking *any* capacity for action would likewise lack any organizing *focus* for experience; that is, any structure by means of which particular features within experience could be picked out as *salient* and *differentiated.* Action thus plays a crucial role in the possibility of experience and thought, and of mental life of any sort, and it is through consideration of the requirements that attend on the capacity for action, which is to say, on the possibility of agency, that we can arrive at a clearer and more detailed understanding of the connections between experience, thought, and spatiality. The connections between agency and spatiality, and between spatiality, thought, and experience, are not simple. As with much of this investigation, a network of interconnected concepts is implicated. Consequently, the connections that must be followed involve not just one but a number of different strands.

The first of these strands concerns the necessity for any creature capable of directed and organized behaviour to have some grasp of the distinction between itself and the world, and so between subjectivity and objectivity. This distinction, simple though it may seem, appears in a number of different forms, one of which is that between subjective and objective *space*. The grasp of subjective space is, as evident in Chapter 2, directly ties to the possibility of action, but since the issue here is the very connection between action and spatiality, this spatialized form of the distinction between subjectivity and objectivity cannot be assumed. The same is true for certain other concepts implicated in agency, but which carry with them immediate and obvious connotations of spatiality. Thus, although the distinction between self and world is also implicit in the concept of body-image or body-schema, which concept is also directly implicated in action, that same concept cannot be taken for granted as usually understood, since it too already depends on the spatial and embodied existence of a subject as something grasped by that subject.

Yet the concept of body-image or body-schema is nevertheless worthy of further consideration, if only briefly, since the grasp of such a concept – or, to avoid begging the question in regard to spatiality, an analogue of it – would seem essential to any capacity for action. Shaun Gallagher has noted a good deal of confusion and obscurity surrounding uses of 'body-image', 'body-schema', and other similar terms in the literature.[2] Following Gallagher, I will use the term body-image to mean 'either a conscious representation of the body or a set of beliefs about the body', and distinguish that from the term body-schema, meaning 'a subconscious system. . . that plays an active role in monitoring and governing posture and movement'.[3] Clearly, both body-image and body-schema may have a role in action. The role of the body-schema, however, is particularly important, since, in order to be able to engage in bodily behaviour in an oriented and directed fashion, it is important that the acting creature be able to monitor the positioning and posture of its body, and parts of its body, and that it have some grasp of its gross bodily structure, so as to plan and direct its movements in the world. As humans, we call upon such bodily 'knowledge' all the time as, for instance, when we duck to avoid an overhanging branch, or when we eat some delicate foodstuff held in the fingers without biting ourselves. In this respect, we may view the body-schema as being already implicated in the idea of a creature's subjective space.[4]

Inasmuch as the body-schema, in particular, is important in enabling and controlling action, any creature capable of action must possess some grasp of itself – distinct from the world in which it is located – and thereby monitor the changes in itself that are relevant to its behaviour. Moreover, only if a creature can grasp its behaviour in terms of bodily changes – thus related to body-schema and perhaps also to body-image – will it even be possible for such a creature to act. To be capable of action is, at the very least, to be capable of bringing about some change in the world through a change in oneself. Only through 'knowing' how to bring about such self-changes can one know how to bring about changes in anything else. For creatures who have a grasp of their own embodiment, that must mean 'knowing' (though not necessarily in any conscious sense) how to bring about changes in their own bodies. It must mean having some grasp of the causal mechanisms internal to themselves. This is true in our case, but that we have a grasp of such mechanisms, and draw upon it, is not something to which we would normally give any conscious reflection. Equally, it is seldom the case that we pay conscious attention to what we actually do with our bodies in acting, and our actions usually are not dependent upon such conscious attentiveness (although there are notable exceptions such as learning some new skill or technique[5]). For this reason, we do not conceptualize actions in terms of basic bodily movements, such as 'moving my hand to the glass, raising and tipping the glass to my lips, and swallowing the water in my mouth', but rather in terms of the worldly change that is the goal of the action, in this case, my drinking of the water. Such action relies on the acting creature's grasp of various dependencies among events, and between events in itself and events in the world around it, but importantly such action also relies on grasp of the difference between the world and things in the world *on* which it acts, and that which forms a part of itself *through* which, or *by means of* which, it acts.

We might call the 'trying to bring about', which is involved in acting, an event of 'willing'. Talk of 'willing', 'trying to bring about', or some 'act of volition' can, however, easily obscure the fact that such willing does not, in itself, provide the *means* by which some enacted intention modifies an object or event that is otherwise distinct from it. Therefore, when I decide to take a drink of water from the glass before me, it is not that my willing forms the causal bridge between my intending to drink and my drinking. Rather, it is that my willing is made effective through my being able to take hold of the glass with my hand, raise it to my lips, tip it forward just enough to allow water to flow into my mouth, and then perform the muscular contractions necessary for me to swallow. Indeed, it is unclear that the concept of willing has any content independent of the particular capacities through which it is exercised, and those capacities are understood through their causal intermeshing with other objects and events in the world. To understand what it is *to will* something, then, is to understand what it is *to do* something – even in cases where the doing may fail or be frustrated.[6] Hence, it is furthermore unclear whether I can even intend something, rather than merely desire that it be the case, unless I also have some idea of how to go about doing what is required to effect such something.

In emphasizing the need for a creature to have a grasp of how to bring things about by bringing things about in its own body, I am not suggesting that in acting we first 'will' some bodily movement, which then brings something about in the world – as if action always involved a sort of double occurrence in which what we do is only the first of those occurrences, namely, making something happen internally to our bodies, and the second occurrence is something apart from that. There is only one occurrence at issue in action and that is the occurrence that is the bringing about, which may be of an intended or, in the case of thwarted action, an unintended outcome, but which is, in both cases, a bringing about of something in the world. Nor am I suggesting that willing always involves a doing or trying to do and that such willing or trying to do itself presupposes a grasp of how one might go about such doing. To suppose that I might will, or try to do, something yet not know how to go about doing it – not know any possible means to the intended end – is incoherent. This is not to say that one must grasp the entire causal structure of some action or event, rather that one must have a basic grasp (even if not a fully conscious one) of the causal structure through which the intended outcome can be effected, or at least initiated.

The distinction between self and world is not only important as it figures in the structure of action but also as it is necessary for action to be conceptualized *as* action. To act is to bring things about in a purposeful and directed fashion. It involves *activity* or *agency*, and, in this respect, action is to be contrasted with a state of passivity, that which merely happens to one and which one simply observes. To be capable of action is to be capable of distinguishing, within one's experience, between active and merely passive effects. A lack of such capability would make controlling or directing action impossible, since it would effectively undermine the knowledge of one's own powers and capacities – whether to affect changes in the world or in oneself – on which the ability to act depends. One particularly good, though very limited, example of this basic point is cited by James Russell. He writes:

> Fruit flies. . . produce an 'optokinetic reaction,' meaning that they turn in the direction of world movements: if a stimulus moves to their left they produce a leftward movement. Now consider the consequences of the animal's being unable to distinguish between self-caused and world-caused changes in the visual input. A stimulus moves leftwards across the animals' visual field, the fly moves its head to the left, the visual field appears to move to the animal's right, so the fly moves to the *right*, causing the visual field to appear to move to the left. . . Clearly, if the fly were treating the apparent, self-caused movements of the visual field as real movements it would become as paralysed as Buridan's ass each time it made the optokinetic reaction. It must, therefore, be capable of coding self-generated changes in visual output *as* such.[7]

The fruit fly case is used by Russell to support a more general thesis to the effect that, in the absence of a grasp of the distinction between self and world (or between changes in perceptual inputs that are the result of one's activity as against one's passivity) action is impossible. A creature that lacked such a grasp would be completely paralysed. My additional claim is that such a creature would lack not only a capacity for action but also a capacity for mental life.

Although he directs much attention to the idea of agency, the distinction between self and world – or between subjectivity and objectivity – is also a central focus of Strawson's discussion in *Individuals*. There, he explains his version of this distinction as obtaining 'between those particular occurrences, processes, states or conditions which are experiences or states of consciousness of one's own, and those particulars which are not experiences or states of consciousness of one's own, or of anyone else's either, though they may be objects of such experiences'. He adds: 'Thus, if a tree is struck by lightning, that is one kind of happening; and if I see the tree being struck by lightning; that is another kind of happening. The knife entering my flesh is one kind of event, and my feeling the pain is another.'[8] Strawson subsequently proceeds to ask what is required in order for this distinction to be grasped. More specifically, his interest is in identifying the conditions under which it is possible for a creature to be capable of identifying thoughts about 'objective particulars', where such particulars are understood as 'particulars distinguished by the thinker from himself and from his own experiences or states of mind, and regarded as actual or possible states of those experiences'.[9] In essence, Strawson asks after the prerequisites for a certain grasp of objectivity, even if it is an objectivity that differs, in certain respects, from that employed by, for instance, Nagel.[10]

So far, I have been careful to put the distinction between self and world that is implicated in the Strawsonian notion of objectivity – and its necessary implication with agency – in ways that leave open the question of any connection between that distinction and any concept of spatiality (whether in general or in particular). There is good reason to suppose, however, that, in conceptual terms, objectivity cannot be divorced from objective *space*. Indeed, as Gareth Evans points out, it is often assumed that to have a concept of things as existing objectively and, therefore, independently of any subject is to have a concept of things as existing in space. He notes that 'the connection between space and objectivity lies so deep in our conceptual scheme that many philosophers pass from "objective" to "outer" without even noticing the question they beg. The subjective being regarded as what is "in the mind," the objective becomes what is "without the mind," and then it is easy to say with Hobbes that if we have a conception of a thing without the mind, we have a conception of space.'[11] Evans does not, in fact, argue against the implication of a concept of spatiality in the concept of objectivity, but he does encourage the exploration of the reasons for, and the nature of, this connection. It is precisely such an exploration that

Strawson undertakes in *Individuals*, with his attempt to describe the world of a creature that lacks a grasp of space but possesses a grasp of objectivity. In the 'conceptual scheme' vocabulary of Strawson (a vocabulary that has problems of its own), the question is: 'Could there be a scheme, providing for a system of objective particulars, which was wholly non-spatial?'[12]

Strawson notes that this question, along with the general form of his inquiry – and, in part, its content – is reminiscent of Kant.[13] In fact, Strawson's discussion, and Evans's own position, develops and builds upon a set of fundamentally Kantian intuitions about the connection between spatiality and objectivity; an important theme in Kant's writing from the Critical and the pre-Critical periods. Kant takes the idea of separate and distinct existence at a time to depend necessarily on the concept of space, such that 'objective' and 'spatial' turn out to be co-referring expressions. This point is obscured by often ambiguous language, making it appear as though Kant is begging the question at issue in a way similar to that noted by Evans, when he repeats the observation that Kant equivocates between using 'outer' to mean 'spatial' and also 'objective'.[14] Thus, in his 'Inaugural Dissertation' of 1770, Kant writes: 'I cannot conceive anything as located outside me unless I represent it as in a space different from the space in which I myself am, nor can I conceive things as outside one another unless I arrange them in different parts of space.'[15] Again, in the *Critique of Pure Reason*, he comments that 'space is the condition. . . under which alone outer intuition is possible for us'.[16] If 'outer' here is taken to mean 'spatial' then these assertions seem quite trivial and otiose. Only if 'outer' means 'objective' – at least in the sense of possessing a separate and distinct existence – do such assertions have any point, and, if in this sense, then they do indeed have a very significant point to them.

In Kant, we seem to find the basis to argue that only with a grasp of space is it possible to understand particulars as both distinct and co-existing, and such an argument seems to lie at the heart, for instance, of the B Edition's 'Refutation of Idealism'. A very similar argument, as Onora O'Neill points out, is also found in the early work of Bertrand Russell, who writes that: 'the possibility of a diversity of simultaneously existing things. . . cannot be given by time alone, but only by a form of externality for simultaneous parts of one presentation. We could never, in other words, infer the existence of diverse but interrelated things, unless the object of sense-perception could have substantial complexity, and for such complexity we require a form of externality other than time.'[17] However, the claim that only the externality of space allows for the simultaneous differentiation necessary for objectivity is one that requires a certain amount of unpacking before we can see what is really at issue.

Strawson's treatment of this question begins with his construction of an imaginary world, called the 'No-Space world,'[18] which is grasped in purely auditory terms. He thus acknowledges that we can grasp some spatial properties of things through hearing, and notes that 'where sense-experience is not only auditory in character, but also at least tactual and kinaesthetic as well – or, as it is in most cases, tactual and kinaesthetic and visual as well – we can then sometimes assign spatial predicates on the strength of hearing alone'.[19] Nevertheless, he denies that it follows from this that there would be any spatial concepts in a form of experience that was purely auditory in character. Sounds, according to Strawson, 'have no intrinsic spatial characteristics',[20] and no set of auditory experiences alone 'would suffice to generate spatial concepts'.[21] This last point is one that we may wish to dispute – as does Onora O'Neill, for instance[22] – but we can, at least for the moment, grant the point to Strawson.

In its general form, the concept of objectivity is tied to the concept of independence from the particular perspective of the experiencing, thinking subject. For Strawson, a more specific form appears in the notion that what exists objectively continues to exist when not being perceived. The question whether there are objective particulars in a purely auditory world can thus be understood to consist, in large part, in the question whether such a world can accommodate the existence of particulars when they are unperceived. The latter, of course, depends on the possibility of being able, not merely to identify particulars, but also to re-identify them as numerically identical – that is, as the same particular encountered on some previous occasion. In order for particulars to be understood as continuing to exist while unperceived – such that those particulars can be identified and re-identified – Strawson argues that what is required is 'a dimension other than the temporal in which unperceived particulars could be thought of as simultaneously existing *in some kind of systematic relation to one another*, and to perceived particulars'.[23] Ordinarily, one would turn to space as providing such a dimension, but since he claims that 'the idea of place, and with it that of a spatial system of objects, cannot be given a meaning in purely auditory terms',[24] Strawson argues for some *'analogy of Space'*,[25] or spatial analogue, sufficient to allow particulars to be located in relation to one another and, thereby, to allow a required analogue of distance ('of *nearer to* and *further away from*') and position.[26]

Such a spatial analogue can be provided in a purely auditory world, so Strawson claims, through the existence of a 'sound of a certain distinctive timbre. . . [that] is heard continuously, at a constant loudness, though with varying pitch. . . [and that] is unique in its continuity'.[27] He compares this 'master-sound' to the whistle one sometimes hears in a malfunctioning radio as the ever-present accompaniment to the other sounds it is meant to produce. As one moves from frequency to frequency, and from one station to another, the whistle also changes in pitch, such that each station can be associated with the distinct pitch of its accompanying whistle.

In similar fashion, the master-sound is heard continuously as the background to every other sound; different sounds can thereby be 'located' at different points on the master-sound; and, through the ordering afforded by the ordering of pitch, each sound can be located as at some definite position in relation to every other sound.[28] The introduction of the master-sound thus provides a unitary dimension within which a multiplicity of other sounds can be 'laid out', and within which those sounds can be grasped as existing simultaneously but independent of one another. Strawson takes this analogue of space as sufficient to allow for the possibility of a system of objective particulars and, so, for the possibility of particulars that may exist unperceived. Whether it is sufficient to allow for a distinction between self and world is, however, another matter.[29] On Strawson's account, a system of objective particulars implies nothing about the existence of a subject as distinct from those particulars. It seems to provide merely a framework that allows the characterization of particulars, both perceived and unperceived, as existing at some location on the master-sound. This presents a problem for Strawson, one to which he pays relatively little attention.

Evans sees Strawson's argument aligned with the Kantian connection between objectivity and spatiality, and Strawson does appear to repeat the claim, found in Kant and in Bertrand Russell, that, in Russell's words quoted above, 'the possibility of a diversity of simultaneously existing things. . . cannot be given by time alone, but only by a form of externality'. Where Strawson differs from Kant and Russell is in his view that such externality need only take the form of an 'analogy of Space', rather than being spatial in any 'literal' sense. Given the ambiguity that attaches to the notion of space, one might question the basis for Strawson's contrast of the literal and the analogical – a contrast that might raise problems of its own. In any case, it seems that Strawson does not provide only an analogue of space, because, in order for the master-sound to function as an analogue, a prior concept of spatiality is required.

Strawson emphasizes, as noted above, that purely auditory experience is itself insufficient to generate spatial concepts. With the introduction of the master-sound, however, it seems that he must mean only that purely auditory experience is incapable of generating any spatial concepts in the 'literal' sense, yet nonetheless capable of generating analogues of those concepts. This is somewhat puzzling (especially since Strawson's purely auditory world seems to provide no basis for grasping any 'literal' sense of spatiality). How can one grasp an analogical sense when one has no grasp of the literal? Furthermore, why should we take the master-sound to be an analogue of *space* at all? In the auditory world, we are presented only a temporally ordered sequence of sounds: one continuous tone that rises or falls in pitch, together with a variety of other sounds that accompany it. Indeed, from the point of view of any experiencing subject, such a world is experienced solely in terms of varying sounds accompanied by a tone of fluctuating pitch. Surely, this purely temporal experience could only be construed as having a non-temporal aspect to it if one *already* had prior access to a concept of non-temporal dimensionality. With that, the idea of the master-sound could then be used to give content to this notion of non-temporal dimensionality, but it seems that the master-sound is inadequate to do this in its own terms.

Such inadequacy is made especially clear in the notion that we are supposed to think of the various pitches that the master-sound can carry as positions to which an experiencing creature can move. Thinking of that sort is problematic, since Strawson's envisaged auditory experience provides only the idea of change in experience, and, since not every change in experience involves movement, no grasp of mere *experiential change* can count as a grasp of *positional change*. Indeed, it seems likely that the very idea of treating changes of pitch that the master-sound carries as being analogous to changes of position only arises because of a prior grasp of spatiality; that which provides a model for such an interpretation of those changes. Evans is thus not far wrong – although the grounds he adduces for the claim are slightly different – when he says that 'the space Strawson extracted out of the concept of objectivity is the space he smuggled into it'. Or, in terms of the argument I have presented, the master-sound provides an 'analogy of Space' only in that it assumes a prior concept of space.

One of the persistent tendencies in thinking about space, a tendency that undoubtedly derives from the primacy accorded to the scientific understanding of space, is to treat it as properly just a *particular* form of non-temporal dimensionality. There is, however, no reason to suppose that space and time are anything other than the basic forms of dimensionality *as such* – of simultaneous or co-present dimensionality, in the case of space, and of sequential or successive dimensionality, in the case of time. Although, rather than thinking of them as separate forms, time and space should probably be seen as constitutive of dimensionality proper, inasmuch as they are tied together. Thus, a point in space has no dimensionality except through time, and a point in time has no dimensionality except through space (this indicates the artificiality of the idea of a point in space or time, as well as the necessity of thinking time and space to be always conjoined). If space is indeed thought of in this way – in terms of the idea of co-present dimensionality – then to have a grasp of a dimension in which there can exist independent and simultaneous particulars is precisely to have a grasp of space. Strawson, it seems, assumes a 'literal' conception of spatiality as just a particular form of simultaneous or co-present dimensionality, namely, that understood in terms of the simultaneous dimensionality of *physical* extension. He is thus led to posit the need for a grasp of dimensionality that is other than, but 'analogous' to, the spatial.

Presumably, this is also what leads him to suppose that one can generate a form of simultaneous dimensionality from non-spatial experience. If one takes simultaneous dimensionality to be identical with spatiality, then experience that is too impoverished to provide for a grasp of spatial dimensionality will also be too impoverished to provide for any form of simultaneous dimensionality. Furthermore, if that is so, then it is likely that auditory experience is not alone in lacking the resources required here. Perhaps no single sensory modality can provide any real analogue of the simultaneous dimensionality that is spatiality.

Consider the case of vision – a modality that is, I suspect, often assumed unproblematically to entail a grasp of spatial dimensionality. In fact, the visual field provides no proper sense of dimensionality, since it offers no way of conceptualizing the relations between elements within it. Purely visual experience provides only an array of colours and shades. Discrimination of simultaneous particulars is not yet a grasp of any proper dimension within which those particulars can be located. Those colours and shades cannot even be grasped as located 'above' or 'to the right of' oneself or one another since those orientations are not given in purely visual terms but depend on a grasp of the whole body in space (the sensation of depth in visual experience is similarly a function of more than visual input alone). One might be able to grasp the overall pattern of particulars, but that does not suggest a grasp of dimensionality as much as it does an ability to grasp the visual field in terms of a single unitary presentation. In this respect, when Strawson claims that 'the momentary states of the colour-patches of the visual scene visibly exhibit spatial relations to each another at a moment',[30] he seems to assume too much. This becomes especially apparent when he contrasts that claim with the case of sound, saying that 'the momentary states of the sound-patches of the auditory scene do not audibly exhibit the auditory analogue of spatial relations to each other at a moment'.[31] The visual array is a set of qualitatively discriminable particulars that together make up a differentiated visual field. Vision is therefore little different from any other sensory modality. Although Strawson is dubious about talk of an auditory or tactile field,[32] if by such a field we mean simply an array of discriminable and simultaneously presented sensory particulars, then such a field is possible for each sensory modality. Moreover, to the extent that each modality is paired with a certain sensory array or field, each modality affords nothing more than the bare dimensionality associated with the presentation of discriminable particulars within a unitary but 'flat' and isotropic field. Inasmuch as a proper sense of dimensionality can only be derived from auditory experience when gained in conjunction with the experience of the other senses, the full dimensionality from any sense can only be derived in conjunction with the others.

I noted above that Strawson does not regard the system of objective location that he describes, at least in its bare form, as sufficient for a distinction between self and world. He acknowledges that a grasp of the latter distinction would suffice for a grasp of the former notion, but a grasp of the existence of objective particulars alone will not, he claims, suffice for a grasp of the distinction between self and world. Strawson sees an 'attractive' line of reasoning that would have it otherwise, on the grounds that the distinction between observed and unobserved particulars surely implies a distinction between self and world, especially since the distinction between observed and unobserved appears to depend on observers 'thinking of *themselves* as being at different places at different times'.[33] Nevertheless, Strawson posits that this line of resistance can and should be resisted. He then advances a means for drawing the distinction 'parallel in other respects to the ordinary "observed-unobserved" distinction' which has no need to call upon any idea 'such as we ordinarily express by the first person singular pronoun and associated forms'.[34] The means proposed is a form of report-writing that records individual auditory experiences but makes no reference to the integration of those experiences with any larger experiential whole. The series of reports so generated are of the form: 'N was observed at L followed by M.'[35] The reports are completely 'objective' in that they enable the association of a particular with a location independent of any reference to an observer – or so it appears. Yet, if this is supposed to be a way by which to draw a distinction 'parallel' to that between observed and unobserved, then it seems to be a dismal failure. Within the reports, there is no distinction between observed and unobserved, since those reports contain no reference, at all, to what is unobserved. Indeed, Strawson's use of the phrase 'was observed' seems problematic, since, although the phrase need contain no reference to the observer, it is obvious that there was just such an observer. The system of objective particulars that, generously understood, is enabled by the use of the master-sound is a system that allows no more than the specification of a series of particulars-at-locations, and, considered in its own terms, provides no basis for any distinction between observed and unobserved.

Naturally, if one introduces the idea of a privileged location within the system – namely, that of the observer – then one can distinguish between what is at the observer's location, and therefore observed, and what is at some other location, and therefore unobserved. Without that introduction, there is no possibility of distinguishing observed from unobserved. Moreover, as already established, for a creature to have a grasp of some objective space – or, equally, in Strawson's terms, any analogue of such a space – the creature needs to be able to relate that space to its own experience, to its own location; that is, it must have a grasp of its subjective space. Thus, inasmuch as a grasp of the existence of objective particulars – including those that exist unperceived – depends on a grasp of some objective system of locations, so it must also depend on a grasp of one's location in relation to that system. It must therefore depend on a grasp of both objective and subjective spaces and, so, on a grasp of the distinction between self and world, between subject and object.

At one point, Strawson appears to propose a distinction, and a way of understanding that distinction, that is seemingly at odds with my emphasis on the necessary relation between a grasp of agency and a grasp of the distinction between self and world. From within the framework of the 'No-Space world', Strawson suggests a distinction with respect to the movement of such a creature (movement that will be movement up and down the master sound) between the creature's moving and the creature's being moved – between active and passive movement. Strawson seems to claim that the creature's grasp of such a distinction need not entail any grasp of the distinction between itself, as agent, and that which is other than itself and on which, or with respect to which, it acts. His proposal is that the 'reports' of experiences simply need to be capable of a distinction like that present in 'scientific papers, in which a distinction is nevertheless made between what was *done*, and what was found to happen [and]. . . we shall not need, in the language of the reports, a distinction between a personal and an impersonal form'.[36]

What Strawson's considerations here leave out, however, is precisely the question as to how a creature could be capable of acting in the 'No-Space world' without a grasp of the distinction between itself and the world in which it acts. The possibility of such action is, on the account I advanced earlier, essential to the possibility of that creature being capable of any thought or experience. Moreover, the possibility of action raises many more questions about the world that Strawson envisages. How, for instance, would a creature inhabiting the 'No-Space world' grasp its own embodiment in that world, and what form would that embodiment take? Strawson gestures towards some of these problems near the end of his discussion, but he concludes that, so far as such complications are concerned, 'the fantasy, besides being tedious, would be difficult, to elaborate'.[37] Evans, too, briefly considers the complications introduced by the preconditions for agency. With respect to the conception of the world that the subject – Evans calls him Hero – would need to possess in Strawson's auditory universe, he writes that 'sounds would have to occupy space, and not merely be located in it, so that the notions of force and impenetrability would somehow have to have a place, and we may well wonder whether we can make sense of this without providing Hero with an impenetrable body and allowing him to be an agent in, and manipulator of, his world'.[38] Without completely rejecting this approach, Evans adds that 'perhaps this is the wrong line to pursue'. Yet much of his discussion of Strawson draws attention to the way in which any adequate conception of the 'No-Space world' would need to draw upon a much richer set of interconnected concepts than Strawson seems to allow – concepts that seem to be most tightly knotted around the idea of agency.

The centrality of agency to the possibility of thought and experience was noted earlier. In addition, we can now begin to see how agency is connected to spatiality through a certain minimal notion of objectivity and, therefore, how the possibility of thought and experience might also be dependent on spatiality and objectivity. The connection between spatiality and objectivity, however, requires further exploration – an exploration that depends itself on additional clarification of the nature of agency and its preconditions, in particular, the connection between agency and causality. Indeed, it is the notion of causality that plays a large part in enabling a richer and more detailed conception of the connection between agency, objectivity, and spatiality. The grasp of agency, along with the very capacity to act, is indeed inseparable from a grasp of oneself as causally embedded in the world. On some accounts, however, the concept of causality is secondary to the concept of agency, that being precisely the point of agent-centred theories of action and of causation, according to which the idea of causation is dependent upon, or derived from, a particular conception of agency as an event of 'bringing about'. Timothy O'Connor states that 'the core element of the concept [of causality] is a *primitive* notion of the production or "bringing about" of an effect',[39] and this is arrived at through the experience of such bringing about in one's own productive agency. Moreover, just as agency provides experience of the power to bring about, it also provides experience of the baulking of such 'bringing about' by factors that would appear to be beyond our control. The experience of agency thus seems to provide the basis for a grasp of both causal power, as it is given in and through our own bodies, and of resistance to such power, as it is experienced in the resistance of the world to our bodily exertions. Such a view is advanced explicitly by Thomas Baldwin, who writes that 'it is through the experience of agency that we get a grasp of bodily power, and thus of causation'.[40]

An important premise in Baldwin's account is the previously discussed idea that action is not to be understood as involving some act of will apart from bodily movement but as encompassing such movement: 'The experience of agency is, therefore, not simply one of acts of will regularly, but mysteriously, conjoined with bodily movements; it is one of acts of will that extend themselves to those parts of the body that are under direct control of the agent' and the experience of agency is the 'irreducible experience of bodily power'.[41] Baldwin claims that the experience of bodily power is an experience of possibility – a direct experience of bringing about – while the experience of worldly resistance to bodily exertion is an experience of impossibility. Since such impossibility is seen to be grounded in what lies outside ourselves – in external forces that act upon us – it brings with it the idea of an objective realm that is causally effective in blocking the successful exercise of our bodily powers. On this basis, Baldwin arrives at the conclusion that the grasp of causation is dependent on our experience of power and resistance, of possibility and impossibility, in the exercise of agency.[42] Yet although the grasp of causality is closely tied to the grasp of agency, there is reason to dispute Baldwin's further claim that the grasp of causality is grounded in, or arrived at through, the grasp of agency.

Baldwin focuses, to a large extent, on the experience of touch as the primary modality in which the resistance of the world and its objects is evident – 'e.g., my experience now as I press against the table'.[43] He later extends this experience of resistance analogously to other sensory modalities, notably sight: 'By finding that some aspects of the content of visual experience, unlike its direction, are not subject to the will, a subject encounters a kind of impossibility within visual experience (a visual analogue of tactile resistance).'[44] Although sensory receptivity is, to a greater or lesser extent, dependent on some capacity for agency (even if only a capacity to orient one's sense organs to sources of perceptual stimulation), mere sensory receptivity does not count as the active exercise of any bodily power; a fact made clear in the discussion of Strawson's 'No-Space world'. Moreover, just as the mere receipt of sensory stimuli does not count as agency, neither does any single sense – neither touch or vision – deliver any experience of power or resistance, or of possibility or impossibility.

When I press my hand against a table and experience its resistance, my grasp of this as resistance derives from a combination of immediate sensory information and my more general grasp of the causal powers of both my body and objects in the world. That is, in order to grasp the act of pressing my hand against the table as both an exercise, or attempted exercise, of a bodily power and as an instance of resistance to such power, I already need to grasp a network of concepts including the concept of causality. Agency is thus not the basis for the grasp of causality. Instead, the capacity for agency depends on a grasp of causal structure. Indeed, it is generally difficult to see how one could understand oneself as 'bringing something about' unless one already had a grasp of oneself as capable of operating as a cause. This does not mean, however, that agency is secondary to causality (the reverse of the position promoted by Baldwin and proponents of some agent-centred theories of causation), but rather that agency and causality are both part of a larger network of concepts. Just as notions of objective and subjective space are neither reducible one to the other, and yet also implicate one another in various ways, the same is true of the concepts of causality and agency. The same 'topographical' structure applies as that which I sketched out in Chapter 1, and as that which also seems to obtain between concepts of subjective and objective space.

The notion of causality as part of the necessary background that embeds agency is a point that Baldwin seems briefly to consider (but to which he apparently gives little attention) when he introduces the idea of causality as grounded in the experience of agency. Baldwin cites Heidegger's criticism of

Max Scheler's claim that 'the having of existence as something that is there is. . . based. . . alone upon the resistance of the entity originally experienced solely in the act of striving'.[45] Although Heidegger notes his agreement with certain aspects of Scheler's position (notably, his rejection of the idea that the grasp of things is primarily based upon 'intellectual functions'), he also points out that the experience of resistance is not the basic phenomenon here, saying 'resistance is a phenomenal character which already presupposes a world'.[46] This point does not merely operate against any attempt to take resistance as a fundamental concept, but also against any attempt to take the experience of bodily action as fundamental – whether such action is understood in terms of the exercise or the baulking of bodily powers.[47]

Baldwin's argument for the grounding of causality in agency is presented as part of a larger argument for the claim that objectivity and agency are closely connected. Baldwin claims, in fact, that to conceive a creature as capable of experiencing an objective world is also to conceive of that creature as an agent,[48] and he argues for this claim on the basis of considerations not dissimilar to those adduced above. Although not entirely explicit, the reasoning that underlies Baldwin's approach seems to consist in two parts. First, that a creature incapable of action would be one to which beliefs would not be attributable on the grounds that beliefs are essentially states defined by their role in the explanation of action.[49] Second, that a creature lacking beliefs would be a creature that could not be understood as capable of perception or, at least, would not be capable of enjoying 'objective perceptions'.[50] The latter inference depends on the claim that 'in assigning objective content to a perception, we think of it as a representation for the subject of features of its environment, and to think of it as such is precisely to think of the role of the perception in the subject's cognitive economy'.[51]

Baldwin's discussion of the connection between agency and objectivity eventually leads on to his investigation of the further connection between agency and causality – the latter being the focus of the discussion above – but prior to that he briefly considers the connection between the terms additional to agency here, namely, objectivity and causality. In so doing, Baldwin refers to Gareth Evans, who countenances the possibility that an investigation of agency might serve to illuminate the connection between spatiality and objectivity. Baldwin claims that the spatial location of some experience is not sufficient to establish the objectivity of that experience (citing, as an example, the case of pains that are experienced as located, but which are not objective features in that they are not independent of the subject's experience[52]). He then adds that 'if one does not rely on the spatiality of the objects of objective experience to provide a context for discussion of the relationship between objectivity and agency, then some other point of entry is required. . . I suggest that considerations of causality provide one'.[53] Continuing the argument, Baldwin posits that experience can be grasped as objective only if grasped as causally related to the things in the world that are the objects of experience, and, on this basis, he attempts to show that the grasp of causality derives from the experience of agency. In rejecting this idea that causality is somehow reducible to agency, I also implicitly reject the idea that causality, itself, provides any alternative means of understanding objectivity, other than one which sees it as essentially connected with spatiality. Indeed, a closer consideration of the connection of objectivity and causality provides the ground on which the interconnection of both with spatiality, as well as with agency, can be exhibited.

The connection between agency, causality, and objectivity does not reside merely in the need for perceptual states – or indeed for other states such as beliefs – to be causally connected with those objects that are also part of the content of those states, but which are otherwise independent of the perceiver or believer. Agency, perception, and belief require a grasp of objects as existing independently of the subject, but they also require that the sensory particulars through which those objects are grasped are organized in such a way that they can be understood as sensations that relate to objects in the first place. Accordingly, the idea of a creature that grasps its world 'objectively', simply through the grasping of certain sensory particulars as located within that world, is fundamentally incoherent. If we accept, on the basis of the arguments already advanced, that agency is essential for the possibility of thought and experience, then the capacity for agency is dependent on the agent being possessed of an organized field of experience within which to act; that is, on experience being organized in a way that connects with the agent's grasp of its own possibilities for action and of the possibilities available within the world. An agent whose experience cannot be correlated with a grasp of its own powers of agency will be an agent incapable of acting, and an agent whose grasp of its powers of agency are completely disconnected from the world will be equally so.[54]

Only if experience is appropriately ordered, and different elements within experience are seen to stand in certain relations to one another, is it possible to order one's actions so as to bring about changes within the field of experience. In short, agency requires the grasp of an objective order that is given in experience, and so given in a way accessible to the agent. Indeed, it seems that experience itself, in requiring an ability to refer experience to objects in the world, also requires the ordering of sensory particulars around concrete objects, which, in turn, combine different experienced properties into a single unified appearance. Thus, I experience the flat and smooth surface before me as also solid and heavy, as marked with various lines and whorls, as having a glossy finish that reflects the light, as capable of supporting the weight of other objects and parts of my body, and as placed on top of other structures that support the said surface in a position some distance above the floor. What I see in front of me is the varnished, wooden desk at which

I sit, and my experience is organized in terms of the desk as a concrete object before me. The organization of the various experienced properties – smoothness, heaviness, reflectivity, and so forth – in terms of their inter-related presentation as part of a single object, reflects the same sort of inter-relation that is characteristic of thought and experience in general; the same sort we saw exhibited in the inter-relation of memory as part of a single life, in the inter-relation of beliefs and other attitudes, and in the inter-relation of action with other actions and with attitudes and experiences. Significantly, such inter-relation is not only that between elements of *experience*, but also that found in the object, and the objective elements, which are themselves *experienced*. It is also an ordering that is fundamentally tied to a grasp of causal relations.

The grasp of the inter-relation of properties in the object cannot be merely an abstract grasp of features, as if nothing more than portrayals. Take the example of a painting – perhaps one produced by a devotee of photo-realism, but nevertheless a painting – a still-life of some assemblage of everyday things, fruit, tools, cans of soup. We experience the elements in the painting as interconnected, but that experience is very different from the way in which we experience the elements when they are united in reality. In a painting of apples or pears, the elements stand in different causal relations to one another, and to the picture as a whole, than do the elements that make up some actual assemblage of apples or pears. Grasping a painting as a painting and a pear as a pear is not so much a matter of properly categorizing what is presented (the figural presentations may be very similar) but more of grasping both the different causal interconnections among the elements and one's own different causal relation to the object. The unification of elements or properties in an object is thus a matter of their causal integration and of the object's integration into a larger causal structure.

There is, however, a line of argument that could be interposed at this point to upset the supposed need for experience to be organized around objects; one which might even be taken to operate against the idea that a grasp of space requires a grasp of both objective and subjective space. John Campbell, for instance, seems to argue that we can have some sort of grasp of an objective space without a grasp of objects. Campbell takes issue with the Strawsonian claim that the identification and re-identification of places depends on the identification and re-identification of objects (and vice versa).[55] Instead, he presents the idea of a system for the re-identification of places that relies not on the re-identification of objects but of features.

Campbell's example, however, seems not to represent a case where there is any grasp of space, nor any model for an account of experience that would be independent of a grasp of subjectivity and objectivity. It is an example that could certainly apply to a purely mechanical system, and, perhaps on some versions, to Strawson's exclusively auditory world, but it is otherwise problematic. The 'subject' in this system guides its activities by simply following a set of in-built instructions that require it to keep certain features constant or to follow a certain sequence of features. A human navigator could, for instance, guide his course by keeping some simple feature constant – 'steer always with the wind at your back'; 'keep on a course that has the setting sun at your right shoulder'. Such a feature-based guidance system is, however, inadequate to model any conceptual grasp of space and position, or to serve as a navigational system, except when conjoined with other capacities. It might be said that a pigeon has this sort of minimal 'grasp' of navigation, but even it is a grasp embedded within a broader set of experiential capacities that require a richer characterization than suggested by Campbell's example. Thus, although a navigational space, and a set of places within it, can be structured in this feature-based fashion, it can only model a grasp of space when embedded in a set of other capacities that include the capacity for some minimal grasp of objects. Agency and the very possibility of experience requires, then, that sensory particulars be ordered in a way that enables the creature to whom those particulars are presented, to grasp the interconnections between particulars and between the world and the creature's own active capacities. This understanding not only enables a better grasp of the connection between agency, objectivity, and causality, but also a better grasp of the way in which all three connect with spatiality.

The concept of objectivity stands in a crucial relation to that of causality, both in terms of the ordering of action and experience, and in terms of objectivity itself. To grasp something as an object is precisely to grasp the way in which a set of parts are combined together, and such combination is fundamentally dependent on causal connection. This is not only true so far as an object's temporal parts are concerned – two temporally distinct components are part of a single object only if there is some appropriate causal connection between them – but also in relation to spatially extended objects. Indeed, the sort of causal connection most important for agency seems to be precisely the connectedness seen to obtain between parts of the same object at a time and between parts of different objects at a time. Furthermore, only if we have a grasp of objects as spatially extended can we have a grasp of the way in which modification of one thing can result in a modification of something else. This is, of course, exactly what we must be able to do in acting, whereby we effect a change in something that exists contemporaneously with us by effecting a change in our bodies.

In this respect, too, it is the spatial differentiation of our bodies that enables us to grasp the possibility of a differentiation in action that can, in turn, be related to differential effects in the world. Only inasmuch as I can grasp differences in myself – that is to say in my own body, however such differences are perceived – can I bring about different changes in myself, and my grasp of these bodily differences is tied to my ability to grasp the various causal connections that obtain between my world and myself. Something of this same point is evident in Kant's emphasis on the way in which a grasp of spatiality is tied to our grasp of bodily differentiation and orientation. He posits that 'our geographical knowledge, and even our commonest knowledge of the position of places, would be of no aid to us if we could not, by reference to the sides of our bodies, assign to regions the things so ordered and the whole system of mutually relative positions'.[56]

In this respect, it is notable that a large part of the problem with Strawson's 'No-Space world' concerns the manner in which a creature with only an auditory sense could possibly grasp its orientation within an exclusively auditory word – even given the presence of the master-sound. Since the master-sound provides a means of establishing direction, given a point from which those directions are taken, and so a creature within the auditory world could presumably grasp differences in pitch between one location and another and thereby grasp the idea of a certain direction, either up or down the scale: *this* sound stands in a direction of lower pitch (where the idea of 'lower than' is understood in purely mathematical terms) from *that* sound. How, though, could this difference in perceptual discrimination translate into a difference in capacity to control movement? Such control of movement would be impossible without some differentiation internal to the creature itself – some internal differentiation that allows for external orientation. A purely auditory world, however, or any world that is presented in terms of only one sensory dimension,[57] would seem incapable of providing the resources to support such differentiation and orientation.

Within a purely auditory world, it would seem impossible to have a grasp of one's body, either as extended in space or as possessing a certain bilateral asymmetry, and, without that, it would seem impossible to orient oneself in terms of ahead, behind, above, below, to the right, and to the left – let alone to be able to grasp one's body as possessed of differentiated causal capacities. In the absence of such a grasp of bodily capacities or orientation, it would be impossible to exercise one's capacities for action in the coordinated and directed fashion that such action would require. Embodiment – one's extended and differentiated location in space – and the grasp of such embodiment would thus seem essential to the possibility of agency, and therefore of experience and thought. Sarah Furness summarizes these matters:

> A disembodied intelligence could have position, but no extension, hence no discernible parts, therefore it cannot rotate. It would have no extension and therefore no sides or directions; there is no possibility for it to discriminate

> any distinction within itself. A disembodied intelligence would be unable to know either its own position or the position of anything else, because it could not assign itself position. . . or an orientation. There could be no possibility of such consciousnesses even looking in different directions. . . an intelligence with position but no extension would not be capable of making any distinction between the fact of experience and what it experienced; that is, it would not be capable of even a minimal distinction between subjectivity and objectivity.[58]

I would only add that such an 'intelligence' would not be one to which any mental life could be attributed, and therefore would not be an 'intelligence' at all.

Inasmuch as the capacity for action is tied to the capacities of the body, so the particular capacities for action of any particular creature are evident in the particular differentiation of that creature's body.[59] Moreover, the complexity of the body, and of bodily movement, itself reflects the complexity of behaviour of which the creature is capable. It is indeed the case, as Ludwig Wittgenstein puts it, that 'the human body is the best picture of the human soul',[60] although this claim need not be restricted only to the human. Grasping the capacities for action that are present in one's own body is a large part of what is involved in the grasp of one's own subjective space. Grasping such a space is just a matter of grasping the possible dimensions of action that arise out of one's own capacities for agency and receptivity in conjunction with a particular worldly situation – a situation that is itself disclosed in relation to, and by means of, those capacities. Agency depends, then, on a grasp of events and objects, including the structure of one's own body, laid out within a complex spatio-temporal structure that is the very frame of action. Indeed, the possibility of agency resides in the possibility of just such a complex structure, within which are related both subjective and objective elements.

Of course, since the possibility of agency is tied to the possibility of mental life, we are returned to the idea that the structure of mental life is dependent on the structure of spatio-temporal embodiment within an objective world. The structure and possibility of mental states – memory, desire, belief, and others – is inseparable from the structure and possibility of active involvement with the world and with the very structure of the world manifested through such involvement. Somewhat provocatively, one might say that to have beliefs (or any other mental state) is to have a capacity for embodied and oriented agency, which is most directly expressed as a capacity for a certain sort of complex but organized movement. To have knowledge or an understanding of the world in general, then, is fundamentally a matter of being able to act and move within that world, and do so in a certain complex and organized fashion. One might go on to suggest – perhaps even more provocatively – that epistemology is actually an inquiry into the possibility of movement and agency. In fact, a sense of 'knowledge' that captures the idea of its connection to agency and movement – and to spatiality and locality – is found, somewhat curiously, in contemporary London. There, prospective cab-drivers must pass a test called 'The Knowledge'. It is not a test of driving skills, but of a candidate's familiarity with the urban geography of central London, more particularly with the 15,842 streets, and the public buildings and amenities on those streets, which lie within a six-mile radius of Charing Cross. This sense of knowledge is tied closely to a quite particular locale, but for a London cabbie 'The Knowledge' is not merely that of street names and locations – even if formalized as routes or 'runs' from one place to another – but above all else it is a knowledge of and ability to move around a particular region.[61]

It is easy to view, and perhaps dismiss, this sense of knowledge as simply a specific form of navigational or narrowly 'spatial' knowledge. 'The knowledge' of the London cab-driver, however, can also be seen as illustrative of the fundamental grounding of knowledge, not in an abstract grasp of propositions (though language does have an important role to play in the possibility of knowledge), but in bodily capacities for action and movement – in the concrete grasp of one's own located existence and the spatio-temporal structure of the world. Moreover, it illustrates the way in which a grasp of particular location and spatio-temporal structure cannot be divorced from a capacity for navigation and movement. Having a grasp of one's location, or of the larger space in which one finds oneself, is essentially tied to a capacity to navigate within that space and move from location to location. A cab-driver's grasp of locations within the City of London is a grasp of just such moves, or 'runs', from one location to another. Particular locations are connected through a grasp of the pathways between them, and the grasp of the connection between locations is essentially a matter of grasping those pathways. For creatures whose grasp of the world can only ever be partial, the interconnection of locations within a space must indeed be based in the creature's own grasp of the pathways that go from the one location to the other. The unity of a particular space is thus grasped, in large part, through the unity of action and movement that is possible within that space. In the case of subjective space, such unity is tied to the subject's concrete capacities for movement and action, but in the case of objective space, it is tied to a much more abstract grasp of the sheer possibilities of movement.[62] Returning to the theme of a 'spatialized' epistemology, one might say, as a consequence of these considerations, that a creature without any capacity to find its way in the world is also a creature that lacks without any capacity for knowledge, either of the world or of itself.

Spatiality and embodiment – and so, also, the idea of the locality in which action is embedded – are essential to the possibility of agency. Moreover, since agency is, in turn, indispensable in the structure of subjectivity, then subjectivity itself can be seen as dependent on spatiality and embodiment. Quassim Cassam writes that 'self-consciousness. . . is intimately bound up with awareness of the subject "as an object" – not as an "immaterial" substance but as a physical object in a world of physical objects'.[63] Certainly, the idea of the subject is inextricably tied to the idea of an organized, differentiated body located within an objective space, even as the ordering of mental life – and therefore the psychological organization of the subject – is grounded in the ordering of the space and spaces in which the subject is located and with respect to which the subject is defined. Hence, subjectivity cannot be the ground for subjective space, because any particular subject is identified only in relation to its own located, oriented, *spatialized* agency. Even the idea of the biological organism – say, the human animal – does not provide an autonomous ground for the subjective space of action associated with such an organism. The organism – or creature – and the space of action that belongs to it are interdependent notions, and neither can be understood apart from the other.

Subjectivity is thus tied to spatial differentiation and cannot provide any simple, independent grounding for such differentiation – including the differentiation of subjective space. This is so because subjectivity is established only through forms of agency and activity that call upon forms of both subjective and objective space. Moreover, if subjectivity cannot ground even subjective spatiality, neither can space (whether subjective or objective) provide any ground for subjectivity. That is, subjectivity cannot be reduced to some purely spatial structure, since spatiality, in the rich sense at issue here, cannot be grasped as independent of the agency and activity of the subject. Indeed, as seen in Chapter 2, spatiality is not a simple concept to be explicated through subjective or objective analyses alone, but is embedded within the more complex unity of place. The existence of the subject is, one might say, 'simultaneous' with the existence of the complex forms of spatiality – 'simultaneous' with the existence of embodied, spatialized agency. The interdependence of subjectivity and spatiality is, in this respect, analogous to the interdependence of subjective and objective spatiality. Just as these two forms of spatiality must be understood as embedded within the more encompassing structure of place, so too must the interdependence of subjectivity and spatiality be understood as an interdependence of elements within a more encompassing 'topographical' structure.

Notes

1 Erwin Strauss, *The Primary World of the Senses*, trans. Jacob Needleman (New York: Macmillan, 1963), 235.

2 Shaun Gallagher, 'Body Schema and Intentionality', in *The Body and the Self*, ed. José Luis Bermudez, Anthony Marcel, and Naomi Eilan (Cambridge, MA: MIT Press, 1995), 227.

3 Ibid., 228.

4 For more on the idea of body-schema and its role in action as well as its relation to space, see David Morris, *The Sense of Space* (New York: SUNY Press, 2004).

5 A rather more extreme example is to be seen in the case of Ian Waterman, who, after suffering a rare neurological disease, was able to regain the capacity for movement through careful attention and conscious control of his limbs. See Jonathan Cole, *Pride and a Daily Marathon* (Cambridge, MA: MIT Press, 1995).

6 The idea of a close connection between willing and acting is to be found in Arthur Schopenhauer, *The World as Will and Representation*, trans. E.F.J. Payne, vol. 1 (New York: Dover, 1966), 101ff; and, as Thomas Baldwin notes in his 'Objectivity, Causality, and Agency', in *The Body and the Self*, 116, such connection is also found in Brian O'Shaughnessy, *The Will* (Cambridge: Cambridge University Press, 1980).

7 James Russell, *Agency: Its Role in Mental Development* (Hove: Erlbaum [UK] Taylor and Francis, 1996), 76–77. Russell's reasoning follows that of von Holst and Mittelstaedt who undertook the basic research in this area. Russell cites the reference to their work in C.R. Gallistel, *The Organization of Action: A New Synthesis* (Hillsdale, NJ: Lawrence Erlbaum Associates Inc., 1980).

8 P.F. Strawson, *Individuals* (London: Macmillan, 1959), 61.

9 Ibid., 61.

10 Unlike Nagel, Strawson is not concerned with the possibility of an objective way in which things might be that is beyond any possibility of experience. Instead, his concern is with a concept of objectivity as it might be grasped by a creature in distinguishing experience from the objects of experience. On this, see Gareth Evans, 'Things Without the Mind – A Commentary upon Chapter Two of Strawson's Individuals', in *Collected Papers* (Oxford: Clarendon Press, 1985), 251–252.

11 Ibid., 249.

12 See Strawson, *Individuals*, 62.

13 Ibid., 62.

14 The observation is made originally by Onora O'Neill in 'Space and Objects', *Journal of Philosophy* 73 (1976): 30.

15 'Dissertation on the Form and Principles of the Sensible and Intelligible World [1770]', in *Kant's Inaugural Dissertation and Early Writings on Space*, trans. John Handyside (Chicago, IL: Open Court, 1929), §15A, 59.

16 Immanuel Kant, *Critique of Pure Reason*, in *The Cambridge Edition of the Works of Immanuel Kant*, trans. Paul Guyer and Allen Wood (Cambridge: Cambridge University Press, 1988), A26–B42.

17 See Bertrand Russell, *Foundations of Geometry* (New York: Dover, 1956), 186; see also Russell's comments on the preceding page, and O'Neill's comments in 'Space and Objects', 43.

18 Strawson, *Individuals*, 63.

19 Ibid.

20 Ibid., 65.

21 Ibid., 66.

22 O'Neill, 'Space and Objects', 33–34.

23 Strawson, *Individuals*, 75.

24 Ibid., 74.

25 Ibid., 74–75.

26 Ibid., 75.

27 Ibid., 75–76.

28 Evans claims that the ordering of pitch, which the master-sound provides, plays no real part in Strawson's discussion. This seems to me mistaken – without the ordering of pitch there can be no way of providing content for the idea of distance that Strawson takes to be essential here. Evans is right, however, that one could provide such an ordering without appeal to the ordering of pitch at all, through the idea of an ordered system of locations in which each location is defined in terms of its relation to other locations – thus location p is defined as that which must be traversed in order to move from o to q. See Evans, 'Things Without the Mind', 225.

29 See Strawson, *Individuals*, 81.

30 Ibid., 80.

31 Ibid.
32 Ibid., 65.
33 Ibid., 81.
34 Ibid., 82.
35 Ibid., 82–83.
36 Ibid., 83–84.
37 Ibid., 85.
38 Evans, 'Things Without the Mind', 280.
39 Timothy O'Connor, 'Agent Causation', in *Agents, Causes and Events*, ed. Timothy O'Connor (New York: Oxford University Press, 1995), 175.
40 Baldwin, 'Objectivity, Causality and Agency', 115–116. Baldwin's position is close to that developed by D. Gasking, 'Causation and Recipes', *Mind* 54 (1955): 479–487; and also by Georg Henrik von Wright, *Explanation and Understanding* (Ithaca, NY: Cornell University Press, 1971).
41 Baldwin, 'Objectivity, Causality and Agency', 115.
42 For a fuller account of Baldwin's position, see especially ibid., 116–121.
43 Ibid., 113.
44 Ibid., 121.
45 Max Scheler, *Die Formen des Wissens und die Bildung* (Bonn: Friedrich Cohen, 1925), 47n24; cited in Heidegger, *History of the Concept of Time*, trans. Theodore Kisiel (Bloomington, IN: Indiana University Press, 1985), 221.
46 Heidegger, *History of the Concept of Time*, 222.
47 I suspect that Baldwin is misled into thinking that Heidegger's position is not directed against the idea that agency is fundamental, here, by the fact that Heidegger does give a central role to our practical involvement with things in the constitution of the world. But this does not imply that our experience of agency is the basis for our grasp of the world, only that experience of agency is a necessary part of the structure of the world. In fact, one can only have a grasp of agency through a grasp of the 'worldhood of the world' as such. Indeed, this seems a large part of what is at stake in Heidegger's discussion of Scheler – a discussion in which Heidegger is concerned both to acknowledge his agreement with Scheler's rejection of any purely intellectual apprehension as the basis for a grasp of the world, and to insist on the need for the grasp of the world to be prior, in one sense, even to the experience of willing.
48 Baldwin, 'Objectivity, Causality and Agency', 107–108.
49 Ibid., 108.
50 Ibid., 107.
51 Ibid., 108. Baldwin adds: 'Without an acknowledgment of their potential cognitive role, they [perceptions] are as nonintentional, as contentless, as the rings on a tree whose width covaries with the type of weather endured by the tree.'
52 This seems, in fact, to be mistaken. If pains are located in this way, then so, surely, are other secondary properties also located in the same way, and therefore must, by the same reasoning, be viewed as subjective. But this merely shows that we can treat almost all experiences as located in the world inasmuch as the objects or events that give rise to them are located in the world, or we can treat such experiences as merely mental entities that are, none of them, located at the places in the world we take them to be.
53 Baldwin, 'Objectivity, Causality and Agency', 110.
54 Notice that the postulation of a Cartesian demon or mad scientist who ensures that an agent's attempted actions are successful, even though the causal connections expected by the agent do not obtain, is nevertheless ensuring that the requisite correlation of agency with world is maintained (the demon's interventions could be taken to constitute a limited version of the universe as envisaged by occasionalism). If this is done consistently, then the agent can still control its actions through the regular (but unrecognized) intervention of the demon; if the intervention is inconsistent then the agent cannot be said to have any capacity for controlled behaviour nor for action simplicitur.
55 See John Campbell, 'The Role of Physical Objects in Spatial Thinking', in *Spatial Representation*, ed. Naomi Eilan, Rosaleen McCarthy, and Bill Brewer (Oxford: Blackwell, 1993), 65–95; Strawson makes the claim at *Individuals*, 37.

56 'On the First Ground of the Distinction of Regions in Space', in *Kant's Inaugural Dissertation and Early Writings on Space*, 23.

57 So, a world presented only visually, or exclusively through tactile sensations, would be limited in analogous ways to the world envisaged by Strawson. The problem is not so much the restriction of Strawson's world to the auditory but rather its restriction to a single sensory modality.

58 Sarah Furness, 'A Reasonable Geography: An Argument for Embodiment' (PhD Dissertation, University of Essex, 1986), 255–256, and 218. See also Elisabeth Ströker, *Investigations in Philosophy of Space*, trans. Algis Mickunas (Athens, OH: Ohio University Press, 1987), 61ff. As Ströker comments, there: 'It is decisive for the space of action that it be constituted through a corporeal being.'

59 Although issues of sexuality and gender – which figure heavily in many discussions of spatiality in feminist literature in particular – are not central themes in the account developed here, it is easy to see how the necessary connection between bodily differentiation, agency, and subjectivity could be used as the basis for a 'sexed' account of spatiality. Moreover, since the constitution of the 'spaces' in which human agents find themselves is not dependent solely on bodily differentiation, but in a more general respect, also derives from other forms of structuring including forms of social practice, so the agent's space of action might be understood as potentially a 'gendered' space also.

60 Ludwig Wittgenstein, *Philosophical Investigations*, trans. G.E.M. Anscombe (Oxford: Blackwell, 1974), 178.

61 'The Knowledge' was dramatized in a Euston Films television production made in 1979. *The Knowledge*, written by Jack Rosenthal and directed by Bob Brooks, recounts the experiences of a group of 'knowledge boys' as they try for the green cab driver's badge. The play emphasizes The Knowledge as something that can only be learnt by actually travelling the runs themselves. As one character explains (played by Nigel Hawthorne) 'the only way to learn The Knowledge is by climbing on your bike and doing the sod!' The Knowledge, which so far has survived the advent of the mini-cab, Uber, and GPS, is administered through an office of the London Metropolitan Police and was established in its present form with the introduction of motorized cabs around the turn of the twentieth century.

62 Although the latter, while not derived from the subjective experience of movement, is nevertheless only possible in relation to it, and in this respect the relation between the grasp of movement in one's own case, and of movement in general, mirrors the relation between the grasp of subjective and objective space.

63 Quassim Cassam, *Self and World* (Oxford: Clarendon Press, 1997), 198. There are a number of themes in Cassam's discussion that mirror lines of argument also pursued here.

Further reading

Cassam, Quassim. *Self and World*. Oxford: Clarendon Press, 1997.

Evans, Gareth. 'Things Without the Mind – A Commentary upon Chapter Two of Strawson's *Individuals*.' In *Collected Papers*. Oxford: Clarendon Press, 1985.

Kant, Immanuel. *Kant's Inaugural Dissertation and Early Writings on Space*. Translated by John Handyside. Chicago, IL: Open Court, 1929. (Although the Handyside volume is useful in bringing together all of Kant's writings on space, many of the writings included there can be found in other editions [and in newer translations], most notably in the *Cambridge Edition of the Works of Immanuel Kant*.)

Morris, David. *The Sense of Space*. New York: SUNY Press, 2004.

Russell, James. *Agency: Its Role in Mental Development*. Hove: Erlbaum (UK) Taylor and Francis, 1996).

Strauss, Erwin. *The Primary World of the Senses*. Translated by Jacob Needleman. New York: Macmillan, 1963.

Strawson, P.F. *Individuals*. London: Macmillan, 1959.

6 Self and the space of others

> When a self does appear it always involves an experience of another; there could not be an experience of a self simply by itself. . . When a self does appear in experience it appears over against the other, and we have been delineating the condition under which this other does appear in the experience of the human animal, namely in the presence of that sort of stimulation in the co-operative activity which arouses in the individual himself the same response it arouses in the other.
>
> (George Herbert Mead, *Mind, Self and Society*[1])

The grasp of objectivity requires a grasp of spatiality as that within which objects can be not only situated and related, but also distinguished from one another and from the creature whose attitudes and actions are directed towards those objects. The grasp of other persons is no different – it too requires a grasp of the externality of space. The idea of a connection between the subjectivity of others and spatiality is something explicitly recognized by Henri Bergson. He writes: 'the intuition of a homogenous space is already a step towards social life. . . probably animals do not picture to themselves, besides their sensations, as we do, an external world quite distinct from themselves, which is the common property of all conscious beings. Our tendency to form a clear picture of this externality of things and the homogeneity of their medium is the same as the impulse which leads us to live in common and to speak.'[2] The explicit association of the spatial and the social is also present in the work of Emmanuel Levinas. There, however, the idea appears embedded in a slightly different vocabulary – specifically, in terms of a connection between the notions of 'alterity' (otherness) and exteriority. The encounter with the 'Other', the experience of the 'face to face', as Levinas presents it, is thus seen as an encounter with what lies outside of me and within the realm of the spatial. 'Man as other comes to us from the outside, a separated – or holy – face. His exteriority, that is, his appeal to me, is his truth. . . The face to face is a final and irreducible relation which no concept could cover without the thinker who thinks that concept finding himself forthwith before a new interlocutor; it makes possible the pluralism of society.'[3] The connection between spatiality and the subjectivity of others arises in at least two ways. First, it arises because of the need to situate the other outside of oneself, in a space that is external to oneself – the connection between spatiality and the subjectivity of others being, in many respects, analogous to the connection that obtains between spatiality and the existence of objects. Second, it arises because the idea of subjectivity is tied to the notion of situated and embodied agency, such that any subject, whether oneself or another, must be grasped as spatially situated and embodied.

The idea of what might be called 'other-subjectivity' is thus dependent on the concept of objectivity and some concept of subjectivity. But what concept of subjectivity is involved here? Is the notion of 'other-subjectivity' clearly distinct from the idea of oneself as subject – what might analogously be termed 'self-subjectivity'? Or can it be arrived at simply through a grasp of one's own subjectivity in conjunction with the idea that multiple locations might exist within an objective space? If the latter, then one might understand others through understanding the possibility of oneself as being located at other positions than the one currently occupied, which, in turn, suggests that the grasp of the subjectivity of others would be secondary to the grasp of the subjectivity of oneself. This not only seems to legitimate a particular solution to the traditional problem of other minds, but also to suggest that the understanding of others is, in general, primarily a matter of empathy or 'simulation'. Moreover, it seems to portray the contrast between self and world as the fundamental structure in the possibility of thought and experience – the contrast between self and other being secondary to it. Certainly, given their necessary implication in the possibility of experience or thought, a grasp of objectivity and a grasp of one's own subjectivity will be essential to the grasp of the subjectivity of others. Yet dependence need not be a one-way relationship, and the fact that other-subjectivity depends upon objectivity and self-subjectivity need not preclude a dependence that also operates in the other direction.

In Chapter 2, I noted that the grasp of objective space is a grasp of space that must extend beyond one's past or future experiences of that space *and* that must also extend beyond any other creature's experience of space. This may lead one to suppose that the idea of objective space already brings with it the idea of space as inter-subjective. Inasmuch as the idea of objective space involves the idea of a multiplicity of positions or locations within such space, one might suppose that objective space also involves the idea of a multiplicity of possible perspectives correlated with those locations. This multiplicity of possible perspectives – perspectives akin to one's own *as* perspectives and yet differently located – might then be thought to be just what is involved in the idea of other-subjectivity. On this account, objective space would already be a space that is inter-subjective, such that, combined with the idea of one's own subjective space (with which the idea of objective space is always linked), it immediately yields a concept of other possible subjective spaces that are not one's own but are correlated with the many other locations within objective space.

Such a line of reasoning is very attractive, but it is also mistaken. There is too great a distance between the bare idea of a multiplicity of locations and the idea of a multiplicity of possible subjective spaces. Furthermore, while one can certainly grasp the possibility of each of those multiple locations being a location correlated with some possible perspective of one's own, that is not quite the same as the idea that those locations might be correlated with subjective spaces other than one's own. The grasp of a subjectivity associated with a different *location* does not amount to a grasp of a location associated with a different *subjectivity*. To grasp the idea of a subjectivity other than one's own is to grasp the possibility of a subjectivity that is contemporaneous with one's own, yet other than one's own. This is not to say that one cannot also grasp the possibility of another subject who exists at an earlier or later time than oneself, but only that the difference at issue here is one that must be such that it can obtain with respect to creatures existing at the same time, as well as with respect to creatures not merely to those existing at another time. Although I can certainly grasp different 'perspectives' associated with different locations through a grasp of the way in which I may be located at different positions, this is not a grasp of the possibility of differently located but contemporaneous perspectives, and, as such, it cannot constitute a grasp of what is involved in the idea of the subjectivity of others. Equally, I can grasp the perspective associated with my current location, but that does not constitute a grasp of the idea that some creature *other* than myself could instead be located where I am now and possess the same perspective on the world.

To illustrate this point, consider the following. Suppose I am located in some portion of an objective, physical space, able to move around in that space and occupy different locations. Suppose, as well, that this space is one that can be grasped in the manner of Strawson's purely auditory world (accepting, for the moment, the basic premises of that world). In that case, my movement in space would be captured in terms of my ability to move along the master-sound and occupy different positions in relation to that sound. As Strawson presents matters, I could use the master-sound to position other 'objects' distinct from me; objects that I could grasp as continuing to exist even when not being perceived by me. I could also grasp the way in which my perspective of the 'No-Space world' changed as I moved around within it, albeit in a restricted fashion. Thus, I could grasp the idea of different objects that exist simultaneously with me at different locations, as well as the idea of different perspectives associated with different locations at different times – such differences in perspective being a consequence of my own movement. There is, however, nothing in this framework that would require or enable my grasp of the idea of different perspectives associated with different locations at the *same* time. Since I can only be at one location at any one time, the idea of a difference in location is also the idea of a difference in time – even if this is only implicit. In this respect, were Strawson's master-sound sufficient to allow for a grasp of the distinction between self and other – understood as a distinction between self and objects – and therefore able to satisfy the conditions for what Strawson calls, in this narrow sense, a 'non-solipsistic consciousness', it would not obviously satisfy the conditions for a 'non-solipsistic consciousness' in the broader sense that includes a grasp of the distinction between self-subjectivity and other-subjectivity.

The conclusion to which we are led by these considerations is that the idea of subjectivity contains two irreducibly distinct components: the idea of self and the idea of otherness. These components may well be mutually dependent, as both may also be dependent upon the idea of objectivity, but neither do they allow of any reduction nor priority between them. The irreducibility of other-subjectivity to self-subjectivity, or, to put matters somewhat differently, the fact that the former cannot be derived from the latter, is indicated by the seductiveness of solipsistic views – at least of that form of solipsism that consists in denying the knowledge of other persons. Such solipsism arises, in part, from the way in which one's own subjectivity, or the view from one's own perspective, rules out simultaneous access to any other subjectivity or to any view from other perspectives. The singularity of one's own subjectivity or perspective – the complete lack of direct experiential access to any perspective other than one's own – is not metaphysically mysterious (deriving from nothing more than the fact that I cannot be in more than one location at a time). It provides a way of explaining, at least in part, why the contrast between self and other may be regarded as an encounter with what is completely 'other' – a point given special emphasis by writers such as Levinas. Of course, the mistake that solipsism embodies is that of supposing that a grasp of the subjectivity of others ought to take the same form as a grasp of one's own subjectivity. Yet, just as the grasp of objectivity is distinct from the grasp of subjectivity, the grasp of self-subjectivity is distinct from the grasp of other-subjectivity. Subjectivity and objectivity are interdependent concepts, and the same is true of self-subjectivity and other-subjectivity. As a consequence, all three concepts – of self, of others, and of objects – must be understood as interdependent and irreducible.

In the previous chapter, I argued that an organism capable of agency needs to have a grasp of objects as having a complex structure – complex both in the unifying of various properties into a single 'presentation' and in their causal structure. Indeed, the idea of an object is clearly the idea of something that can function as that which Donald Davidson has called a 'common cause'[4] – something that possesses a variety of causal properties such that it can give rise to simultaneous but different effects, including differing presentations of itself to different observers. In this respect, the idea of the object as common cause would seem to imply the possibility of simultaneous observation of differing, perhaps even *prima facie* inconsistent, aspects of the same object. Thus, the same flat, coloured surface may appear to be differently coloured to differently placed observers; the same branch half-immersed in a lake may appear bent one way to an observer from above the water and bent another way to an observer below the water; the same item of food or drink may taste bitter to one person and sweet to another. Cases such as these – where divergent perceptions are nevertheless grasped as being related to a single object – provide particularly dramatic exemplifications of the point at issue. The same idea, however, is instantiated whenever different observers converge on a single object as the common cause for their individual perceptions and as the common object of their thoughts and experiences.

Given the argument of the previous chapter, the idea of objects as capable of giving rise to co-present particulars – different but simultaneous perceptions that, inasmuch as they are perceptions of the same object, have a common objective cause – has to require a grasp of concepts of spatiality and causality. In order to identify some object as a common cause, it is necessary to be able to situate that object in relation to the observers to whom it is causally, and so also intentionally, related, and, of course, to have some grasp of the way in which that object and those observers are embedded in a larger causal framework. This reinforces the importance of spatiality and causality to the concept of objectivity, a concept that calls upon, not just notions of spatiality and causality, but also subjectivity – of both self and other. The interdependence of a grasp of objectivity and a grasp of subjectivity has already been central to much of the discussion in previous chapters. What is now evident is that the interdependence between subjectivity and objectivity is not merely a two-way dependence but one that obtains between at least three distinct notions: self-subjectivity, other-subjectivity, and objectivity. It is furthermore one that can be understood as organized in relation to two contrasting conceptual pairs: subject and object, and the inter-subjective pairing of self and other.[5] Only with a grasp of the possibility of different but simultaneous perspectives on the world – that is, a grasp of simultaneously existing but distinct subjective spaces, which implies a grasp of one's own subjectivity and that of others – can one properly grasp the concept of an object as capable of giving rise to distinct but simultaneous presentations.

Certainly, a solitary creature, with no concept of others, would have difficulty making sense of how the same object could present different views at the same time, since such a creature could have no conception of any view other than its current view. Such a creature might well grasp the possibility of an object giving rise to different views over time, corresponding to its different encounters with the object, but this requires only the idea of a common cause *over time* (a cause whose differing presentations might be due to changes in the object), not the idea of a common cause *at a time* (a cause whose differing presentations are due to differences in the observers rather than in the object). Indeed, it would seem that the idea of objectivity requires some grasp of the way in which the same object can have differential but simultaneous effects on different observers, and, in this respect, objectivity seems inseparable from the idea of other-subjectivity. Similarly, if grasping one's own subjectivity depends on being able to situate oneself objectively, it would also seem to depend on being able to grasp oneself in a way that includes reference to the idea of others – others like oneself but nevertheless distinct.

The interconnection between the concepts of self-subjectivity, other-subjectivity, and objectivity implies that they come as a package deal – to have a grasp of one is to have a grasp of all. Indeed, something very close to this claim is present in Davidson's work, though in slightly different terms. In 'Three Varieties of Knowledge', he writes:

> The philosophical conception of subjectivity is burdened with a history and a set of assumptions about the nature of mind and meaning that sever the meaning of an utterance or the content of a thought from questions about external reality, thus creating a logical gap between 'my' world and the world as it appears to others. This common conception holds that the subjective is prior to the objective, that there is a subjective world prior to knowledge of external reality. It is evident that the picture of thought and meaning I have sketched here leaves no room for such priority since it predicates self-knowledge on knowledge of other minds and of the world. The objective and the inter-subjective are thus essential to anything we call subjectivity, and constitute the context in which it takes form.[6]

Davidson thus rejects the possibility that any one of the three elements at issue here – he presents them as subjectivity, inter-subjectivity, and objectivity – could stand as the foundation for the others. The three elements are interdependent and irreducible. Davidson's argument for this conclusion is presented in terms similar to those I have employed in the discussion above. Indeed, the idea of objects as a 'common cause' is one that originates with Davidson's development of the idea of objectivity as arising on the basis of what he calls *triangulation*.

The idea of triangulation was already referred to in Chapter 1 in relation to the practice of topographical surveying. Ordinarily, triangulation is a technique for the determination of relative location that operates through the relations between landmarks located at the three points of a triangle. Through the taking of sightings and measurements of distance between some of the landmarks one is able to determine the angles and distances for all of them. The idea is first illustrated in relation to map-making by Gemma Frisius in his *Libellus de locorum describendum ratione* (*Booklet concerning a way of describing places*) attached to the 1533 edition of his *Cosmographia* (see Figure 7). Rather than applying it to the determination of location, however, Davidson applies it to the problem of the determination of the object to which an agent or speaker is attitudinally or intentionally oriented, and so also to the problem of the determination of the contents of an agent's or speaker's attitudes.

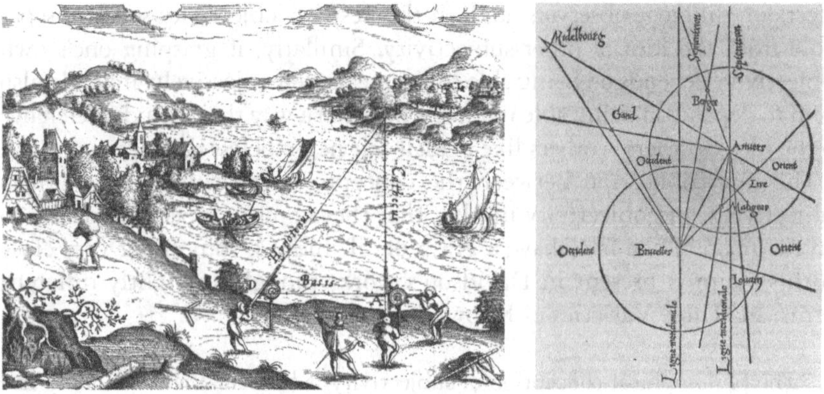

Figure 7 *Left*: Levinus Hultius, 'Measuring the width of a river by triangulation', from *Theoria et praxis quadrantis geometrici. . . das ist, Beschreibung, Unterricht und Gebrauch des gevierdten geometrischen und anderer Instrument* (Amsterdam, 1594).
Right: The page from Gemma Frisius's *Libellus de locorum describendum ratione* (attached to the 1533 edition of Frisius's *Cosmographia* [Antwerp]) in which Frisius first illustrated the idea of triangulation. This illustration, which uses a line between the cities of Brussels and Antwerp as the base, was hypothetical since the cities triangulated are not close enough to be in line of sight from one another.

Consider, for example, the case of a child standing before a table to which the child's attention appears to be directed. If we were to take a line from the child to the table, then at what point on the line would the object of the child's attention be located? It might be at the point where the table is physically located (that is, it might be the table itself to which the child is directed); it might be at the surface of the child's sense organs; or it might even be located at some point in the 'inner space' of the child's mind. Elsewhere, Davidson puts this same problem in slightly different terms. Adopting the view that we should identify the objects of attitudes by reference to their causes, he asks: 'But which of the many possible causes is the right one? Events in the nervous system, patterns of stimulation of the nerve-endings, or something further out?'[7] If we look only to the resources available to one solitary creature, it seems that we have no basis on which to locate the object at any one point over another and, therefore, no basis on which the object can be identified. Davidson's claim is that only if we have two creatures, and so have two lines from creature to object, and have as well a baseline that consists in a certain similarity of response on the part of those creatures (the entire structure therefore mirroring the structure of triangulation in the ordinary topographic situation), can we then look to the object as located at the intersection of the two lines. As Davidson explains:

> The child finds tables similar; we find tables similar; and we find the child's responses in the presence of tables similar. It now makes sense for us to call the responses of the child responses to tables. Given these three patterns of response we can assign a location to the stimuli that elicit the child's responses. The relevant stimuli are the objects or events we naturally find similar (tables) which are then correlated with responses of the child we find similar. It is a form of triangulation: one line goes from the child in the direction of the table, one line goes from us in the direction of the table, and the third line goes from us to the child. Where the lines from child to table and us to table converge 'the' stimulus is located. Given our view of child and world, we can pick out 'the' cause of the child's responses. It is the common cause of our response and the child's response.[8]

The inter-subjective space opened up between two creatures confronting the same object is a space that enables a grasp of the object itself and thereby enables a grasp of an objective space that is inter-subjectively accessible.

Although Davidson does not present it in these same terms, it seems that the image of 'triangulation' depends largely on the notion, already discussed, that a solitary creature has no means to pick out objects except through encountering and re-encountering them over time. Such successive encounters, however, provide only a set of successive presentations, not any object that is common to those presentations. In this respect, one cannot appeal to a single creature 'triangulating' with itself through a comparison of present and past encounters.[9] Such a notion does not deliver what is needed here, namely, the idea of multiple simultaneous presentations that are the result of a single cause, and yet it is just such an idea that is an important part of the concept of objectivity. Indeed, it is just this idea that may be said to underlie the concept of error and of disagreement. Only if I can grasp how the same object can present at least two 'faces' – one grasped by me and one grasped by another, either or both perhaps being true or false – can I grasp the possibility that how I see things, now, is neither the only way in which they can currently be seen, nor necessarily the way things currently are. Successive encounters over time require no such idea of the same object as underlying apparently inconsistent or simultaneously multiple presentations. Only if a creature can grasp the possibility of the same object presenting itself differently at the same time – which entails having a grasp of a form of subjective presentation that is similar to, but distinct from, its own – can such a creature properly be said to have a grasp of objectivity.

Of course, it might be thought that the only requirement, here, is the *idea* of a subjectivity other than one's own – that so long as a creature can grasp the mere possibility of other-subjectivity in contrast to self-subjectivity, then it will be capable of grasping the idea of objectivity. Yet, at issue in this discussion is not some abstract notion of objectivity and subjectivity, but rather a grasp of objectivity and subjectivity as they might apply in concrete thought and experience. Thus, so far as the concept of objectivity, for instance, is concerned, what is at stake is the possibility of grasping *particular* objects. In fact, Davidson's introduction of the idea of inter-subjectivity, as necessary to the possibility of objectivity, is in terms of the need to refer to some other creature, with similar responses, as the means by which *particular* objects can be picked out as the common causes of those responses. The turn to inter-subjectivity thus arises in relation to certain problems of interpretation and self-interpretation (in relation to the possibility of grasping oneself or another as a subject) that require a capacity to pick out particular objects, and so also require an involvement with other creatures within an actual, rather than abstract, location – a location that is also an inter-subjective place.

Inasmuch as objectivity, self-subjectivity, and other-subjectivity form a closely bound triad of concepts, so any creature that has a grasp of one must have a grasp of all. But as I noted in Chapter 2, merely having a grasp of, for instance, objective space, need not imply any grasp of the concept of such a space. We may need to make reference to some concept of objectivity, and therefore to concepts of self and other, in explaining the behaviour of many creatures – but to speak of them as having some 'grasp' of objectivity or subjectivity need not commit us to the attribution of any conceptual grasp of such notions. The more complex a creature's behaviour, however, the more complex must be its grasp of itself, of other creatures, and of the objects that make up its world. Indeed, a particularly high level of behavioural complexity is possible only for creatures that are capable of a conceptual grasp of themselves or their world and, thereby, also capable of reflecting upon and interpreting their own mental states and the mental states of others. Only with such capabilities can organisms experience any sophisticated mental life or have states with propositional content. Such conceptualization, reflection, or interpretation, however, requires that the organism be able to identify the autonomous objects (those whose existence is not dependent on the existence of the organism) to which its mental states are directed. Now evident is that this ability requires the capacity to interact with other creatures as well as with objects in the world. Consequently, determining the contents of mental states, whether in one's own case or in the case of others, is identical with determining the autonomous objects of thought, and this cannot be done except in an inter-subjective space; that is, through a grasp, not only of one's own subjectivity, but also that of others.

'What makes the idea of an autonomous object available to us?' asks Davidson, and he answers, 'Its availability requires, above all, the corroboration of others, others who are tuned to the same basic events and objects as we are, and who are tuned to our responses to those events and objects.'[10] Such corroboration naturally depends on the possibility of communication. Corroboration and communication are, however, tied to the abilities to construct and to understand specific presentations of things that are free of any particular experiential perspective, and that are accessible from outside of any such perspective. Any creature that can correlate its responses with the responses of others, and also relate those responses to the common objects encountered in the world, must therefore have a capacity to grasp and present things in an essentially communicable and inter-subjective form (a form not tied to any particular subjectivity). Such a form of presentation was encountered earlier in the discussion of that form of 're-presentation' that is characteristic of maps and diagrams. Yet the idea of such an 'objective' and inter-subjective mode of presentation – according to which a subject has access to a concrete experiential presentation of what is essentially a non-experiential and conceptual grasp of things (a map, a diagram, or, in the most general sense, a sign or sequence of signs), and by means of which sophisticated communicative interaction is possible – lies precisely at the heart of the concept of the linguistic. There is, in this respect, an essential connection between the capacity for a complex mental life, the capacity for a sophisticated grasp of oneself and other like organisms and common objects of the world, and the capacity for language – a connection that is also explicitly noted by Davidson.[11]

McGinn, as noted in Chapter 2, adopts the view that there is a 'radical discontinuity' between perception and conception (between, as one might crudely say, 'seeing and believing'), writing that 'conception. . . is not explicable in terms of an imagined perceptual point of view, indeed it is not strictly a point of *view* at all'.[12] The capacity for conceptual thought – to employ concepts in their generality, to grasp connections between concepts, to group and re-group particulars according to different conceptual frameworks, to redeploy old concepts and invent new ones – would seem to be dependent on, if not identical with, a capacity to grasp oneself and the world in a way that is not restricted to one's own experiential awareness or particular subjective space. Indeed, this point was already implicit in the discussion of Nagel's 'view from nowhere'. The ability to detach from one's own perspective is dependent on a capacity for conceptual abstraction that must entail a grasp of objectivity (though, contra Nagel, this involves precisely a capacity to achieve a grasp of the world that is not a 'view from nowhere', nor a 'view' at all). This capacity is, in turn, interconnected with capacities for complex forms of communication and abstract presentation, wherein language, conceptuality, and inter-subjectivity – as well as the very possibility of states capable of having propositional content – can be seen to be interwoven with the notion of objectivity in such a way that the possibility of each is dependent on the possibility of the others.

Objective space is an essentially impersonal or 'anonymous' space, devoid of perspectivity and in which no particular location has any priority over another. The 'anonymity' of objective space, and of objectivity, is thus important in enabling the possibility of inter-subjectivity. I cannot experience the subjectivity of another in the same way I experience my own subjectivity. That I cannot do so is not owing to some peculiar metaphysical feature of persons or selves, but to nothing more than the fact that I cannot grasp things from two perspectives at once, and whatever perspective from which I do grasp things is necessarily *my* perspective (much the same point as that which arose, in Chapter 3, in relation to the ownership of one's mental states). One grasps the subjectivity of other individuals, in fact, through being able to match one's own responses to those of others and through being able to locate others, both within an objective space to which each has access and in relation to a set of common objects and events. I am, moreover, able to represent myself as a subject just in virtue of my capacity, not simply to *experience* things for myself, but also to similarly *locate* myself, both within an objective space and in relation to those same objects and events. Thus, it is precisely through my access to the 'anonymous' and impersonal realm of objectivity that I am able to grasp the concept of others, and through which I am also able to grasp the concept of myself. I am able to represent myself and others through my ability to grasp all from within the same framework – 'anonymous', objective, and therefore also inter-subjective.

In this respect, I am able to conceive of myself through my ability to conceive of my subjectivity – my subjective space – as dependent on a particular location within and experience of the world, which is just one of a multitude of possible locations and experiences. Inasmuch as the grasp of objectivity and of objective space is indeed a grasp of the world as anonymous and impersonal – and yet also a world on which there are a multiplicity of possible perspectives, in which my own is included – so it is a grasp of the world as belonging to no-one and to everyone. In a similar fashion, the grasp of inter-subjectivity that is implicated with a grasp of objective spatiality involves a grasp of subjective space that is neither one restricted to a grasp of my own subjectivity nor one that merely sets the subjective space of my experience over and against a set of other possible such spaces from which it is distinguished. Rather, it is a grasp of subjective space that understands all as located within a single framework, none occupying a more central or privileged position. The concept of inter-subjectivity thus encompasses the entire range of subjective spaces – of perspectives or points of view – understood in relation to an objective space.

The idea that an understanding of inter-subjectivity involves understanding the possibility of a plurality of subject-positions within an objective framework, each of which must in turn be understood through its relation to both the objective world and the other subjects around it, may suggest that an understanding of inter-subjectivity requires that one leave one's subjectivity behind. Similarly, one might suppose that, in grasping space as objective, one loses a sense of one's subjective space – and even of the broader sense of place as that within which both subjectivity and objectivity are located. Certainly, if the conceptual connections I have attempted to chart are accepted, then it must also be accepted that, in arriving at a concept of oneself, one is involved in thinking of oneself in a way that abstracts from one's perspective on the world. In conceiving of oneself, one also, to some extent, conceives of oneself as 'other than' oneself. There should be no mystery about this. A creature with such an understanding of itself is also a creature capable of a certain sort of self-alienation (though exactly what form that takes may well vary depending on culture and situation and may, indeed, never be given explicit expression). It is a creature that can think beyond its own subjective space, into a multiplicity of other possible spaces, without losing a sense of its own subjectivity. The capacity to think beyond one's own space is interdependent with the capacity to think within that space. A creature that has a capacity for any form of self-understanding has a capacity to grasp, not merely the anonymous sameness that obtains between itself and others, but also the difference that obtains there. The idea or concept of inter-subjectivity is thus essentially interconnected and interdependent with the network of other concepts that includes both the concept of our own subjectivity and the subjective space that goes with it, and the concept of a purely objective order that is expressed in the related concept of objective space.

To return to a familiar point, the concept of objective space is not arrived at through extrapolation from the concept of subjective space nor from some process of detachment from subjectivity, but instead belongs to a network of related, but nevertheless irreducibly distinct, concepts that also includes subjectivity – both of self and of other. Moreover, if objective space is not conceptually derived from any subjective space, neither is the concept of the subjectivity of others derived or extrapolated from a grasp of one's own subjectivity whether conceptual or otherwise. We do not first grasp ourselves as subjects and then grasp the subjectivity of others. Instead, we come to understand our own being, as subjects, at the same time as we develop an understanding of the subjectivity of others, at the same time, that is, as we arrive at an understanding of sociality. It is thus not through some empathic or sympathetic ability that we grasp the possibility of other subjective spaces – of the existence of other persons – but through our grasp of the objectivity of the space in which we are situated. Much the same is true for the grasp of oneself. The grasp of the concept of objective space is necessarily interconnected with a grasp of the concepts of self-subjectivity and other-subjectivity and so with a grasp of inter-subjectivity. This is not to deny that empathy and sympathy are important elements in our understanding of others (they may well be essential components in any form of ethical life) but rather to stress that empathy, for instance, is only possible on the assumption that we already grasp the existence of those with whom we empathize. Through a grasp of the idea of different situation within objective space – within an extended spatio-temporal framework – we can grasp the possibility of a difference in experience through a difference in situation and orientation. In empathy, we imagine the ramifications of such a difference – we 'put ourselves in the other's shoes' – but such empathic thinking, although important to our thinking about others, does not constitute that in which our thinking about others is founded.

Grasping the existence of other creatures is a matter of situating those creatures in relation to ourselves and the objects we encounter in the world. This interdependence applies as much to our grasp of ourselves as to our grasp of others. Indeed, to be a creature that is capable of identifying its own beliefs and attitudes is to be a creature that is capable of forming a concept of itself and, correlated with this, a concept of other persons, of external objects, and of the world within which all are situated. Moreover, inasmuch as having a grasp of this set of concepts is inseparable from the capacity to communicate with other persons and to act in relation to other persons and objects, and inasmuch as this necessarily depends on a capacity to achieve some unified and coherent view of things, both in relation to their spatial location and their ordering over time (including, of course, the causal inter-relations between things), one might say that having a grasp of the concept of oneself is a matter of achieving some unified understanding of oneself *as well as* of other persons, objects, and the world. Such understanding involves a capacity to conceive of things objectively and to apply that objective conception to one's subjective experience.

In Chapter 3, I noted that the self cannot properly be understood as some substance that underlies mental states and to which those states can be attributed, nor as something that is independent of the actions attributed to it and that somehow guides or directs those actions. On the account that I have advanced in this chapter, the self is to be understood as constituted only through the complex unity of actions and attitudes that are, themselves, constituted in terms of their relations to one another and, most importantly, through their relation to objects and persons in the world – and so through being tied to certain situations and operations within that world. To have a conception of oneself and a sense of one's own identity – one's 'ipseity', or selfhood, to use Ricoeur's term[13] – is to have a sense, not of some simple and underlying self that is one's own, but of a particular place within the world. Such a sense of place consists in having a grasp of a conceptually complex structure – a structure that encompasses different forms of spatiality, concepts of self and others and an objective order of things – which demands to be articulated linguistically. The connection between having language and having a sense of place is not just a matter of the connection between language and conceptuality. Rather, it is a matter of the necessary inter-subjectivity of place, along with the structuring of subjectivity (underlying the subjectivity of self and of others), both in terms of the structure associated with the propositionality of mental content and that associated with the narrativity of mental life as such. In this respect, an explicit turn to more literary and poetic explorations of place, which characterizes the following two chapters, can be seen to reflect the inseparability of a sense of place from its linguistic and narrative articulation.

Before moving on, however, there is one further issue that should be addressed – an issue that, like the conclusion to the preceding chapter, concerns epistemology. Although philosophers have offered accounts that seek to characterize the nature of knowledge in its generality – accounts that often distinguish, for instance, knowledge *how* (the knowledge associated with skills and 'know-how') from knowledge *that* (the sort of propositional knowledge usually defined in relation to the idea of justified true belief) – the question concerning the possibility of knowledge has often taken on quite different forms depending on what the object of knowledge is taken to be. The question of the nature and possibility of our knowledge of other persons, for instance, has often been taken to be quite separate from that concerning, for instance, our knowledge of ourselves or our knowledge of the external world. It has been said of Descartes that he attempted to make our knowledge of the external world secure by grounding it in self-knowledge (in the *cogito*), but that in doing this, he only made such worldly knowledge even more insecure. Yet if self, others, and world are indeed bound together in the way I have sketched – such that to have a grasp of oneself is to have a grasp of the world and, thereby, the ordering of that world, as well as to have a grasp of others – then the question concerning the nature and possibility of knowledge of self, others, or world must be a single question with a single answer. Indeed, the question of knowledge does not differ according to whether it is knowledge of ourselves, other persons, or the world that is at issue. There is only one question or 'problem' of knowledge (if it is indeed a 'problem' at all), and that question is identical with the question as to how thought and experience – and mental content in general – are possible. Indeed, this is something alluded to in Davidson's own treatment of these matters. The tripartite structure that he outlines as obtaining between the concepts of subjectivity, inter-subjectivity, and objectivity is the same structure that unites the knowledge of self, knowledge of others, and knowledge of objects – the 'three varieties of knowledge' that provide the title of Davidson's paper quoted earlier in this chapter.[14]

The very possibility of knowledge or of experience requires that the content of experience be connected, in a number of ways, with an objective ordering of the world. Indeed, only through grasping a creature as situated within an objective world of which it has some grasp, can such a creature be understood as possessed of any sort of mental life. This is true in respect of our understanding of ourselves as much as in respect of our understanding of others. It seems, then, that grasping the connections between spatiality, causality, and agency, and between subjectivity and objectivity, also entails recognizing the incoherence of any form of global scepticism that would render dubious our grasp of the world in which we are situated. Such scepticism could be threatening only at the cost of rendering dubious the very fact that we are possessed of thoughts and experiences, and in that case, scepticism itself becomes a dubious notion. Scepticism is nothing if not a casting in doubt of the veracity of our thoughts and experiences, but if that entails a casting in doubt of our very having of thoughts and experiences (which is what this argument would suggest), then the sceptical doubt must extend to that which is the very focus of sceptical inquiry. Genuine scepticism becomes a doubting even of the possibility of sceptical doubt, and such scepticism seems to relapse into silence.

It might seem, however, that this argument holds a very simple error. Perhaps the ideas at issue do indeed possess the interconnected character that has become apparent, and yet this sheds no real light on the problem of scepticism or of the possibility of knowledge or experience. What has been shown may well be that we must *think* these concepts together, and so must *think* of ourselves as embodied creatures, located in an objective space, if we are to think of ourselves as capable of thought and experience, but this shows nothing at all about whether these thoughts correspond to how things really are. That we must *think* things to be in this way demonstrates nothing about whether or not things *are* indeed as we suppose them to be. The objection suggested here is well-known. It has been advanced as a standard form of response to any 'transcendental' argument that would attempt to exhibit certain features of experience as necessary to experience itself, and thereby undermine scepticism. Accordingly, the arguments that I have advanced might be viewed as 'transcendental', inasmuch as they attempt to derive conclusions about the preconditions for knowledge, experience, and thought on the basis of an implicit assumption that there is knowledge, experience, and thought.[15] It might be claimed, therefore, that such arguments can only deliver conclusions of a hypothetical character. If we are to think of ourselves as having thoughts and experiences, then we must think of ourselves as embodied, situated, and so forth, but this can show nothing about whether we are actually embodied or situated in this way. Or, if it can show this, then it must rely on invoking some verificationist premise to the effect that the way things *seem* is the way things *are*.[16]

As a general rule the fact that we may think of things in a certain way – and perhaps find it necessary or useful to think in that way – has little or no bearing on whether things actually are that way. We are all familiar, for instance, with heuristic procedures in a variety of disciplines and activities that involve adopting a particular way of doing or thinking about things, which fail to reflect the underlying structure of those things or processes. However, the sorts of connections and ways of thinking that typically characterize 'transcendental' arguments, and that are at issue in the discussion here, are not ways of thinking that we adopt in virtue of their heuristic usefulness. Instead, they are, for the most part, mutually constitutive of one another and of the realm within which they have their application. Thus, the concept of belief, for instance, has no content independent of its interconnection with concepts of subjectivity *and* of objectivity and inter-subjectivity. Since the concepts of belief, attitude, and action, of subjectivity and of objectivity, and of self and world are embedded in a network of concepts, such that no concept can stand alone, it is only when we have access to the entirety of that conceptual system that we can have the capacity to formulate questions, to advance answers, to doubt, hope, fear, or believe. Of course, a very similar point is central to Wittgenstein's well-known rejection of scepticism in *On Certainty*: 'Our doubts depend on the fact that some propositions are exempt from doubt, are as it were like the hinges on which those turn.'[17]

The challenge here need not come only from traditional forms of epistemological scepticism. A similar challenge might issue from a reductive, physicalist approach. Thus, it may be argued that while we do, as a matter of fact, or perhaps must, as a matter of necessity, understand ourselves in terms of a complex of 'folk-psychological' concepts that includes belief and attitude, action and judgment, and self and other, this mode of understanding actually obscures our real nature as purely physical systems. The fact that we have difficulty in applying a purely physical analysis to our own case tells us nothing, it might be argued, about our real nature. Yet, to suppose that resort to the language of belief and desire, action and judgment, and narrative and place is simply a feature of our understanding of ourselves, rather than a feature of how we actually are, is to misunderstand the way in which what we are is determined, in large part, by our self-conception and the language of our self-understanding. That we do indeed believe, desire, judge, and act is the starting point for our attempts at self-understanding. Moreover, since these concepts form a single interdependent system, to suppose that such concepts could or should be dispensed with in favour of a set of purely physicalist concepts, which would alone be adequate to describe and explain human existence, is really to suppose nothing more than that we do not really believe, desire, judge, or act at all. It is, in fact, only on the basis of the recognition of our character as thinking, judging, and acting creatures that we can begin to interrogate our own nature or, indeed, that we can begin to interrogate the nature of the place in which we find ourselves, in which we find other persons, and by means of which the world itself comes into view.

Notes

1 G.H. Mead, *Mind, Self and Society* (Chicago, IL: University of Chicago Press, 1934), 195.

2 Henri Bergson, *Time and Free Will*, trans. F.L. Pogson (London: George Allen and Unwin, 1910) 138; see also ibid., 97.

3 Emmanuel Levinas, *Totality and Infinity*, trans. Alphonso Lingis (Pittsburgh, PA: Duquesne University Press, 1969), 291.

4 A notion originally deployed by Davidson in 'A Coherence Theory of Truth and Knowledge', in *Truth and Interpretation*, ed. Ernest LePore (Oxford: Basil Blackwell, 1986); but which later appears at a number of places in his work, including 'The Second Person', in *Subjective, Intersubjective, Objective* (Oxford: Clarendon Press, 2001), 107–122.

5 Most triadic structures can, of course, also be treated as composed of overlapping sets of paired components. Davidson, as will be seen from the discussion below, sets out a triadic structure that he presents in terms of the three-way contrast between subjectivity, inter-subjectivity, and objectivity. The advantage of keeping to such a triadic structure is that it maintains the emphasis on the

equal importance of all three components, and their mutual interdependence, in a way that might otherwise be obscured by the use of a more binary structure.

6 Davidson, 'Three Varieties of Knowledge', in *Subjective, Intersubjective, Objective*, 218–219.

7 Donald Davidson, 'Reply to Burge', *Journal of Philosophy* 85 (1988): 665.

8 Davidson, 'The Second Person', 119. See also Davidson's comments in 'Rational Animals', in *Subjective, Intersubjective, Objective*, 105.

9 A counter-argument to the Davidsonian position along these lines is advanced in John Heil, *The Nature of True Minds* (New York: Cambridge University Press, 1992), 217–219.

10 Davidson, 'The Third Man', in *Truth, Language, and History* (Oxford: Clarendon Press, 2005), 160.

11 'Our sense of objectivity is the consequence of another sort of triangulation, one that requires two creatures. Each interacts with an object, but what gives each the concept of the way things are objectively is the base line formed between the creatures by language. The fact that they share a concept of truth alone makes sense of the claim that they have beliefs, that they are able to assign objects a place in the public world.' See Davidson, 'Rational Animals', 105. See also Davidson, 'Thought and Talk', in *Inquiries into Truth and Interpretation* (Oxford: Clarendon Press, 1984).

12 Colin McGinn, *The Subjective View* (Oxford: Clarendon Press, 1983), 80–81.

13 See Paul Ricoeur, *Oneself as Another*, trans. Kathleen Blamey (Chicago, IL: University of Chicago Press, 1992), 116; and also Ricoeur, 'Narrative Identity', in *On Paul Ricoeur: Narrative and Interpretation*, ed. David Wood (London: Routledge, 1991), 189. Ricoeur emphasizes this notion of identity as selfhood in contrast to identity as 'sameness'.

14 In fact, Davidson published a later version of that paper with the title 'Subjective, Intersubjective, Objective' (the same title used for the third volume of his collected essays) in *Current Issues in Idealism*, ed. Paul Coates and Daniel D. Hutto (Bristol: Thoemmes Press, 1996), 155–178.

15 For a more detailed discussion of the nature of transcendental arguments, and of transcendental reasoning in general, see my 'The Transcendental Circle', *Australasian Journal of Philosophy* 75 (1997): 1–20.

16 The best-known version of this objection is to be found in Barry Stroud, 'Transcendental Arguments', *Journal of Philosophy* 65 (1968): 241–256, where Stroud takes Strawson's arguments in *Individuals* as a particular focus for his discussion. See also Judith Jarvis Thomson, 'Private Languages', *American Philosophical Quarterly* 1 (1964): 20–31; and A.J. Ayer, 'The Concept of a Person', in *The Concept of a Person and Other Essays* (New York: St Martin's Press, 1963), 110.

17 Ludwig Wittgenstein, *On Certainty*, ed. G.E.M. Anscombe and G.H. von Wright, trans. Denis Paul and G.E.M. Anscombe (Oxford: Blackwell, 1977), §341. Another way of putting the point at issue here is as follows. Suppose we take scepticism, at least in its most basic, modern form (a form that is, in many respects, more extreme, as well as differently oriented, compared to that of the ancients), as just the thought that 'everything might be other than we think it to be'. What then are we to make of such a thought and of the sentence that expresses it? If we are to take this sceptical idea seriously, and if we are to take seriously the possibility that everything could be other than we take it to be, then the very sentence we use to express this thought could be other than we take it to be; the thought itself – even that there is a thought – could be other than it seems. At this point scepticism comes to seem not a position that actually has any content but merely a perpetually reiterated 'what if…', whose meaning remains almost completely and utterly obscure.

Further reading

Bergson, Henri. *Time and Free Will*. Translated by F.L. Pogson. London: George Allen and Unwin, 1910.

Davidson, Donald. *Subjective, Intersubjective, Objective*. Oxford: Clarendon Press, 2001.

Davidson, Donald. *Truth, Language, and History*. Oxford: Clarendon Press, 2005.

Levinas, Emmanuel. *Totality and Infinity*. Translated by Alphonso Lingis. Pittsburgh, PA: Duquesne University Press, 1969.

Mead, G.H. *Mind, Self and Society*. Chicago, IL: University of Chicago Press, 1934.

7 The unity and complexity of place

> Place always opens a region in which it gathers the things in their belonging together... Place is not located in a pre-given space, after the manner of physical-technological space. The latter unfolds itself only through the reigning of places of a region.
>
> (Martin Heidegger, 'Art and Space'[1])

The very possibility of being a creature that can experience the world and have thoughts about the world is dependent on being a creature that has the capacity to act in relation to objects within the world. This, in turn, is dependent on being a creature that has a grasp, not only of the subjective space correlated with its own capacities and with features in its immediate environment, but also of the objective space within which the creature and its environmental surroundings are located. To be a creature that has such a grasp is also to be a creature that can distinguish between its own perspective on the world and that of others. So, to be a creature that is capable of worldly experience and of thought is not merely to be a creature located in a physically extended space. It is to be a creature that finds itself always situated within a complex but unitary place – a place that encompasses the creature itself, other creatures, and a multiplicity of objects and environmental features.

The idea of place at issue here cannot be understood merely in terms of the notion of physical extension or simple location that is so often associated with the narrow conception of space that is so often assumed, but neither, as should be evident from the preceding discussion, can it be understood entirely apart from such a conception. Similarly, the idea of spatiality that has emerged in connection with this richer concept of place is also a richer concept than that of physical extension. Up until this point, however, the focus of my discussion has been on the elements that constitute the structure of place, rather than on place as such. Consequently, concepts such as spatiality, subjectivity, and objectivity have most often occupied centre stage. It is now time to bring place itself more directly and concretely into view. Since there are, as seen in Chapter 1, few philosophical sources to which appeal can be made in such an endeavour, much of the following discussion will look to the appearance of place in contexts outside of philosophy, especially in literature and, in particular, in the work of Marcel Proust. Proust's *In Search of Lost Time* is particularly useful in this respect, since that work (already invoked in the Introduction) provides a literary exploration of the concepts of place, self, space, and time that incorporates, though in a very different and sometimes almost kaleidoscopic form, a number of themes that are central to the understanding of place. Moreover, in the exploration of the life on which *In Search of Lost Time* focuses, we can also see the elaboration of a concept of place that enables the unifying of that life, and of the world in which it is lived, while also preserving a sense of its multiplicity and complexity. The way this concept of place is developed, however, is in close relation to the concept of time, and the very regaining of time that is the novel's aim is possible only in and through place.

In the first volume of Proust's *In Search of Lost Time*, there appears one of the most famous and oft-quoted passages in modern literature, a passage in which Proust describes the sudden and unexpected flood of recollection that comes with the taste of a crumb of cake soaked in tea:

> And suddenly the memory revealed itself. The taste was that of the little piece of madeleine which on Sunday mornings at Combray (because on those mornings I did not go out before mass), when I went to say good morning to her in her bedroom, my aunt Léonie used to give me, dipping it first in her own cup of tea or tisane. . . And as soon as I had recognised the taste. . . immediately the old grey house upon the street, where her room was, rose up like a stage set to attach itself to the little pavilion opening on to the garden which had been built out behind it for my parents (the isolated segment which until that moment had been all that I could see); and with the house the town, from morning to night and in all weathers, the Square where I used to be sent before lunch, the streets along which I used to run errands, the country roads we took when it was fine. . . in that moment all the flowers in our garden and in M. Swann's park, and the water-lilies on the Vivonne and the good folk of the village and their little dwellings and the parish church and the whole of Combray and of its surroundings, taking on shape and solidity, sprang into being, town and gardens alike, from my cup of tea.[2]

In Search of Lost Time is not primarily a work of nostalgic recollection, but is instead a project of recovery and reclamation. It is a project in which the life of the narrator, Marcel, is rediscovered and regained through the recovery of a time that encompasses the past – including the persons, places, and events that make up that past – as it is brought into close conjunction with the present and opens into the future. The experience of the madeleine is the experience, in a moment, of such a time; a time once lost and now, if only briefly, regained. The recovery of the unity of Marcel's life, which is to say, the recovery of Marcel's life as such, is thus identical with the recovery of time. In spite of the original English translation of the work's title as *Remembrance of Things Past*, the focus of Proust's search is not the *past* (*la passé*), but *time* (*le temps*), as the French title itself indicates – *In Search of Lost Time* (*A la recherche du temps perdu*) – and so the final volume of Proust's work takes the form of a finding again, a regaining, of time – hence its title as *Time Regained* (*Le temps retrouvé*).

It is the experience of time as encompassing an entire realm of experience – a life or a significant part of a life – that is characteristic of the pivotal experiences in Proust's magnum opus, particularly the experiences of 'involuntary memory'. All of those experiences involve the 'embodiment of time', such that, in a single moment, an entire world is opened up. So, at the very end of the novel, when Marcel, considers beginning a novel of his own, he says of the work he proposes, as Proust could say of his own work: 'If I were given long enough to accomplish my work, I should not fail, even if the effect were to make them resemble monsters, to describe men as occupying so considerable a place [*place*] compared with the restricted place which is reserved for them in space [*éspace*], a place, on the contrary, prolonged past measure, for simultaneously, like giants plunged into the years, they touch the distant epochs through which they have lived, between which so many days have come to range themselves – in Time.'[3] It would seem that, in this respect, time has taken on the form of an open region – a place – within which a life is constituted and particular places, persons, and things are given identity and form. Consequently, Georges Poulet takes Proust's search for lost time as also a search for lost place. The task that Proust aims to accomplish is thus a task directed towards the regaining of time through the 'localization' of memory: 'It is not only a certain period of its childhood that the Proustian being sees rise up from its cup of tea; it is also a room, a church, a solid topographical whole, which no longer wanders, which no longer wavers.'[4] It is in this recovery of time in place that Marcel's life is also recovered.

In spite of the difficulties in making any simple or straightforward correlation between French and English when it comes to terms like space and place (an issue already noted in Chapter 1), one nevertheless finds in Poulet's treatment of Proust a clear focus on a concept of place that, as Poulet puts it, 'cannot be reduced to pure localization in space' ('ne peuvent être réduits à de pures localisations dans l'espace'[5]). Indeed, in keeping with the breadth of meaning associated with the French *espace*, Poulet's own talk of 'space' is, for the most part, already such as to implicate place. Poulet thus argues for a reading of Proust according to which the recapture of time is achieved through its rendering in the form of *space* – *espace* in the French original – a space that is not apart from the topographic or topological (Poulet refers directly to 'the Proustian topology' (*la topologie proustienne*).[6] He writes:

> At the moment the Proustian novel is ended. . . then the discontinuous multiplicity of episodes, identical until this moment to a series of isolated and juxtaposed pictures, is found to make room in the mind of him who embraces everything within it, for a coherent reality of images that relate the one to the others, are mutually lighted up, and, so to speak, *compose themselves*. . . at the moment when it ends, and where, retrospectively, it reveals itself in its wholeness, Proust's novel has ceased to be temporal; exactly like a history of France *in images*, it is no longer a history; it is a collection of images, which, if brought together, furnishes a place [*lieu*] and forms an *illustrated space* [*espace illustré*]. . . '*Time for him is like space*,' he writes of one of his characters, Jean Santeuil. And in the same way, one can say of his novel what he himself said of a certain place [*lieu*] called Guermantes, which like the Church of Combray, was full of memories: '*Time has taken there the form of space*' ['Le temps y a pris la forme de l'espace'][7] [see Figure 8].

It is the spatial, according to Poulet, that provides the necessary frame of unity in Proust. The spatial affords a realm in which 'elements. . . [may]. . .

Figure 8 The interior of the church of Saint-Jacques in Illiers-Combray – photograph by Patrick Tourneboeuf, reproduced by permission. Proust describes the church in Combray as 'an edifice occupying, so to speak, a four-dimensional space – the name of the fourth being Time – extending through the centuries its ancient nave, which bay after bay, chapel after chapel, seemed to stretch across and conquer not merely a few yards of soil, but each successive epoch from which tit emerged triumphant' (*In Search of Lost Time*, 83 – for Proust's entire ecstatic description, see 80–85).

be exteriorised, the ones relatively to the others, and aligned, the ones beside the others'.[8] In the establishing of such a unity, time, as that which encompasses past as well as present, is regained. Thus, Poulet treats the primary method of Proust's work to be essentially one of juxtaposition – in contrast with 'displacement' or 'superposition' – and juxtaposition is precisely a matter of the simultaneous presentation of particulars that is possible only through spatiality. 'What is it to juxtapose? It is to place one thing *beside* another,' writes Poulet. In contrast, superposition 'requires the disappearance of the one so that the appearance of the other may take place. . . To superimpose the successive images of human beings, therefore, is to act like the reality of time does; it is to hide away what no longer is, in order to make place for what is coming to be.'[9] Here, Poulet emphasizes the same aspect of spatiality that was so important to the discussion in Chapters 6 and 7: only the exteriority of space can provide a frame within which a multiplicity of elements can be grasped as existing in simultaneous juxtaposition.

It is notable that this emphasis appears to be opposed (and Poulet himself claims as much) to those Bergsonian accounts of Proust that take the time searched for to be the 'real time' of pure duration.[10] Indeed, this Bergsonian position might be generalized so as to argue against either Poulet's reading of Proustian time in terms of space, or the idea of time as a form of place, on the grounds that such approaches do not regain time but do away with it altogether. In addition, one could argue that Poulet's apparent prioritization of space over time is problematic even from within the Proustian framework itself. It would seem, for instance, that, on Poulet's account, time is not regained so much as obliterated (or displaced) by space. Moreover, although the distinction of place from space is not always clear-cut (especially in Poulet's discussion), it is notable that, in the passage from *Time Regained* quoted above, Proust does appear to distinguish time, space, and place such that what is regained through the recovery of time is not merely a *space* but a place 'so considerable. . . compared with the restricted place. . . in space'.[11] It is the idea of a place, rather than a *mere* space that seems the crucial notion here, and given Poulet's own use of concepts and images of localization and place, this is surely a conclusion with which Poulet himself ought to be in agreement. It should be noted too that this emphasis on *place* does not mean that *space* is thereby excluded either. In emphasizing place, what is emphasized is a concept that includes, but is not limited to, the notion of simultaneous dimensionality that is central to spatiality, even as it also still allows for the dynamic unfolding that is characteristic of time. In fact, what is really at work here is not so much the prioritizing of space or time alone, nor their obliteration, but rather the bringing of both back within the compass of place, and so the recovery of space and time from the loss of both that occurs in their seeming separation from one another (which may occur through the prioritization of either apart from the other).

The recovery of time that is the particular task of *In Search of Lost Time* is indeed identical, as Poulet makes clear, with the establishing of a *place* – the sort of open but unitary region that has already figured in my own discussion, and within which various elements are inter-defined and jointly constitute the place itself. It is such a place that encompasses and defines Marcel's life, as well as the lives of others, and that likewise encompasses and defines the many particular places with which Marcel's existence is entwined. Yet, this is not the establishing of a region that stands opposed to time, nor one in which time is displaced by or transformed into space. Notwithstanding Poulet's occasional arguments to the contrary, the place that is established through Proust's narrative – a narrative that Marcel envisages at the end of *Time Regained* – is one that must reconcile both time and space and thereby achieve the rediscovery of time, rather than its obliteration. Poulet clearly directs our attention to the way in which the exteriorization of images and experiences within a spatial frame allows those images and experiences to be, in Poulet's phrase, 'mutually lighted up'. While it is certainly true, as the more abstract analyses in Chapters 5 and 6 demonstrated, that such a 'co-presence' of particulars requires spatiality, it is equally true that it requires temporality. Thus, the unfolding of appearances in Proust always occurs as an unfolding of co-present particulars, and such co-presence is only possible in space, yet, since it is also a necessarily dynamic rather than static process, it always calls upon time as well (and so upon what Poulet treats as the displacement associated with the temporal). In this respect, Proust's achievement is to display the disclosure of the multiplicity and unity of experience, and therefore of the world, as something that occurs through the spatio-temporal unfolding of place.

Some of the complexity of place has already been evident in my emphasis on the way in which place cannot be reduced to any one of the elements situated within its compass, but must instead be understood as a structure comprising spatiality *and* temporality, subjectivity *and* objectivity, self *and* other. These elements are established only in relation to each other and thus only within the topographical structure of place. In Proust, the focus is not on the structure of place as such, but on the role of place in the formation of the self and, at the same time, on the establishing of a world in which both self and other, self and object, are encountered. Yet it is not that self and world are each somehow brought into being just in the epiphanic moment that Marcel experiences with the taste of the madeleine. The epiphany that is identical with that moment of 'involuntary memory' reveals something that was always already there – not something that 'comes to be' only in that moment – namely, the character of Marcel's life as a complex and differentiated unity that conjoins the past to the present, that is articulated in and through the places in which that life has been lived, and that is to be understood in terms of a single encompassing 'place', within which the reality of things can appear. What Marcel discovers is thus the character of his life as it always was, not merely as it is experienced in a sudden, unifying 're-membering' of place. This point is particularly important in Poulet's analysis in which 'spatialization' – exemplified by what occurs with the taste of the madeleine – is shown to be essential to the experience of epiphanic remembrance, and, more importantly, to the very possibility of experience itself.

Poulet's contrasting of the idea of juxtaposition with that of displacement was noted briefly above. The prioritization of space in Poulet's account (a prioritization that Poulet also attributes to Proust) is explicitly intended to address the problem arising from the way in which the 'displacement' of particulars that occurs in time also seems to entail the obliteration of each preceding particular and, therefore, the loss of any enduring presence. Proust's extravagant description of the almost 'slow motion' approach of Marcel to Albertine in the act of a kiss exemplifies the point: 'so now, during this brief journey of my lips towards her cheek, it was ten Albertines I saw; this one girl being like a many-headed goddess, the head I had seen last, when I tried to approach it, gave way to another'.[12] In this proliferation of Albertines, and their successive displacement one by another, the problem is that the 'real' Albertine would seem to be lost forever. Poulet's solution (again one he attributes to Proust) is that the reality is not to be found in the succession of particulars alone, but only in the possibility of their juxtaposition – their unification, or 'gathering together', within a time that is like space, and in which different particulars can be placed side by side so as to be unified and integrated, even while remaining distinct. The problem that Poulet presents here has its analogue in the problem that I explored more prosaically in Chapters 5 and 6 concerning the impossibility of arriving at any adequate grasp of objectivity without a grasp of the possibility of simultaneous but distinct aspects of the same object. Both my account and that of Poulet can be taken to indicate the impossibility of any grasp of objectivity within a purely temporal frame. Poulet's account clearly leads towards the necessity for some forms of spatialization. My consideration of analogous problems leads to recognition of the need for a complex set of concepts, including spatiality *and* temporality. Yet this latter conclusion can be seen as capable of being drawn out of Poulet's account also, particularly in the role he assigns to both juxtaposition *and* to displacement.

Although Poulet presents the proliferation of particulars in time as problematic, he is keenly aware of the way in which Proust presents the real as given precisely through such proliferation and differentiation. This is part the problem in response to which *In Search of Lost Time* attempts, indeed constitutes, a solution. On the Proustian account, the world presents itself as a stream of constantly *displaced* particulars, and so it would seem that the reality of things is continually being lost, continually slipping away from us, continually given over to a past that cannot be regained. In the extravagant example of the kiss, Marcel loses any sense of the real Albertine amongst the multiplication of particulars. The continual proliferation and displacement of particulars sets a problem for the possibility of a unified grasp of the world, for any unity in experience, yet it is precisely out of such proliferation that experience arises as a possibility. Experience is a matter of grasping multiple and multi-faceted elements – objects, events, and persons – gathered together as part of a single, complex world. Poulet's contention is that the unity of multiple particulars evident in experience, and in which a grasp of the world consists, is achieved through spatiality and juxtaposition, but the spatiality that Poulet seems to have in mind is one inextricably tied to movement, to activity, and to the displacement that calls upon temporality.

Given that the fundamental problem in Proust is one of unity in the face of multiplicity, and given Poulet's emphasis on spatiality and juxtaposition, as the solution to this problem, then, at least for Poulet, the question immediately arises: in what does the unity of space consist? At one point, Poulet puts this question in terms of the interconnection of places understood, in a somewhat abstract sense, as separate locations. He asks, 'How to put in communication places that only exist independently of one another?' and immediately answers, 'By local movement, displacement of space.'[13] For Poulet, it would seem that displacement may set the problem, yet is itself part of the solution. A completely static space, a space that allowed nothing more than the simultaneous presentation of images, would not be a space that offered any possibility for the unification of those images. Such unification requires connection, and such connection is possible only through the displacement of space that is tied to *movement* and, therefore, to time. Such movement remains a movement *within* place – like a vibrancy that is internal to it – rather than being the constant movement that occurs in the experience of the seemingly inexorable passage of ordinary time. As such, the emphasis on movement, or on what Poulet refers to as 'local movement' (which we may indeed take to be the movement that belongs to place), does not constitute the reinstatement of displacement or superposition over juxtaposition. Instead, it is their unification in place, but also therefore, within the bounds of place.

Poulet uses a number of key passages from *In Search of Lost Time* to illustrate the unity of place and space as something articulated in terms of activity or movement, and, indeed, to show the unity of objects (and, we might say, of the subject) as also tied to such activity. One such passage presents a description of three spires as seen by Marcel from a moving carriage – first, a view 'of the twin steeples of Martinville, bathed in the setting sun', and, then, a view 'of a third steeple, that of Vieuxvicq, which, although separated from them by a hill and a valley, and rising from rather higher ground in the distance, appeared none the less to be standing by their side'.[14] Through changing views, the three spires are brought close and thereby brought not only close *to each other* but also close *to Marcel himself*. The twisting and turning movement of the carriage thus brings together the spires of Martinville, the spire of Vieuxvicq, and the person of Marcel, all within a unitary, if complex, frame. In another passage, the same ideas are evident, though with greater emphasis on the unification that is apparently achieved through spatial displacement. Watching, from a moving railway carriage, the changes in sky and landscape that accompany the gradual rising of the sun, Marcel tells how he spent his time 'running from one window to the other to reassemble, to collect on a single canvas the intermittent, antipodean fragments of my fine, scarlet, ever-changing morning, and to obtain a comprehensive view and a continuous picture of it'.[15] Of this passage, in its entirety, Poulet writes:

> It is no longer a question here of bringing two objects together; it is a question of bringing them nearer in such a way that both of them, which are opposite, fragmentary, and bounded in time as in extent, form a totality and a continuity. . . Thus objects, beings, places [*les lieux*], lose their exclusiveness without losing their originality. Each thing is in rapport with an infinity of others; each being, like each place [*lieu*], offers an infinity of possible positions, from the one to the other of which one sees them pass.[16]

Movement allows for a multiplication of the aspects that the same object or scene presents to us, but if such multiplication were all that resulted, we would be lost in a chaos of such presentations. Movement is always grasped from within a particular subjective point of view – thus related to that point of view and to the capacities for activity with which that point of view is associated – and it is mapped out with respect to an objective space, in which both the subject and the objects surrounding the body can be situated. It is by means of movement, or activity in general, that space is grasped in its complexity, but it is the possibilities for movement that enable the ordering of things in space, since such ordering is always an ordering dependent on our own capacities for moving and acting.[17] In Proust, then, and on the basis of the analyses advanced in Chapters 5 and 6, it is evident that the world and the things within it, including our selves, are able to be grasped and understood precisely through the capacity for spatialized, embodied activity.

Since juxtaposition and displacement, as Poulet deploys these notions, can be correlated with concepts of space and time, the relation between juxtaposition and displacement in Proust can be seen as exactly analogous to the relation between spatiality and temporality that became evident in

Chapter 5. Indeed, juxtaposition and displacement seem to be identical to spatiality and temporality, understood as forms of co-present and successive dimensionality and seen as similarly interdependent concepts. Just as space and time together allow for the appearance of objects, it is only through both juxtaposition and displacement that it is possible for there to be a differentiated but unitary array of particulars. Spatiality and temporality could then be understood as corresponding to forms of dimensionality generated in terms of, respectively, juxtaposition and displacement, and so as interrelated aspects of the single dimensionality that is integral to activity and fundamental to the idea of place. On such an account, activity is not prior to spatiality or temporality. Instead, activity is a form of ordering that can be understood as dependent on both spatial and temporal dimensions, while spatiality and temporality can be viewed as forms of ordering established in and through activity.

Tying spatiality and temporality to activity in this way does not, however, mean that it is space and time only *as subjectively grasped* that are at issue here. A creature's capacities for active involvement in the world – a creature's capacities as an agent – are dependent, as became evident in Chapter 5, not only on particular capacities for physical movement, but also on one's grasp of the causal interconnection of the world. So far as the particular capacities that make for the possibility of agency are concerned, one's grasp of such causal interconnection is, in part, relative to oneself.[18] The structuring of subjective space is thus a matter of the causal structure of that space understood in relation to one's own causal capacities. Yet, when one thinks of the world objectively, one no longer thinks of it in terms such as 'too heavy for me to lift' or 'able to support my weight' or 'obscuring my line of sight' but rather in terms of causal properties and capacities that are independent of any reference to oneself (thereby mirroring the character of objective space as a space conceived independently of any particular location within it). So, while one's subjective space is structured around notions of activity that are themselves tied to conceptions of causality indexed to oneself, one's grasp of objective space is structured around notions of 'event' (under which the idea of activity is subsumed) that are tied to an abstract concept of causality, not indexed to oneself. The dimensionality of space and of time (each an aspect of the unitary dimensionality of place) are thus interconnected to concepts of activity and event, and to concepts of causality, in different ways according to the different spatial and temporal structures at issue.

The concepts of juxtaposition and displacement, deployed by Poulet, are no less complex in their relation nor any less interdependent than the concepts of causality and dimensionality or of subjectivity and objectivity. Juxtaposition and displacement cannot be opposed to one another in any simple contrastive relation, because they are inextricably bound together. Displacement allows for the generation of a multiplicity of particulars, and juxtaposition allows a multiplicity of particulars to be brought together. In bringing things close, juxtaposition enables the multiplicity generated in displacement to be grasped as a multiplicity of distinct particulars that are nevertheless interconnected in certain quite specific, even if prolific, respects. Multiplicity is thus essential to the method of juxtaposition, just as juxtaposition is necessary for unification. Poulet can therefore write that the unity of particulars achieved by Proust through displacement and juxtaposition is achieved, 'not by a simplification, but on the contrary by a multiplication of the aspects offered by opposing objects; as if it were only in taking consciousness of the inexhaustible variety they present that one could arrive at understanding their true nature'.[19] Poulet presents such multiplication as arising within a structure that he treats in spatial/topological terms. He conceives of space itself, not only as necessarily interconnected with displacement and movement, and so with temporality, but as a rich structure that involves much more than physical extendedness. Poulet's account of 'Proustian space' presents space as something almost tangible and enveloping, a densely packed structure of overlapping and intersecting views and regions, a space of multiplication, of activity, and of movement.

The way in which Poulet connects space so strongly with movement and activity is sufficient to suggest that the concept of space at issue here cannot be reduced to a notion of objective or physical space alone. Such a limited conception could not, as argued in Chapter 2, be adequate to the complex structure of spatiality that arises in conjunction with the idea of active subjectivity. This is a point that the phenomenologist Erwin Strauss also emphasizes, though in a slightly different way from either Poulet's account or mine. Strauss focuses on the way in which the ordering of space is an ordering established in relation to a creature's possibilities for movement. He writes:

> The space enclosed by the walls of a room becomes an inner space. . . only for a being which in its totality relates itself to the totality of the world and who encounters the limits of the possibilities of its actions; the boundaries of the room are that which cuts a man off from the totality of his world. Because he has the possibility of stepping beyond those boundaries, the walls and door become limits. Because he has the power of relating himself, as an individual, to the totality of the world, then the limits themselves must be pervasive and many-sided. The boundaries are relative to the action system of the bound person.[20]

Such considerations lead Strauss to claim that 'the relation of within and without is not a spatial phenomenon, it is a phenomenon of the scope of action'.[21] Indeed, this claim is part of his larger argument against any view according to which 'within and without are thought of as objective, general spatial relations'.[22]

The relation of 'within and without' and the associated notion of 'boundary' to which Strauss gives special attention – both of which can be seen implicated with a general notion of 'containment' – are of special importance in the investigation of place. The concept of place is essentially the concept of a *bounded* but open region, *within which* a set of interconnected elements can be situated. That such a concept necessarily involves a form of 'containment' – enclosedness within bounds – was noted in Chapter 4, in the discussion of the 'nested' character of place. One can certainly understand the idea of one point in space having a location that belongs to a set of possible locations; the latter comprising a certain abstractly conceived area of space. We can also analyse an object as having certain possibilities for movement that are restricted by the physical structure of the immediate environment in which it is physically located. The notion of containment, however, properly goes beyond any such minimal sense of inclusion (which can be understood in a purely formal sense alone). Containment involves the establishing of a certain differentiated form of spatiality and associated directionality, able to be expressed in terms of 'within', 'without', 'internal', and 'external', and incompatible with the abstracted notion of space as an extended and homogenous field. Such directionality and, with it, the important role played by notions of inside and outside in our grasp of place and space, is directly tied to the necessarily perspectival (and so also active and embodied) character of the experience of space discussed in Chapter 2.

The idea of place that is evident in Proust, as well as in Poulet's account of 'Proustian space', implicates notions of both containment and boundedness. Marcel's Combray (one of the key places in Proust's novel) possesses its own boundaries within which appear house and pavilion, park and garden, square and street, and even Combray itself. In this respect, place cannot be conceived either as a static backdrop to action and experience nor as some framework above and apart from the array of elements that it encompasses. The character of place as bounded, and also as both contained and containing (through the way in which places are embedded or nested within other places, even while embedding other places and things in turn), is alone sufficient to make for a complex structure, and this is a complexity over and above that associated with place as it encompasses the differentiated structure of subjectivity and objectivity, dimensionality, and activity. Places always open up to disclose other places within them – as every house contains its nooks and crannies, as well as its rooms, as every garden contains spots and corners, as every stretch of country has its sites and locales, as every town has its streets and neighbourhoods. Equally, from within any particular place, one can always look outwards to find oneself within some much larger expanse – just as one can look from the room in which one sits to the house in which one lives, and from there to the town or the region to which one belongs (see Figure 9).

Figure 9 John Glover, *Hobart Town, taken from the garden where I lived*, 1832, oil on canvas, Dixson Collection, State Library of New South Wales. Here the house and its interior spaces are nested within the garden, which in turn opens out to the town, and then on to the wider landscape of the river and surrounding hills, with the encircling horizon (and the larger world it beckons towards) in the far distance.

As evident in Poulet's discussion of Proust, the grasp of space – and so of place – is tied to activity. In this respect, any concrete sense of place is most closely tied to concrete capacities to act and to be acted upon (since the capacity to be affected by one's surroundings is an important element in action and in the grasp of space and place). One result of this is that the less a place is encompassed by our capacity to act or to react, the more abstract must be our grasp of that place. For instance, a move from room to apartment, or to building, to neighbourhood, to city, to state or province, to country, and so on, is not a move in which the places cited, each being contained within the other, are all of the same character. In general, a move to more encompassing places is also a move to greater abstractness. The same is true of a move downwards, to ever smaller 'places'. Indeed, there is a sense in which a move either upwards or downwards takes us away from *place*, towards an increasingly abstracted sense of *space*. The connection between place and activity, then, puts certain constraints on place; constraints that are reflected in the bounding of places in ways that, as Strauss explicitly points out, are tied to the boundaries on capacities for action and, of course, for reaction. Nevertheless, even given these bounds on place, there remains no determinate delimitation that attaches to places as such. The bounding of place is not the bounding associated with any simple spatial demarcation.

Inasmuch as place can be understood as tied to a field of activity and response, so analyses that treat supposedly nomadic peoples as somehow living in a way that is not tied to place in any strong sense can be seen to depend on a mistaken and static understanding of the nature of place as well, perhaps, of nomadism itself. Places are established (though not exclusively) in relation to activity, and the area in which a 'nomadic' people lives and across which they regularly travel can thus be understood as itself a single place spread across an extended region of integrated activity, or else as a closely integrated network of regularly traversed (regularly 'enacted') places. Of course, as Krim Benterrek, Stephen Muecke and Paddy Roe point out, it may be something of a cultural bias that leads us to suppose that belonging to the land entails a settled form of existence – they emphasize that the nomad is precisely 'the one who doesn't leave the country'.[23] Thus, in Kenneth White's work, the nomadic refers precisely to a mode of engagement with place, and certainly not to any mode of disengagement from place or indifference towards it. It is through journeying out into the world that place is encountered, and though such journeying always involves a place departed from, even if not always returned to, so journeying always stands in relation to sojourning, as movement and rest implicate each other. For White, it is not the nomad who is apart from place but the obsessive stay-at-homer, the one who refuses to see the necessary implication of the home-place with the foreign, who fails to see, even in the home-place, the horizon that opens up to the world beyond.[24] Nomadism aside, it is also worth noting that just as place is always active, always mobile, so the relation to place is not established merely by the fact, as recorded in a passport or identity paper, of birth at a certain location and at a certain time and date. The entry into place may be said to begin at birth, but it is the articulation of the relation to place as that occurs in the activity of a life, and that therefore also involves a multiplicity of places, as it implicates the world, that constitutes the genuine reality of human being-in-place.

Places offer themselves in a multiplicity of aspects that thereby reflect the various ways in which those places can be situated relative to other places, the diverse orientations and perspectives that are possible within the bounds of a particular place, and the very openness of place as a structure that allows the appearance of things within it. Places can turn outwards to reveal other places, but they can likewise turn inwards to reveal their own character or the character of the subject who identifies with that place. In this latter respect, the possibility of taking a place to be variously oriented, to be folded either inwards or outwards (or, as it might also be put, to 'unfold' in a way that reveals something of its own structure or features of the world) is part of what enables Merleau-Ponty to speak, in the quotation to which I referred in the introduction, of the world as being wholly inside and I as wholly outside myself.

This 'folded' character of place is made notably evident by the way in which a particular place can appear within the very bounds that it also opens up. This is something about which I shall have more to say in the next chapter, but here it is important to see how, for instance, the place that is Marcel's Combray can be that within which a multiplicity of particulars appear, as well as itself appearing as a 'particular' (within, as it were, the boundary of appearance that it does itself establish). Place allows for the appearing of place within it, and this is so in two respects. First, as that within which experience is possible, place is thereby experienced *as the place of experience*, which is to say, of any experience whatsoever. Second, and perhaps more prosaically, place can appear *as itself something experienced* – as I can experience this or that place – and this experience of place, which is always of *a* place, will itself bring an experience of other places with it (in virtue of the necessary entanglement of places). As it can be itself the object of experience, so place, which is to say specific places, can also be grasped conceptually or representationally – whether by means of a name, a description, a map, an image, or whatever), and so grasped in abstraction from the concrete particularity, or perhaps better, the 'singularity',[25] of the place.

That places can be represented in this way is itself crucial to the possibility of their identification and re-identification – at least in the developed sense of place at issue here (although one might argue that identification and re-identification of particulars always relies on some capacity for representation[26]). The capacity for conceptualization and representation, whether it be of places, ourselves, or anything else, and which is itself tied to language, is indeed essential to the possibility of any sophisticated grasp of self, of others, of objects – or of place. In representation, however, we do indeed also abstract that which is represented from the concreteness of its presentation. As we typically identify places through the ways in which we abstractly represent them, so we often come to identify places with their abstracted representations. In effect, we readily confuse the map with the territory, and in doing so we also tend to treat places as abstracted and represented identities (reducing places to mere locations or even to images and symbols), rather than attending to the concreteness with which those places originally present themselves. As a result, we can indeed be led to view places as the static backdrops to action and experience, rather than as the very ground and frame for such.[27]

Place has a complex and differentiated structure – as Poulet's discussion of Proust makes very clear – and this complexity and differentiation is not only a matter of the elements that place encompasses (space and time, subjective, intersubjective, and objective), but also of the various aspects that belong to it. Place is thus both containing and contained, open and bounded, folded inwards and outwards, of the homely and the strange, concretely experienced and abstractly represented. The fact of such complexity leads to an inevitable multiplicity in the ways in which place can be grasped and understood. Place may be viewed in terms that emphasize the concrete features of the natural landscape, that give priority to certain social or cultural features, or that emphasize place purely as experienced. Indeed, much writing about place takes up place, and particular places, only through one or another such mode of presentation. Yet, since these different ways of grasping the structure of place are grounded in the complexity of place as such, no single way of grasping place can exhaust its complexity or entirely ignore that complexity. Consequently, the treatment of place as a subjective structure – as a matter of 'emotional reminiscence' or personal feeling – draws on *one* element within the structure of place and attempts to understand place in a way that gives priority to that element, but it does not constitute an exhaustive characterization of that structure, nor can it proceed in a way that entirely obliterates the objective. Indeed, even the Proustian exploration, in *In Search of Lost Time*, cannot be viewed as a purely subjective exploration that concerns only the accumulation of memory and personal experience in the life of Marcel. To remain within the purely subjective would be to remain within the realm of loss and displacement alone. The regaining of 'lost time', the regaining of a life, is indeed the regaining of a sense of the reality of things that transcends the subjective and encompasses particular places, persons, objects, actions, and events.

Recognition of the complexity of place should direct our attention to the very unity in which place also consists. The complexity of place does not entail a dispersion of elements, but rather enables their 'gathering together' – their interconnection and unification – in such a way that their multiplicity and differentiation can be both preserved and brought to light. The differentiated and complex unity of place reflects the complex unity of the world itself. It also reflects the complex unity, given focus through a creature's active involvement with respect to particular objects and events, that makes for the possibility of memory, of belief, of thought, and of experience. Only within place is the unity necessary for subjectivity established. The necessary dependence of subjectivity on place is given special emphasis in Proust, where the exploration and reconstitution of the self is at one with the exploration and reconstitution of place, and where persons are always and only encountered in and through the places they inhabit. The idea that subjectivity in general, and the nature and identity of individual persons in particular, is to be understood only in relation to place and the particular places in which the subject is embedded has been a theme throughout much of the preceding discussion, and was, of course, the idea with which this book began. The next chapter will focus more directly on this idea, providing a more detailed account of the interconnection of person with place as this arises in the formation of self-identity and self-conception.

Notes

1 Martin Heidegger, 'Art and Space', trans. Charles Seibert, *Man and World* 1 (1973): 4.
2 Marcel Proust, *In Search of Lost Time*, trans. C.K. Scott Moncrieff and Terence Kilmartin, rev. D.J. Enright, vol. 1, *Swann's Way* (London: Chatto & Windus, 1992), 63–64.
3 Proust, *In Search of Lost Time*, vol. 6, *Time Regained*, 531–532.
4 Georges Poulet, *Proustian Space*, trans. Elliott Coleman (Baltimore, MD: Johns Hopkins University Press, 1977), 16.
5 Ibid., 33; or Georges Poulet, *L'Espace proustien* (Paris: Gallimard, 1963), 50.
6 In this regard, the French, and especially Poulet's own use of notions of place and space, has the advantage over the English precisely in that it does not treat space and place as necessarily separated from one another, but rather allows for their interconnection, even while it also does not ignore the need, in some cases, for their distinction.
7 Poulet, *Proustian Space*, 103–105; or *L'Espace proustien*, 131–135.
8 Poulet, *Proustian Space*, 106. In a similar vein, George Stambolian comments that 'all of Marcel's lost time has been spatialized in the present'. See his *Marcel Proust and the Creative Encounter* (Chicago, IL: University of Chicago Press, 1972), 190.
9 Poulet, *Proustian Space*, 91–92.
10 See ibid., 105–106.
11 In the original French: 'une place si considérable, à côté de celle si restreinte qui leur réservée dans l'espace'. See Marcel Proust, *À la recherche du temps perdu, vol. 3, Le temps retrouvé* (Paris: Gallimard, 1954), 1048. As noted earlier, Poulet also, on occasion, contrasts space with place. See especially *Proustian Space*, 32–33. Proust's characterization of the place at issue in this passage as one 'prolonged past measure' –'une place...prolongée sans mesure' – may strike one as somewhat odd given the way in which place seems to be necessarily tied to a certain openness within bounds. The crucial idea here is surely not of a place without bounds but of a place without internal limits, whose dimensions can never be exhausted – a place that, instead of imprisoning, releases into an immeasurable wealth of experience and of memory.
12 Proust, *In Search of Lost Time, vol. 3, The Guermantes Way*, 499; or *A la recherche du temps perdu, vol. 2, Le côté de Guermantes*, 365. See Poulet, *Proustian Space*, 85–88.
13 Poulet, *Proustian Space*, 73.
14 Proust, *In Search of Lost Time, vol. 1, Swann's Way*, 254.
15 Proust, *In Search of Lost Time, vol. 2, Within a Budding Grove*, 317.
16 Poulet, *Proustian Space*, 80; or *L'Espace proustien*, 102–103. Poulet also notes that this passage is 'of importance almost without equal'.
17 Poulet comments that 'there is no need to be moved oneself, nor to be in a moving vehicle' for the phenomenon of multiplication and unification that is at issue here to be possible – 'it suffices to see the sunlight change places on a landscape, in order that the latter modify itself gradually before our eyes, as if we turned ourselves about to see it better'. See *Proustian Space*, 81–82. The movement that is at issue here is thus not merely the movement associated with gross change of place; it is, in general, only through, and in relation to, our own capacities for movement of both our bodies and parts of our bodies that space and the objects within it can be grasped. But one should add that this itself operates against the background of the other forms of movement that also occur in language and, so, in the intersubjective space of our relation to others, as well as in relation to objects.
18 In John Campbell's terms, it is a grasp of causal concepts that are 'causally indexical'. See his *Past, Space, and Self* (Cambridge, MA: MIT Press, 1994), 43–46.
19 Poulet, *Proustian Space*, 80.
20 Erwin Strauss, *The Primary World of the Senses*, trans. Jacob Needleman (New York: Macmillan, 1963), 243. Strauss recognizes that this seems to entail the conclusion that 'strictly speaking, one could not say of dead things that they are in a space, say, or in a room'.
21 Ibid., 244.
22 Ibid., 241. Inasmuch as Strauss can be viewed as privileging activity over spatiality, then he would seem to be adopting a view clearly reminiscent of Heidegger's treatment of spatiality, in *Being*

and Time, as a secondary or derivative element in the structure of being-in-the-world. Moreover, Strauss's emphasis on the impossibility of relation within a space that is divorced from the idea of movement or activity is also present in Heidegger who claims that within a purely Cartesian space there can be no proper connectedness between things. See Heidegger, *Being and Time*, trans. John Macquarrie and Edward Robinson (New York: Harper & Row, 1962), §12, H55. It is notable that Heidegger fails to recognize the way in which this creates certain problems for his own insistence (*Being and Time*, §12, H54) on understanding the idea of the 'being-in' associated with 'containment' as involving a Cartesian view of space as objective physical extension. For more on issues of place and space in Heidegger, see my *Heidegger's Topology* (Cambridge, MA: MIT Press, 2006), esp. chap. 3. There, I discuss the problems that arise in relation to the analysis in *Being and Time*.

23 Krim Benterrek, Stephen Muecke, and Paddy Roe, *Reading the Country: Introduction to Nomadology* (Fremantle, WA: Fremantle Arts Centre Press, 1984), 224, and 15.

24 See, for example, White, *The Nomad Mind*, trans. Sam La Védrine (Liverpool: Liverpool University Press, forthcoming 2018); and also *The Wanderer and His Charts: Exploring the Fields of Vagrant Thought and Vagabond Beauty* (Edinburgh: Polygon, 2010).

25 See my 'Place and Singularity', in *The Intelligence of Place: Topographies and Poetics*, ed. Jeff Malpas (London: Bloomsbury, 2015), 65–92.

26 Inasmuch as the capacity to identify and re-identify particulars is tied, even if indirectly, to the capacity for a grasp of space and of spatial location (as has been evident from earlier discussions, especially those in Chapter 5), then the capacity for such identification and re-identification would seem to be underpinned by exactly the sort of cognitive mapping that enables spatial navigation and positioning (although it should be remembered that such mapping can operate independently of any direct awareness of it).

27 It is this latter tendency, not merely in relation to place, but to our experience in general, that leads Proust to argue against any tendency towards abstraction in literature, and to emphasize the particular and the concrete. In this respect, as Proust himself makes clear, the 'search for lost time' that is undertaken in *In Search of Lost Time* – the search that is also a search for place – is, in turn, a search that attempts to reclaim the reality – the essence – of things through art. Thus, Proust writes of 'the greatness... of true art' as lying in a certain reconnecting with the reality of our lives: 'We have to rediscover, to reapprehend, to make ourselves fully aware of that reality, remote form our daily preoccupations, from which we separate ourselves by an ever greater gulf as the conventional knowledge which we substitute for it grows thicker and more impermeable, that reality which it is very easy for us to die without ever having known and which is, quite simply, our life. Real life, life at last laid bare and illuminated.' See *In Search of Lost Time, vol. 6, Time Regained*, 298; or *À la recherche du temps perdu, vol. 3, Le temps retrouvé*, 895. And this 'laying bare' and 'illuminating' of the reality of life is brought about, not through some reductive account of their fundamental character, but through the unification – by means of a spatialized and temporalized dimensionality, by means of the displacement and juxtaposition – of a dense multiplicity of elements.

Further reading

Malpas, Jeff, ed. *The Intelligence of Place: Topographies and Poetics*. London: Bloomsbury, 2015.

Poulet, Georges. *Proustian Space*. Baltimore, MD: Johns Hopkins University Press, 1977.

Proust, Marcel. *In Search of Lost Time*. Translated by C.K. Scott Moncrieff and Terence Kilmartin. Revised by D.J. Enright. London: Chatto and Windus, 1992 (or any other edition).

White, Kenneth. *The Wanderer and His Charts: Exploring the Fields of Vagrant Thought and Vagabond Beauty*. Edinburgh: Polygon, 2010.

8 Place, past, and person

> It is indeed my life that I am staking here, a life that tastes of warm stone, that is full of the sighs of the sea and the rising song of the crickets.
>
> (Albert Camus, 'Nuptials at Tipasa'[1])

Subjectivity, as seen in Chapters 3 and 4, is to be understood as an interplay of elements that are organized specifically in relation to the concept of agency, rather than as some underlying ground in which the unity of those elements is independently founded. One of the consequences of this (a consequence already explored to some extent in Chapters 5 and 6) is that subjectivity cannot be grasped independently of a larger structure that not only encompasses other subjects but also the objects and events of the world. It is, we can say, in the dense structure of place that subjectivity is embedded, and since subjectivity is only to be found within such a structure, there is a necessary dependence of subjectivity on the other elements within that structure and on the structure as a whole. Up to this point, much of the discussion has been focused on mapping out the topography of the more general structure within which subjectivity – and the possibility of thought and experience – is constituted. The more specific connection between subjectivity and place, according to which the very content of a subject's mental life and the character of a subject's self-identity and self-conception are tied to the places in which the subject finds itself, is something that has not been fully explored (though it was already a theme in Chapter 4). It is now time to take up this connection as a central theme.

The dependence of subjectivity on place is something already glimpsed as an important element in Proust's *In Search of Lost Time.* There, this dependence often appears most clearly in relation to the binding of persons and places in *memory* – one recalls not just the person but person *and* place, and both as part of the same image, part of a single remembrance. As Poulet writes: 'Beings surround themselves with the places where they find themselves, the way one wraps oneself up in a garment that is at one and the same time a disguise and a characterization. Without places, beings would be only abstractions. It is places that make their image precise and that give them the necessary support thanks to which we can assign them a place in our mental space, dream of them, and remember them.'[2] This binding of person to place in memory would seem to mirror the more general inter-relation between memory and place noted in Chapter 4: memories, particularly memories that have some personal or autobiographical component, are typically keyed to particular spaces and places.[3] That we often remember persons in relation to specific places and surroundings, in characteristic poses or moods that imply a certain situation, exemplifies this more general phenomenon.

The binding of memory to place, and so to particular places, can be seen as a function of the way in which subjectivity is necessarily embedded in place – in spatialized and embodied activity. That persons 'surround themselves with the places where they find themselves' is thus indicative of the character of both memory *and* subjectivity. The very identity of subjects, both in terms of their own self-definition and their identity as grasped by others, is inextricably bound to the particular places in which they find themselves and in which others find them, yet, in a more general sense, it is only within the overarching structure of place as such that subjectivity is possible. Quite often, in fact, Proust writes of persons as if they were tied to places in some such very basic fashion – not as *remembered* only in relation to place, but as *being who and what they are* through their inhabiting of particular places and their situation within particular locations; what I termed, in the Introduction, 'Proust's Principle.' The principle is one suggested by the very nature of Proust's search in *In Search of Lost Time*. Marcel's identity is inextricably tied to the places in which his life has been lived, such that the recovery of self can only take the form of a recovery of place – both a recovery of specific places as well as the recovery of an encompassing place, within which his life can be grasped as a whole.

This dependence of self-identity on place derives, of course, both from the general characterization of subjectivity as a structure that is topologically embedded in a world of other subjects and multiple objects, and from the more particular way in which the mental life of the subject is dependent on the subject's active engagement with the surrounding environment and, therefore, on its situatedness within a particular place. The more specific dependence of self-identity on particular places is an obvious consequence of the way in which self-conceptualization and the conceptualization of place are interdependent elements within the same structure. Our identities are thus bound up with particular places, or localities, through the very structuring of subjectivity and mental life within the overarching structure of place. Particular places enter into our self-conception and self-identity because it is only in, and through, our grasp of the places in which we are situated that we can encounter objects, other persons, or, indeed, ourselves. In this respect, it is important to recognize that, in arguing for self-identity and self-conception as necessarily entwined with the self's being-in-place, it is not any simple psychological claim that is at issue – one to the effect that we generally *think of ourselves* as defined by reference to the particular places in which we have lived or about which we have certain strong memories or attachments (such a psychological claim may indeed be true, but it can be viewed as consequential upon the more basic point at issue).[4] Instead, the argument advanced here is that we are the sort of thinking, remembering, experiencing creatures we are only in virtue of our active engagement in place; that the possibility of mental life is necessarily tied to such engagement, and therefore to the places in which we are so engaged; and that, when we come to give content to our concepts of ourselves and to the idea of our own self-identity, place, and locality play a crucial role. Our identities are, one can say, intricately and inevitably place-bound.

That our relation to place is both intricate and inevitable is not something to which we often pay a great deal of attention. After all, though it seems obvious, the places in which we live are always with us, and usually they demand our attention only in unusual circumstances – when our situation radically changes, for instance, or when we find ourselves in certain moods and frames of mind. Moreover, in many of the most basic respects, our dependence on place is something that always remains implicit or that can only be explicated with great difficulty. It is nevertheless a characteristic feature of much of our thinking about ourselves that place occupies an especially significant role. Indeed, since our subjectivity is inseparably tied to place, our self-identity and self-conceptualization (and our conceptualization of others) can only be worked out in relation to place and our active engagement in place – and this is so whether or not we give explicit recognition to the fact. In being worked out in this way, however, self-identity is not thereby tied to any simple location within some purely static space. This is evident from the arguments of the preceding chapters, and it is also implicit in the emphasis on self-identity as worked out in relation to 'active engagement'. Certainly, in Proust, it is quite clear that the binding of persons to places is not a matter of the subject being held within some unchanging space or location, like an insect preserved in amber. Finding themselves in place, subjects also find themselves within space *and* time, and so the articulation of a sense of self-identity, which is often presented in terms of a search for place, is invariably a search that is both spatial and temporal.

In a passage in which the notion of 'presence' invokes part of what is here at issue in talk of place, the theologian Paul Tillich writes:

> The mystery of the future and the mystery of the past are united in the mystery of the present. Our time, the time we have, is the time in which we have 'presence.' But how can we have presence? Is not the present moment gone when we think of it? Is not the present the ever-moving boundary line between past and future? But a moving boundary is not a place to stand upon. If nothing were given to us except the 'no more' of the past and the 'not yet' of the future, we would not have anything. We could not speak of the time that is *our* time; we would not have 'presence.'[5]

What is at issue in this passage is partly what Proust also addresses. The problem is one that is inevitable if time is understood as mere succession – as a constant super-positioning of one moment in relation to another. The solution to the problem as Tillich expresses is to be found in an expanded notion of the present – in what might be understood as a spatialised present. Such a direction of thought leads us, however, away from the notion of a pure temporality, and into a much broader topography or topology. It is this notion that is arguably at work wherever one finds the assertion of the 'moment' as that expansive realm in which genuine existence is to revealed – an idea found not only in Tillich, but also, to some extent, in Heidegger, in Nietzsche, in Goethe, and perhaps even among the Stoics and Epicureans.[6] What appears is, as in Proust, the opening up of place as that which encompasses even time.

As the Proustian recovery of time is achieved through the recovery of place, so the engagement with place, even outside Proust, is also an engagement with time. A particularly good example of this point is to be found in Sally Morgan's *My Place*.[7] The book recounts Morgan's search to uncover her own and her family's history. Morgan's story is a very personal one – as much about Morgan's relationship with her mother and grandmother, as about her relationship to the past – but it is also a story that has significance beyond Morgan's immediate family, since the book makes a significant contribution to the discourse around post-European Aboriginal Australia.[8] The culmination of the book is the account of Morgan's visit, with her mother, to Corunna Downs Station, a pastoral holding in the Pilbara region of northwest Australia, the place and region from which her mother's family originally came. Describing a portion of the visit, Morgan writes:

> Mum and I sat down on part of the old fence and looked across to the distant horizon. We were both trying to imagine what it would have been like for the people in the old days. Soft, blue hills completely surrounded the station. They seemed to us mystical and magical. We easily imagined Nan, Arthur, Rosie, Lily, and Albert, sitting exactly as we were now, looking off into the horizon at the end of the day. Dreaming, thinking. 'This is a beautiful place,' Mum sighed. I nodded in agreement. Why did she tell me it was an ugly place? She didn't want me to come. She just doesn't want to be Aboriginal. We both sat in silence. . . We all felt very emotional when we left from Doris' house. . . We kissed everyone goodbye and headed off towards Nullagine. Mum and I were both a bit teary. Nothing was said, but I knew she felt like I did. Like we'd suddenly come home and now we were leaving again. But we had a sense of place, now.[9]

This passage presents a number of interesting points. One of the more obvious concerns the way in which, as in Proust (notwithstanding differences in style and language), the identity and images of persons are intimately bound to the particular places with which their lives are associated, with 'Nan, Arthur, Rosie, Lily, and Albert' seeming to be part of the landscape of Corunna. The fact that this is expressed, as such matters usually are, in terms of a relation between person and named location – in this case Corunna – should not be allowed to obscure the more complex set of interconnections that the use of the name invokes. More significant perhaps, and this is a feature not only of this particular passage but of the book as a whole, is that Morgan chooses to describe what is gained by her visit to the Northwest and the discovery of her Aboriginal background, in terms of a return *home* and the recovery of a 'sense of *place*'. This is so even though Morgan's journey is as much a journey in search of a past, and a family history, as it is a journey to and around a particular region (although it is not insignificant that the discovery of this sense of place and of time is indeed accomplished through such a physical journeying). In gaining a sense of place, Morgan discovers a sense of her own *identity*; an identity in which the landscape of Corunna, and all that is associated with it, has a quite special role.

The use of the phrase 'sense of place' is itself worthy of comment, especially since this phrase – to which I have made little reference in the previous discussion – appears so frequently in discussions of place and of the human relation to place.[10] 'Sense of place' can refer to both the felt qualities of a place that give it a distinctive character (to 'sense' as in 'sensed') and to the idea of a place as the distinctive place it is and, so, as encompassing its identity as a place (to 'sense' as it connotes 'meaning').[11] If this phrase is not one to which I have had much recourse here, then the reason is simply that the notion remains somewhat ambiguous, and the ambiguity is difficult to resolve. Moreover, not only does the use of the term tend to reinforce commonplace assumptions concerning the subjectivity of place (so the sense of place is just the felt or meaningful character associated with certain spatial locations or regions),[12] but it also tends to focus attention only on the idea of place as that which is indeed sensed or made sense of in this explicit fashion. A large part of the argument here has been that the connection to place goes beyond merely that which we explicitly recognize, operating in a way that extends much deeper and is more pervasive. There is no doubt, however, that the idea of a sense of place is both significant and widespread. It is an idea that ought to be seen to reinforce the account of the fundamental role of place that is the main focus of this volume. Moreover, it is also an idea that can be seen to be underlain by exactly the analysis of the complex nature of place that has been developed over previous chapters – that analysis, taken as a whole, can be read as precisely an analysis of that in which the sense of place (which is indeed a certain grasp of place) is founded, and in which it may also be said to consist.

The connection of a sense of identity with a past, which is what is at issue in Morgan's talk of 'sense of place', and so also with a narrative or set of narratives (which belong neither solely to the person nor the place, but connect both), is one of the key ideas that Morgan's work reinforces – all the more so since Morgan's work, embeds her story, which is about her place, with the stories of others who also stand in relation to that same place (in fact those other stories – those of Arthur, Gladys, and Daisy – are given as separate inclusions within the overall structure of Morgan's book). This does not mean, as noted above, that self-identity can be reduced to the simple identification of person with place, or to some set of images or memories of place, but it does illustrate the way in which the fundamental grounding of subjectivity and of mental life in place, is mirrored by the subject's own self-conceptualization in terms of place and location. Yet, in addition to this, Morgan's work also exemplifies the way in which having a sense of the *past*, and the narratives that go with it, is tied to a sense of *place* and to identifiable localities. Indeed, given the already established close interconnection of subjectivity – and so of narrativity and memory – with embodied and *spatialized* activity, it is difficult to see how matters could be otherwise.

To have a sense of the past, to have both a cognitive and felt grasp of it *as past* and *as a distinct past*, is not just a matter of having a grasp of some temporally ordered sequence of experience. The ordering of experience – the ordering of the mental itself – is both temporal *and* spatial. It is an ordering established through the agent's active involvement within a concrete, spatio-temporal, intersubjective frame and with respect to particular objects and locations (including the causal connections that structure relations between them) within that frame. To have a sense of the past is always, then, to have a sense of the way in which present and future conditions are embedded in a complex 'history' that is articulated only in terms of particular individuals and concrete objects as they interact in relation to certain places.[13] To have a sense of one's own past is to have a grasp of one's present and future in relation to the 'story' of one's embodied activity within the places in which one lives and with respect to the objects and persons in those places. The past cannot be prised away from the places – that is, from objects and persons as they interact within particular spatio-temporal regions – with respect to which that past is established. This is true of the past that can be recounted as part of a personal biography, and of the past that is articulated through communal narrative and history (neither being wholly independent of the other).

The past cannot be grasped independently of place. Only in place can there be a creature capable of grasping past, present, or future, and only within the compass of place can there be the spatio-temporal ordering of things on which a grasp of the past depends. This dependence of the past on place is reflected, in a quite particular fashion, in a phenomenon already encountered in Poulet's discussion of Proust; namely, the way in which the past, even time itself, can be seen as taking on an embodied and spatialized form in features of the surrounding environment. To repeat Poulet's comment in respect of one of the key places in Proust's narrative, Guermantes: since, like the Church of Combray, 'it is full of memories, it seems that, there, time has taken the form of space'.[14] In similar fashion, though at a level that could be seen to implicate the communal and not merely the personal, William Faulkner, in 'The Jail', writes of the way in which one building carries within it the accumulated history and experience of a town:

> And so, being older than all, it had seen all: the mutation and the change: and in, in that sense, had recorded them. . . invisible and impacted, not only beneath the annual inside creosote-and-whitewash of bullpen and cell, but on the blind outside walls too, first the simple mud-chinked log ones and then the symmetric brick, not only the scrawled illiterate repetitive unimaginative doggerel and the perspectiveless almost prehistoric sexual picturing-writing, but the images, the panorama not only of the town but of its days and years.[15]

In Faulkner, as in Proust, the temporal is found – spatialized, materialized, and *memorialized* – in the objects around us in the present.[16] Although, as noted earlier, Poulet sometimes treats this as a transformation of time into space, it is better to view this 'objectification' of time, and the past, as indicative of the way in which, at the most general level, both temporality and spatiality are always given together in the unitary dimensionality of place – a unitary dimensionality that is also material, and indeed this is just what materiality is: *the singular appearing of place*. In place, and only in place, can we encounter the possibility of past and future, of nearness and distance, of temporality and spatiality – only within the complex unity of place is any such encounter even possible.

Just as a sense of the past is tied to a sense of place, so is memory – personal and autobiographical memory – tied to place. Moreover, just as memory is, in certain important respects, tied to narrativity, so is the connection between memory and place indicative of a parallel connection between place and narrative. The integration of memory is a central element, as seen earlier, in the integration of mental life, which is a prerequisite of subjectivity and for self-identity. Additionally, the integration of memory – particularly of personal and autobiographical memory – depends on the capacity to locate memories within a variety of narrative structures. Of course, there is also a certain interdependence, since the capacity to construct such narratives is itself dependent on the capacity to remember, and the more far-reaching one's memories, the richer and more complex will be the possibility for narrative integration of one's life. This does not imply any problematic circularity between memory and narration, but rather is indicative of the way in which memory and narration, along with so many of the concepts at issue here, must be seen as interdependent elements within a single structure. A sense of self-identity (and, in a certain respect, it is just a sense of self-identity that makes for self-identity as such[17]) is therefore tied to the capacity for memory and narration. Given such connections between memory, narrative, and a sense of self-identity, and given also the already noted connection between memory, narrative, and place, one can readily see why a sense of self might be closely tied to a sense of place, and why a sense of time and of the past might be similarly tied. Even if we look to the capacity to plan and to one's ongoing projects as partly determinative of a sense of self-identity, those plans and projects remain rooted in a narrative that encompasses a past as well as future. Of course, as was evident earlier, place enables the encounter with both self *and* other, and as it does this, so too does it enable memory and narrative to extend beyond the personal alone to become something that belongs to a community and a culture – it enables, in fact, the possibility of a genuine *history* and a living *tradition.* The material forms of culture provide the basis on which rest the possibility of shared remembrance and communal story. In this respect, the public monument or memorial is merely an attempt to embed memory in the fabric of communal life by the only means in which any memory can be so embedded – through its materialization.[18]

The importance of memory to self-identity, and the connection of memory with place, illuminates a feature that is present in *In Search of Lost Time*, as well as in much ordinary experience; namely, the way in which self-reflection very often takes the form of reflection on, and remembrance of, past places and things (which can often approach a form of nostalgia[19]), and, in conjunction with this, the way in which the experience of places and things from the past is very often an occasion for intense self-reflection. This is perhaps particularly evident in cases of childhood memories and in relation to childhood places (not just memories and places from childhood but from any of the formative times in our lives). The way in which such memories and places often become more important to us as we age, and the strong feelings (whether fondness or, sometimes, revulsion) that are typically associated with the places of our growing up and early life can be seen as indicative of the founding role of those places, not only in our narratives about ourselves, but also in the establishing of our sense of self-identity (and these tendencies are often reflected at a collective level in term of communal and even national self-formation and self-reflection). It is perhaps not surprising that such past places often take on an idealized form. The connection between the memory of childhood and the idea of the idyllic character of past places (in contrast to the debasement of the present) is something noted by Raymond Williams,[20] and in New Zealand literature Bruce Mason's *The End of the Golden Weather* provides an excellent example of the intimate association of childhood, and so of the past, with place. Mason invites his reader 'to join [him] in a voyage into the past, to that territory of the heart we call childhood. Consider, if you will, Te Parenga. A beach, three-quarters of a mile long, a hundred yards wide at low water. . . This is Te Parenga: my heritage, my world.'[21] Here, Mason's imagery of place and movement are as notable as the connection he invokes between a sense of past – of home or heritage – and a grasp (or perhaps a 'sense') of place. Sometimes, of course, this focus on the past and the home can become problematic – but it is so only when it is tied to an obsessive turn away from the wider world to which even our being-placed at-home ought properly to open us. It is indeed only from out of a place in which we are 'at home' – in which, in other words, we are able to find a sense of ourselves – that the world can open to us.[22]

The connection between the formation of self-identity and the grasp of place is also reflected in the way in which, as we grow older, and as our capacity to construct broader narratives of our lives and our access to autobiographical memories increases (a phenomenon that may well be tied to an increasing sense of self-identity and capacity for self-narration), past places and things associated with the past become more important. This almost commonplace feature of memory and ageing is something recognized within psychological studies of autobiographical memory. Clare Cooper Marcus notes that 'while adolescents are most likely to cherish stereos or sports equipment (egocentric, present experience), their grandparents are most likely to cherish family photos or significant items of furniture (past association and reminders of family networks)', and this leads her to suggest that, as a practical consequence, 'allowing an older person to bring their own furniture into an otherwise impersonal housing scheme or retirement home is critically important for establishing a sense of personal continuity. Depriving them of such objects may be cutting off a part of the self.'[23]

Once we understand the way in which subjectivity is tied to embodied and materialized activity, and to particular places, then we can well understand how the separation from places and possessions may be, almost literally, a separation from parts of oneself (which is why immigration and exile are often so difficult) – and not only from oneself. A particularly interesting aspect of these observations is the emphasis on certain objects as bringing with them important inter-subjective associations. It may well be the case that the development of a sense of identity of self can be mapped as the development of a sense of the identity of others. This would be entirely consistent with the way in which, as seen in the discussion here, the development of the concepts of self and other are necessarily tied together. Regardless of the extent to which such a parallel in the development of a concrete sense of self- and other-identity may be given empirical support, what is clear is that our encounter with ourselves and with others, and our grasp of the identity of ourselves and others, is always situated and articulated with respect to particular places and specific objects and surroundings. Indeed, the general thesis at issue here – that memory and identity are tied to spatiality, embodiment, and worldly location – is one that should be familiar from a wide range of literary and poetic works, as well as from many other sources, including a number of empirical psychological studies.[24]

Subjectivity – the subjectivity of the self as well as the inter-subjectivity found in culture and society – is something necessarily worked out in terms of embodied and spatialized activity, in terms of the personal and cultural narratives that are essentially connected with such activity, and therefore in and through the structure of place. Yet, as already noted, place is itself worked out and articulated through the narratively structured activity of human subjects, both individually and collectively, within an objective physical environment. This is, indeed, an important theme in *In Search of Lost Time.* Not only does Proust see persons as tied to places, but for him, places themselves take on the attributes of persons. 'There is,' he writes, 'something individual about places [*il y a quelque chose d'individuel dans les lieux*].'[25] One could well say of the places to which Proust attends, as Heaney says of the Lake District landscape that preoccupied Wordsworth, that they too are both 'humanized and humanizing'. Indeed, the 'humanized', 'personalized' character of place can be viewed as indicating, first, the character of places as unitary structures possessed of a certain identity and particularity of their own (something expressed in the giving of a name) and, second, the obtaining of a certain *interdependence* between place and person.

Since place is not to be reduced simply to a region of space, the identity of any particular place is determined, not in terms of any simple set of clearly defined parameters, but by means of a complex of factors deriving from the elements encompassed by that place itself. Places are established in relation to a complex of subjective, inter-subjective, and objective structures that are inseparably conjoined within the overarching structure of place as such. Thus, the identity of the place that is Marcel's Combray (a place that is, of course, half fictional and half real) or Wordsworth's Lake District, or any other place one might care to name, must be understood in terms of complex conjunction of factors including the natural landscape, the pattern of weather and of sky, the human ordering of spaces and resources, and also those individual and communal narratives with which the place is imbued. While the possibility of human involvement in the world is given only in and through such a place, the unity of the place is also evident in, and articulated by means of, the organized activity of the human beings who dwell within it. As I pointed out in the Introduction, such interdependence does not make place subjective. Place remains a structure that cannot be grounded in the existence of an independent subject. In addition, the unity and identity of a place is worked out only in relation to the human subject as actively involved with its objective surroundings and within an inter-subjective context. The dependence of place on subjectivity, and on objectivity and inter-subjectivity, is a dependence (properly an interdependence) that results from the character of place as a structure that necessarily encompasses all of these elements and in which the elements are themselves constituted.

The partial dependence of the ordering of space and place on subjectivity is reflected, in a particularly important way, in the role of narrative in such ordering. Narrative is that which can be seen as structuring, in a similar fashion, both memory and self-identity, as well as the places – the landscapes – in which self-identity is itself worked out and established.[26] This invoking of narrative is not, however, meant to suggest the priority of some universal 'narrative principle'. It is merely to indicate, once again, the way in which the sorts of structures that we encounter as determinative in the organization of self and mind are also structures that are determinative of our understanding of the world. Likewise, those that are determinative in the possibility of action, and so through action, are structures that are determinative of the places in which action is possible. We understand a particular space through being able to grasp the sorts of 'narratives of action' that are possible within that space. We understand a place and a landscape through the historical and personal narratives that are marked out within it, that give the place a particular unity, and that establish a particular set of possibilities within it.

At one level, the ordering of a place through narrative forms (there being no such single or dominant form) is itself tied to the material instantiation of a culture and a society – in cultures like our own, through the shaping of space and environment that occurs with the construction of rooms, houses, offices, public buildings, roads, and so on; and in cultures that stand in a less obtrusive relation to the land, through the establishing of pathways and sites. These structures order and reorder space in ways that establish and constrain the actions and lives of the individuals who inhabit that space. Indeed, as they order and reorder space, so they also order and reorder the possible forms of subjectivity in that space. This is an important element in Foucault's treatment of power as something exercised through the disciplining of bodies and the structuring and organization of space (an idea often taken to be exemplified in the image of the 'Panopticon' – the system of all-round surveillance – that Foucault takes from the work of Jeremy Bentham).[27] It is also an idea given particular attention, though in rather different form, through the Heideggerian analysis of equipmentality and the structure of the ready-to-hand.[28] Henri Lefebvre's work provides a further instance of the close connection between forms of mental and social ordering and spatial organization.[29] At still another and very different level, the ordering of the land is a matter not just of the imprinting of specific forms of activity or social organization onto the physical environment but rather of the land as carrying in the very forums in which it appears – in pathways, monuments, sites, and landscape itself – a cultural memory and storehouse of ideas. Thus, in almost any inhabited region, one finds the stories that define the culture (or the cultures) of the people that live there to be 'written in' the places and landmarks around them in a way that is reminiscent of the Wordsworthian conception of poetry as 'memorial inscription'.

Just as personal memory and identity is tied directly to place and locality, so too are cultural 'memory' and identity tied to landscape and the physical environment. Perhaps the most striking and best-known example of this is the way in which, for Aboriginal Australians, the landscape is marked out with narratives – or songs – and thus 'sung' into being.[30] Such embedding of narrative in landscape is not, however, peculiar to Aboriginal culture. While the cultural forms are very different, Tim Robinson's detailed account of the history and topography of the island of Aran[31] reveals its landscape to be deeply etched by the narratives and the lives of the people of those islands such that the island comes to be what it is through stories told and lives lived. Every cultural landscape is established in a way that is essentially similar to that exemplified in the dense 'topography' mapped out by Robinson, or that contained in the songs and stories of Australian Aboriginal peoples. Embedded in the physical landscape is a landscape of personal and cultural history, of social ordering and symbolism, and, just as Robinson finds it impossible to tell the stories of Aran without also telling the story of Aran's geology and geography, the narratives of the land, as encultured and humanized, cannot be prised away from its physical structure. In this respect, it should be emphasized that the narratives at issue here cannot be understood as mere subjective *impositions* onto a place or landscape. Just as the narratives that structure subjectivity are directly tied to action and movement, so too are the narratives that belong to places and landscapes (to which the narratives that are internalized in subjectivity are connected) tied to the possibilities that are inherent in those places and landscapes, and that are part of their very fabric – a genuine narrative is thus no more a mere imposition onto a landscape than is a map of it.

Most often, of course, narrative is understood, not as connected to space or place, but along with memory, as tied much more specifically to time. Indeed, Paul Ricoeur's *Time and Narrative* takes, as one of its main themes, the idea that narrative is central to the understanding of temporality and only it can overcome the 'aporeitic' character of time – for instance, the dispersal of time into past, present, and future, or the difficulty of reconciling 'phenomenological' with 'cosmic' time. Time and space can only be properly understood together, as interconnected forms of *dimensionality*, and so too narrative must be understood as connected not to time alone but also to space. Just as narrative provides a means to grasp and articulate the unity of a space or region, narrative itself is necessarily worked out in relation to such spatial and topographic structures. This theme was implicit in the discussion of the last few paragraphs, as well as in the earlier introductory idea of the novel having its origins in the travelogue; an idea that can also be seen to derive directly from the arguments, developed in the course of this book, for the necessary role of spatial and topographic concepts in the possibility of thought and of experience. Indeed, the 'aporietic' character of time, which Ricoeur takes up, can be seen to reflect similar issues of loss, displacement, and multiplicity that are part of the problematic of Proust's project in *In Search of Lost Time*; issues resolved, there, through a narrative of 'topographical' unity that is as much spatial as temporal.[32]

Acknowledging the ambiguity that does indeed attach to talk of 'sense', one can nevertheless say, in summary of much of the above discussion, that to have a 'sense' of self is also to have a 'sense' of place. Of course, the fact of such a connection may be seen, and sometimes is seen, as largely a consequence of biological or evolutionary factors.[33] It should be clear, however, based on the considerations set forth here and in earlier chapters, that I take such approaches to be essentially mistaken. The significance of place should not be construed as just a contingent feature of human psychology or biology, but instead as rooted in the very structure that makes possible the sort of experience or thought exemplified in the human (though this is not to rule out the possibility that certain particular features of our response to place may be contingent). The idea, then, that identity is tied to place (and so to a spatio-temporal realm in which persons and things can be encountered and a world can be grasped) is one, not just in which a sense of identity might be tied up with a certain 'emotional reminiscence', but from which is derived an understanding that the very character of subjectivity, both general and particular, and the very content of our thoughts and feelings are necessarily dependent on the place and places within which we live and act. At the end of his *Landscape and Memory*, Simon Schama quotes a passage from the works of Henry David Thoreau: 'It is vain to dream of a wildness distant from ourselves. There is none such. It is the bog in our brain and bowels, the primitive vigor of Nature in us, that inspires that dream.'[34] It is indeed vain to dream of a wildness distant from ourselves, but equally, the landscape that is in us – that we find in 'myth and memory', as Schama says elsewhere – is the same landscape that we find around us and that provides the stuff of our dreams, thoughts, and feelings. That landscape is not only formed, to a greater or lesser extent, through our activity within it, but is itself constitutive of our character and identity. The landscape in which we find ourselves, and through we which we are defined, is thus as much a part of what we are – of our minds, our actions, and our selves – as is the food we eat and the air we breathe. One might thus speak here of a form of 'romantic materialism' that comes with the recognition of the place-bound character of human being – such romantic materialism being itself expressed the commitment to 'Proust's Principle.'[35] The essence of romantic materialism is precisely the idea that what is felt, thought, and remembered (the 'romantic' if you will) is given only in and through the placed materiality of the world – in earth and stone, in air and water, in flesh and bone, in light and sound – while at the same time that materiality is taken up into and imbued with the romantic. There is no tearing of these apart, any more than one can truly tear apart the world.

Indeed, the grasp of place, and so also of the materiality of things, is important, not just to a grasp of self or of others, but to the grasp of the world itself. As indicated earlier, the very possibility of understanding, or of knowledge, resides in locatedness and a certain embeddedness in place. Indeed, as 'The Knowledge' of the London cab-driver might indicate,[36] perhaps one ought to think of knowledge as always a form of such locatedness or 'placing' – as always a knowledge in and of place. In a passage from his 'The Autobiography', the Northamptonshire poet John Clare writes of an episode from his childhood in which he uses 'knowledge' in a way that echoes this connection of knowledge and locality:

> I had often seen the large heath calld Emmonsales stretching its yellow furze from my eye into unknown solitudes. . . & my curiosity urgd me to steal an opportunity to explore it that morning. . . So I eagerly wanderd on & rambled along the furze the whole day till I got out of my knowledge when the very wild flowers seemd to forget me & I imagind they were the inhabitants of new countrys the very sun seemd to be a new one & shining in a different quarter of the sky still I felt no fear my wonderseeking happiness had no room for it. . . & when I got back into my own fields I did not know them everything lookd so different.[37]

Once again, in the emphasis on being 'beyond or out of one's knowledge', we find a sense of knowledge that ties knowledge closely to a familiar physical location.[38] Thus, 'to know' is not merely to be acquainted with something, nor does it primarily involve a grasp of a body of true and justified propositions. Instead, it is a matter of one's locatedness within a particular region; a matter of being able to find one's way within such a region; and, perhaps above all else, at least for Clare, a matter of dwelling or of being 'at home'. In this sense, one's 'knowledge' is the region in and through which one's life is established and defined (perhaps this is the real meaning of home when it appears, as it so often does, in discussions of place, self, and identity). Such 'knowledge' can often be named. For Clare, it took the name of Helpstone; for Proust's Marcel, we might say, it often takes the name of Combray. Such 'knowledge' makes possible not only the specific knowledge of particular things but also that in which one's very life is grounded. Thus, for Marcel, the regaining of such 'knowledge' was a regaining of a life, while in Clare's case, its loss seems to have been connected with his own loss of sanity and of self.[39]

In Clare's poetry there is a strong sense, not only of the character of a particular place and the places found within it, as well as of Clare's own deep feeling for that place, but also of its fragility and vulnerability; all the more so, given his own experience of its destruction through enclosure.[40] Certainly places perdure (especially relative to human lives), and many indigenous peoples would argue that they perdure eternally (because the underlying structure of place is the underlying structure of the world as established in the very beginning). Yet the character of places can certainly change, as may the relations between places, and since the identity of places can never be made wholly determinate, their perdurance must surely also remain often unclear.[41] Since our lives are inseparably and intricately bound to the places in which we find ourselves, the susceptibility of those places to change, if perhaps not to complete obliteration,[42] is indicative of a corresponding susceptibility to change and also loss in our own lives and identities. Human beings are fragile beings, and their fragility is a direct consequence of their intricate and complex entanglement in the plural and dynamic relationality of place. In the poetry of Wordsworth this appears in a particularly interesting fashion. Although it is possible to see Wordsworth's poetic development as centred on ideas of place, dwelling, and home (ideas all present in, for instance, 'Michael', the poem that figured in this book's Introduction), one can also find a preoccupation – one that runs throughout Wordsworth's writing – with the idea of finding a dwelling-place, a home, that will endure in a way that no earthly home can. Thus, John Kerrigan writes that 'Wordsworth's entire career was shaped by his need to find a dwelling-place which would not fade,'[43] and he divides Wordsworth's poetic development into three: an early phase in which Wordsworth looks to the dwelling place of the 'croft and cottage'; a middle phase that arises out of an awareness of the insecurity and fragility of such 'stone-built dwellings' and that looks, instead, to the grave and the tomb as an 'immutable place to dwell'; and, finally, a late phase in which even the tomb has come to seem all too transient a home, and the poet has turned his thoughts to truly eternal dwellings and to the chapel and the church as earthly images of a heavenly abode.[44] In this respect, the Wordsworthian 'search for place' can be seen as a search for escape from loss and vulnerability. Yet there is a clear irony here. If the principle that I described in the introduction as 'Proust's Principle', and that I said could as easily be a principle attributable to Wordsworth himself – namely that human identity is inseparable from place and locality – then the fragility and mortality of human life is nothing other than the fragility and mortality that attaches to the places and spaces of human dwelling – and is just as inevitable.[45]

The Wordsworthian longing for a secure dwelling place, one that would not succumb to decay and desertion, is a longing that, while it can be seen to arise out of a keen awareness of the significance of place, also represents an implicit denial of that significance, because to seek an escape from the transience and fragility of place is to seek an escape from place itself. As evident in Proust, the places in which human lives are enmeshed are places constituted through both 'juxtaposition' and 'displacement', through activity and movement. Not only, then, do the places and spaces of human dwelling change and disintegrate, but they are themselves disclosed only through processes that bring change and alteration in their wake. Indeed, such places and spaces are disclosed only in relation to movement, to agency, and, one might say, to change. The idea of an eternal place or dwelling would require a very different conception of what human dwelling, and human thought and experience, might be. The idea of a place immune to change, immune to decay and disintegration, is the idea of a 'place' in which nothing at all can appear – neither self nor others, neither the things of the world nor even the place itself. In this respect, the idea of 'eternity' – of a life lived without end – may be incompatible with the idea, not merely of human dwelling, but also of dwelling as such; incompatible with the very possibility of thought and experience. Certainly, it would seem that to be a creature capable of engaging with the world in the way that is paradigmatic of human existence, is to be a creature possessed of a necessarily fragile and limited existence.[46]

Recognizing our inextricable tie to our surroundings means recognizing our own finitude and mortality. Furthermore, since our mortality is a consequence of our necessarily placed existence (and therefore is not to be understood merely in terms of the inevitably of our deaths), it is also the case that such placedness is a necessary condition of our very capacity to experience. Our mortality, our capacity to think and feel, and our embeddedness in place are bound together as part of the same structure that makes us what we are. Wordsworth's inability to come to terms with mortality is an inability to come to terms with the essentially placed character of human existence. It thus represents a form of estrangement from that in which his life was nevertheless grounded – an estrangement from place. Death is not some 'accident' to which we just happen to be unusually (in fact, invariably) prone. To be who and what we are is to be creatures whose placed existence brings death inevitably in its wake. Though it may seem trivial to say, we can only fear death because we are creatures who die. Yet this also means that to recognize who and what we are – to grasp ourselves in relation to the place and places in which we dwell and in which our existence is rooted – is also to recognize our mortality as something essential to us, something that belongs to us as we belong to it; just as place also belongs to us and we to it. A grasp of the essential character of our mortality need not obviate the fear of death (fear is seldom so simple a response), but it should entail a proper recognition of both the place of death and the place of our own lives. In this respect, it involves no brooding upon or 'valorizing' of either death or the transience of things, because such responses would precisely withhold from death, and our lives, their proper place.[47]

The Proustian search for time, for place, and for a life – a search undertaken through the many pages of *In Search of Lost Time* – is necessarily one that arises only as a consequence of the inevitable experience of loss. If it achieves any resolution to the distress induced by that experience, it is a resolution that is brought about, not through a discovery of some eternal mode of dwelling outside of the earthly world in which we find ourselves, but precisely through a better understanding of the densely woven unity of life as lived, and of the places, persons, sights, and sounds with respect to which such a life is constituted (the face of a loved one, the line of hills on a distant horizon, the familiar room in which one sleeps, the taste of warm stone, the sound of crickets ... and so on). Only thus – in the concreteness of an embodied, located, bounded existence – can we come to understand that in which the value and significance of a life is to be found. Since every such life is a life lived amidst a richness that cannot be protected from vulnerability and loss, every such life is defined by the experience of both the wonder and the fragility of place – by the experience of place lost and regained, by the experience of place as 'humanized and humanizing'.

Notes

1 Albert Camus, 'Nuptials at Tipasa', in *Lyrical and Critical Essays*, ed. Philip Thody, trans. Ellen Conroy Kennedy (London: Hamish Hamilton, 1967), 69.

2 Georges Poulet, *Proustian Space*, trans. Elliott Coleman (Baltimore, MD: Johns Hopkins University Press, 1977), 26–27.

3 Bachelard takes our memories to be 'housed', as we ourselves are, in the very buildings in which we live. See Gaston Bachelard, *The Poetics of Space*, trans. Maria Jolas (Boston, MA: Beacon Press, 1969), 8.

4 The commonplace talk of 'sense of place' (which is seldom explicated) often ends up being taken in just this psychological fashion and so as something less than is at issue in the analysis developed above.

5 Paul Tillich, *The Eternal Now* (New York: Charles Scribner's Sons, 1963), 130.

6 Pierre Hadot has an excellent discussion of matters relating to this idea of the expansive moment in '"Only the Present is our Happiness": The Value of the Present Instant in Goethe and in Ancient Philosophy', in *Philosophy as a Way of Life*, trans. Arnold I. Davidson (Oxford: Blackwell, 1995), 217–237. Much the same idea is at work in R.C. Zaehner's discussion of Proust and the 'eternal present' in *Mysticism: Sacred and Profane* (Oxford: Oxford University Press, 1961). Outside of his volume on Proust, Poulet takes up a similar theme in French thought, in the writings of Montaigne, Baudelaire, and others (including Proust), through the exploration of the idea of a creative 'act of time' that is also the 'death of time'. See Poulet, *Studies in Human Time* (New York: Harper, 1959). In fact, as should

be evident from the discussion here, what is really at issue is the idea of place as that out of which both space and time emerge, but in which both are held. What comes first, therefore, is not space or time, but place. Something like this idea also seems to be at work in the idea of the *Augenblick*, which appears in Kierkegaard and Nietzsche, as well as in Heidegger. See, for example, Koral Ward, *Augenblick: The Concept of the Decisive Moment in 19th- and 20th-Century Western Philosophy* (Aldershot: Ashgate, 2008). See also Hannah Arendt's use of this idea in *The Life of the Mind*, vol. 1 (San Diego, CA: Harcourt, Brace and Co., 1971), 202–211; and my discussion in '"Where Are We When We Think?" Hannah Arendt and the Place of Thinking', *Philosophy Today* (forthcoming 2018).

7 Sally Morgan, *My Place* (Fremantle, WA: Fremantle Arts Press, 1989).

8 In the year of its publication, 1987, *My Place* won the inaugural Human Rights and Equal Opportunity Commission humanitarian award and, in the following year, the *Western Australia Week* literary award for non-fiction. Morgan's story was attacked (along with many other tellings of Aboriginal history and experience) by Keith Windschuttle in *The Fabrication of Aboriginal History, vol. 3, The Stolen Generations 1881–2008* (Sydney: Macleay Press, 2009).

9 Morgan, *My Place*, 228–230.

10 Two important works that deploy this phrase are: Steven Feld and Keith H. Basso, eds., *Senses of Place* (Santa Fe, NM: School of American Research Press, 1996); and Lucy Lippard, *The Lure of the Local: Senses of Place in a Multicentered Society* (New York: New Press, 1997).

11 'Sense of place' also brings to mind the idea of the 'spirit of place', or *genius loci*, which has a long history in Western thought and culture, as well as having its counterparts in other traditions. The term *genius loci* comes from the Latin and refers to the Roman notion of the protective divinity of a particular place or locality. The notion became especially important in garden and landscape design in the eighteenth and nineteenth centuries (and later). As Alexander Pope famously writes in Epistle IV to Richard Boyle, Earl of Burlington:

> Consult the genius of the place in all;
> That tells the waters or to rise, or fall;
> Or helps th' ambitious hill the heav'ns to scale,
> Or scoops in circling theatres the vale;
> Calls in the country, catches opening glades,
> Joins willing woods, and varies shades from shades,
> Now breaks, or now directs, th' intending lines;
> Paints as you plant, and, as you work, designs.

12 Hence the idea of place as space plus subjectivity, which was discussed in Chapter 1 (30–31), appears once again, and indeed those who give most attention to the idea of a sense of place are often those who, like Yi-Fu Tuan, take place to be a matter of humanized or meaningful space.

13 A similar point can be seen to lie behind Campbell's claim that 'one does not think of memory as constituting an independent type of epistemic access to one's surroundings. It can function to give one knowledge of one's past life because it depends on other ways of knowing about one's environment through perception.' See John Campbell, *Past, Space, and Self* (Cambridge, MA: MIT Press, 1994), 221.

14 Poulet, *Proustian Space*, 105.

15 William Faulkner, 'The Jail', in *The Portable Faulkner*, rev. ed., ed. Malcolm Lowry (New York: Viking Press, 1967), 666. The recording of the past in the spatialized environment is, of course, interdependent with memory and history. As David Lowenthal emphasizes: 'Memory, history and relics offer routes to the past best traversed in combination. Each route requires the others for the journey to be significant and credible.' See Lowenthal, *The Past is a Foreign Country* (Cambridge: Cambridge University Press, 1985), 249.

16 The idea that time is indeed to be found in space takes on an especially extreme, but intriguing, form in Michael Lyton's claim that the 'source of time is shape'. See Michael Leyton, *Symmetry, Causality, Mind* (Cambridge, MA: MIT Press, 1992), 3. Leyton argues that the past is given only through objects and, in particular, through the physical shape of objects (since it is shape that records past events and processes). Memory, therefore, is the extraction of the past from the spatial and topological structure of objects.

17 Since self-identity (which here does not mean simply the way in which a thing is the same as itself) just is the having of a sense of one's self as oneself.

18 Although not developed in the way set out here, Maurice Halbwachs's account of collective memory (which is the starting point for much contemporary work on the subject) gives explicit recognition to the role of space and materiality. See Halbwachs, *The Collective Memory*, trans F.J. Ditter and V.Y. Ditter (New York: Harper & Row Colophon Books, 1980), 128–157. The emphasis on materiality that follows from recognition of the centrality of place as developed here converges with the recent explosion of work (focused especially in archaeology, anthropology, museum studies, and increasingly in sociology) in what has come to be known as 'material culture studies'. See Dan Hicks and Mary C. Beaudry, eds., *The Oxford Handbook of Material Culture Studies* (Oxford: Oxford University Press, 2010).

19 See note 39 below.

20 See his classic study, Raymond Williams, *The Country and the City* (London: Chatto & Windus, 1973), esp. 297–298.

21 Bruce Mason, *The End of the Golden Weather: A Voyage into a New Zealand Childhood* (Wellington: Victoria University Press, 1970), 31. The special role of certain childhood memories of place is also beautifully illustrated in a passage from one of Virginia Woolf's autobiographical writings: 'If life has a base that it stands upon, if it is a bowl that one fills and fills – then my bowl without a doubt stands on this memory. It is of lying half asleep, half awake, in bed in the nursery at St. Ives. It is of hearing the waves breaking...of hearing the blind draw its little acorn across the floor...of lying and hearing this splash and this light.' See Woolf, *Moments of Being: Unpublished Autobiographical Writings*, ed. Jeanne Schulkind (Brighton: The University Press, 1976), 64–65. As Tennyson writes in one of his letters: 'A known landscape is to me an old friend that continually talks to me of my own youth and half-forgotten things.' See quote by Geoffrey Grigson in the introduction to *The Faber Book of Poems and Places*, ed. Grigson (London: Faber & Faber, 1980), 31.

22 Ideas of home and heritage can indeed become associated with an obsessively introverted perspective or with forms of xenophobic resistance to the unfamiliar and the foreign. There is, not surprisingly, much critical literature on this topic, and often that literature argues against notions of home, and even place, on the grounds that such notions are inherently given over to introversion or xenophobia. See, for instance, the critique of the specifically German articulation of ideas of place and home as expressed in the notion of *Heimat*, or 'homeland', in Peter Blickle, *Heimat: A Critical Theory of the German Idea of Homeland* (New York: Camden House, 2002). It would, however, be a serious mistake to take such 'pathologies of place' as the norm and, on that basis, reject place as inherently problematic or dangerous. To do so would be likely, in fact, to reinforce those same pathologies or else create new ones, since it would be to refuse what is a basic structure of human being and of the world as such.

23 Clare Cooper Marcus, 'Environmental Memories', in *Place Attachment*, ed. Irwin Altman and Setha M. Low (New York: Plenum Press, 1992), 101. On the issue of memory and identity, see also Louisa Chawla, 'Childhood Place Attachments', in Altman and Low, *Place Attachment*, 63–86.

24 The phenomenon of place attachment is a particularly rich source of psychological material. For a discussion that approaches these issues from the perspective of clinical application (at least in one particular area), see also Michael A. Godkin, 'Identity and Place: Clinical Applications Based on Notions of Rootedness and Uprootedness', in *The Human Experience of Space and Place*, ed. Anne Buttimer and David Seamon (London: Croom Helm, 1980), 73–85; and, specifically in relation to schizophrenia, see Harold F. Searles, *The Nonhuman Environment* (New York: International Universities Press, 1960).

25 Marcel Proust, *In Search of Lost Time, vol. 1, Swann's Way*, trans. C.K. Scott Moncrieff and Terence Kilmartin, rev. D.J. Enright (London: Chatto and Windus, 1992), 142; or *À la recherche du temps perdu, vol. 1, Du côté de chez Swan* (Paris: Gallimard, 1954), 185.

26 The exploration of both landscape and memory in explicit relation to large-scale cultural narratives (and perhaps, given the very personal tone of the book's opening sections, to much more personal narratives as well) is a central theme in Simon Schama, *Landscape and Memory* (London: HarperCollins, 1995).

27 Michel Foucault, *Discipline and Punish: The Birth of the Prison* (New York: Vintage Books, 1979).

28 See Heidegger, *Being and Time*, trans. John Macquarrie and Edward Robinson (New York: Harper & Row, 1962), H102ff.

29 See Henri Lefebvre, *The Production of Space*, trans. Donald Nicholson-Smith (Oxford: Blackwell, 1991). In *Places on the Margin* (London: Routledge, 1991), Rob Shields emphasizes both the role of spatialization in forms of social practice and differentiation and the necessary interplay of individual and collective structures, as well as bodily and environmental factors, in spatialized social formations.

30 Although its treatment is somewhat romanticized, this is a central theme in Bruce Chatwin, *Songlines* (London: Pan, 1988). See also Krim Benterrak, Stephen Muerke, and Paddy Roe, *Reading the Country: Introduction to Nomadology* (Fremantle, WA: Fremantle Arts Press, 1984).

31 Tim Robinson, *Stones of Aran: Labyrinth* (Harmondsworth: Penguin, 1995).

32 For a direct comparison of Ricoeur and Proust, see Rhiannon Goldthorpe, 'Ricoeur, Proust and the Aporias of Time', in *On Paul Ricoeur: Narrative and Interpretation*, ed. David Wood (London: Routledge, 1991), 84–101.

33 For a brief summary of some accounts that attempt to explain the centrality of place in memory and experience by reference to such factors, see Robert B. Riley, 'Attachment to the Ordinary Landscape', in Altman and Low, *Place Attachment*, 14–15.

34 Quoted in Schama, *Landscape and Memory*, 578.

35 The phrase 'romantic materialism' is also used by Gillian Beer, though with a somewhat different sense from mine, in her *Darwin's Plots: Evolutionary Narrative in Darwin, George Eliot, and Nineteenth-Century Fiction*, 3rd ed. (Cambridge: Cambridge University Press, 2009), 36–41.

36 See the discussion in Chapter 4, 139.

37 John Clare, 'The Autobiography', in *The Prose of John Clare*, ed. J.W. and Anne Tibble (London: Routledge and Kegan Paul, 1951), 13.

38 The use of 'knowledge' that we find in Clare, an echo of which seems to persist in 'The Knowledge' of the London cabbie (see Chapter 4), does not appear in standard dictionaries such as the *Oxford English Dictionary*, but it does appear in the *English Dialect Dictionary* of 1905, where we find: 'Knowledge, sb.... Slang. 1. Range, remembrance, view; esp. in phr. to get beyond or out of one's knowledge, to lose one's way.' See *The English Dialect Dictionary*, vol. 3, ed. Joseph Wright (Oxford: Oxford University Press, 1905), 485. The sources for this use of the word are noted as being from Lancashire, Nottinghamshire, Leicestershire, and Warwickshire (neither London nor Clare's Northamptonshire are mentioned, although Northamptonshire does border on Leicestershire).

39 The enclosure movement was responsible for the destruction of the familiar landscape of Clare's Northamptonshire home, and much of his poetry reflects his antagonism towards the changes in the land and the changes in attitudes to the land that were occurring in his day. Clare ended his days in an asylum, and while his mental instability was clearly the result of a complex of factors, the destruction of the landscape to which he was so deeply attached undoubtedly had a deep effect on him. For a more detailed analysis of Clare, his life and poetry, see John Barrell, *The Idea of Landscape and the Sense of Place 1730–1840: An Approach to the Poetry of John Clare* (Cambridge: Cambridge University Press, 1972). Barrell points to some important differences between the sense of place as it arises in Clare and the sense of place in writers such as Wordsworth and Hardy. See also John Lucas's discussion of Clare and Wordsworth in 'Places and Dwellings: Wordsworth, Clare and the Anti-picturesque', in *The Iconography of Landscape*, ed. Denis Cosgrove and Stephen Daniels (Cambridge: Cambridge University Press, 1989), 83–97.

40 See especially John Lucas, 'Places and Dwellings', 89ff. Lucas focuses, in particular, on two of Clare's poems in his discussions: 'The Flitting' and 'To a Fallen Elm'.

41 The perdurance of place is something emphasized by Casey in his response to the first edition of this book (Cambridge: Cambridge University Press, 1999), found in 'Converging and Diverging In/On Place', *Philosophy and Geography* 4, no. 2 (2001): 225–230. My reply is found in 'Comparing Topographies: Across Paths/Around Place: A Reply to Casey', *Philosophy and Geography* 4, no. 2 (2001): 231–238. See also my 'The Remembrance of Place', in *The Voice of Place: Essays and Interviews Exploring the Work of Edward S. Casey*, ed. Azucena Cruz-Pierre and Don Landes (London: Bloomsbury, 2013), 103–126. Precisely because I take place to be dynamic and indeterminate, I find it hard to put the same emphasis on perdurance as does Casey.

42 It is notable that the obliteration or destruction of places has commonly been used as a tool of genocide and as a weapon of war. Indeed, it was so used by the Romans, most famously in their destruction of Carthage. It was used by the Nazis against Jewish communities and against communities in occupied territories that offered resistance to such occupation. It is currently being used in many places of the world as a means to destroy or undermine communities and cultures through the destruction of the material basis of those communities and cultures, including the destruction of buildings and sites, or restriction of access to them. The embeddness of culture in place, and the destruction or control of place as one of the means by which authority is imposed and maintained, is a key reason for the intractability of the political situation in Israel and Palestine. There is now an increasing literature on this general topic, undoubtedly partly spurred on by the destruction of sites of cultural significance by the Taliban in Afghanistan and by ISIS in Syria. See Robert Bevan, *The Destruction of Memory: Architecture at War* (London: Reaktion, 2006); Lawrence Davidson, *Cultural Genocide* (New Brunswick, NJ: Rutgers University Press, 2012); Helen Walasek and Amra Hadžimuhamedović (contributions by Richard Carlton, Valery Perry, and Tina Wik), *Bosnia and the Destruction of Cultural Heritage* (London: Routledge, 2015); Peter G. Stone and Joanne Farchakh Bajjaly, eds., *The Destruction of Cultural Heritage in Iraq* (Woodbridge: The Boydell Press, 2008).

43 John Kerrigan, 'Wordsworth and the Sonnet: Building, Dwelling, Thinking', *Essays in Criticism* 35 (1985): 45–75.

44 See ibid., esp. 50–51.

45 If the experience of loss is an inevitable accompaniment of the experience of place, then the experience of 'lost places' – as described by Peter Read in *Returning to Nothing* (Cambridge: Cambridge University Press, 1996) – will be a characteristic feature of human life irrespective of culture or location, and so too will be the experience of nostalgia, which is properly understood as precisely the pain (*algos*) experienced in the loss that is part of the experience of home (*nostos*). On this latter point, see my 'Philosophy's Nostalgia', in *Heidegger and the Thinking of Place* (Cambridge, MA: MIT Press, 2012), 161–176. In *The Memory of Place: A Phenomenology of the Uncanny* (Athens, OH: Ohio University Press, 2012), Dylan Trigg argues, not only for the necessary interconnection of place, memory, and self, but also for the uncanny character of place – every place is thus a haunted place.

46 For a more detailed argument to this conclusion, see my 'Death and the End of Life', in *Heidegger and the Thinking of Place*, 177–198.

47 For an account that emphasizes the connection between a proper sense of place (through dwelling) and a sense of mortality, see Karsten Harries, *The Ethical Function of Architecture* (Cambridge, MA: MIT Press, 1997), esp. 254–267.

Further reading

Altman, Irwin, and Setha M. Low, eds. *Place Attachment*. New York: Plenum Press, 1992.

Barrell, John. *The Idea of Landscape and the Sense of Place, 1730–1840: An Approach to the Poetry of John Clare*. Cambridge: Cambridge University Press, 1972.

Feld, Steven, and Keith H. Basso, eds. *Senses of Place*. Santa Fe, NM: School of American Research Press, 1996.

Donohoe, Janet. *Remembering Places: A Phenomenological Study of the Relationship between Memory and Place*. Lanham, MD: Lexington Books, 2016.

Morgan, Sally. *My Place*. Fremantle: Fremantle Arts Press, 1989.

Schama, Simon. *Landscape and Memory*. London: HarperCollins, 1995.

Trigg, Dylan. *The Memory of Place: A Phenomenology of the Uncanny*. Athens, OH: Ohio University Press, 2012.

9 Place and world

> We all suffer, in this 21st century, from an insane amount of exchangeable images and exchangeable stories, and a terrible withdrawal from first-hand experience. It leads, slowly but steadily, to an ongoing loss of reality, and to the loss of belief once more, in the story-telling capacity of places. According to the indigenous people of Australia, places die if they are not kept alive, and so do we, along with them. In my book, they're damn right.
>
> (Wim Wenders, 'In Defense of Places'[1])

The poem with which this book began, Wordsworth's 'Michael', is set in a world that, in spite of its burgeoning urbanization and industrialization,[2] is still a world that appears as, one might say, essentially *local*. The same might be said of the world that Proust evokes – certainly of Combray and the countryside to which it belongs. The world we find ourselves in today, however, is one that is routinely described as *global*, a world in which sameness seems to proliferate across places, and in which even movement between places often occurs at a speed and frequency such that it is barely noticed. Does this mean that, in the global contemporary world, place has indeed died or been obliterated? Does it mean that the connection between persons and places that has been such a central theme of this book is no longer relevant – that it belongs to something past, rather than to the present or the future?

Certainly, the seeming loss of place in the contemporary world is a widespread theme in academic and popular writing, as well as a commonly observed phenomenon in ordinary experience. In the conclusion to *Place and Placelessness*, one of the most significant works on the topic of place of the last fifty years, Edward Relph writes of placelessness as describing 'both an environment without significant places and the underlying attitude which does not acknowledge significance in places. It reaches back into the deepest levels of place, cutting roots, eroding symbols, replacing diversity with uniformity and experiential order with conceptual order',[3] and he adds that 'our experience of the landscapes we live in is increasingly becoming an attitude of placelessness'.[4] Although *Place and Placelessness* was published in 1976, Relph's observations were not unprecedented, expressing a sense of the loss of place that was already widespread. Indeed, it is a sense of loss adumbrated even in Wordsworth[5] – 'Michael' is itself a poem about dispossession and alienation as much as it also concerns the depth of the relation to place. At the time they were made, Relph's observations thus echoed those of other past and contemporary writers, and they have been echoed in turn by many since. The seeming trend towards both the genericization and homogenization of places and the removal – some would say the 'freeing'[6] – of individuals from the specificity of place and locale is therefore a phenomenon of long-standing. Yet it is a phenomenon that has also undoubtedly been exacerbated in more recent years by a range of factors, including the increasing power and reach of modern corporations and the rise of digital media and communication systems.

Frequently, the 'loss of place' is put in terms of a loss of *authentic* place, and this requires some direct comment in its own terms. The idea of authenticity at work here, though commonplace, is also extremely problematic. Sometimes it amounts to no more than another way of speaking of the loss of places – so places are replaced by something else that is not place even though it may masquerade as place. Yet the notion of authenticity often brings with it something more than just this, and even to imply a distinction between places – between those that are authentic and those that are not – that can, in itself, lead to a mistaken understanding of the nature of place, as well as support certain forms of privileging of places with harmful consequences. The very idea of the authentic brings with it a sense of both extremity and authority – of a determinate and determining character to things. Yet the relationality of place carries with it a degree of *indeterminacy*, even of *resistance to determination* – including the determination that comes with the idea of the authentic.[7] Moreover, if place is as fundamental as my arguments here would suggest, and is so all-encompassing of the possibility of appearing, then this holds for place absolutely, not only for some places as distinct from others. The derelict building is no less a place than is the lived-in apartment, the factory no less than the garden, the mining site no less than the national park. Place does not itself distinguish between the 'authentic' and the 'inauthentic', the good and the bad, the human and the wild, the modern and the traditional.

Undoubtedly, there are those who take the phenomenon of 'placelessness', and the seeming loss of place (whether or not associated with the idea of the authentic) to represent a real change in the formation of the world and of human life in the world. On such a view, the world of today is a world in which place has indeed given way to space, and, more particularly, to the space of unbounded extensionality in which everything is related to everything else across a seemingly unbroken field of transfer and flow (a concept of space partly derived from the idea of objective spatiality as distinct from space as intersubjective or subjective). To suppose that such a seemingly radical change could have occurred over the last few centuries would also be to suppose that what is at issue here is something essentially *contingent* – that place and the relation to place is variable according to time, and also, therefore, *according to place*. That the very statement of contingency in this way invokes the relation to place that is said to be contingent ought to indicate the oddity of supposing that the relation to place can be anything other than a necessary relation. Any contingency can only affect the way in which the relation to place is manifest, the way it is played out in concrete circumstances and instances, rather than the basic fact of that relation.

The fundamental and necessary role played by place follows from the interconnection between place, space, and time, as well as between these concepts and the concepts of self, agency, attitude, and memory – interconnections identified and delineated over preceding chapters. The necessity that appears here might thus be characterized as a *conceptual* necessity: it arises because of the way the concepts at issue depend upon and entail one another. So, for example, the possibility of agency can be said to be dependent on both a grasp of subjective and objective space, not as a result of any empirical considerations, but because the modes of space at issue are, as it were, 'built in' to the very possibility of agency itself. In fact, the conceptual interconnection that appears here is analogous to the interconnection of elements within the structure of place. Thus, as suggested in Chapter 1, the investigation undertaken in this volume has actually been an investigation of a certain interconnected region or place – a conceptual region – which, it turns out, is the region or place that belongs to place, and so also to space, time, agency, self, and so forth. One might think of that region as akin to a *constellation*,[8] but a constellation whose elements cannot be separated from the relations that connect them; a constellation whose structure is essentially topographic. Moreover, if we do indeed talk of a conceptual region, and of the structure and relations as conceptual, then this does not mean that the investigation is *merely* conceptual or that it pertains *only* to concepts rather than to the world. There is no conceptuality apart from the world, and part of what follows from the account developed previously is that conceptuality, and so also *thinking*, is not separable from the spatialized materiality of things – is not separable from the embodied and active presence of the thinker, or agent, in the world.

Given that the fundamental structure of place and the relation to it cannot be treated as anything other than a *necessary* structure, the basic structure of place and the relation to place must indeed remain much the same now as it has been in the past. That this is so is reinforced by consideration of the fact that the apparent loss of place, to which Relph and others draw attention, is something that itself occurs topologically, which is to say that it occurs *in and through the experience of places*. That it should be so is, of course, just what one would expect given the necessity just alluded to. If we distinguish between, on the one hand, *place as a general and encompassing structure* – the complex bounded and interwoven structure of spatiality and temporality – and, on the other hand, place as it refers to *individual places*, each of which has its own character (a distinction already presaged in the discussion in Chapter 8), then it is easy to see how place must persist, even in the face of the apparent loss of place. Places can be objects of experience – as I experience this place or that place – but place is also that within and out of which experience arises. Any experience of the world, along with the appearing of things within the world, will thus always be from within the embrace of place. What is described as the loss of place is therefore more properly described as an experience of place in which place is seemingly effaced in its very presentation. I find myself *here*, and yet, in being here, I find nothing that marks off this place as distinctive – that marks it off as just the place that it is. Consider this example, which will be familiar to many: except for differences in the clothing and ethnicity of the shoppers, being in a shopping mall in Beijing may be almost indistinguishable from being in a shopping mall in Sydney, from being in a shopping mall in Dubai, from being in a shopping mall in Houston – the same shops, the same products, the same architecture. Here is the experience of being in a place that nevertheless also appears in such a way that it obscures its very character as a place, and so one can say that the experience is almost like being nowhere at all.

This loss of distinctiveness is partly an experience that arises because of the proliferation of what Marc Augé has called 'non-places',[9] a term that properly refers to places that are transitional – places of transience rather than long-term attachment, places we pass through – and so are exemplified not only by the shopping mall but also by the supermarket, the petrol station, the airport. We may also say of these 'non-places' (and I use the term in quotation marks since they are indeed places, if of a particular kind) that they are typically and increasingly places determined by the operation of globalized capital. Nowhere is this clearer than in the case of the airport, which has itself merged with the shopping mall to become representative of a world in which everyone is constantly on the move at the same time as they constantly consume.[10] Indeed, the convergence evident here – exemplified also in the case of the petrol station, which now often combines food outlet and mini-supermarket – is characteristic of the operation of modern technology, the hallmark of which is indeed the bringing together of both things and places. The most obvious manifestation of this is the internet, which is routinely presented as bringing the entire world to one's fingertips (via mobile phone, tablet, or laptop) and thereby opening up the world to us, no matter where we might be. In fact, mobile technology does not actually remove the constraints of location in quite the way that is often presented but instead changes certain aspects of the way we experience and act in relation to the spaces and places in which we find ourselves, and, at the same time, such technology alters and reconfigures aspects of those same spaces and places.[11]

The contemporary sense of the loss of place is thus a result of the proliferation of 'non-places', and the increasing role of such places in everyday life, as well as the convergence of things and places that occurs both through the bringing together of things and activities that were once separate, and through the connecting of spaces and places that were once apart. The latter phenomenon is one that Joshua Meyrowitz discussed in the 1980s, even prior to the advent of mobile digital technology, by reference to the breaking down of the social and cultural boundaries between places through new visual technologies, especially television.[12] So, for instance, television news reportage gives direct visual access to places that would otherwise remain inaccessible, often breaking down the barriers between public and private spaces, and between spaces that are socially or politically segregated from one another. New media and communications technologies have exacerbated many of the tendencies identified by Meyrowitz, who was himself building on ideas and so identifying tendencies already present or adumbrated in Marshall McLuhan's work.[13] The seeming breakdown of previous spatial and topographic structures is a phenomenon to which new forms of transportation also contribute. The rise of cheap air travel, for instance, has significantly reconfigured relations of distance and proximity, and that reconfiguration has brought with it important social, cultural, and economic changes.[14]

Given the considerations advanced in previous chapters, the way in which technology operates spatially and topographically should indeed be unsurprising. A key idea in the overall argument of this book has been that action, thought, and experience can only be understood as arising in relation to the complex structure of place. This is not only true at the level of the individual, but also at levels beyond the individual – at the level of the social, the economic, the political (a point that should have been evident from the preceding discussion, since it is already implied by the interdependence that obtains between subjectivity, objectivity, and intersubjectivity). In each case, particular forms of action or agency – and the structures of meaning, significance, memory, and experience that come with these – involve specific modes of spatial and topographic intervention and configuration. Sometimes this will be simply in terms of the specific items, structures, or events that are brought close and thereby made salient, and sometimes it will be in terms of the way such closeness and distance themselves operate or cease to operate. In riding a bicycle, for instance, one is engaged in a very specific form of action, employing a specific technology, and usually within a fairly narrow range of circumstances and conditions. In keeping with the analysis developed in Chapter 2, one can say that the act of riding a bicycle brings with it a specific configuration of subjective and objective spaces at the same time as it also brings close, and so makes salient, certain features of the environmental context (the surface over which one rides, for instance, is brought much closer when riding a bicycle than when travelling in a car, and differently from on foot). The construction of cycling networks within an urban planning context similarly involves a different set of spatial and topographic understandings, experiences, and saliencies, than are primarily evident to the road engineer or the city manager. One could undertake the same sort of analysis with respect to newer technologies – the laptop computer, the mobile phone, the driverless car.

The way different spatialities and topographies are invoked in relation to such technologies is itself a function, not merely of the attitudes, habits, and orientations of individual human actors, but of the larger spatial and material complex or 'assemblage' within which those actors are embedded, and that include things, networks, and events as much as persons or systems of social relations. Such complexes or 'assemblages' themselves stand in relationship to places, since they are indeed spatialized and materialized, and so are articulated topographically, both in and through specific places, and in ways that may also encompass multiple places. Since the operation of these spatialized and topological structures is neither wholly determined by human agents nor able to be entirely encompassed by them, those structures can be viewed in ways that are partially independent of human agency, whether individual or collective. Thus, writers such as Bruno Latour have been led to talk of such assemblages, or of the things that belong to them, as possessed of an agency of their own,[15] but this may be seen to extend the concept of agency in a way that does violence to the other concepts with which agency is enmeshed – and so is conceptually obscuring even if also, in some ways, imaginatively productive. It is better simply to acknowledge the fact that such assemblages and things, understood always relationally, have effects that are neither intended by nor under the control of the agents with whom those assemblages are enmeshed and who are enmeshed with them.

The spatial and topographic reconfigurations that accompany new technologies bring changes in modes of action and in the arrangement of things, but also in the formation of the self, both individual and collective. Perhaps the most obvious example is found in the operation of contemporary social media, which has significantly altered the character of social interaction, and even of social life more generally,[16] as well as reshaped the ways in which we narrate and remember. The present-oriented character of social media – evident in the immediate recording and uploading of events and images and thoughts, the immediacy of responses to them, and the constant updating of posts and rapid shifting of attention from one post to the next – can be seen to exemplify something very similar to the phenomenon of displacement that appears in Proust. Although posts can be scrolled back, it is the latest post that takes precedence for attention over all others. The embedding of individual posts within the larger network of posts also has the effect of making the details of personal life open to all, and, in a certain sense, depersonalizing them. The narratives that appear become everyone's narratives, often replicating other narratives, and sometimes, in the case of those most addicted to online social interaction, deliberately so. Social media has the effect of a radical externalization of personal life – the self being articulated through online communication and interaction – that is also an obscuring of the internality of the self. Such an obscuring is directly connected to the obscuring or effacing of place. The loss of a sense of place is a loss of a sense of the distinctiveness of places, and that loss of distinctiveness is closely tied up with a loss of the sense of the internality of places – such internality being bound to the singular identity of places. Without a sense of internality, there is neither a strong sense of place nor a clear sense of self, but since self and place remain, their character becomes confused and uncertain.

The way in which the sense of the loss of self may be tied to a sense of the loss of place, and the regaining of self to a regaining of place, was a central theme in the last chapter. Consideration of the topographic and spatial effects of modern technology on action and the self merely reinforces that basic point. Taking up new technologies is not like donning a new set of clothes – as if the technology were something completely external that could be put on or off at will, without making any real difference to the body (or the self) beneath. Technologies change us through changing the material forms in which our lives are embodied and expressed – through changing the ways in which space, time, and place are experienced and appear. This point has significant implications, not just for the consideration of modernity or the technologies that reign within it, but also for all manner of human life and activity. When we act, we act in ways that are both shaped *by* and also, to some extent, shaping *of* the specific character of the places, times, and spaces in which we are embodied and located (although here it should be noted that place itself, which is the general structure within which all of this occurs, remains determinative of both the shaping of persons and the shaping of places by persons – all such shaping occurs, and can only occur, *in and through place*). The ways in which we shape places thus have a direct effect on the shapes of our very lives and the lives of those around us. This has special significance for those practices that are explicitly oriented towards the spatial and topographic (or topological) – practices such as architecture, landscape design, urban and regional planning, interior design, and even furniture and fashion design. Inasmuch as those practices deal directly with the place, time, and space of things, which are the very materiality of things, they shape the things themselves, and so shape the possibilities that are made available for human life. To design and build a house, to construct a garden or plan a town, to craft a chair or sew a gown, is also to touch on the shape of action, the form of experience, the contour of thought. Yet even when the spatial and topographic are not directly or explicitly thematized in some practice, place is no less relevant or influential. Any and every action, any and every intervention in the world, is always placed and thereby affected by place as well as affecting place. So, too, place is always affecting of human being, even if only the being of the one who acts. Place is the very medium of our lives; that which supports us, that within which we encounter one another, and that which gives us space in which to move and time for such movement.

The fundamental role played by place is indeed unchanged by technology (because, as already noted, technology depends on place and our relation to place in order to function, even as it also obscures place). Yet, although limited in this way, the changes wrought by modern technology in respect of place, and so of space and time, remain quite radical and far-reaching. One of those changes is in the convergence of places that was noted earlier – the way different places are entangled together in the same places. Another is the frequently noted phenomenon of time–space compression, originally advanced by geographer David Harvey,[17] and taken up by others since. Harvey derives the idea both from Marx's account of the annihilation of space by time in the operation of capital,[18] and from Heidegger's account of the abolition of the near and far that occurs in technological modernity.[19] In similar fashion, Paul Virilio argues that the primary characteristic of modernity is speed.[20]

Given the way in which the rise of modern science, as well as modern technology, has been closely tied to the rise of the idea of space as pure extension – the idea of space encountered in the first chapter of this book – one can view modernity, in general, as determined by that very same mode of spatiality. The supposed 'placelessness' of the modern world can thus be seen as a reflection of the dominance of an almost purely spatialized view – and a spatialized view that is based not in any *subjective* mode of spatiality but rather in the levelled-out spatiality that belongs with *objectivity*. To the extent that place itself is allowed to appear in that view, it is as a mere *location* within such an objective spatiality. Thus, within the structures of contemporary capitalism, within modern financial and managerial frameworks, within the digital media and communications networks of today, appear no genuine 'places', but only the representation of unbounded spaces containing nodes, lines, and flows (see Figure 10) – and this mode of spatiality is dominant in the writing and thinking even among those who attempt to theorize and critique the structures of modernity.[21] Not only are there those who valorize this mode of spatiality,[22] but even where it is the object of critique, the assumption that this mode of spatiality is inevitable and ubiquitous in contemporary life means that there is no real basis on which any genuine critique can be based. If the modern world is indeed a 'space of flows' (to use Manuel Castells's phrase),[23] then that is just what it is, and we must accommodate ourselves to it. If it results in a change to the character of human experience, then that is simply the way things are, and, once again, we can only accommodate ourselves to that change. The possibility of real critique depends, in fact, on recognizing the way in which the mode of spatiality, through which modern technological capitalism articulates and presents itself, is indeed inconsistent with the properly placed character not only of human being but of all experience and all appearing – even, if we attend closely enough, the appearing of modern technological capitalism. Critique, in this instance, depends on revealing the way the modern spatialization of the world hides the topographical character of the world, as well as the topography in which that spatialization is itself embedded.

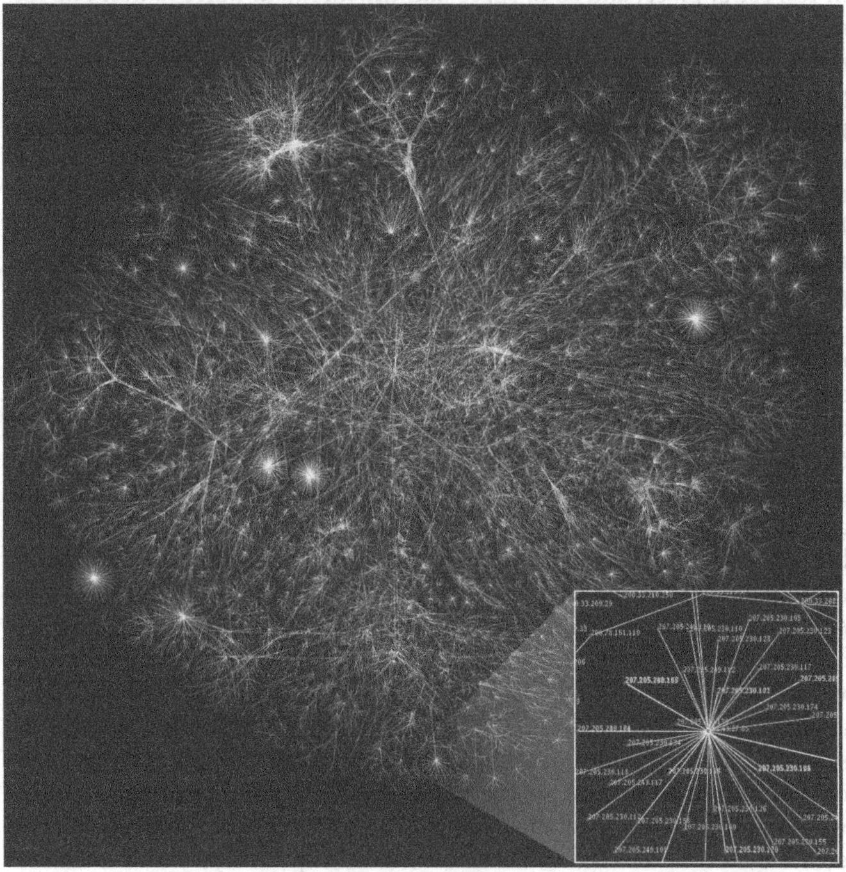

Figure 10 Partial map of the internet derived from data as of 15 January 2005 at opte.org. Each line connects two nodes, representing two IP addresses with the line's length representing the delay between them. The image is available at https://en.wikipedia.org/wiki/Internet_Mapping_Project (accessed 21 August 2017).

What the consideration of technological modernity demonstrates, in spite of its own contrary self-representation (since the rhetoric of modernity is so often about precisely the *escape* from place), is indeed the necessity of place for all appearance, and so also the way the world itself opens up only in and through place. And it is not just one unique place that is at issue here – 'The centre starts from everywhere,'[24] writes Kenneth White, and so too does the world have its beginning in any and every place, even though the exact way this occurs may be different in different places. Just as the horizon of the visual field is not that which prevents vision but precisely that which enables it – the abolition of the horizon being the erasure of vision rather than its freeing-up – so place and being-placed is that which enables the opening up of the entirety of the world. Thus, the essential *boundedness* of place allows the entry into the *unboundedness* of the world. In this way, too, place appears as the first and most primordial form of liminality, the latter term deriving from the Latin for threshold, *limen*, and connecting with the Latin *limitem* or *limes*, meaning limit or bound;[25] and place appears as essentially advental, as in 'arrival', 'event', 'happening', or more literally, a 'coming to'. To be in place is therefore to be *at the threshold of the world* and to be taken up *in the happening of world.* The relation between place and world, between limit and openness, limit and opening, is frequently overlooked or misconstrued – whether because of the obscuring effects of technology or as a result our own tendency to introverted obsession with ourselves.[26] Yet even though places may seem to change, place as such remains, and so too does the essential relation of place and the human. The world begins in place, but so too do we.

Notes

1 Wim Winders, 'In Defense of Places', on Directors Guild of America website, November 2003, accessed 22 June 2017, www.dga.org/Craft/DGAQ/All-Articles/0311-Nov-2003/In-Defense-of-Places.aspx.

2 Indeed, a central theme in 'Michael' is that of dispossession and alienation – something experienced by the old shepherd Michael himself as a result of his son's departure, from the hillsides in which he was raised, for 'the dissolute city' and its 'evil courses'. See William Wordsworth, 'Michael: A Pastoral Poem', in *Lyrical Ballads*, vol. 2 (London: Longman and Rees, 1800), 223.

3 Edward Relph, *Place and Placelessness* (London: Pion, 1977), 143.

4 Ibid., 145.

5 And also, as it happens, in Proust – in fact, Relph's discussion of placelessness, at the end of his book, begins with a quotation from *In Search of Lost Time*. See ibid., 144.

6 See, for example, Barry Wellman, 'Physical Place and Cyber Place: The Rise of Personalized Networking', *International Journal of Urban and Regional Research* 25 (2001): 227–252. There, Wellman talks of the way that modern mobile communication technology offers 'liberation from place'.

7 See my 'From Extremity to Releasement: Place, Authenticity, and the Self', in *The Horizons of Authenticity: Essays in Honor of Charles Guignon's Work on Phenomenology, Existentialism, and Moral Psychology*, ed. Hans Pedersen and Lawrence Hatab (Dordrecht: Springer, 2015), 45–62.

8 Dieter Henrich uses the idea of constellation in his work on the early history of German idealism, where it is used to refer to the systematic relations between groups of thinkers. See Henrich,

Konstellationen: Probleme und Debatten am Ursprung der idealistischen Philosophie (1789–1795) (Stuttgart: Klett-Cotta, 1991). Here, however, the term is used to refer to constellations of concepts; though see also Martin Mulsow and Marcelo Stamm, eds., *Konstellationsforschung* (Berlin: Suhrkamp, 2005), where the term is also sometimes used in a similar sense of conceptual constellation.

9 See Marc Auge, *Non-Places: An Introduction to Supermodernity*, trans. John Howe (London: Verso, 1995).

10 Some of the criticism of Auge's work has been based on observing precisely this aspect of the way the airport operates and so to assert that they are not only transitional. That airports are complex places need not, however, be denied – the point is rather that the sort of places that they are is indeed such as to efface their very character as places, and this enables a different way of capturing their being as 'non-places'. The effacement of place that occurs in places like airports is itself directly tied to the way those places draw together different types of places and so blur the boundaries between places.

11 See Malpas, 'The Place of Mobility: Individualization, Relationality, and Contemporary Technology', in *Mobile Technology and Place*, ed. Rowan Wilken and Gerard Goggin (London: Routledge, 2012), 26–38.

12 See Joshua Meyrowitz, *No Sense of Place: The Impact of Electronic Media on Social Behavior* (New York: Oxford University Press, 1985).

13 Especially Marshall McLuhan, *Understanding Media: The Extensions of Man* (Cambridge, MA: MIT Press, 1964).

14 The launch of the journal *Mobilities* in 2006 reflects the extent to which mobility (including not only the mobility associated with transportation but also of new communication and information technologies) has itself become a key research topic. See Kevin Hannam, Mimi Sheller, and John Urry, "Editorial: Mobilities, Immobilities and Moorings," *Mobilities* 1, no. 1 (2006): 1–22.

15 See, for example, Bruno Latour, *Reassembling the Social: An Introduction to Actor-Network-Theory* (Oxford: Oxford University Press, 2005).

16 On this general topic, see especially the work of Sherry Turkle – including *Life on the Screen: Identity in the Age of the Internet* (New York: Simon and Schuster, 1995); and *Alone Together: Why We Expect More from Technology and Less from Each Other* (New York: Basic Books, 2011).

17 See David Harvey, *The Condition of Postmodernity: An Enquiry into the Origins of Cultural Change* (Cambridge, MA: Blackwell, 1990), part 3, esp. 260–307.

18 Karl Marx, *Grundrisse: Foundations of the Critique of Political Economy*, trans. Martin Nicolaus (Harmondsworth: Penguin, 1973), 539.

19 See Martin Heidegger, 'The Thing', in *Poetry, Language, Thought*, trans. Albert Hofstadter (New York: Harper and Row, 1971), 163–164.

20 See Paul Virilio, *Speed and Politics: An Essay on Dromology* (New York: Semiotext(e), 1977).

21 An argument I advance in more detail in 'Putting Space in Place: Relational Geography and Philosophical Topography', *Planning and Environment D: Space and Society* 30 (2012): 226–242.

22 Within geography, much of Nigel Thrift's work seems to provide an example (if somewhat ambiguously) of this sort of valorization. See, for example, Thrift, *Non-Representational Theory: Space, Politics, Affect* (London: Routledge, 2008). In contemporary architecture, in which pure spatial form seems often to have triumphed over any genuine attentiveness to place, such valorization appears widespread. Zaha Hadid's work is commonly cited as an instance of this, but other examples abound. One might argue that the increasing dominance of digital and computational methods in architecture – which emphasize the spatial just inasmuch as they also emphasize the measurable and quantifiable – have exacerbated architecture's tendency towards pure spatial formalism. On this, see especially Alberto Pérez-Gómez, *Attunement: Architectural Meaning After the Crisis of Modern Science* (Cambridge, MA: MIT Press, 2016). It is reasonable to ask, however, whether the contemporary methods of architecture could be used differently – whether the digital and computational could be redeployed, perhaps against their own tendencies, to return us to forms of genuinely emplaced design. On this issue, see also Randall Lindstrom and Jeff Malpas, 'The Modesty of Architecture', in *Architecture and Political Theory*, ed. Duncan Bell and Bernardo Zacka (forthcoming 2018).

23 Manuel Castells, *The Informational City: Information Technology, Economic Restructuring, and the Urban-regional Process* (Oxford: Blackwell, 1989).

24 Kenneth White, 'Passage West', in *Open World: The Collected Poems 1960–2000* (Edinburgh: Polygon, 2003), 394.
25 See Massimo Cacciari, 'Place and Limit', in *The Intelligence of Place*, ed. Jeff Malpas (London: Bloomsbury, 2015), 13–22.
26 For one possible antidote to such a tendency, see Randall Lindstrom's treatment of *kenosis* in 'Kenosis Creativity Architecture' (PhD dissertation, University of Tasmania, 2015), http://eprints.utas.edu.au/22742/.

Further reading

Auge, Marc. *Non-Places: An Introduction to Supermodernity*. Translated by John Howe. London: Verso, 1995.

Meyrowitz, Joshua. *No Sense of Place: The Impact of Electronic Media on Social Behavior*. New York: Oxford University Press, 1985.

Relph, Edward. *Place and Placelessness*. London: Pion, 1977.

Yurkle, Sherry. *Alone Together: Why We Expect More from Technology and Less from Each Other*. New York: Basic Books, 2011.

Virilio, Paul. *Speed and Politics: An Essay on Dromology*. New York: Semiotext(e), 1977.

Conclusion

Topography and the place of philosophy

> Before we walked, like Demokritus, in empty space, whither we had flown on the butterfly-wings of metaphysics, and there we had conversed with spiritual beings. Now, since the sobering power of self-recognition has caused the silky wings to be folded, we find ourselves again on the ground of experience and common sense. Happily, if we look at it as the place allotted to us, which we never can leave with impunity, and which contains everything to satisfy us as long as we hold to the useful.
>
> (Immanuel Kant, *Dreams of a Spirit-Seer*[1])

The journey that has been undertaken over the past nine chapters began with the idea of place and the necessary locatedness of experience in place, and it has ended with an exploration of the way in which place itself opens up into the world – even into the world of modernity, where place is obscured and sometimes denied. This journey has involved a series of overlapping excursions across a unitary terrain whose shape and structure has been gradually disclosed by our travels through it. What could thus be said of these explorations is much the same as what Wittgenstein says of his own inquiries in *Philosophical Investigations*:

> The philosophical remarks in this book are, as it were, a number of sketches of landscapes which were made in the course of these long and involved journeyings. The same or almost the same points were always being approached afresh from different directions, and new sketches made. Very many of these were badly drawn or uncharacteristic marked by all the defects of a weak draughtsman. And when they were rejected a number of tolerable ones were left, which now had to be arranged and sometimes cut down, so that if you looked at them, you could get a picture of the landscape. Thus this book is really an album.[2]

And, like the album to which Poulet compares Proust's *In Search of Lost Time*, this book has attempted to uncover (through a variety of sketches of the same landscape, through juxtaposition and displacement, through traverse and triangulation), not an 'empty space', but a single, complex, and interconnected region – the very region in which our own identity is grounded, and in which the encounter with other persons and with the things of the world is possible.

Inasmuch, then, as this book has been centrally concerned with the concept of place, so it has aimed to use that concept to inquire into the structure of experience and human subjectivity, as well as to explore the idea of place itself. In the course of those inquiries and explorations, a particular 'place' or territory has also been laid down; one that encompasses, not merely certain discussions in epistemology and metaphysics, and in the philosophy of mind and of language, but also in literary and psychological appropriations of ideas of place and locality. The topographical character of this book is thus evident in its deployment of place as a theoretical or even 'methodological' concept, in the appearance of place as a focus of inquiry, and in the interconnecting of a variety of different disciplinary 'locations' within a single compass. Of course, the very idea of 'topography' that I have employed here might be thought problematic if for no other reason than that it may appear to bring with it a certain 'circularity'. Each element within the topographical structure at issue here supposedly finds its unity in its relation to other elements – every element depends on every other. To take an example from the discussion of Proust in Chapter 6 the unity achieved through juxtaposition apparently depends on displacement, yet the unity achieved through displacement, in turn, depends on juxtaposition. It is not, however, obvious why such apparent 'circularity' should be taken to be problematic. The triangular structure to which Davidson refers, for instance, and which encompasses subjectivity, inter-subjectivity, and objectivity, is a single structure made up of three elements, each of which is dependent on the others but is no less intelligible for that. The structure is understood as one constituted precisely through the interplay of different elements, the unity of which is simply given through their structural interconnection.[3]

The topographical structure at issue in my discussion (a structure that is, to some extent, exemplified in Davidsonian 'triangulation') is one constituted through the interplay of a number of elements that are, themselves, constituted only as part of that structure – much as the different elements in a painting take on a particular character and identity only in the context of the total composition. Those elements, and the structure as a whole, can be causally explained in terms of the physical properties of certain underlying objects and processes, but understood purely as physical objects and processes, there is no painting and no experience, there is no thought and no place. Indeed, while it is a widespread philosophical and scientific tendency to seek to reduce complex structures to more primitive levels of analysis, such reductions typically involve a shift in that which is the focus of explanation. Therefore, they do not explain so much as change the subject. One cannot become a great painter solely through the mastery of the chemical and physical properties of paint, brush, and canvas, because, ultimately, one must master the 'vocabulary' of art itself. Similarly, there is something different about explaining the structure of a painting by reference to its physical composition, rather than by reference to the artistic and cultural milieu in which it was created. The very same lesson applies to philosophical inquiry in general, to the inquiry into human thought and experience that is arguably at the very heart of philosophy, and to thinking itself.

Merleau-Ponty notes the necessity of stepping outside of our normal 'involvement' with the world in order to be able to make that involvement the subject of philosophical inquiry.[4] And yet, although we step back from that place 'here, in the midst of things' that gives philosophy its origin and ground, philosophy cannot afford ever to lose sight of that place. Properly understood, philosophy is topographical, not only because the topographical structure described above determines the very structure and methodology of philosophical inquiry, but also because place itself is the primary focus of philosophical inquiry (even when this goes unrecognized). Thus, although this book is described as a philosophical topography, the truth is that philosophy is itself a form of topography. The starting-point for philosophical reflection is not a world of empty space or inhuman objects, nor a realm of purely subjective sensation or 'sense-data'. Instead it is a world given in relation to activity; an objective world grasped from a subjective viewpoint, a world of other persons and a world in which we find ourselves. Thus, it is to *this* world, and to the place in which it unfolds, that our philosophical explorations must always be addressed, and to which they must always return. The turn back to this world, and so to this place, otherwise all too easily forgotten or overlooked, is what constitutes philosophy as properly self-reflexive – it is not just a matter of the turn back to the self, but of a turn back to the place in which the self appears, from which the world emerges. That this world, this place, must be kept clearly in view is not only important if philosophy is adequately to address the questions that concern philosophy as such, but also if it is to be capable of addressing the concerns of other disciplines (not just the concerns of, for instance, the physical sciences) and of a wider public. In the contemporary climate, in which philosophy can easily be seen as one of the disciplines most removed from those spaces in which the real business of the world takes place, it is all the more important that philosophy be able address itself, not only to its own place within contemporary culture, but also to the concrete locations of contemporary life.[5]

In this respect, however, it may be thought that my work here remains within a fairly abstract frame – a frame removed, for instance, from concrete social and political issues, from issues of gender and sexuality. Certainly, what has been attempted in these pages is the delineation of an account of experience and thought – as characteristically exemplified in human existence – that exhibits the grounding of such experience and thought in place, as well as something of the complex structure of place. Although that project is perhaps overly ambitious, it has undoubtedly left, more or less untouched, a whole series of further issues. What, for instance, might be the implications of this sort of topographical account for our understanding of moral and political matters? To what extent is our relation to place inflected by considerations of gender, class, or culture? Is there anything to draw from these considerations in more practical matters concerning our relation to the spaces and places in which we dwell? In fact, there is already a considerable and expanding literature that addresses just such questions as these – a literature, and a set of questions, to which I cannot do justice here. In this regard, my aim has been a relatively limited one. I have tried to fill a quite particular gap in the philosophical treatment of space and place, and to provide a more adequate philosophical foundation for ideas concerning the centrality of topographic and spatial notions, which now cut across such a wide range of disciplines and so many different areas of human thought and activity. Consequently, this project need not be viewed as in any way incompatible with other projects that attempt to fill out more particular, especially socio-cultural, features of our relation to place. It may, however, be viewed as providing a framework within which some of those projects can be more readily defined and oriented.

Indeed, the latter point suggests that there is at least one respect in which this book might be seen as significant to certain issues concerning the ethics, and also the *politics*, of place. In much contemporary discussion, place is a notion that has been viewed with a great deal of suspicion – as a naive affectation or as arising out of some sedentary conservatism.[6] But if the arguments of the preceding pages are taken seriously, then place cannot be dismissed in this way, nor can it be taken unproblematically to give support to any particular form of conservatism. Indeed, the complex structure of place – its resistance to any simple categorization or characterization, its encompassing of both subjective and objective elements, and its necessary interconnection with agency – suggests that the idea of place does not so much bring a certain ethics and politics with it but rather defines the very frame within which the ethical and political must be located. It is only from a grasp of that place within which ethics and politics both arise that we can even begin to think about the possibility of either in a way that would do justice to the character of our existence as, fundamentally, an existence in and through place.

Notes

1 Immanuel Kant, *Dreams of a Spirit-Seer*, trans. E.F. Goerwitz (London: Swann Sonnenschein & Co, 1900; repr., London: Thoemmes Press, 1992), 114.

2 Ludwig Wittgenstein, *Philosophical Investigations*, trans. G.E.M. Anscombe (Oxford: Blackwell, 1974), ix.

3 In his discussion of Strawson's *Individuals* (and referring to a theory whose viability has been the focus of discussion), Evans writes: 'Although each person in a large circle can be sitting upon the knees of the person behind him, this is not a feat which only two or three people can manage. Perhaps the objection is not that there is a circle in a theory... but that the circle is too small.' See, Gareth Evans, 'Things Without the Mind', in *Collected Papers* (Oxford: Clarendon Press, 1985), 266. Perhaps, considering the Davidsonian triangle, three elements are just enough.

4 See Merleau-Ponty, *The Phenomenology of Perception*, trans. Colin Smith (London: Routledge & Kegan Paul, 1962), xiii.

5 For more on the relation between place and philosophy, see some of the essays in the first section of my *Heidegger and the Thinking of Place* (Cambridge, MA: MIT Press, 2012); and 'Re-Orienting Thinking: Philosophy in the Midst of the World', in *Commonplace Commitments: Thinking Through the Legacy of Joseph P. Fell*, ed. Peter S. Fosl, Michael McGandy, and Mark Moorman (Lewisburg, PA: Bucknell University Press, 2016), 169–186; as well as my discussion with Edward Casey, 'A Phenomenology of Thinking in Place', in *Thinking in the World*, ed. Jill Bennett and Mary Zournazi (London: Bloomsbury, forthcoming 2017).

6 This is so, as I noted earlier, in some of Doreen Massey's discussion of place, and it has certainly been a feature of much of David Harvey's treatment of the concept. See also some of the papers in Jonathan Boyarin, ed., *Remapping Memory: The Politics of Time/Space* (Minneapolis, MN: University of Minnesota, 1994), especially Boyarin's opening essay 'Space, Time and the Politics of Memory', 1–37.

Further reading

Casey, Edward S., and Jeff Malpas. 'A Phenomenology of Thinking in Place.' In *Thinking in the World*, edited by Jill Bennett and Mary Zournazi. London: Bloomsbury, 2018.

Glossary

Action purposive behaviour (as distinct from mere behaviour, 'activity', or effect upon).

Agency the capacity to act and so also the capacity proper to agents; sometimes agency (rather like 'action') is used in a very general sense to mean little more than the capacity to influence or have effect upon, but here it is used more specifically to refer to the capacity for action (that is to say, for genuinely purposive behaviour).

Allocentric space a space whose shape or structure is given by some feature or features of the environment other than the acting body.

Anisotropic space (v. isotropic space) a space that varies according to direction or orientation.

Anomalous monism the view, originating in the work of Donald Davidson, that although mental events are physical events, there is no one-to-one identity between them, and no strict laws that connect them.

Attitude the stance taken with respect to some content as specified by a sentence or 'proposition' (and so the attitudes at issue here are often referred to as 'propositional attitudes'); belief is an instance of an attitude, namely, that of holding something to be true.

Belief a type of attitude; also a type of mental state; more specifically, the holding of something (typically as expressed by a sentence or 'proposition') to be true; beliefs do not come singly, but always as part of larger networks of beliefs.

Conceptual v non-conceptual that which involves or pertains to concepts (any form of genuinely reflexive behaviour or cognition is conceptual); the conceptual is often contrasted with the non-conceptual which does not involve or pertain to concepts (a creature may exhibit oriented and directed behaviour even while it lacks any capacity for conceptualization).

Chora Classical Greek term that has a variety of senses including space or room 'in which a thing is', place, spot, field, country, land, territory, estate, proper position (within, for instance, a social or military hierarchy). As also noted in relation to *topos*, Classical Greek does not sharply distinguish place from space, and so both *chora* and *topos* carry spatial as well as topographic connotations.

Dimensionality openness or extension; the most basic form of dimensionality is space.

Displacement or Superposition v (Juxtaposition) the placing or positioning of one thing over another in such a way as to effectively obliterate it.

Egocentric space literally, space as centred on a subject or 'ego'; often used as a synonym for subjective space.

Externalism the view that the contents of an agent's mental states are determined by entities and events in the external environment of the agent.

Holism when applied to attitudes or mental states, the idea that those states do not come singly, but always as part of a larger body of states – as part of a larger whole (e.g. belief is holistic inasmuch as to have one belief is to have many beliefs); holism implies relationality.

Intentionality when used in relation to mental states, the character of those states as being directed towards an object; when used in relation to action, the character of action as determined in relation to a desired end (action is thus intentional behaviour).

Intersubjective space the space of engagement with others.

Intersubjectivity the quality of being related or pertaining to the engagement with others.

Isotropic space (v anisotropic space) a space that is invariant regardless of direction or orientation (from the Greek *iso*, meaning equal, and *tropos*, meaning direction or way).

Juxtaposition (v Displacement or Superposition) the placing or positioning of one thing alongside another so that both appear together.

Mental content the content associated with mental states (e.g. the content of the belief that 'London is pretty' is that London is pretty).

Mental event an event belonging to the mind; occurrences of believing, desiring, thinking, hoping, remembering are all instances of mental events.

Mental state a state belonging to the mind; belief, desire, thought, hope, or memory are all instances of mental states. As used here, mental states can be understood as either episodic or dispositional (as occurring at a time or over time); as underlain by behavioural patterns and tendencies; and as potentially reinterpretable in terms of mental *events*.

Objective space the space of objects as they are apart from any subject and in which no location or feature has priority over any other.

Objectivity the quality of being related or pertaining to objects.

Philosophical topography a philosophical inquiry that proceeds topographically, that is, that exhibits the unity of a conceptual region through the mapping of the inter-relations between the elements that are given within that region and that also constitute it; philosophical topography also names the inquiry into the nature and significance of place.

Place at its most basic, a bounded openness or opening; when treated as derivative of space, place becomes a mere location in space, or a location that has some subjective quality of meaning attached to it; in its fullest sense, space is that complex and yet unitary structure that encompasses space and time, subjective and objective; empirically, place appears in those many different places, often named, in which persons and things are situated, and within and between which they move.

Region sometimes identical with place, but also sometimes referring to an interconnected set of places.

Sense of place the felt or meaningful character of a place that makes it distinctive as a place.

Space dimensionality, 'room' or extension, whether physical or non-physical; openness.

Spatiality the quality of being related or pertaining to space.

Subject literally (from its Latin origin), and in its most general sense, 'that which underlies', but more specifically, that which stands over against objects; often identical with the self.

Subjective space the space established by the capacities of an acting subject and directly keyed to those capacities.

Subjectivity the quality of being related or pertaining to the subject.

Superposition see *Displacement*.

Topoanalysis a term used by Gaston Bachelard in *Poetics of Space*: the analysis or investigation of place or places, especially, in Bachelard's case, interior and domestic spaces (the house, the room, the cupboard) of human life; in Bachelard, topoanalysis is invariably an analysis of the places of the self.

Topography in its literal sense, the description of place or places; in relation to surveying, the measuring and recording of some part of the surface of the Earth, and so of some region or landscape; also the character of a region or landscape as given in its surface.

Topology literally, the underlying structure of place or the inquiry into that structure; often understood, in contemporary terms, as any spatially oriented study that attends to the formal structure of those relations (deployed this way, though differently in each case, in geometry and some areas of geography); in Heidegger, the saying of place, and especially the saying of the place of being (topology of being).

Topophilia a term used by Bachelard in *Poetics of Space* (but also by other writers): the love of place or places.

Topopoetics the taking up of place and places within a poetic context, the poetizing of place or poetics of place.

Topos Classical Greek term that originally has a variety of senses including place, position, region, location, site, burial-place, or an element in rhetoric. It is also closely related to the notion of a bounding surface. In contemporary English, it is sometimes used as a near synonym for place. As also noted in relation to *chora*, Classical Greek does not sharply distinguish place from space, and so both *topos* and *chora* carry spatial as well as topographic connotations.

Bibliography

Adams, Percy. *Travel Literature and the Evolution of the Novel.* Lexington, KY: University Press of Kentucky, 1983.

Agnew, John A., and James S. Duncan, eds. *The Power of Place.* Boston, MA: Unwin Hyman, 1989.

Agnew, John A., 'The Devaluation of Place in Social Science.' In Agnew and Duncan, *The Power of Place*, 1–28.

Algra, Keimpe. *Concepts of Space in Greek Thought.* Leiden: E.J. Brill, 1995.

Altman, Irwin, and Setha M. Low, eds. *Place Attachment.* New York: Plenum Press, 1992.

Aristotle. *The Complete Works of Aristotle.* Edited by Jonathan Barnes. Princeton, NJ: Princeton University Press, 1984.

Atkins, Kim, ed. *Narrative Identity and Moral Identity: A Practical Perspective.* London: Routledge, 2008.

Auge, Marc, *Non-Places: An Introduction to Supermodernity.* Translated by John Howe. London: Verso, 1995.

Ayer, A.J. *The Concept of a Person and Other Essays.* New York: St Martin's Press, 1963.

Bachelard, Gaston. *The Poetics of Space.* Translated by Maria Jolas. Boston, MA: Beacon Press, 1969.

Baddeley, Alan, Andrew Thornton, Siew Eng Chua, and Peter McKenna. 'Schizophrenic Delusions and the Construction of Autobiographical Memory.' In *Remembering Our Past*, edited by David Rubin, 384–428. Cambridge: Cambridge University Press, 1996.

Baldwin, Thomas. 'Objectivity, Causality and Agency.' In Bermudez, Marcel, and Eilan, *The Body and the Self*, 107–126.

Barclay, Craig R. 'Remembering Ourselves.' In *Memory in Everyday Life*, edited by G.M. Davies and R.H. Logie, 285–309. Amsterdam: Elsevier, 1993.

Barrell, John. *The Idea of Landscape and the Sense of Place 1730–1840: An Approach to the Poetry of John Clare.* Cambridge: Cambridge University Press, 1972.

Barrell, John. *The Dark Side of the Landscape.* Cambridge: Cambridge University Press, 1980.

Bate, Jonathan. *Romantic Ecology: Wordsworth and the Environmental Tradition.* London: Routledge, 1991.

Baxter, James K. *In Fires of No Return: Poems*. London: Oxford University Press, 1958.

Benterrak, Krim, Stephen Muecke, and Paddy Roe. *Reading the Country: Introduction to Nomadology*. Fremantle, WA: Fremantle Arts Centre Press, 1984.

Berdoulay, Vincent. 'Place, Meaning and Discourse in French Language Geography.' In Agnew and Duncan, *The Power of Place*, 124–139.

Bergson, Henri. *Time and Free Will*. Translated by F.L. Pogson. London: George Allen and Unwin, 1910.

Berkeley, George. *Of the Principles of Human Knowledge*, part 1, §10. In *Philosophical Works, Including the Works on Vision*, edited by M. Ayers, vol. 2, 79. London: Dent, 1975.

Bermudez, José Luis, Anthony Marcel, and Naomi Eilan, eds. *The Body and the Self*. Cambridge, MA: MIT Press, 1995.

Bevan, Robert. *The Destruction of Memory: Architecture at War*. London: Reaktion, 2006.

Bilgrami, Akeel. *Belief and Meaning: The Unity and Locality of Mental Content*. Cambridge, MA: Blackwell, 1992.

Bilgrami, Akeel. 'Review of Jerry A. Fodor: *A Theory of Content and Other Essays* and Jerry A. Fodor and Ernest Lepore: *Holism: A Shopper's Guide*.' *Journal of Philosophy* 92 (1995): 330–344.

Bird, Jon, Barry Curtis, Tim Putnam, George Robertson, and Lisa Tickner, eds. *Mapping the Futures*. London: Routledge, 1993.

Blomfield, Reginald A. *History of French Architecture, 1661–1774*. London: G. Bell and Sons, 1921.

Bloom, Harold, ed. *Seamus Heaney*. New Haven, CT: Chelsea House, 1986.

Bochner, Salomon. 'Space.' In *Dictionary of the History of Ideas*, 295–307. New York: Charles Scribner's Sons, 1973.

Boyarin, Jonathan. 'Space, Time and the Politics of Memory.' In *Remapping Memory: The Politics of Timespace*, edited by Jonathan Boyarin, 1–37. Minneapolis, MN: University of Minnesota Press, 1994.

Brentano, Franz. *Psychology from an Empirical Standpoint*. London: Routledge & Kegan Paul, 1973.

Brockmeier, Jens, and Donal A. Carbaugh, eds. *Narrative and Identity: Studies in Autobiography, Self and Culture*. Amsterdam: John Benjamins Publishing, 2001.

Burge, Tyler. 'Cartesian Error and the Objectivity of Perception.' In *Subject, Thought and Context*, edited by Philip Pettit and John McDowell, 117–136. Oxford: Clarendon Press, 1986.

Burge, Tyler. 'Individualism and Self-Knowledge.' *Journal of Philosophy* 85 (1988): 649–663.

Burge, Tyler. 'Individualism and the Mental.' In *Midwest Studies in Philosophy*, vol. 4, edited by P.A. French, T.E. Uehling, Jr., and H.K. Wettstein, 73–121. Minneapolis, MN: University of Minnesota Press, 1979.

Buttimer, Anne, and David Seamon, eds. *The Human Experience of Space and Place*. London: Croom Helm, 1980.

Cacciari, Massimo. "Place and Limit." In Malpas, *The Intelligence of Place*, 13–22.

Cameron, Patsy. *Grease and Ochre: The Blending of Two Cultures at the Colonial Sea Frontier*. Hobart, Tas: Fullers, 2011.

Campbell, John. *Past, Space, and Self*. Cambridge, MA: MIT Press, 1994.

Campbell, John. 'The Role of Physical Objects in Spatial Thinking.' In Eilan, McCarthy, and Brewer, *Spatial Representation*, 65–95.

Camus, Albert. 'Nuptials at Tipasa.' In *Lyrical and Critical Essays*, edited by Philip Thody, translated by Ellen Conroy Kennedy, 51–56. London: Hamish Hamilton, 1967.

Carr, David. 'Narrative and the Real World: An Argument for Continuity.' *History and Theory* 25 (1986): 117–131.

Carter, William C. *Marcel Proust: A Life*. New Haven, CT: Yale University Press, 2000.

Casey, Edward S. *The Fate of Place*. Berkeley, CA: University of California Press, 1996.

Casey, Edward S. *Getting Back into Place*. Bloomington, IN: Indiana University Press, 1994.

Casey, Edward S. and Jeff Malpas. 'A Phenomenology of Thinking in Place.' In *Thinking in the World*, edited by Jill Bennett and Mary Zournazi. London: Bloomsbury, forthcoming 2018.

Casey, Edward S. *Remembering*. Bloomington, IN: Indiana University Press, 1989.

Casey, Edward S. 'Smooth Spaces and Rough-Edged Places: The Hidden History of Place.' *Review of Metaphysics* 51 (1997): 267–296.

Cassam, Quassim. *Self and World*. Oxford: Clarendon Press, 1997.

Castells, Manuel. *The Informational City: Information Technology, Economic Restructuring, and the Urban-regional Process*. Oxford: Blackwell, 1989.

Cavell, Marcia. *The Psychoanalytic Mind: From Freud to Philosophy*. Cambridge, MA: Harvard University Press, 1993.

Chatwin, Bruce. *The Songlines*. London: Pan, 1988.

Chawla, Louisa. 'Childhood Place Attachments.' In Altman and Low, *Place Attachment*, 63–86.

Clare, John. *The Prose of John Clare*. Edited by J.W. Tibble and Anne Tibble. London: Routledge & Kegan Paul, 1951.

Clark, Andy. *Supersizing the Mind: Embodiment, Action, and Cognitive Extension*. Oxford: Oxford University Press, 2008.

Cicero. *De oratore*. Translated by E.W. Sutton and H. Rackham. Loeb ed. Cambridge, MA: Harvard University Press, 1942.

Clauss, Ludwig Ferdinand. *Die nordische Seele: Eine Einführung in die Rassenseelenkunde*. Munich: J.F. Lehmanns, 1932.

Cole, Jonathan. *Pride and a Daily Marathon*. Cambridge, MA: MIT Press, 1995.

Cosgrove, Denis, and Stephen Daniels, eds. *The Iconography of Landscape*. Cambridge: Cambridge University Press, 1989.

Cornford, F.M. *Plato's Cosmology*. London: Routledge & Kegan Paul, 1937.

Countless Signs: The New Zealand Landscape in Literature. Compiled by Trudie McNaughton. Auckland: Reed Methuen, 1986.

Cresswell, Tim. *Place: A Short Introduction*. Chichester: Wiley-Blackwell, 2004.

Davidson, Donald. *Essays on Actions and Events*. Oxford: Clarendon Press, 1980.

Davidson, Donald. *Inquiries into Truth and Interpretation*. Oxford: Clarendon Press, 1984.

Davidson, Donald. *Problems of Rationality*. Oxford: Clarendon Press, 2004.

Davidson, Donald. *Subjective, Intersubjective, Objective*. Oxford: Clarendon Press, 2001.

Davidson, Donald. *Truth, Language, and History*. Oxford: Clarendon Press, 2009.

Davidson, Donald. 'Reply to Burge.' *Journal of Philosophy* 85 (1988): 664–665.

Davidson, Donald. 'Reply to Suppes.' In *Essays on Davidson: Actions and Events*, edited by Bruce Vermazen and Jaakko Hintikka, 247–252. Oxford: Clarendon Press, 1986.

Davidson, Donald. 'Subjective, Intersubjective, Objective.' In *Current Issues in Idealism*, edited by Paul Coates and Daniel D. Hutto, 155–178. Bristol: Thoemmes Press, 1996.

Davidson, Donald. 'The Problem of Objectivity.' *Tijdschrift Voor Filosofie* 57 (1995): 203–219.

Davidson, Lawrence. *Cultural Genocide*. New Brunswick, NJ: Rutgers University Press, 2012.

Deleuze, Gilles. *Proust and Signs*. New York: G. Braziller, 1972.

Deleuze, Gilles, and Felix Guattari. *A Thousand Plateaus: Capitalism and Schizophrenia*. Translated by Brian Massumi. Minneapolis, MN: University of Minnesota Press, 1987.

Dennett, Daniel C. *Content and Consciousness*. London: Routledge, 1993.

Descartes, René. *Principia Philosophiae*. In *Oeuvres de Descartes*, edited by Charles Adams and Paul Tannery, VIII-1. Paris: Librarire Philosophique, J. Vrin, 1982. Translated by John Cottingham, Robert Stoothoff, and Dugald Murdoch in *The Philosophical Writings of Descartes*, vol. 1 (Cambridge: Cambridge University Press, 1985).

Donohoe, Janet, ed. *Place and Phenomenology*. London: Rowman & Littlefield International, 2017.

Donohoe, Janet. *Remembering Places: A Phenomenological Study of the Relationship Between Memory and Place*. Lanham, MD: Lexington Books, 2014.

Dreyfus, Hubert, and Charles Taylor. *Retrieving Realism*. Cambridge, MA: Harvard University Press, 2015.

Edson, Evelyn. *Mapping Space and Time: How Medieval Mapmakers Viewed Their World*. London: British Library, 1977.

Eilan, Naomi, Rosaleen McCarthy, and Bill Brewer, eds. *Spatial Representation*. Oxford: Blackwell, 1993.

Einstein, Albert. 'The Problem of Space, Ether and the Field in Physics.' In *Ideas and Opinions*, translated by Sonja Borgmann, 276–285. New York: Crown, 1956.

El-Bizri, Nader. 'On *Khôra*: Situating Heidegger between the *Sophist* and the *Timaeus*.' *Studia Phaenomenologica* 4 (2002): 73–98.

Elden, Stuart. 'Heidegger's Hölderlin and the Importance of Place.' *Journal of the British Society for Phenomenology* 30, no. 3 (1999): 258–274.

The English Dialect Dictionary. Edited by Joseph Wright. Oxford: Oxford University Press, 1905.

Entrikin, J. Nicholas. *The Betweenness of Place*. Baltimore, MD: Johns Hopkins University Press, 1991.

Evans, Gareth. *The Varieties of Reference*. Edited by John McDowell. Oxford: Clarendon Press, 1982.

Evans, Gareth. *Collected Papers*. Oxford: Clarendon Press, 1985.

Faulkner, William. *The Portable Faulkner*. Rev. ed. Edited by Malcolm Lowry. New York: Viking Press, 1967.

Febvre, Lucien. *A Geographical Introduction to History*. London: Kegan Paul, Trench, Trubner & Co., 1925.

Feld, Steven, and Keith H. Basso, eds. *Senses of Place*. Santa Fe, NM: School of American Research Press, 1996.

Fodor, Jerry. *Psychosemantics*. Cambridge, MA: MIT Press, 1987.

Fodor, Jerry, and Ernest LePore. *Holism: A Shopper's Guide*. Oxford: Blackwell, 1992.

Fodor, Jerry, and Ernest LePore, eds. *Holism: A Consumer Update*. Amsterdam: Rodopi, 1993.

Foucault, Michel. *Discipline and Punish: The Birth of the Prison*. New York: Vintage Books, 1979.

Foucault, Michel. 'Of Other Spaces.' *Diacritics* 16 (1986): 22–27.

Freud, Sigmund. 'Screen Memories.' In *The Complete Psychological Works*, vol. 3, *Early Psycho-Analytic Publications (1893–99)*, translated by James Strachey, 299–322. London: Hogarth Press, 1966.

Frisius, Gemma. *Libellus de locorum describendum ratione*. In *Cosmographia* (Antwerp, 1533).

Furness, Sarah. 'A Reasonable Geography: An Argument for Embodiment.' PhD dissertation, University of Essex, 1986.

Gallagher, Shaun. 'Body Schema and Intentionality.' In Bermudez, Marcel, and Eilan, *The Body and the Self*, 225–244.

Gammage, Bill. *The Biggest Estate on Earth. How Aborigines Made Australia*. Sydney: Allen and Unwin, 2011.

Gasking, D. 'Causation and Recipes.' *Mind* 54 (1955): 479–487.

Gibson, J.J. *The Ecological Approach to Visual Perception*. Boston, MA: Houghton Mifflin, 1979.

Glacken, Clarence J. *Traces on the Rhodian Shore*. Berkeley, CA: University of California Press, 1967.

Godfrey-Smith, Peter. 'Finding Your Way Home.' *Boston Review*, 14 September 2015. Accessed 14 August 2017. http://bostonreview.net/books-ideas/peter-godfrey-smith-dreyfus-taylor-retrieving-realism.

Godkin, Michael A. 'Identity and Place: Clinical Applications Based on Notions of Rootedness and Uprootedness.' In Buttimer and Seamon, *The Human Experience of Space and Place*, 73–85.

Goldthorpe, Rhiannon. 'Ricoeur, Proust and the Aporias of Time.' In Wood, *On Paul Ricoeur: Narrative and Interpretation*, 84–101.

Grant, Edward. *Much Ado About Nothing: Theories of Space and Vacuum from the Middle Ages to the Scientific Revolution*. Cambridge: Cambridge University Press, 1981.

A Greek-English Lexicon. Rev. ed. Compiled by Henry George Liddell and Robert Scott. Oxford: Clarendon Press, 1968.

Grigson, Geoffrey, ed. *The Faber Book of Poems and Places*. London: Faber & Faber, 1980.

Grosz, Elizabeth. *Space, Time and Perversion: The Politics of Bodies*. New York: Routledge, 1995.

Guide dans la monuments de Paris. Paris: Paulin et Le Chevalier, 1855.

Guignon, Charles. *Heidegger and the Problem of Knowledge*. Indianapolis, IN: Hackett Publishing, 1983.

Hadot, Pierre. *Philosophy as a Way of Life*. Translated by Arnold I. Davidson. Oxford: Blackwell, 1995.

Hahn, Lewis Edwin, ed. *The Philosophy of Donald Davidson*. Library of Living Philosophers XXVII. Chicago, IL: Open Court Press, 1999.

Halbwachs, Maurice. *The Collective Memory*. Translated by F.J. Ditter and V.Y. Ditter. New York: Harper & Row Colophon Books, 1980.

Harries, Karsten. *The Ethical Function of Architecture*. Cambridge, MA: MIT Press, 1997.

Hartman, Geoffrey. *Beyond Formalism: Literary Essays, 1958–1970*. New Haven, CT: Yale University Press, 1970.

Harvey, David. *Justice, Nature and the Geography of Difference*. Cambridge, MA: Blackwell, 1996.

Harvey, David. *The Condition of Postmodernity: An Enquiry into the Origins of Cultural Change*. Cambridge, MA: Blackwell, 1990.

Harvey, David. 'Between Space and Time: Reflections on the Geographical Imagination.' *Annals of the American Association of Geographers* 80 (1990): 418–434.

Harvey, David. 'From Space to Place and Back Again: Reflections on the Condition of Postmodernity.' In Bird et al., *Mapping the Futures*, 3–29.

Hauser, Marc D., Noam Chomsky, and W. Tecumseh Fitch. 'The Faculty of Language: What Is It, Who Has It, and How Did It Evolve?' *Science*, New Series 298, no. 5598 (2002): 1569–1579.

Heaney, Seamus. *Seeing Things*. London: Faber & Faber, 1991.

Heaney, Seamus. *Preoccupations: Selected Prose, 1968–1978*. London: Faber & Faber, 1984.

Heidegger, Martin. *Being and Time*. Translated by John Macquarrie and Edward Robinson. New York: Harper & Row, 1962.

Heidegger, Martin. *Elucidations of Hölderlin's Poetry*. Translated by Keith Hoeller. New York: Humanity Books, 2000.

Heidegger, Martin. *History of the Concept of Time*. Translated by Theodore Kisiel. Bloomington, IN: Indiana University Press, 1985.

Heidegger, Martin. *On Time and Being*. Translated by Joan Stambaugh. New York: Harper & Row, 1972.

Heidegger, Martin. *On the Way to Language.* Translated by Peter D. Hertz. New York: Harper & Row, 1971.

Heidegger, Martin. *The Question Concerning Technology and Other Essays.* Translated by William Lovitt. New York: Harper & Row, 1977.

Heidegger, Martin. *Wegmarken, Gesamtausgabe.* Vol. 9. Frankfurt: Klostermann, 1976.

Heidegger, Martin. *What is a Thing?* Translated by W. B. Barton, Jr. and Vera Deutsch. Chicago, IL: Henry Regnery, 1967.

Heidegger, Martin. 'Art and Space.' Translated by Charles Seibert. *Man and World* 1 (1973): 3–5.

Heidegger, Martin. 'Hebel – Friend of the House.' Translated by Bruce V. Foltz and Michael Heim. *Contemporary German Philosophy* 3 (1983): 100–101.

Heidegger, Martin. 'Seminar in Le Thor 1969.' In *Four Seminars*, translated by Andrew Mitchell and François Raffoul. Bloomington, IN: Indiana University Press, 2004.

Heidegger, Martin. 'The Thing.' In *Poetry, Language, Thought*, translated by Albert Hofstadter, 161–180. New York: Harper and Row, 1971.

Heil, John. *The Nature of True Minds*. Cambridge: Cambridge University Press, 1992.

Henrich, Dieter. *Konstellationen: Probleme und Debatten am Ursprung der idealistischen Philosophie (1789–1795).* Stuttgart: Klett-Cotta, 1991.

Hicks, Dan, and Mary C. Beaudry, eds. *The Oxford Handbook of Material Culture Studies*. Oxford: Oxford University Press, 2010.

Hultius, Levinus. *Theoria et praxis quadrantis geometrici. . . das ist, Beschreibung, Unterricht und Gebrauch des gevierdten geometrischen und anderer Instrument.* Amsterdam, 1594.

Hutto, Daniel D., ed. *Narrative and Understanding Persons*. Royal Institute of Philosophy Supplement 60. Cambridge: Cambridge University Press, 2007.

Ihimaera, Witi. *Tangi*. Auckland: Heinemann, 1973.

Isidore of Seville. *Etymologiae*. Augsburg: Gunther Zainer, 1472.

Jammer, Max. *Concepts of Space: The History of Concepts of Space in Physics*. 2nd ed. Cambridge, MA: Harvard University Press, 1970.

Janz, Bruce, ed. *Place, Space and Hermeneutics*. Dordrecht: Springer, 2017.

Johnson, Mark. *The Body in the Mind.* Chicago, IL: University of Chicago Press, 1987.

Johnston, R.J. *Geography and Geographers: Anglo-American Human Geography since 1945*. 4th ed. New York: Edward Arnold, 1991.

Joyce, James. *Ulysses*. Rev. ed. Edited by Danis Rose. London: Picador, 1997.

Kant, Immanuel. *Critique of Pure Reason*. In *The Cambridge Edition of the Works of Immanuel Kant*, translated by Paul Guyer and Allen Wood. Cambridge: Cambridge University Press, 1988.

Kant, Immanuel. *Kant's Inaugural Dissertation and Early Writings on Space*. Translated by John Handyside. Chicago, IL: Open Court, 1929.

Kant, Immanuel. *Dreams of a Spirit-Seer*. Translated by E.F. Goerwitz. Reprint, London: Thoemmes Press, 1992. Originally published 1900 by Swann Sonnenschein & Co.

Kay-Robinson, Dennis. *The Landscapes of Thomas Hardy*. Exeter: Webb & Bower, 1984.

Kerrigan, John. 'Wordsworth and the Sonnet: Building, Dwelling, Thinking.' *Essays in Criticism* 35 (1985): 45–75.

Kripke, Saul. 'A Puzzle About Belief.' In *Meaning and Use*, edited by A. Margalit. Dordrecht: Reidel, 1979.

A Latin Dictionary founded on Andrew's Edition of Freund's Latin Dictionary. Edited and revised by Charlton T. Lewis and Charles Short. Oxford: Clarendon Press, 1879.

Latour, Bruno. *Reassembling the Social: An Introduction to Actor-Network-Theory*. Oxford: Oxford University Press, 2005.

Lea, Hermann. *Thomas Hardy's Wessex*. London: Macmillan, 1977. Originally published in 1913.

Lefebvre, Henri. *The Production of Space*. Translated by Donald Nicholson-Smith. Oxford: Blackwell, 1991.

Levinas, Emanuel. *Totality and Infinity*. Translated by Alphonso Lingis. Pittsburgh, PA: Duquesne University Press, 1969.

Ley, David, and Marwyn S. Samuels, eds. *Humanistic Geography: Prospects and Problems*. London: Croom Helm, 1978.

Leyton, Michael. *Symmetry, Causality, Mind*. Cambridge, MA: MIT Press, 1992.

Lilburne, Geoffrey R. *A Sense of Place: A Christian Theology of the Land*. Nashville, TN: Abingdon Press, 1989.

Lindstrom, Randall S. 'Kenosis Creativity Architecture.' PhD dissertation, University of Tasmania, 2015, http://eprints.utas.edu.au/22742/.

Lindstrom, Randall, and Jeff Malpas. 'The Modesty of Architecture.' In *Architecture and Political Theory*, edited by Duncan Bell and Bernardo Zacka Forthcoming.

Lucy Lippard. *The Lure of the Local: Senses of Place in a Multicentered Society*. New York: New Press, 1997.

Lowenthal, David. *The Past is a Foreign Country*. Cambridge: Cambridge University Press, 1985.

Lucas, John. 'Places and Dwellings: Wordsworth, Clare and the Anti-Picturesque.' In *The Iconography of Landscape*, edited by Denis Cosgrove and Stephen Daniels, 83–97. Cambridge: Cambridge University Press, 1989.

Lukermann, F. 'The Concept of Location in Classical Geography.' *Annals of the American Association of Geographers* 51 (1961): 194–210.

Mach, Ernst. *Space and Geometry in the Light of Physiological, Psychological and Physical Inquiry*. Chicago, IL: Open Court, 1906.

MacIntyre, Alasdair. *After Virtue: A Study in Moral Theory*. London: Duckworth, 1981.

MacMurray, John. *The Self as Agent*. London: Faber & Faber, 1957.

Malpas, Jeff. *Donald Davidson and The Mirror of Meaning*. Cambridge: Cambridge University Press, 1992.

Malpas, Jeff. *Heidegger and the Thinking of Place: Explorations in the Topology of Being*. Cambridge, MA: MIT Press, 2012.

Malpas, Jeff. *Heidegger's Topology: Being, Place, World*. Cambridge, MA: MIT Press, 2006.

Malpas, Jeff. 'The Beckoning of Language: Heidegger's Hermeneutic Transformation of Thinking.' In *Hermeneutical Heidegger*, edited by Ingo Farin and Michael Bowler, 203–221. Evanston, IL: Northwestern University Press, 2016.

Malpas, Jeff. 'Constituting the Mind: Kant, Davidson and the Unity of Consciousness.' *International Journal of Philosophical Studies* 7, no. 1 (1999): 1–30.

Malpas, Jeff. 'Five Theses on Place (and Some Associated Remarks): A Reply to Peter Gratton.' *Il Cannocchiale* 62 (2017): 69–81.

Malpas, Jeff. 'From Extremity to Releasement: Place, Authenticity, and the Self.' In *The Horizons of Authenticity: Essays in Honor of Charles Guignon's Work on Phenomenology, Existentialism, and Moral Psychology*, edited by Hans Pedersen and Lawrence Hatab, 45–62. Dordrecht: Springer, 2015.

Malpas, Jeff. '"The House of Being": Poetry, Language, Place.' In *Heidegger's Later Thought*, edited by Günter Figal, Diego D'Angelo, Tobias Keiling, and Guang Yang. Bloomington, IN: Indiana University Press, forthcoming 2018.

Malpas, Jeff. 'Is There an Ethics of Place?' *Localities* 2 (2012): 7–32.

Malpas, Jeff, with Karsten Thiel. 'Kant's Geography of Reason.' In *Kant's Geography*, edited by Stuart Elden and Eduardo Mendieta, 195–214. New York: SUNY Press, 2011.

Malpas, Jeff. 'Place and Hermeneutics: Towards a Topology of Understanding.' In *Inheriting Gadamer: New Directions in Philosophical Hermeneutics*, edited by Georgia Warnke, 143–160. Edinburgh: Edinburgh University Press, 2016.

Malpas, Jeff. 'Place and Placedness.' In *Situatedness and Place: Multidisciplinary Perspectives on the Spatio-temporal Contingency of Human Life*, edited by Thomas Hünefeldt and Annika Schlitte. Dordrecht: Springer, forthcoming 2018.

Malpas, Jeff. 'Place and Situation.' In *The Routledge Companion to Philosophical Hermeneutics*, edited by Jeff Malpas and Hans-Helmuth Gander, 354–366. London: Routledge, 2015.

Malpas, Jeff. 'The Place of Mobility: Individualization, Relationality, and Contemporary Technology.' In *Mobile Technology and Place*, edited by Rowan Wilken and Gerard Goggin, 26–38. London: Routledge, 2012.

Malpas, Jeff. 'Putting Space in Place: Relational Geography and Philosophical Topography.' *Planning and Environment D: Space and Society* 30 (2012): 226–242.

Malpas, Jeff, with Günter Zöller. 'Reading Kant Geographically: From Critical Philosophy to Empirical Geography.' In *Contemporary Kantian Metaphysics: New*

Essays on Space and Time, edited by Roxana Baiasu, Graham Bird, and A. W. Moore, 146–166. London: Palgrave Macmillan, 2011.

Malpas, Jeff. 'The Remembrance of Place.' In *The Voice of Place: Essays and Interviews Exploring the Work of Edward S. Casey*, edited by Azucena Cruz-Pierre and Don Landes, 63–72. London: Bloomsbury, 2013.

Malpas, Jeff. 'Re-Orienting Thinking: Philosophy in the Midst of the World.' In *Commonplace Commitments: Thinking Through the Legacy of Joseph P. Fell*, edited by Peter S. Fosl, Michael McGandy, and Mark Moorman, 169–186. Lewisburg, PA: Bucknell University Press, 2016.

Malpas, Jeff. 'Self-Knowledge and Scepticism.' *Erkenntnis* 40 (1994): 165–184.

Malpas, Jeff. 'Space and Sociality.' *International Journal of Philosophical Studies* 5 (1997): 53–79.

Malpas, Jeff. 'Thinking Topographically: Place, Space, and Geography.' *Il Cannocchiale* 62 (2017): 125–154.

Malpas, Jeff, ed. *The Intelligence of Place: Topographies and Poetics*. London: Bloomsbury, 2015.

Marcus, Clare Cooper. 'Environmental Memories.' In Altman and Low, *Place Attachment*, 87–112.

Martin, Lauren, and Anna J. Secor. 'Towards a Post-Mathematical Topology.' *Progress in Human Geography* 38 (2013): 420–438.

Marx, Karl. *Grundrisse: Foundations of the Critique of Political Economy*. Translated by Martin Nicolaus. Harmondsworth: Penguin, 1973.

Mason, Bruce. *The End of the Golden Weather: A Voyage into a New Zealand Childhood*. Wellington: Victoria University Press, 1970.

Massey, Doreen. 'Power-Geometry and a Progressive Sense of Place.' In Bird et al., *Mapping the Futures*, 59–69.

McDowell, John. *Mind and World*. Cambridge, MA: Harvard University Press, 1994.

McGinn, Colin. *The Subjective View*. Oxford: Clarendon Press, 1983.

McLuhan, Marshall. *Understanding Media: The Extensions of Man*. Cambridge, MA: MIT Press, 1964.

Mead, George Herbert. *Mind, Self and Society*. Chicago, IL: University of Chicago Press, 1934.

Melville, Hermann. *Redburn: His First Voyage*. New York: Doubleday, 1957.

Menin, Sarah, ed. *Constructing Place: Mind and Matter*. London: Routledge, 2003.

Merleau-Ponty, Maurice. *The Phenomenology of Perception*. Translated by Colin Smith. London: Routledge & Kegan Paul, 1962.

Meyers Konversations-Lexikon: Ein Nachschlagewerk des allgemeinen Wissens. Leipzig und Wien: Bibliographisches Institut, 1895–1898.

Meyrowitz, Joshua. *No Sense of Place: The Impact of Electronic Media on Social Behavior*. New York: Oxford University Press, 1985.

Mill, John Stuart. *An Examination of Sir William Hamilton's Philosophy*. Edited by J.M. Robson. Toronto: University of Toronto Press, 1979.

Mink, Louis O. 'History and Fiction as Modes of Comprehension.' *New Literary History* 1 (1969–70): 541–558.

Morgan, Sally. *My Place*. Fremantle, WA: Fremantle Arts Press, 1989.

Morris, David. *The Sense of Space*. New York: SUNY Press, 2004.

Mulsow, Martin, and Marcelo Stamm, eds. *Konstellationsforschung*. Berlin: Suhrkamp, 2005.

Myers, Fred R. *Pintupi Country, Pintupi Self*. Canberra: Australian Institute of Aboriginal Studies, 1986.

Nagel, Thomas. *The Possibility of Altruism*. Oxford: Clarendon Press, 1970.

Nagel, Thomas. *The View from Nowhere*. Oxford: Oxford University Press, 1986.

National Inquiry into the Separation of Aboriginal and Torres Strait Islander Children from their Families (Commonwealth of Australia). *Bringing Them Home: Report of the National Inquiry into the Separation of Aboriginal and Torres Strait Islander Children from their Families*. Sydney: Human Rights and Equal Opportunity Commission, 1997.

Neisser, Ulric and Eugene Winograd, eds. *Remembering Reconsidered: Ecological and Traditional Approaches to the Study of Memory*. Cambridge: Cambridge University Press, 1988.

Neisser, Ulric. 'Five Kinds of Self-knowledge.' *Philosophical Psychology* 1 (1988): 35–59.

Neisser, Ulric. 'Domains of Memory.' In *Memory: Interdisciplinary Approaches*, edited by P. Solomon, G.R. Goethals, C.M. Kelley, and B.R. Stephens, 67–83. New York: Springer, 1989.

Neisser, Ulric. 'Nested Structure in Autobiographical Memory.' In *Autobiographical Memory*, edited by David C. Rubin, 71–81. Cambridge: Cambridge University Press, 1986.

Neisser, Ulric. 'What is Ordinary Memory the Memory Of?' In Neisser and Winograd, *Remembering Reconsidered*, 356–373.

Newton, Isaac. *Sir Isaac Newton's Mathematical Principles of Natural Philosophy and His System of the World*. Translated by Andrew Motte. Revised by Florian Cajori. Berkeley, CA: University of California Press, 1934.

Nicolson, Harold. *Some People*. London: Pan Books, 1947.

The Nobel Assembly at Korlinska Institutet. '2014 Nobel Prize in Physiology or Medicine.' Press Release, 6 October 2014. Accessed 14 August 2017. www.nobelprize.org/nobel_prizes/medicine/laureates/2014/press.html.

Norberg-Schulz, Christian. *The Concept of Dwelling*. New York: Rizzoli, 1985.

Nuttall, Mark. 'Place, Identity and Landscape in North-west Greenland.' In *Mapping Invisible Worlds, Cosmos, Yearbook of the Traditional Cosmology Society 9*, edited by Gavin D. Flood, 75–88. Edinburgh: Edinburgh University Press, 1993.

Nuzzo, Angelica. *Ideal Embodiment: Kant's Theory of Sensibility*. Bloomington, IN: Indiana University Press, 2008.

O'Connor, Timothy. 'Agent Causation.' In *Agents, Causes and Events*, edited by Timothy O'Connor. New York: Oxford University Press, 1995.

O'Keefe, John, and Lynn Nadel. *The Hippocampus as a Cognitive Map*. Oxford: Clarendon Press, 1978.

Old Cumbria Gazetteer. 'Greenhead Gill (Ghyll).' Accessed 28 August 2017. www.geog.port.ac.uk/webmap/thelakes/html/lgaz/lgazfram.htm.

O'Neill, Onora. 'Space and Objects.' *Journal of Philosophy* 73 (1976): 29–45.

O'Shaughnessey, Brian. *The Will*. Cambridge: Cambridge University Press, 1980.

The Oxford English Dictionary. 2nd ed. Prepared by J.A. Simpson and E.S.C. Weiner. Oxford: Clarendon Press, 1989.

Parker, Sue Taylor, Robert W. Mitchell, and Maria L. Boccia, eds. *Self-Awareness in Animals and Humans: Developmental Perspectives*. Cambridge: Cambridge University Press, 1994.

Parkes, Don, and Nigel Thrift. *Times, Spaces, and Places: A Chronogeographic Perspective*. Chichester: John Wiley & Sons, 1980.

Parkes, Don, and Nigel Thrift. 'Putting Time in its Place.' In *Timing Space and Spacing Time, vol. 1, Making Sense of Time*, edited by Tommy Carlstein, Don Parkes, and Nigel Thrift, 119–129. London: Edward Arnold, 1978.

Peirce, C.S. 'How to Make Our Ideas Clear.' In *Collected Papers of Charles Sanders Peirce, vol. 5, Pragmatism and Pragmaticism.* Cambridge, MA: The Belknap Press, 1935.

Pérez-Gómez, Alberto. *Attunement: Architectural Meaning After the Crisis of Modern Science.* Cambridge, MA: MIT Press, 2016.

Plato. *The Collected Dialogues.* Edited by Edith Hamilton and Huntington Cairns. Princeton, NJ: Princeton University Press, 1963.

Poulet, Georges. *Studies in Human Time*. New York: Harper, 1959.

Poulet, Georges. *L'espace proustien*. Paris: Gallimard, 1963. Translated by Elliott Coleman as *Proustian Space* (Baltimore, MD: Johns Hopkins University Press, 1977).

Proust, Marcel. *À la recherche du temps perdu*. Paris: Gallimard, 1954. Translated by C.K. Scott Moncrieff and Frederick Blossom as *Remembrance of Things Past* (New York: Random House, 1932–1934), and revised by D.J. Enright as *In Search of Lost Time* (London: Chatto & Windus, 1992). Translated by Lydia Davis, Mark Treharne, James Grieve, John Sturrock, Carol Clark, Peter Collier, and Ian Patterson as *In Search of Lost Time* (London: Allen Lane, 2002).

Putnam, Hilary. 'The Meaning of "Meaning".' In *Mind, Language and Reality: Philosophical Papers*, vol. 2, 215–271. Cambridge: Cambridge University Press, 1975.

Ranganath, C., and L.-T. Hsieh. 'The Hippocampus: A Special Place for Time.' *Annals of the New York Academy of Science* 1369 (2016): 93–110.

Ratzel, Friedrich. *Anthropogeographie*. Stuttgart: J. Engelhorns Nachf., 1921–1922.

Read, Peter. *Returning to Nothing: The Meaning of Lost Places*. Cambridge: Cambridge University Press, 1996.

Relph, Edward. *Place and Placelessness.* London: Pion, 1977.

Ricoeur, Paul. *Time and Narrative.* Translated by Kathleen McLaughlin and David Pellauer. 3 vols. Chicago, IL: University of Chicago Press, 1984–1988.

Ricoeur, Paul. *Oneself as Another*. Translated by Kathleen Blamey. Chicago, IL: University of Chicago Press, 1992.

Ricoeur, Paul. 'Life in Quest of Narrative.' In Wood, *On Paul Ricoeur: Narrative and Interpretation*, 20–33.

Ricoeur, Paul. 'Narrative Identity.' In Wood, *On Paul Ricoeur: Narrative and Interpretation*, 188–200.

Riley, Robert B. 'Attachment to the Ordinary Landscape.' In Altman and Low, *Place Attachment*, 13–35.

Robinson, Hoke. 'Kant on Embodiment.' In *Minds, Ideas and Objects*, North American Kant Society Studies in Philosophy 2, edited by Phillip D. Cummins and Guenter Zoeller, 329–340. Atascadero, CA: Ridgeview Publishing, 1992.

Robinson, Tim. *Stones of Aran: Labyrinth*. Harmondsworth: Penguin, 1995.

Rose, Deborah Bird. *Dingo Makes Us Human: Life and Land in an Australian Aboriginal Culture*. Cambridge: Cambridge University Press, 1992.

Röska-Hardy, Louise S. 'Introduction – Issues and Themes in Comparative Studies: Language, Cognition, and Culture.' In *Learning from Animals? Explaining the Nature of Human Uniqueness*, edited by Louise S. Röska-Hardy and Eva M. Neumann, 1–12. Hove: Psychology Press, 2009.

Routledge Encyclopedia of Philosophy. www.rep.routledge.com/.

Russell, Bertrand. *Foundations of Geometry*. Cambridge: Cambridge University Press, 1897.

Russell, Bertrand. *Our Knowledge of the External World*. London: George Allen & Unwin, 1926.

Russell, James. *Agency: Its Role in Mental Development*. Hove: Erlbaum [UK] Taylor & Francis Ltd, 1996.

Russell, James. 'At Two with Nature: Agency and the Development of Self-World Dualism.' In Bermudez, Marcel, and Eilan, *The Body and the Self*, 127–152.

Sacks, Oliver. *The Man Who Mistook His Wife for a Hat*. London: Pan, 1986.

Samuels, Marwyn S. 'Existential and Human Geography.' In Ley and Samuels, *Humanistic Geography*, 222–240.

Schacter, Daniel L. *Searching for Memory*. New York: HarperCollins, 1996.

Schama, Simon. *Landscape and Memory*. London: HarperCollins, 1995.

Schatzki, Theodore R. *The Timespace of Human Activity: On Performance, Society, and History as Indeterminate Teleological Events*. Lanham, MD: Lexington Books, 2010.

Scheler, Max. *Die Formen des Wissens und die Bildung*. Bonn: Friedrich Cohen, 1925.

Schopenhauer, Arthur. *The World as Will and Representation*. 2 vols. Translated by E.F.J. Payne. New York: Dover, 1966.

Seamon, David, and Robert Mugerauer, eds. *Dwelling, Place and Environment*. New York: Columbia University Press, 1989.

Searles, Harold F. *The Nonhuman Environment – In Normal Development and in Schizophrenia*. New York: International Universities Press, 1960.

Seddon, George. *Sense of Place*. Nedlands, WA: University of Western Australia Press, 1972.

Sheldrake, Philip. *Spaces for the Sacred: Place, Memory, and Identity*. Baltimore, MD: Johns Hopkins University Press, 2001.

Shields, Rob. *Places on the Margin: Alternative Geographies of Modernity*. London: Routledge, 1991.

Slote, Michael. 'Causality and the Concept of a Thing.' *Midwest Studies in Philosophy* 4 (1979): 387–400.

Smart, J.J.C. 'Space.' In *The Encyclopedia of Philosophy*, edited by Paul Edwards, vol. 7/8, 506–511. New York: Macmillan, 1967.

Smith, Ailsa Lorraine. 'Taranaki Waiata Tangi and Feelings for Place.' PhD dissertation, Lincoln University, 2001.

Sopher, David E. 'The Structuring of Space in Place Names and Words for Place.' In Ley and Samuels, *Humanistic Geography*, 251–268.

Sorokin, P.A. *Sociocultural Causality, Space, Time*. Durham, NC: Duke University Press, 1943.

Spacks, Patricia Meyer. *Imagining a Self*. Cambridge, MA: Harvard.University Press, 1976.

Spence, Donald P. 'Passive Remembering.' In Neisser and Winograd, *Remembering Reconsidered*, 311–325.

Stambolian, George. *Marcel Proust and the Creative Encounter*. Chicago, IL: University of Chicago Press, 1972.

Stanford Encyclopedia of Philosophy. https://plato.stanford.edu/.

Stone, Peter G., and Joanne Farchakh Bajjaly, eds. *The Destruction of Cultural Heritage in Iraq*. Woodbridge: The Boydell Press, 2008.

Strauss, Erwin. *The Primary World of the Senses*. Translated by Jacob Needleman. New York: Macmillan, 1963.

Strawson, P.F. *Analysis and Metaphysics*. Oxford: Oxford University Press, 1992.

Strawson, P.F. *Individuals*. London: Macmillan, 1959.

Stehlow, T.G.H. *Aranda Traditions*. Melbourne, Vic: Melbourne University Press, 1947.

Ströker, Elizabeth. *Investigations in Philosophy of Space*. Translated by Algis Mickunas. Athens, OH: Ohio University Press, 1987.

Stroud, Barry. 'Transcendental Arguments.' *Journal of Philosophy* 65 (1968): 241–256.

Swain, Tony. *A Place for Strangers: Towards a History of Australian Aboriginal Being*. Cambridge: Cambridge University Press, 1993.

Swinburne, Richard. *Space and Time*. London: Macmillan, 1968.

Te Rangi Hiroa [Sir Peter Buck]. *The Coming of the Maori*. Wellington: Māori Purposes Fund Board, 1949.

Textbook of Topographical Surveying. 4th ed. London: Her Majesty's Stationery Office, 1965.

Thomson, Judith Jarvis. 'Private Languages.' *American Philosophical Quarterly* 1 (1964): 20–31.

Thoreau, Henry David. *The Writings of Henry D. Thoreau: Journal, Vol 3: 1848–1851*. Edited by Robert Sattelmeyer, Mark R. Patterson, and William Rossi. Princeton, NJ: Princeton University Press, 1990.

Tillich, Paul. *The Eternal Now*. New York: Charles Scribner's Sons, 1963.

Thrift, Nigel. *Non-Representational Theory: Space, Politics, Affect*. London: Routledge, 2008.

Tolkien, J.R.R. *The Hobbit*. London: George Allen and Unwin, 1937.

Tolkien, J.R.R. *The Lord of the Rings*. 3 vols. London: George Allen and Unwin, 1955.

Tolman, Edward C. 'Cognitive Maps in Rats and Men.' *Psychological Review* 55 (1948): 189–208.

Trakakis, N.N. 'Deus Loci: The Place of God and the God of Place in Philosophy and Theology.' *Sophia* 52 (2013): 315–333.

Tuan, Yi-Fu. *Topophilia*. Englewood Cliffs, NJ: Prentice-Hall, 1974.

Tuan, Yi-Fu. *Space and Place*. Minneapolis, MN: University of Minnesota Press, 1977.

Tuan, Yi-Fu. 'Geopiety: A Theme in Man's Attachment to Nature and to Place.' In *Geographies of the Mind: Essays in Historical Geosophy*, edited by David Lowenthal and Martyn J. Bowden, 11–39. New York: Oxford University Press, 1976.

Turkle, Sherry. *Life on the Screen: Identity in the Age of the Internet*. New York: Simon and Schuster, 1995.

Turkle, Sherry. *Alone Together: Why We Expect More from Technology and Less from Each Other*. New York: Basic Books, 2011.

Vassilieva, Julia. *Narrative Psychology: Identity, Transformation and Ethics*. Dordrecht: Springer, 2016.

Vidal de la Blanche, Paul. *Principles of Human Geography*. Translated by M.T. Bingham. New York: Henry Holt, 1926.

Villela-Petit, Maria. 'Heidegger's Conception of Space.' In *Critical Heidegger*, edited by Christopher Macann, 134–157. London: Routledge, 1996.

Virilio, Paul. *Speed and Politics: An Essay on Dromology*. New York: Semiotext(e), 1977.

von Wright, Georg Henrik. *Explanation and Understanding*. Ithaca, NY: Cornell University Press, 1971.

Walasek, Helen, and Amra Hadžimuhamedović, with contributions by Richard Carlton, Valery Perry and Tina Wik. *Bosnia and the Destruction of Cultural Heritage*. London: Routledge, 2015.

Walter, E.V. *Placeways: A Theory of the Human Environment*. Chapel Hill, NC: University of North Carolina Press, 1988.

Wellman, Barry. 'Physical Place and Cyber Place: The Rise of Personalized Networking.' *International Journal of Urban and Regional Research* 25 (2001): 227–252.

White, Kenneth. *The Nomad Mind*. Liverpool: University of Liverpool Press, forthcoming 2018.

White, Kenneth. *On Scottish Ground*. Edinburgh: Polygon, 1998.

White, Kenneth. *The Wanderer and His Charts*. Edinburgh: Polygon, 2004.

White, Kenneth. *Open World: The Collected Poems 1960–2000*. Edinburgh: Polygon, 2003.

Williams, Raymond. *The Country and the City*. London: Chatto & Windus, 1973.
Wittgenstein, Ludwig. *Philosophical Investigations*. Translated by G.E.M. Anscombe. Oxford: Blackwell, 1974.
Wittgenstein, Ludwig. *On Certainty*. Edited by G.E.M. Anscombe and G.H. von Wright. Translated by Denis Paul and G.E.M. Anscombe. Oxford: Blackwell, 1977.
Wittgenstein, Ludwig. *Wittgenstein's Lectures on the Philosophy of Mathematics, Cambridge 1939*. Edited by Cora Diamond. Hassocks: Harvester, 1976.
Wood, David, ed. *On Paul Ricoeur: Narrative and Interpretation*. London: Routledge, 1991.
Woolf, Virginia. *Moments of Being: Unpublished Autobiographical Writings*. Edited by Jeanne Schulkind. Brighton: The University Press, 1976.
Wordsworth, William. *Lyrical Ballads*. Vol. 2. London: Longman and Rees, 1800.
Wynn, Mark R. *Faith and Place: An Essay in Embodied Religious Epistemology*. Oxford: Oxford University Press, 2009.
Yates, Frances. *The Art of Memory*. London: Routledge & Kegan Paul, 1966.
Yoon, H.K. *Maori Mind, Maori Land: Essays on the Cultural Geography of the Maori People from an Outsider's Perspective*. Bern: Peter Lang, 1986.
Young, Julian. 'Heidegger's Heimat.' *International Journal of Philosophical Studies* 19 (2011): 285–293.
Zaehner, R.C. *Mysticism: Sacred and Profane*. Oxford: Oxford University Press, 1961.
Zumthor, Peter. *Thinking Architecture.* Boston, MA and Basel: Birkhäuser, 1999.

Index